"No one can criticize Dan Esty and his talented colleagues for not thinking big: there are ideas in this book that will appeal to anyone—and maybe a couple that will raise your hackles. It's the kind of spirited, discipline-crossing, deep dive that will help reorient a sometimes-stale environmental debate!"
—Bill McKibben, author of *Falter: Has the Human Game Begun to Play Itself Out?*

"This thoughtful and challenging book sets out how we can close the talk and action gap, making it essential reading for anyone that cares about the future of our planet and humanity."
—Paul Polman, former CEO and Chairman, Unilever

"*A Better Planet: Forty Big Ideas for a Sustainable Future* creates forty opportunities to start accelerating the transition to a better planet today. The direction is clear; now we need to work together, at scale."
—Peter Bakker, President and CEO, World Business Council for Sustainable Development

"Comprehensive, balanced, thought-provoking, thorough and, above all, readable! This book will become a must-have for anyone who wants to understand what has happened, and is happening, to our environment, why we should care, and what we can do about it."
—Christine Todd Whitman, Governor of New Jersey, 1994–2001, and Administrator of the Environmental Protection Agency, 2001–2003

"*A Better Planet* offers insightful and practical solutions to the complex, multifaceted climate change challenge—and ones with potential bipartisan appeal! This book deserves consideration by anyone who cares about moving us toward a clean-energy future."
—Ryan Costello, Member of the U.S. House of Representatives, 2015–2019

"A masterful summation of and reflection on past environmental efforts—and a valuable outline of principles to guide and inspire a new era of progress."
—William K. Reilly, Administrator of the Environmental Protection Agency, 1989–1993

A BETTER PLANET

EDITED BY DANIEL C. ESTY

WITH A FOREWORD BY INGRID C. BURKE

# A Better Planet

BIG IDEAS FOR A SUSTAINABLE FUTURE

Yale UNIVERSITY PRESS   NEW HAVEN AND LONDON

Yale University Press books may be purchased in quantity for educational, business, or promotional use. For information, please e-mail sales.press@yale.edu (U.S. office) or sales@yaleup.co.uk (U.K. office).

Set in Scala type by Westchester Publishing Services.
Printed in the United States of America.

Library of Congress Control Number: 2019941070
ISBN 978-0-300-24624-7 (hardcover: alk. paper)

A catalogue record for this book is available from the British Library.

This paper meets the requirements of ANSI/NISO Z39.48-1992 (Permanence of Paper).

10 9 8 7 6 5 4 3 2 1

To the generations of Yale graduates who have contributed to
building a sustainable future—and to all those who inspired them

# CONTENTS

## FOREWORD

Ingrid C. Burke

Perhaps the most important challenge of this century centers on whether humans can obtain the necessary resources to flourish in a manner that is sustainable for future generations without causing irreversible damage to the planet. How do we obtain the requisite food, clean and sufficient water, energy, clean air, and access to green and wild places for our own health? How do we steward the biological diversity of the planet? As far as we know, we are the only species with capabilities to answer these questions: imagining the future, identifying problems, generating complex knowledge and tools, creating technological solutions and incentives, having empathy for others of our species who may have much worse challenges, governing our societies, and more. There are many worrisome trends in the environment at this time. But because of our human capacity for thought and action, we have enormous opportunities to generate knowledge and then deliver processes and policies for sustainable natural resource use with support for social equity and environmental justice.

Human health and the environment are inextricably linked, and much of the linkage occurs through the use of natural resources, the consequences of extracting those resources, and the impacts on air, water, land, and ecosystem quality and integrity. Individuals who are in positions to develop and implement policies or business practices to protect the environment for human health tend to be in a minority that is distant from the key challenges that arise from those linkages, generally living in conditions that are among the best in the world. This phenomenon of distant threats creates potential for lack of will in governance for environmental protection, as has been evident in the inertia associated with climate change policy for the United States. But the distant threats are becoming closer for everyone. We are experiencing rapidly increasing rates of environmental disasters that endanger human life, from hurricanes and forest fires to heat waves, drought, and flooding. In a more and more urbanized world, pressure mounts on rural lands for food, energy, and fiber resources to support cities. Waste accumulates on land and in the sea at remarkable rates. And environmental pollution—a "very near threat"—disproportionately affects the lower-income populations across the globe.

Why a book about environmental protection, and why right now? Why dialogue, collaboration, and leadership by experts?

It is an ideal time for new ideas to guide environmental protection, ideas that rely on science and rigorous analysis, prioritize environmental protection for those either currently near or far from the threats of irreversible environmental damage, generate opportunities for economic investment and welfare, and are tractable. This book presents such big ideas from different perspectives and areas of expertise.

The authors are scholars and practitioners working in business, government, and the nonprofit world, as well as a few graduate students. The concepts, frameworks, and solutions advanced here offer great promise for moving society toward a sustainable future. Of course, it might seem odd to put forward a book based on this belief in our current political moment, marked by substantial public distrust of experts, and indeed, of elite institutions such as my own. Experts are perceived by some to be out of touch, far from the real problems that face everyday citizens, and even biased toward one or another political perspective. But this lack of trust is inconsistent in its forms. Public appreciation for what science and technology can bring us remains strong when it comes to curing illness, engineering solutions that result in enhanced communication over smartphones and the internet, and delivering new and exciting modes of transportation. But resistance rises with regard to solutions that seem to address distant threats or that carry some short-term hardship in return for a longer-term benefit. To some extent, we experts may have brought some of this distrust on ourselves, through developing tremendous depth in knowledge and tools, but perhaps not as much skill in communicating that knowledge or its relevance to the invested citizens.

This book addresses the gap between expert innovation and perceived useful knowledge for environmental protection in two ways. First, the essays are the result of scholarly and practical thinking and writing that have been through the Yale Environmental Dialogue, which is to say presented to diverse audiences who engaged in spirited dialogue about the ideas, providing feedback to be incorporated and adding value for all readers. Second, our authors have been selected as experts who can communicate across levels of expertise, political perspectives, and the range of values that exist about environmental protection.

Catalyzing the movement of these innovative ideas into solutions demands leadership. Leaders in the realms of business, government, industry, and land management have the opportunity through this book to learn about current and future trends in the environment and envision new ways forward that prioritize human and environmental health, many of which can also lead to increased economic growth. It is an exciting time to be reshaping the dialogue about the environment that brings all political viewpoints to the same table, with common goals for a sustainable future, and catalyzes solutions through innovation.

# Introduction

Daniel C. Esty

IN THE 1960S, the Naugatuck River in central Connecticut ran red, purple, green, and yellow depending on the dyes being used that day by the Uniroyal factory along its banks to make Keds sneakers. The emissions from the facility not only affected the color of the water but also imparted a distinct odor to the air. Nonetheless, the factory provided employment and economic security to hundreds of families—jobs and prosperity that are much harder to find today amid the industrial decay of the struggling communities of the Naugatuck River valley.

The river is much cleaner now. People with fishing poles line its banks on summer weekends, and kids jump off rope swings into the water to swim—something that was never done while I was growing up nearby. In fact, in those days a dip in the river was sure to be followed by a trip to the doctor for a tetanus shot.

The Naugatuck River runs clear today because of an enormous commitment to environmental protection that we as a society have undertaken over the past fifty years. The United States adopted a Clean Air Act in 1970 and a Clean Water Act in 1972, both of which imposed significant emissions controls on industrial facilities across the land. We followed those first sweeping federal environmental laws with additional statutes aimed at curbing chemical exposures, toxic material mismanagement, and haphazard disposal of hazardous waste. Americans today in every state breathe cleaner air, drink safer water, face less pollution exposure, and enjoy swimming, fishing, hiking, and camping in parks and wilderness areas that are a direct legacy of this nation's environmental efforts.

Flash forward four decades, and you might expect to see Congress holding congratulatory hearings to celebrate the pollution control and conservation progress that has been made. But instead, significant numbers of senators and representatives take to the floor of Congress to denounce the Environmental Protection Agency, call for its authority and budget to be slashed, and decry the job losses and economic burdens they believe the agency's regulatory agenda has saddled society with. At the same time, other senators and representatives rise to express their distress at the nation's failure to control the build-up of greenhouse gases in the atmosphere or address the persistent risks that many citizens still face from pollution exposure.

How can this be? Who is right?

Ironically, both sides have a point. America has made great strides in the environmental realm in the past five decades, but often at high cost. And we face substantial residual pollution harms as well as new challenges that have been given too little attention. Thus, we simultaneously both overregulate and underregulate. Yet for more than a generation, we have been unwilling (or perhaps it would be more accurate to say *unable*) to refine our framework of environmental policy with careful attention to what has worked—and what has not. Nor have we systematically assessed how to balance environmental progress with other priorities such as economic prosperity, mobility, and liberty.

More troublingly, environmental protection has become an arena for bitter partisan battles, leading to inaction on critical agenda items including reframing the nation's energy strategy and confronting the existential threat of climate change. What is going on? Why has a policy area that once enjoyed broad bipartisan support become a source of deep division?

Part of the answer lies in the general trend over the past two decades toward gridlock in Congress, a decline of civility in political debate, and the loss of the spirit of compromise that once marked deliberations in both the House and the Senate.[1] Some of the breakdown can be attributed to the rapidly rising scale and over-riding importance of money in election campaigns. Moreover, the huge investments made by special interests on all sides of the political spectrum in campaign contributions, which they hope will protect their privileged positions from scrutiny, have made policy reform and any sort of change ever more difficult—even when the status quo is plainly not working.

But part of the problem comes from the nature of the environmental policy debate itself. Green groups and their political allies have in too many cases not taken seriously the concerns voiced about the economic burdens, political implications, and countervailing risks and costs of the policies that they seek to advance. Many in the environmental community have furthermore been curiously unreflective and unwilling to admit that some of their policy prescriptions have not delivered the results desired or promised. And some have failed to acknowledge the trade-offs that inescapably must be made as society decides how far to push the environmental agenda. They have thus dismissed or even attacked the use of risk analysis, benefit-cost assessments, and other policy tools that provide an analytically rigorous framework for systematic environmental decision-making.

Those who have pushed back on the environmentalism of the twentieth century have done so for many different reasons, some of which arise from legitimate concerns about the rigidity and excesses of environmental protection as it has come to be practiced across the United States. But other arguments seem less thoughtfully grounded. Indeed, many of those opposed to more vigorous environmental action have been hostile to science, unwilling to look at data, and inattentive to the long-term environmental consequences of certain industrial activities—all of which are essential foundations for rational, successful, and cost-effective environmental policy. Others have exploited the inherent uncertainty in science and the commitment of scientists to ongoing reassessment of the prevailing theories and conclusions to suggest disingenuously that we do not know enough for policymaking to proceed. And some have been all too quick to do the bidding of special interests whose business models depend on *not* paying for the emissions that go up a smokestack or out an effluent pipe or using public lands and resources without fully paying for the value being extracted.

Thus, while some progress has been made in addressing the most egregious environmental harms and natural resource losses, the pace of progress has slowed in recent years. As economists would say, many *externalities* remain *uninternalized*. And while the theory of pollution control and natural resource management has advanced significantly, the practice has not been fundamentally rethought in more than a generation. Simply put, the twentieth-century approach to environmental protection, which remains largely in place, now needs to be modernized.[2]

In the pages that follow, an extraordinary collection of thought leaders—spanning a wide range of political beliefs, disciplinary perspectives, and issue expertise—have offered their big ideas for reigniting environmental progress. They have each been asked to offer concrete suggestions for policy progress and to do so on a basis that could win broad political support. The ideas presented build on a much sharper picture of the environmental challenges that society faces compared with what policymakers knew when our current framework of environmental law and policy took shape in the 1970s and 1980s. These proposals reflect advances in knowledge that the Information Age and era of Big Data have unleashed in many fields, from epidemiology to ecology. The essays in this volume thus provide a menu of innovative suggestions on which America and the world might build over the next several decades in reimagining the response to pollution, land use, natural resource management, and energy challenges.

Some of the proposals are more conceptual in nature—offering new ways to understand or approach critical issues. Others introduce frameworks for analyzing policy options. And yet other essays put forward specific solutions to pressing problems. All of them take seriously the notion that society faces a "sustainability imperative,"[3] which requires that we do all the things we do in new and better ways that minimize environmental degradation, increase short-term economic opportunity, and promote long-term prosperity.

Readers will appreciate, for example, how ecologists now demonstrate the profound interconnections within ecosystems and across species—arguing for a much greater focus on a "systems" perspective in policymaking—rather than the media-specific silos of our existing legal structure. While skeptics may debate the value of science and dismiss statistical studies, the essays in this volume highlight how carefully gathered data and rigorous analysis provide the best possible basis for making good policy choices. And they demonstrate how these choices optimize environmental outcomes at the lowest possible cost while respecting other policy virtues such as simplicity, transparency, flexibility, and predictability.

We have also come a long way in understanding and mapping the assimilative capacity of our ecosystems, including the "planetary boundaries" that demarcate the safe operating space for human activity on Earth.[4] These efforts make clear that we have entered the *Anthropocene,* a new geological epoch defined by humanity's influence on the global environment. Research indicates that human activity risks exceeding planetary boundaries in areas such as climate change, biodiversity loss, and the natural flow of elements like nitrogen and phosphorus. To thrive in the Anthropocene, several authors in the essays that follow make clear that we must overcome the twentieth century's short-term bias in many domains, including business as well as environmental policy. Long-term thinking will be essential to address the range of problems that build up over time, achieve intergenerational equity (especially what some are now calling "climate change justice"), and tend to other dimensions of fairness critical to a sustainable future. Fairness and inclusion also require that we rethink how we talk about the environment, and incorporate new approaches such as the "hip-hop sustainability" proposed by Thomas RaShad Easley in this volume. Others observe that while remaking our environmental strategy around new principles of accountability and a commitment to the "end of externalities," we may want to lean on long-standing normative traditions including foundational legal principles as well as religious values and spirituality.

We also now know that one of the megatrends of our era is urbanization—meaning that the kind of cities we build will determine in fundamental ways whether we can deliver a more sustainable future. We have also come to appreciate the limits of top-down environmental policies—and thus the need for bottom-up strategies that engage mayors, governors, and corporate leaders as well as presidents and prime ministers in the delivery of environmental programs such as clean energy and climate-friendly transportation systems. Moreover, while governments (particularly national governments) were seen as the primary actors in twentieth-century environmental efforts—often deciding what needed to be done, who would do it, and what particular programs would be advanced—we have now learned that "broader engagement" will often represent a better strategy. Moreover, even in policy domains such as land conservation, where government action has been deemed essential, we are realizing that private sector participation and partnerships with nongovernmental organizations may be advantageous.

We further recognize that environmental law and policy cannot be all about "red lights" and "stop signs" that tell people what not to do; we need an equal measure of "green lights" that incentivize both creative individuals and entrepreneurial businesses to bring innovation to bear on pollution control, renewable power generation, and other environmental breakthroughs that society needs. Innovation can also improve environmental governance itself, through new technologies such as the use of machine learning to sharpen regulatory strategies and techniques such as adaptive learning that ensure continuous refinement of policies. Likewise, we have learned that *waste—* of materials or water or energy—need not be accepted as inevitable. Indeed, in many cases, waste should be seen as a valuable resource that can be recaptured and reused. And we now are aware that the right policy incentives can effect this shift in perspective.

Similarly, we now know that, while business seemed like *the* environmental problem in the twentieth century, companies can be part of the solution if given the right price signals and incentives that spur innovation in support of a sustainable future. We understand furthermore that one of the shortcomings of twentieth-century environmental efforts was the failure to ask where the money would come from for all of the investments required in sustainable infrastructure—from renewable power generation to modern drinking water systems. Thus, another key to progress will be mechanisms, such as Green Banks and Green Bonds, to finance investment in sustainable infrastructure. We will also need better corporate environmental/social/governance metrics to help sustainability-minded investors steer their portfolios and capital investments toward sustainable companies and away from those that are environmentally damaging or otherwise unsustainable. Nowhere will this emphasis on sustainable business models be more critical than in food and agriculture—a sector on which all of us depend but of which too little was asked in the past.

The diversity of issues that must be addressed to achieve a sustainable future can seem daunting. But this volume provides a sweeping sense of the fresh thinking about pathways to a sustainable future occurring across the nation and around the world. It offers a starting point for reexamining our environmental strategies and the policy trade-offs that need to be made.

This commitment to reimagining our policy frameworks and fundamentally remaking our future is as old as the project that is America. Indeed, Thomas Jefferson argued that a "little rebellion now and then is a good thing . . . [and] . . . a medicine necessary for the sound health of government."[5] In adopting that same spirit of creative thinking and reform, this book offers a sweeping set of new perspectives and innovative policy approaches that might help put the United States and the world beyond on a more sustainable trajectory. And in doing so, it lays the groundwork for an important debate that we hope you will join.

After reading the essays in this volume, *reflect* on the concepts, frameworks, and solutions they advance. Then tell us what *you* think at http://environment.yale.edu/dialogue. Indeed, our goal is not just to contribute to the substance of the policy dialogue over our environmental future but also to demonstrate how to have such a conversation. So please join us in this debate.

## NOTES

1.  Daniel C. Esty, "Compromise and the Art of the Deal," *Our Daily Planet*, December 15, 2018, https://mailchi.mp/ourdailyplanet.com/our-daily-planet-bright-ideas-compromise-and-the-art-of-the-deal-by-daniel-c-esty?e=a7d68bd0ca.

2.  There is, in fact, a group that calls itself "ecomodernists" and that advances an agenda with some elements that align with the ideas in this volume. See John Asafu-Adjaye et al., "An Ecomodernist Manifesto," www.ecomodernism.org; Ted Nordhaus and Michael Shellenberger, *Break Through: From the Death of Environmentalism to the Politics of Possibility* (Boston: Houghton Mifflin, 2007); Ted Nordhaus, Michael Shellenberger, and Jenna Mukuno, "Ecomodernism and the Anthropocene: Humanity as a Force for Good," The Breakthrough Institute, accessed January 14, 2019, https://thebreakthrough.org/journal/issue-5/ecomodernism-and-the-anthropocene; Steven Pinker, "The Environment," in *Enlightenment Now* (New York: Viking, 2018), 156–90.

3.  David A. Lubin and Daniel C. Esty, "The Sustainability Imperative," *Harvard Business Review*, May 1, 2010, https://hbr.org/2010/05/the-sustainability-imperative.

4.  Will Steffen et al., "Planetary Boundaries: Guiding Human Development on a Changing Planet," *Science* 347, no. 6223 (February 13, 2015): 1259855, https://doi.org/10.1126/science.1259855; Johan Rockström and Mattias Klum, *Big World, Small Planet: Abundance within Planetary Boundaries* (New Haven, CT: Yale University Press, 2015).

5.  Thomas Jefferson, "From Thomas Jefferson to James Madison, 30 January 1787," Founders Online, National Archives, last modified June 13, 2018, http://founders.archives.gov/documents/Jefferson/01-11-02-0095.

# PART ONE NATURE, LAND, AND WATER

# Sustaining Humans and Nature as One

## ECOLOGICAL SCIENCE AND ENVIRONMENTAL STEWARDSHIP

Oswald J. Schmitz

DURING THE COURSE of the Earth's very recent history, our species has rapidly transitioned from being one among millions of species on Earth to being the species that is single-handedly transforming the entire planet to suit its own needs.[1] This planetary transformation has been so rapid and overwhelming that scientists now characterize humanity's impact over this period as the "great acceleration."[2] Humankind continues to speed up its economic productivity and technological advancement, both of which are further accelerating human impacts on nature. These impacts include especially the extraction of natural resources, the domestication of natural wildlands to support agriculture, and the urban and peri-urban built environment. On a finite planet, expanded demand for any given natural resource or land area necessarily leaves less available for the millions of other species with which we share the planet. These limits have profound implications for sustaining all of humanity. They entail most fundamentally humanity's ethical obligations to humankind and all other species with which we share the planet, and furthermore how humanity ought to meet those obligations. A key part of reimagining environmental protection for the twenty-first century and beyond, then, is to think differently about what such an obligation entails scientifically, and the steps that are needed to ensure a sustainable future for all of life on Earth.[3]

Ecology is undergoing a paradigm shift and offering a new set of lessons for us about these obligations. The discipline once contended that nature must be protected from humankind and its relentless drive to dominate and destroy it. That view is giving way to a new vision of humankind and nature working together, each dependent on the other for its existence. The challenge is to implement this vision in the absence of any illustrative case examples. Here, then, I offer thoughts on what putting this view into practice might entail. Fundamentally it requires reconsidering how the entirety of nature as a grand economy should be valued, and thinking about the kind of policy approaches that can ensure that all nature—of which humans are a part— is sustained.

## THE ECONOMY OF NATURE

Ecological science teaches that conceiving a sustainable future requires the fundamental appreciation that we live on a finite planet that supports a grand economy called nature. It is a circular economy that is sustained not by technology but by a mind-boggling variety of technologically irreplaceable plant, animal, and microbial species that are freely able to fulfill their biological roles.[4] These biological roles ensure the perpetual production, consumption, exchange, and recycling of materials and energy—supports to humanity known as *ecosystem services*. Sustaining this economy supports the enduring opportunity to remove renewable natural resources such as mineral nutrients, water, timber, wild plants, and fish and game to support human economic activity and well-being.[5] Sustaining this economy also keeps in place the enduring opportunity to supply ample clean and fresh water, build deep and fertile soils, maintain the genetic variety to produce hardy crops, preserve the means to pollinate those crops, and purify the air by sequestering gaseous emissions, among numerous other ecosystem services that humans rely on to sustain their health and well-being.

The conundrum here is that removing natural resources or transforming landscapes to enhance human well-being paradoxically stands to diminish human well-being over time by compromising the provision of ecosystem services in that place. Reconciling this conundrum arguably stands out as among the foremost environmental policy challenges of our time. It requires coming to grips with how we as humans ought to view our engagement with nature, particularly our role within it. There are effectively two different views on this question.

The reigning view is a despairingly stark one. It sees humankind existing apart from nature, merely treating it as a trove of economically valuable resources or places that can be relentlessly exploited and transformed, thereby putting humanity on a headlong course to ruin nature and ultimately collapse human society. Ecological science has long abetted this view by amassing scientific knowledge to identify and characterize species and ecosystems at risk.[6] The science instigated an era of environmental conservation and natural resource management, and advocacy for outright protection of species and ecosystems, which continues to this day. The conventional policy solution is to enact laws intended to limit the level of damage humans inflict, and to establish parks and nature reserves to restrict human access, thus keeping some of wild nature and its functions and services intact.

Emerging scientific evidence shows, however, that such well-intended safeguards by themselves will not work, because they do not foster the kind of human behavioral changes needed to decelerate humankind's environmental impact. Instead, the perceived license to freely exploit the vast unprotected parts of landscapes leads to continued land transformation that often encroaches right to the borders of the protected areas. Consequently, protected areas increasingly become isolated islands in heavily domesticated landscapes. Isolation jeopardizes the long-term persistence of the very species, ecological functions, and environmental services that these places are intended to protect.

## FROM DESPAIR TO HOPE

An alternative, emerging view from ecology inspires hope by imagining the possibility of humankind (the social) and nature (the ecological) existing together across landscapes, entwined as a "socio-ecological system," in which each part requires the other for its existence.[7] Realizing that possibility, however, requires humanity to engage with nature very differently than it now does. Current ecological science advises rethinking human engagement with nature based on a new ethic of ecosystem stewardship, which proposes that humans have ethical obligations to one another that are mediated through their mutual relationships with nonhuman species and with nature. As a golden rule of sorts, humankind ought then to strive to ensure the integrity, resilience, sustainability, and beauty of all landscapes, both the human-built and natural alike.

Ecosystem stewardship is not the same as conservation, whose goal is merely to preserve and protect species and ecosystems. Nor is it the same as management, whose goal is striking a balance between maximizing natural resource extraction and minimizing damages resulting from exploitation and transformation of nature. An ecosystem stewardship ethic strives for continuous improvement of environmental performance everywhere in support of the simultaneous preservation of species and the production of natural resources and ecosystem services. This means reimagining all places—from the remotest wild areas to the most densely populated urban areas—as complementary, albeit different, forms of nature, each being a part of a greater, integrated circular economy. This ethic informs the objective for many regional and national environmental policies, such as the National Environmental Policy Act in the United States, which requires that government agencies evaluate the environmental impact of their work. Ecological science, however, now teaches that developing sound environmental policies under such processes requires rethinking how humans value and engage with nature.

Developing sound policies requires seeing natural resources as dividends of sustained ecosystem productivity rather than as a stockpile of assets.[8] Environmental policies and regulations ought to be aimed at supporting ecosystem service provisioning, which requires protecting entire ecosystems that make up nature's economy, not triaging and letting go of the parts that humans presume to be useless. By advancing a stewardship ethic, ecologists aim to instill an appreciation that humans must live within, not exceed, the means provided by the rest of the species on Earth, thereby enabling all species to carry out their biological roles.

Changing the mind-set from despair to hope requires letting go of conventional thinking that nature exists in some fragile balance. It requires moving from a conversation of always lamenting humankind's persistent habit of disrupting that putative balance to one that is more consistent with the emerging state of ecological knowledge. Ecological science is now showing that nature is continuously changeable and that many species have greater ability to adapt and be resilient to changes than was once thought, *provided that* their physical and physiological capacities for resilience are not stretched beyond their evolved limitations. Modern ecological science is acquiring better understanding and measures of what those species' limitations are. It is thereby better able to help identify a safe, flexible operating space within which humankind can make choices about using landscapes and sustaining ecosystem functions. Stewardship in turn must make these findings actionable by crafting creative, scientifically defensible policies that minimize threats to species' freedoms to fulfill their biological roles. This in turn creates a portfolio of opportunities to manage, restore, and sustain natural ecosystems and the services they provide for current and future generations. Doing this requires reimagining how to appropriately value nature's economy and devise a compatible policy process that integrates humans into that economy.

## AN EXPANDED VALUATION OF NATURE

Currently, the value placed on any natural resource is typically determined only by what consumers are willing to pay, given supply and demand pricing within markets. When a company sells a manufactured product, its price reflects all of the manufacturing costs, including sourcing raw materials, transforming those materials into goods, getting them to the market, and reinvesting to ensure the machinery driving the manufacturing continues to function. It goes without saying that it would be pure folly economically not to financially account for those costs because it would lead to inevitable bankruptcy. But this is exactly the folly that is playing out in humanity's great acceleration.

A naturally supplied resource, say timber, is effectively a product manufactured by nature. The prices paid for this and other natural resources typically reflect only the market value of the products themselves, including the costs of resource extraction. The prices do not at all factor in the costs of ensuring that the manufacturing process itself is sustained on landscapes—a process contingent on the existence and collective functioning of many species within an ecosystem.[9] For instance, the possibility to extract timber comes about because of the survival and production of forest trees that are adapted to the particular climatic conditions of a region. Tree survival and production is entirely dependent on the presence of fertile soils, which, in turn, results from a multitude of soil-dwelling organisms working to convert raw materials (organic wastes) into mineral nutrients that are essential for the value-added plant production that generates timber. Those organisms also create and preserve the physical conditions for soil to take up and retain water in support of plant production.

Because this chain of functional dependence is often disregarded, its value remains hidden and so is rarely, if ever, factored into economic accounting. Such undervaluation then causes land management and extraction to proceed in ways that ruin the lands that support these species, thereby causing species losses and the consequent erosion of nature's productive capacity. This miscalculation also leads to additional missed opportunities because of the inherent multifunctionality of nature. For instance, tree production also provides an important ecosystem service because it slows climate change by sequestering carbon from the atmosphere that in many ecosystems ends up being stored in living biomass and in dead organic matter in soils. This additional value can be accounted for by pricing the stored carbon. But here again, this simply puts value on the end product, not on the process that creates the product.

Ensuring the long-term sustainability of natural resource supplies and ecosystem services requires that policy decisions be based on a different way to economically value the entirety of nature. Ecological science teaches that it is no longer sensible to guide policy using traditional economic approaches that value natural resources and ecosystem services as stocks of end products. Instead, newer valuation approaches can be applied to account for the full value coming from stocks, and more importantly, flows of resources through *intact,* value-adding chains of interdependent species.[10] These emerging new approaches can lead to more sensible, scientifically defensible policy solutions because they begin to align human economic thinking with the way nature's economy truly works. In nature's economy, natural resources and ecosystem services are the sustained dividends of species freely carrying out their biological roles and multiple functions. Stewardship aims to ensure that species can fulfill those roles.

### STEWARDSHIP IN ACTION

Considering species' roles and the context of multifunctionality requires overcoming the silo-ing that happens when, even under well-intentioned policy processes such as the National Environmental Policy Act, different policy sectors (for example, resource extraction, wildlife management, species conservation, climate change mitigation) act in isolation because of a lack of coordination among them. A case in point, which is not atypical of many landscape-scale policy conundrums, concerns resource extraction, conservation, and management in the boreal forest ecosystem of western Canada. Here conflict arises because one resource sector (oil and gas), through its exploration and extraction activities, indirectly jeopardizes another resource sector (timber) by directly altering the interdependencies among species such as wolves, moose, and caribou. These changes trigger policy responses in a third sector (wildlife) that feed back to negatively impact timber production and forest carbon storage.

In this region, permitted land development for seismic exploration by the oil and gas industry (the responsibility of one government agency overseeing energy and mines) opens up the forested landscape in ways that make it easier for wolves to traverse it more widely. Such expanded movement leads to more frequent killing of woodland caribou prey that are normally hard to find, being isolated in rare old-growth forest habitats across the landscape. Woodland caribou are designated as a threatened wildlife species in need of conservation protection, and increased wolf predation makes caribou harder to protect.

The policy solution (the responsibility of another government agency overseeing wildlife, environment, and parks) is to cull wolves to protect the caribou as well as restore forest on some of the permitted seismic lines to recover habitat. Culling wolves, however, reduces natural controls over moose and deer populations, who then increase their foraging on woody vegetation, which in turn infringes on the profitability of forest production, as well as diminishes the amount of carbon stored in soils (the responsibility of a third government agency overseeing agriculture and forestry). Thus, tasking an agency with only its particular resource sector may end up working in opposition to policies in other sectors. In turn, the response of one agency to the problem created by another creates a landscape-wide "whack-a-mole" effect. In the western Canadian case, oil and gas extraction policy cascades to alter predator-prey relations, which threatens biodiversity conservation. Conservation policy responses cascade to alter natural resource and ecosystem service provisioning.

An ecosystem stewardship approach could help avert these unintended cascading effects by imagining policy entwinement across sectors. Before any action is taken, stewardship would have each sector anticipate how its policies influence all others, mediated by their shared use of the landscape as well as the species and ecosystem functions and services supported by that landscape. This involves developing an a priori reasoning process that conceives interrelated causal pathways of policy and ecological effects. Such reasoning increases the sustainability of the ecosystem in its entirety. In the case here, rather than being consigned to making costly fixes to the problems, such as culling wolves and converting seismic lines back to forest, an entwined policy process could avoid such costly mistakes in the first place. Entwined policy would seek to use ecological science to good effect and plan oil and gas development in ways that have little impact on wolf movement and attendant effects on other wildlife and forest tree species. By treating policy and ecology as an enmeshed system, it becomes possible to develop interrelated policies that can create mutually reinforcing ecological and political outcomes to minimize conflicts and enhance the durability of policy solutions.

Ecosystem stewardship is not, however, intended simply to fall within the purview of government.[11] Stewardship is more than having governments institute policies, laws, and procedures for regulating human behavior, and having citizens merely advocate for competing interests. Stewardship encourages all citizens to share responsibility for environmental decision-making and to be accountable for any consequences that arise from those decisions. Stewardship succeeds when people as individuals—or as members of organizations, communities, or other institutions that compose human social systems—have opportunity to engage with each other and with local, regional, and national governments in the interest of cooperative, coordinated management of ecosystems for long-term sustainability. Sustainability then emerges from the creative choices made within a particular social system and reflects the environmental, social, and economic contexts of that society. This can create the kind of societal buy-in that helps ensure durable environmental policy success. But ecologists cannot go it alone to achieve this objective.

For all of this to be effective, ecologists must engage more deeply with social scientists and humanists to fully understand how to motivate and steer human action in the interest of sustaining nature in its entirety. Such efforts must see to it that citizens take interest and responsibility to stay scientifically informed about what kinds of solutions ecosystems need and how people's particular choices could affect their local environment *and* beyond.[12] Hence, ecological science, too, has a new responsibility to present its understanding of nature not just in highly technical, data-driven ways that are customary in current science-policy approaches, but also in ways that are compelling and accessible to a broader public. Ecosystem stewardship offers the hope and means to ensure sensible sustainability policies so that—to paraphrase Theodore Roosevelt—future generations will be richer, not poorer, because of how we have lived.[13]

**NOTES**

This essay draws on and builds on the author's prior scholarship including *The New Ecology: Rethinking a Science for the Anthropocene* (Princeton, NJ: Princeton University Press, 2016).

1. Yuval Noah Harari, *Sapiens: A Brief History of Humankind* (New York: Harper, 2015).
2. Will Steffen, Paul J. Crutzen, and John R. McNeil, "The Anthropocene: Are Humans Now Overwhelming the Great Forces of Nature?," *Ambio* 36, no. 8 (December 2007): 614–16.
3. Catholic Church, with Sean McDonagh, *On Care for Our Common Home: The Encyclical of Pope Francis on the Environment, Laudato Si'* (New York: Orbis Books, 2016).
4. Schmitz, *The New Ecology.*

5. Schmitz, *The New Ecology*; F. Stuart Chapin, III, Gary P. Kofinas, and Carl Folke, eds., *Principles of Ecosystem Stewardship: Resilience-Based Natural Resource Management in a Changing World* (New York: Springer, 2009).

6. Chapin, Kofinas, and Folke, *Principles of Ecosystem Stewardship*.

7. Chapin, Kofinas, and Folke, *Principles of Ecosystem Stewardship*.

8. Chapin, Kofinas, and Folke, *Principles of Ecosystem Stewardship*.

9. Chapin, Kofinas, and Folke, *Principles of Ecosystem Stewardship*.

10. Eli P. Fenichel, Joshua K. Abbott, and Seong Do Yun, "The Nature of Natural Capital and Ecosystem Income," in *Handbook of Environmental Economics, Volume 4*, ed. Partha Dasgupta et al. (North Holland: Elsevier, 2018), 85–142.

11. Fenichel, Abbott, and Yun, "The Nature of Natural Capital."

12. Fenichel, Abbott, and Yun, "The Nature of Natural Capital."

13. Alfred Henry Lewis, *A Compilation of the Messages and Speeches of Theodore Roosevelt, 1901-1905* (New York: Bureau of National Literature and Art, 1910).

# A Habitable Earth

## PROTECTING BIODIVERSITY THROUGH
## NATURAL SYSTEMS

Thomas E. Lovejoy

CONSERVING BIODIVERSITY—including the full spectrum of plants, animals, and microorganisms across the globe as well as the genetic makeup of each species—has proven to be incredibly challenging because almost all human activity affects biodiversity in some way. It is, however, an essential goal, as biodiversity drives the resilience of ecosystems that sustain all life on Earth, including our own. In a body of work beginning in 1949, the ecologist Ruth Patrick demonstrated that biodiversity reflects not only all natural conditions of watersheds but also all human impacts within them.[1] At the planetary level, we now know that biodiversity also shows the cumulative impact of human activities. In the *planetary boundaries* framework that the sustainability researcher Johan Rockström and his colleagues developed to help define the "safe operating space" for human existence on the planet, biodiversity clearly breaches the boundary line and falls well into the danger zone. Indeed, of the nine planetary boundaries identified, biodiversity appears to be most deeply into negative territory, which follows logically because it reflects the impacts of all the other Earth system stresses as well as being vulnerable directly.[2]

Scientists and diplomats have begun to work at the global scale to set targets for biodiversity protection. Building on various alarming reports about the state of the world's biological diversity—including the World Wildlife Fund's *Living Planet Report,* which found a massive loss of mammalian biomass[3]—their efforts have triggered some important and ambitious initiatives to protect biodiversity. For example, the parties to the global Convention on Biological Diversity have suggested that 30 percent of the terrestrial and marine ecosystems of the planet should be put under protection by 2030 (known as the "30 by 30 target").

These efforts resonate with important visions such as that of the Harvard entomologist Edward O. Wilson's "Half-Earth" proposal to set aside half the surface of the Earth for nature and that of the hundreds of conservationists who have come together to launch a global nongovernmental organization called Nature Needs Half. The Global Deal for Nature and the Leonardo Di-Caprio Foundation's One Earth go beyond biodiversity in the narrow sense to embrace functioning ecosystems across the globe.[4] Most of these initiatives are primarily biodiversity-focused and seek to respond to the imminent risk of loss of major portions of the planet's biodiversity while also spelling out the fundamental ways in which the planet's ecosystems function and provide the *ecosystem services* on which biodiversity and humanity are dependent.

These initiatives stand in stark contrast to the resurgence of triage, namely the idea that we cannot save all species so much as decide which ones make it and which do not. Triage differs from more ambitious approaches to conservation that, instead of lamenting inadequate budgets to save all species, basically argue that the budget for conservation should increase.[5]

Thus the critical challenge going forward centers on how to translate the recognized value of biodiversity into on-the-ground conservation results. Protecting the world's biodiversity will require deepening the public's understanding of the Earth as a living planet made up of *functional landscapes*—which is to say self-sustaining systems that support humanity, allow the world's vast variety of species to thrive, and provide ecosystem services. This will require additional measures and approaches that go beyond classic protected conservation areas yet still strongly benefit biodiversity.

## SELF-SUSTAINING LANDSCAPES

The Amazon River basin represents an important starting point for thinking about a functional landscape. Much of its biodiversity can be protected by the 25 percent of land currently in formal conservation units and the additional 25 percent in demarcated indigenous areas. Yet these lands would be imperiled if the Amazon were not managed as the system that it is. This great system (with 20 percent of the world's river water and more species of fish—3,000—than any other river basin) actually creates half of its own rainfall within the basin. That hydrological cycle originates with moisture moving westward into the basin from the tropical Atlantic. It depends on the existence of rain forest with its complex evaporative surfaces and transpiration power—the movement of water through plants and into the atmosphere. That allows the system to recycle moisture five to six times as the air mass moves to the Andes mountains (where it rises and much of the moisture precipitates out to create the great river system).

The dependence of the Amazon ecosystem on its own engineered water cycle was elegantly demonstrated by the Brazilian scientist Eneas Salati in the 1970s through examining the atomic composition of oxygen in rainwater from the Atlantic to the Peruvian border. His research shattered the existing and long-reigning dogma that vegetation is simply the consequence of climate and has no influence on it whatsoever.

This new understanding led logically to a question: how much deforestation will cause the hydrological cycle to degrade to the point of generating insufficient rainfall to support a tropical rain forest? It was an interesting question but not a pressing one, because the percentage of deforested Amazon land was in the single digits at the time. As deforestation grew, it became more pertinent, and the Brazilian climate scientist Carlos Nobre engaged some scientists to model the question of where the tipping point of Amazon dieback (with much loss of biodiversity) to a savanna state might lie. It was not an easy question, but the result was somewhere in the 30 to 40 percent deforestation range—still seemingly comfortably far off.[6]

In human-environmental interactions there is invariably a temptation to go right up to an environmental limit (ignoring a margin of safety approach), only to be surprised when some other factor pushes the system beyond the tipping point. Today, the Amazon and its hydrological cycle are measurably affected by climate change and extensive use of fire as well as deforestation (now close to 20 percent). Carlos Nobre and I believe that the synergy among these three factors is pushing the Amazon to the very verge of the tipping point for Amazon dieback.[7] Historically unprecedented droughts in 2005, 2010, and 2016 would seem to be the first flickers of system change. Happily, there is an antidote: reforestation can build back a margin of safety for maintenance of the Amazon hydrological cycle.

Given its scale and astounding biological diversity, the Amazon may be among the more dramatic examples of functional landscapes, but it is certainly not the only one. There is an impressive one in the United States, namely, the Dust Bowl. "Systems thinking" did not exist as a term when the explorer John Wesley Powell cautioned in the mid-1800s against unmodified westward expansion beyond the hundredth meridian, which cuts south across the U.S. Great Plains. He rightly foresaw that declining rainfall gradients to the west of that point required a new agricultural model. For a while he succeeded in putting that expansion on hold so science could design a better approach to land use. But before that could be achieved, his land-use legislation was repealed and population and settlement pressed westward.

In due time the cumulative clearing of native vegetation in the course of that settlement produced a subcontinental-scale system change and much of the region's good soils literally disappeared in enormous dust storms that reached even the nation's capital. We would be experiencing them to this day were it not for the programs initiated in the Great Depression and Franklin Delano Roosevelt administrations to replant enough vegetation to get the Dust Bowl under control. Ominously, because of climate change, the drier conditions that started at the hundredth meridian now begin about 190 kilometers farther to the east.

The systems approach has long been applied to freshwater systems as well, but mostly just from a water management perspective for energy generation and water supply. Watershed vegetation has often been recognized as important for generating quality water supplies, such as in the Catskills for New York City; the New Haven Water Company forests for New Haven, Connecticut; or the Tijuca Forest of Rio de Janeiro. The emphasis nonetheless has been on water as a physical substance, not as a habitat for aquatic life forms. Without question, freshwater biodiversity is more overlooked than all terrestrial biodiversity.

The Mekong River, which runs from China to Vietnam, needs management as an ecological system, not just as a freshwater source that can provide energy and drinking water. The dams being constructed in the upper part of the Mekong will be able to supply energy, but their current design will severely affect water and sediment flow, both important to river life. Those in turn are vital to the fisheries that sustain Cambodians and the rice agriculture that in turn sustains Vietnamese.

Another freshwater system that calls out for system management is the Pantanal, South America's greatest wetland—encompassing parts of Brazil (the largest part), Bolivia, and Paraguay. At one point an ambitious *hidrovía* shipping channel system—if built—would have severely impacted the Pantanal's ability to function as an enormous, continental-scale, biologically diverse sponge, absorbing water during the wet times of the year and releasing it gradually through the rest. The *hidrovía* plan was set aside as a consequence, but current threats come from dam projects for some of the tributaries of the Pantanal and agrochemical use in the watersheds that feed it.

It is of course critical to go beyond the local and regional and also apply a systems approach to the climate system, a gigantic challenge for managing life on Earth. This will be dealt with elsewhere in this volume, but it is essential to take 1.5 degrees Celsius of warming as the limit: the planet becomes unmanageable biologically above that because ecological systems will come apart.[8] Equally if not more important will be to engage in large-scale ecosystem restoration to pull back a lot of the planet-warming atmospheric carbon dioxide emitted during ecosystem destruction across the globe. This is not just about restoring forests but also about restoring other ecosystems, including grasslands and coastal wetlands, mangroves, and more, as well as designing agro-ecosystems that do not leak but rather accumulate carbon and become more fertile as a consequence. The potential to remove tens of parts per million of atmospheric carbon dioxide is incredibly powerful in dealing with the climate change juggernaut and avoiding passing 1.5 degrees Celsius. And it puts interesting meaning in the ecologist G. Evelyn Hutchinson's remark that he hoped the various things we were doing to the atmosphere would cancel each other out.

## PROTECTING GLOBAL SYSTEMS

Buried in such a functional landscape approach is the hope of growing global awareness that the planet works as a linked biological and physical system, which must be respected—indeed honored—even as the human population continues to rise and people push to occupy ever-larger swaths of land.

That recognition will, in turn, require systems thinking about socio-economic systems relative to human development. These connections are captured to an important degree in the United Nations' Sustainable Development Goals, which set out economic, social, and environmental targets for the world to reach by 2030. These 17 goals, covering a vast range of policy issues, will require systems thinking and a new global development trajectory. High on the list of approaches that must change to move societies toward a sustainable development model would be our food systems and related land use practices. The University of Minnesota ecologist David Tilman and other scientists have provided insightful analyses of how all the coming billions of additional people can be adequately fed without destroying another square inch of nature.[9] In theory that can be done through a combination of improved agricultural productivity (through careful and judicious use of inputs like fertilizers and pesticides) in particular places, reduction in food waste (40 percent of all food is wasted—not getting to markets in some places or molding in refrigerators in others), and lower-meat diets (recommended by doctors in any case). The fifth and sixth essays in this volume offer additional pathways to a future of more sustainable agriculture through better land stewardship, intensified production, and deployment of technology breakthroughs.

The preceding examples of ecosystem protection, excellent as they are, have value as models for the future only to the extent that they have successfully engaged those with a stake in making economic development decisions. Even within governments it is difficult to have a sustainable and integrated approach to development. The more responsible and visionary regional development banks and the World Bank/International Finance Corporation can make important contributions in the way they engage planning and finance ministries in development of "country plans." And even in those cases the systems being affected may be greater in geographical extent than actual nations—for example, the eight countries of the Amazon or the three countries plus China involved in the Mekong—which will require innovative approaches like the binational commission that guides management of the North American Great Lakes.

Another key to a more sustainable future and better development trajectories will be a new approach to infrastructure. Big infrastructure projects were thought of in the past as great advances for society, such as the Erie Canal, the Transcontinental Railroad, the Panama Canal, and the Itaipu Dam. They unquestionably produced major benefits. Nonetheless, as impressive as their scale was, so was their impact on the ecosystems they touched. In some cases, such as the Three Gorges Dam in China, the impact has been severe. In other cases, the design choices mitigated potential harm. In yet other circumstances, luck may have played a role. For example, the Panama Canal runs on freshwater from Lake Gatun (created by a dam), freshwater that provides a biological barrier between the salt water of the Pacific and Atlantic Oceans. This natural barrier prevents the biodiversity chaos that would otherwise be caused by mixing the biota of the two ocean ecosystems. For example, predatory sea snakes (a Pacific group of marine cobras) are environmentally blocked from the Caribbean.

Society needs a much more *systematic* approach to sustainable infrastructure. To take an example from the Amazon basin, 50-year-old energy plans that propose new river-blocking dams for hydropower should be dropped.

These mega-dams would both block sediment flow carved from the Andes, which is essential for the nutrient base of aquatic systems, and impede the migrations of the multiple large catfish species—the life spans of which range from the oceanic Amazon estuary to the watershed's origin in the Andes. Alternative designs—notably run-of-river dams that do not impede water flow—could produce hydropower with a fraction of ecosystem impact because they allow sediment flow and fish migrations.

Roads are another form of infrastructure infamous for unintended consequences. When I first was in the Amazon in the late 1960s, people were remarking on the spontaneous human settlement and forest clearing along the only road—the Belém-Brasília Highway. As one Brazilian official said to me, the impact of the road was not in the details of its construction; rather, it was in what it enabled. Almost without exception the impact of roads in the tropics has included major unplanned environmental destruction.

An interesting example of a highway that provides transportation with de minimis environmental impact is the Rodovia dos Imigrantes highway in Brazil's São Paulo State. Where it crosses Amazonia's intact Atlantic Forest, it does so as an elevated highway that provides no access to the forest. Its concrete pylons impact 2.5 percent of the land a standard highway would. While more expensive to build, it is far less costly to maintain than a conventional highway in the wet tropics. (Highway projects rarely include the cost of maintenance when being designed.)

Serious attention also needs to be paid to production systems so that products become more often recyclable by nature than not. We have to move away from a worldview in which we produce most anything with little concern for its environmental impact. We continue to invent, produce, and use compounds new to nature, whether plastics, agricultural inputs, or other chemicals. They get introduced—akin to littering—into the environment usually with no environmental evaluation, let alone consideration of the possible interactions between and among them and of the negative effects on biodiversity and ecosystems. It is really not surprising that summer nocturnal insect populations appear to have crashed in North America and Europe in part because of widespread chemical use.

But while better agriculture and infrastructure policies and practices offer a starting point for a new seriousness of purpose around biodiversity, more will be required. In this regard, we must not lose track of what is directly needed for conservation of biodiversity and for the longer-term goal of a biologically diverse planet with robust populations of plants, animals, and microorganisms and functioning ecosystems. Protected areas must be expanded and enhanced as important havens and safe places, but they also need to be embedded in a biodiversity-friendly matrix of land uses. We need to think of a world in which plant and animal populations are not restricted to protected areas but can recover and move across gradients of biodiversity-friendly land uses in response to environmental change (as is already happening in response to climate change). Humanity and biodiversity will be best served when the latter is accorded the wonder, respect, and indeed affection it deserves. We need to embrace a world where human aspiration is embedded in nature and biological diversity, in broader landscapes, freshwater-scapes, and seascapes.

## NOTES

1. Ruth Patrick, "Ecology of Freshwater Diatoms and Diatom Communities," in *The Biology of Diatoms,* ed. Dietrich Werner (Berkeley: University of California Press, 1977), 284–332; Ruth Patrick, "A Proposed Biological Measure of Stream Conditions, Based on a Survey of the Conestoga Basin, Lancaster County, Pennsylvania," *Proceedings of the Academy of Natural Sciences of Philadelphia* 101 (1949): 277–341; Veronica I. Pye and Ruth Patrick, "Ground Water Contamination in the United States," *Science* 221 (1983): 713–18.
2. Johan Rockström et al., "A Safe Operating Space for Humanity," *Nature* 461 (2009): 472–75, https://www.nature.com/articles/461472a.
3. *Living Planet Report 2018: Aiming Higher,* World Wildlife Fund (2018), http://wwf.panda.org/knowledge_hub/all_publications/living_planet_report_2018/.
4. Eric Dinerstein et al., "A Global Deal for Nature: Guiding Principles, Milestones, and Targets," *Science Advances* 5, no. 4 (April 2019), https://doi.org/10.1126/sciadv.aaw2869; Eric Dinerstein et al., "An Ecoregion-Based Approach to Protecting Half the Terrestrial Realm," *BioScience* 67, no. 6 (April 2017): 534–45, doi:10.1093/biosci/bix014; Karl Burkart, "One Earth Climate Model," Leonardo DiCaprio Foundation (2018), https://www.leonardodicaprio.org/one-earth-climate-model/.
5. Thomas E. Lovejoy, "We Must Decide Which Species Will Go Forever," *Smithsonian Magazine* 7, no. 4 (1976): 52–59.
6. Gilvan Sampaio et al., "Regional Climate Change over Eastern Amazonia Caused by Pasture and Soybean Cropland Expansion," *Geophysical Research Letters* 34, no. 17 (September 2007), doi:10.1029/2007GL030612.
7. Thomas E. Lovejoy and Carlos Nobre, "Amazon Tipping Point," *Science Advances* 4, no. 2 (February 2018), https://doi.org/10.1126/sciadv.aat2340.
8. Thomas E. Lovejoy and Lee Hannah, "Avoiding the Climate Failsafe Point," *Science Advances* 4, no. 8 (August 2018), https://doi.org/10.1126/sciadv.aau9981.
9. David Tilman and Michael Clark, "Food, Agriculture and the Environment: Can We Feed the World and Save the Earth?," *Daedalus* 144, no. 4 (Fall 2015): 8–23, https://doi.org/10.1162/DAED_a_00350.

# A Restoration Agenda for Native Forests

Mark S. Ashton and Craig R. Brodersen

BEFORE THE INDUSTRIAL REVOLUTION, native forests covered 6 billion hectares, or about 30 percent of global land surface. Today about 3.9 billion hectares of forests cover the terrestrial surface of the world; of them only about a third remain relatively intact. In the last fifty years, humans have converted extensive areas of tropical and subtropical forest to other land uses, including agriculture, ranching, and plantations, much of which is not sustainable in the long term. Forests in other tropical regions have undergone chronic and repeated exploitation for fuelwood, game, timber, and non-timber forest products. Both deforestation and forest exploitation have converted forests into wastelands, often fire-prone and permanently altered. In temperate regions, many of these same impacts happened before and during the Industrial Revolution at the beginning of the nineteenth century.

Forest restoration must be understood as complex and multi-dimensional due to the diversity of forest systems, the legacies of their past disturbance, competing human demands, the onslaught of invasive insects and pathogens, and forest fragmentation from suburbanization—all compounded by a rapidly changing climate. There has now emerged a global call for restoration of deforested lands, given the growing recognition that forests provide a disproportionate amount of the services—drinking and irrigation water, climate change mitigation, stormwater management, and recreation—that allow humanity to survive in the long term.[1] But how best to advance the restoration agenda remains under debate.

Most of the native forests across the world, over 86 percent, are publicly owned. Public lands are those owned and managed by national, state, and regional governments and government-owned institutions. Much of the public forest land across the world is also claimed by local communities and indigenous peoples. And most of this forest is degraded and/or recuperating and often restricted to the most marginal soils and uplands in the more remote areas of a country. Yet, these forests are still home to the bulk of the world's and each nation's wildlife and biodiversity, still serve as the most important resource for outdoor recreation, and remain critical watersheds for each nation's supply of irrigation and drinking water.

Since the 1970s, ecological science has dramatically improved our understanding of how native forests function over short- and long-term timescales. This foundational knowledge should serve as a template for their restoration. Two main pillars of this increased knowledge base should undergird a global forest restoration agenda: (1) deeper and more refined understanding of the conditions that allow for forest species and genetic diversity to arise, persist, and increase; and (2) completely reworked comprehension of how forests and the trees within them change over time. Together this research should both guide and constrain the third axis of information necessary for native forest restoration: (3) understanding how to achieve social stability within and surrounding native forests. Without social stability, secure land tenure, strong environmental regulation, and robust markets for products and services from native forests, it will be impossible to incentivize their restoration.

## UNDERSTANDING DIVERSITY

To restore forests to their healthy state, we must understand what factors drive the diversity of species that compose them. It was not long ago that ecologists thought that the reason why diversity was the greatest in tropical wet forests, as compared with all other kinds of ecosystems, was because their longer time in evolutionary development promoted higher species diversification, and their more moderate precipitation and temperature allowed for the greatest numbers of species to potentially coexist. Researchers considered simple random chance and time the main mechanisms that accumulated and maintained species diversity and coexistence in such conducive climes. However, much work over the past thirty years has demonstrated that tropical forests, and forests in general, are diverse for many reasons. We now recognize that the most important reasons for diversification are *negative density dependence, niche differentiation,* and *biogeography.*[2]

Negative density dependence is the regulation of a species population by competition for resources with other species, predation, and pathogens. The more dominant and numerous the individuals of a species in a given area, the more prone they are to mortality from these factors, as the increased species population tends to lead to increased population of their predators and pests. Many studies are demonstrating that in ever-moist and warm climates, the fewer related tree species that surround each other, the less chance they have of being predated, browsed by herbivores, or infected by a pathogen.[3] Researchers suspect that this pattern arises because a given habitat can be divided up by numerous species that exploit a specific set of conditions, and that predators (either herbivores or seed predators) tend to specialize on specific species rather than preying on a broad range of potential host plant species. Climates that have more extreme seasonality—such as boreal forests, temperate forests, or deserts—exhibit weaker negative density dependence. This is because many of the pathogens and insects are eliminated by stronger seasonality and accompanying effects of cold or ecosystem *disturbances* like droughts, fires, or floods. This pattern promotes a "monodominance" of fewer tree species that are specialized to survive such climate extremes and disturbances without the pressure of negative density dependence processes. Primary productivity, the total amount of biomass a forest produces in a given amount of time, is generally lower in boreal and temperate regions, but this is more of a function of growing season length and resource availability rather than species diversity. Greater forest diversity generally leads to increased productivity regardless of location, and productivity and carbon sequestration from the atmosphere increase with forest age.

The other important process that has presumably coevolved with negative density dependence is niche differentiation. Studies show that as the heterogeneity of a forest's soils, elevation, hydrology, and disturbance increase, higher numbers of species specialized to particular sites and disturbance regimes—particular differentiated "niches"—arise. Defining the factors that drive species differentiation and at what temporal and spatial scale they occur is critical. For example, there are over five hundred *Shorea* tree species that coexist in Asian tropical rain forests. Although they are all very closely related, species coexist because they have sets of physiological and morphological traits that allow them to outcompete their relatives at different points along gradients of soil types, elevation, and disturbance. As a genus, *Shorea* species have separated from one common ancestor into many distinct species, each with unique sets of adaptions to particular forest niches in both space and time.

The third reason for forest diversification is the history and nature of the biogeography of a region—that is, the way its biological attributes have been shaped by geographic conditions. Continental land masses, given their size and ancient geologies, have inherent higher capacity for diversification as compared with islands that are newer and spontaneously originate through volcanism. Continental evolutionary taxonomies are related to ancient movements in plate tectonics, whereas many volcanic island taxonomies are novel and develop by chance.

Lessons learned from the study of negative density dependence, niche differentiation, and biogeography should be the underpinnings for any kind of future land management—natural forests or their plantation and agricultural analogs. To date, modern forest management principles and best practices are rarely properly implemented. First, understanding the strength of negative density dependence processes in relation to climate should determine the long-term proneness to insects and disease of an agricultural or tree plantation system or native forest. Agricultural-style monocultures of single trees in the tropics, which are now a very important source of the world's supply of food and fiber, bode huge risks of future failure. This situation has arisen largely because economies of scale favor single-species production under current agricultural and plantation practices. Likewise, low-diversity or monodominant temperate and boreal native forests of today are now exposed to warmer climates and are likely prone to greater impacts of insects and disease.

Second, forests and trees that exhibit strong niche differentiation require restoration practices that cater to their specialized site and disturbance requirements. Similarly, in plantation and agricultural systems, species that have been planted because of their economic value have often failed because their owners chose species based on their potential profitability and not on their suitability to local conditions. Thus, future work will be required to move from monocultural practices that are generally at odds with current ecological theory in terms of long-term stability, resiliency, and productivity.

## FOREST SUCCESSION AND STAND DYNAMICS

The second important area to understand arises from the new sub-discipline within silviculture (the applied ecology of growing trees and forests) called *stand dynamics,* which describes the general turnover of tree species that dominate a forest as it progresses in age and development. The necessity that nature should be understood and emulated does not mean that silviculture should blindly follow either the reality of natural processes or abstract theories about them. Most forests and trees have an average lifespan longer than humans. It is therefore difficult to recognize that the natural disturbances that renew forests, often occurring at intervals of centuries, such as fires, windstorms, and insect outbreaks, are usually big and replace entire sections of forests.

Early ecological research speculated that small iterative disturbances were the most common and driving forces of forest *succession,* or species change through time, with tree species of different successional phases of a forest's development iteratively establishing at different times; fast-growing sun-loving species establishing first, and slower-growing more shade-tolerant species establishing later beneath the shade of the fast-growing canopy trees. Some forests are slowly and continuously renewed by minor disturbances, but these are far from the norm. The various patterns in the development of forest vegetation over time and after disturbance are largely dominated by much larger, more intense disturbances. This is now well recognized as an important process especially for more temperate and boreal forest types, where complete processes of forest transitions have been more easily observed by researchers.

Congruent with this understanding, research has shown that species of different successional phases establish and grow together, not sequentially, but grow at different rates, reach the canopy of the forest at different times, and live for different lengths of time. Through these processes, most forests develop over time after disturbances as groups of individuals rather than as a single cohort competing for growing space. When this happens, cohorts grow through phases of growth into a mature forest.[4] After a disturbance has created vacant growing space, the new trees that have become established are in a phase called "stand initiation," the establishment of a new *stand.* When tree crowns become closed, this event starts the second stage of stand development, the "stem exclusion stage." During this stage, the trees start to compete with each other; the more vigorous ones encroach into the growing space of weaker trees that eventually die—usually from lack of light or soil moisture— and additional regeneration of tree species can no longer occur. Unless some disturbance wipes out the stand and starts a new stand initiation stage, an aging stand will gradually enter the "understory re-initiation stage." In this stage, small vacancies from canopy tree death and dieback allow the establishment of new plants beneath. The gradual death of overstory trees and replacement by younger age-classes leads into an "old-growth stage." Forests reach this stage when the original trees are gone and one or more of the new age-classes or cohorts compose parts of the top canopy. Stratified mixtures of species typically develop. Most forests never attain this stage of development because of new disturbance.

What does all this mean for restoration of native forests? It means that the traditional sequential silvicultural practice of small iterative treatments and the creation of small forest openings are in most cases not the most effective forest restoration strategies. For restoration purposes, late- and early-successional trees should be planted together at the same or almost the same time; and restorative treatments to initiate successional dynamics to increase local diversity should often be dramatic but one-time treatments. This approach facilitates the establishment of a single cohort needed to start the maturation of a forest. Across a landscape, forests need to represent all stages of stand development at scales, arrangement, and lengths of developmental time driven by the natural rhythm of nature's disturbance cycle for the biological, geographical, and climate conditions of the region. A silvicultural approach to achieve this scope and scale of restoration will take not only considerable political and economic investment but also education and a long-term commitment to the goal of restoration.

## ECONOMY, CULTURE, AND LAW

Current silviculture, and by implication forest practice, is much more complex and varied now than at any stage in the history of its development. In the more remote forests of tropical Africa and the Amazon, people still practice the silviculture associated with shifting agricultural cultivation systems. In many populated rural regions of the tropics and sub-tropics of underdeveloped regions, *coppice* systems, the practice of tree cutback and regrowth that was once widespread in Europe and northeast Asia, still predominate as the mainstay for fuelwood and charcoal production and as a source fertilizer for crops and fodder for livestock. Much of the developed world now has private land invested in intensive plantation systems for wood production. But by far the largest proportion of forest land is native, fragmented, logged over, or old agricultural land reclaimed as *second-growth* forest and restricted to poorer sites. These native forests are now on the verge of a new economy, particularly in developed nations where their service values for climate and storm mitigation, biodiversity conservation, recreation, and watershed protection are increasingly recognized.

For restoration of these native forests to occur, social stability must underpin forestry and its long-term investment in future products and services. This means a clear recognition of land tenure, adherence to environmental laws, and the presence of strong and diverse markets. Only under these conditions can restored forests for the future flourish. Without this protection, it is difficult to implement restoration with any security of investment.

Developed economies that can provide social stability are therefore an opportune place to practice restoration, silviculture, and forestry on native forests.[5] In such regions, forests have endured the complete economic development continuum of subsistence, exploitation, and conservation. We now need sophisticated site-specific and ecologically based silviculture nested within a framework of secure tenure, law, and markets. Because these forests are on marginal lands, they are slow growing and therefore prone to the vagaries of change in tenure, market, and law. Such social change makes these forests susceptible to near-term exploitation and degradation, even though these forests provide higher economic and social benefits if managed for the long term using the ecological and silvicultural principles we have discussed. One such governance structure that uses market incentives to improve forest management is certification, but even though certifying agencies have been around for twenty-five years, results have met with mixed success.

We provide three case examples that illustrate these principles for restoring native forests: the mixed-coniferous forests of the temperate American West, the native mixed-deciduous forests of northeastern America, and the tropical mixed-dipterocarp forests of Southeast Asia.

*Coniferous Forests of the Sierra Nevada.*    Coniferous forests of the far west have a history of exploitation and heavy logging starting around the beginning of the twentieth century, resulting in even-aged and overcrowded stands that established during a period of higher rainfall and the active suppression of wildfires dictated by U.S. Forest Service policies. Recent lower winter snowfall—combined with longer summer growing seasons, increases in pollutants such as ozone, increased summer and spring temperatures, and earlier snowmelt—led to widespread drought and pollutant stresses among much of the forest. This stress then limited the trees' ability to defend themselves from bark beetle outbreaks. Tree mortality resulting from pollutants, drought, and pests subsequently provided enormous amounts of fuel for future forest fires.[6] While fire at regular intervals is an intrinsic part of the ecology of these habitats, and many species depend on frequent fire for reproduction, the U.S. Forest Service largely promoted long-term fire suppression in this region because of a lack of understanding of local ecology, as well as the development of home construction in and around these forests. The combination of hot, dry periods and human activities has allowed for massive, stand-replacing fires to now occur regularly throughout areas of California, which make these disturbances catastrophic to human life.

Restoration of these forests requires changes in building codes and zoning laws, the creation of strong markets for carbon sequestration and watershed protection, and a governance structure that allows managers to manage with greater, more site-specific creativity. The forests themselves, because of overstocking, need judicious thinning in places to accelerate their development from stem exclusion to understory initiation. Managers also need to reintroduce fire back into the landscape both through purposeful prescribed burning and by allowing nature to self-regulate in more remote areas through natural-origin wildfires. At a larger scale, the forests need to regenerate over time and space at scales defined by historical records of natural disturbance size, frequency, and severity.

*Northeast Oak-Hardwood Forests of America.*   Today's northeastern U.S. oak-hardwood forests, contrary to trends, are largely held by private landowners. These forests arose largely as even-aged mixtures released for growth after old-field pine was cut out in the early 1900s. The pine established on pastures that cultivators abandoned when the wool market collapsed in the 1850s and more people migrated to city centers. Continuous partial cuttings for timber have removed much of the oak, leading to a more moisture-loving shade-tolerant forest largely composed of maple species. In the last half century, the northeast has become warmer and wetter, with more dramatic warming in the winter and only moderate increases over the summer. While the frequency of high-intensity precipitation events has increased, periods between such events—particularly in late summer and fall—receive little rain, making for more frequent and intense droughts. Because of the predicted increase in heavy rainfall events during winter due to climate change, combined with increased microbial soil activity in the summer, the already nutrient-poor soils throughout this region will likely degrade over time. Increasing temperatures are also predicted to cause further shifts in the geographical distribution of species, with increased prevalence of species that currently have their northern limits just to the south.

To promote forest restoration and adaptation, forest managers should focus on developing greater structural, compositional, and age-class complexity. They should use regeneration methods that simulate windstorms and promote the establishment of or creation of growing space for all tree species together, but also increase diversity to make the forest less prone to the processes of negative density dependence. These methods need to create single- or two-aged stands that are managed to arrive at an all-aged forest within the shortest period of time possible. Markets need to facilitate these processes by payments for watershed and carbon services, with stronger regulations to retain forests rather than convert them to other land uses. Such forests will be more resilient to the uncertain effects of climate change, especially in terms of increased temperatures and changes in precipitation.

*Mixed-Dipterocarp Forests of Southeast Asia.*   Trees of the Dipterocarpaceae family dominated the tropical ever-wet regions of Indonesia, Malaysia, and the Philippines before much of the land was heavily logged for the timbers of the dipterocarp trees. Logging started extensively in the 1970s and still continues, with much of the land converted to single-species crops of oil palm, coconut, and rubber. Much of this land is now heavily degraded brush depauperate of the original forest composition and structure. Other areas are extensively degraded after crop failure and have reverted to fire-dependent grass and fern lands.

These are government lands that require strong environmental protection from illegal logging and land clearance. Their restoration is complex and can be iterative, but simply put, degraded brush can be cut back. This cutting will stimulate natural regeneration of the original forest still present in the understory, which together with brush growth can develop as a single cohort of many species that will grow at different rates to eventually form a diverse stand. If the trees required for natural regeneration are not present, managers can plant and release the forest instead. And on grasslands they can establish mixed-species plantations of the same successional groups of species found in the original forest. Fire will obviously need to be controlled, and the plantations will need protection. Restoration will also require that policy makers develop strong markets to pay for biodiversity conservation and non-timber forest products.

These case studies illustrate that diverse parts of the world demand diverse forest restoration solutions. Just as no two forests are the same, no two sets of management practices will resemble each other exactly. But across the world, greater understanding of the factors that drive forest growth and diversity can help us begin to regenerate these crucial ecosystems.

## NOTES

1.  Don Funnell and Romola Parish, *Mountain Environments and Communities* (London: Routledge, 2005).
2.  Joseph S. Wright, "Plant Diversity in Tropical Forests: A Review of Mechanisms of Species Coexistence," *Oecologia* 130, no. 1 (2002): 1–14.
3.  Liza S. Comita et al., "Asymmetric Density Dependence Shapes Species Abundances in a Tropical Tree Community," *Science* 329, no. 5989 (2010): 330–32.
4.  Chadwick Dearing Oliver and Bruce C. Larson, *Forest Stand Dynamics* (New York: John Wiley and Sons, 1996).
5.  Mark S. Ashton and Matthew J. Kelty, *The Practice of Silviculture: Applied Forest Ecology* (New York: John Wiley and Sons, 2018).
6.  Brendan Choat et al., "Triggers of Tree Mortality under Drought," *Nature* 558 (2018): 531–39.

# Private Lands

## THE FUTURE OF CONSERVATION IN AMERICA

Larry Selzer

THE NATURE OF LAND CONSERVATION in America needs to change. Up until this point, we largely have trusted governments to conserve land in its natural state to protect biodiversity and the landscapes we love. In the future, however, if we are to conserve the vast important landscapes needed to protect biodiversity and water quality and become more resilient to climate change, land conservation is likely to focus less on fee ownership by public agencies and more on conservation easements on the lands that lie between our national parks and wildlife refuges—in other words, private lands.

Many factors drive this shift. While a significant number of Americans continue to support land conservation (a 2018 national poll by the National Wildlife Federation revealed that three out of every four Americans support full funding of the Land and Water Conservation Fund for federal, state, and local holdings[1]), many Americans, especially across the western states, are growing more skeptical of significantly increasing the amount of land that is federally owned. Already, 48 percent of the state of Wyoming is owned by the federal government. In Utah it is 64 percent, and in Nevada fully 85 percent of the state is federally owned. Recent high-profile conflicts between those who want to continue their traditional uses of the land, such as ranching, and those who want the land to revert to a more pristine state have reignited the polarizing sentiments of the Sagebrush Rebellion against federal land ownership in the 1970s and 1980s. These conflicts have had a signifi-cant anti-conservation impact on federal and state policymaking, including how much money is appropriated each year by Congress to fund land con-servation.

In addition, there is an increasing mismatch between the cost of landscape-scale conservation and the stagnating public budgets available to finance it. Congress has permanently reauthorized the Land and Water Conservation Fund, the primary federal mechanism for funding land conservation, but it has not significantly increased the amount appropriated in years, and full funding at the authorized level of $900 million per year remains elusive.

Finally, there is a growing recognition that keeping land in private owner-ship, allowing for continued economic use but with important public interest values protected through a permanent conservation easement that restricts how the land is used, is in many ways the ideal outcome for these landscapes. These protected private lands provide for both the environment and the people who depend on them for their livelihoods. They must be a fundamen-tal part of future efforts to expand conservation in America.

This recast conservation strategy will be especially important in the con-text of America's large, privately held working forests—those unfragmented forests that provide timber and other products. The loss of these forests repre-sents the greatest land conservation problem in the country today. In addition to the land conservation impact, the effect of forest loss extends to the irre-placeable climate stability, ecosystem resilience, and economic prosperity benefits that working forests uniquely generate. It is such an immense chal-lenge because of the scale of land in danger (the U.S. Forest Service estimates that as many as 40 million acres of forestland are at risk of development over the next two decades), the amount of money needed to protect the most envi-ronmentally important lands (roughly $5 billion to protect the five million acres that the U.S. Forest Service estimates are of high conservation value), and the speed with which large forestland transactions are completed (in many cases within just 90 to 120 days). There is not enough public money or political will to buy these lands outright, and traditional forms of philanthropy simply cannot mobilize fast enough or at sufficient scale to address this big of a challenge. If we are to protect them into the future, we need new models, new skills, even a new language.

## FROM THE BIRTH OF CONSERVATION TO THE ERA
### OF REGULATION

To understand why we need a new approach to conservation, it is useful to look at the history of the environmental movement in America. With due respect to Ulysses S. Grant, who created the first national park (Yellowstone) in 1872, for me and many others the story of the modern environmental movement begins at the turn of the twentieth century when Teddy Roosevelt was president of the United States. It was a time of tremendous economic expansion; the mantra was "go west," and our nation's vast natural resources were there to be exploited. To build our cities, we clear-cut our forests. To support manufacturing, we extracted minerals and energy without regard for the environmental consequences. For sport or fashion, we hunted species nearly to extinction.

Dismayed by all this, Roosevelt acted. He expanded our emerging system of national parks, created our first national wildlife refuges, and, building on previous work by Presidents Harrison, Cleveland, and McKinley, established the National Forest Service. His efforts, totaling millions of acres of land, launched the first era of the environmental movement, the era of conservation, and today our network of protected lands is the envy of the world. By the mid-twentieth century, however, we faced a whole new set of environmental challenges. Air quality in some cities was so bad that you had to turn on your windshield wipers to remove the soot before you could drive your car. Rivers were so polluted that some turned a different color each day of the week depending on what dye was being used. And widespread use of chemicals like DDT threatened iconic species, such as the peregrine falcon, with extinction.

Then, in 1962, Rachel Carson published her seminal book, *Silent Spring*, which brought public attention to the link between environmental pollution and human health. Her book unleashed a tidal wave of grassroots activism and ushered in the second era of the environmental movement—the era of regulation. As a result, there are now more than 10,000 environmental organizations in the United States and more than 50,000 pieces of legislation and regulation on the federal, state, and local books, including some of the most important laws the country has ever passed—the Clean Air Act, the Clean Water Act, and the Endangered Species Act.[2]

This era was about stopping bad things from happening, and it worked. Industrial pollution has plummeted, laws protect consumers from the most harmful of chemicals, and better land use planning has kept development out of the most fragile ecosystems. Yet, these gains have come with a price. Our half-century reliance on the tools of legislation, litigation, and regulation has now become our Achilles' heel. In too many cases, advocates for the environment can say exactly what they are against, but often have a hard time saying what they are for. Renewable energy is a case in point. For decades the environmental movement has held out renewable energy as the only responsible path forward for energy development. And yet, today, many major renewable energy projects and the transmission lines they need to get the energy to the grid are litigated by environmental organizations. This posture has become a major impediment to innovation and the movement's ability to develop solutions that can be implemented at significant scale. Conserving millions of acres of our nation's last remaining large, intact working forests will require dramatically new approaches.

## A MODEL OF PRIVATE LAND CONSERVATION

What we need is a new kind of environmentalism, defined not by saying no but by saying yes. I call this new era the "era of convergence"—defined by the coming together of two of the most powerful forces in the country today: the environmental movement and the free enterprise system. Only by embracing the tools of the marketplace will we be able to mobilize the capital we need to protect the huge landscapes that are at risk.

Yet, bringing together these two forces is not easy. They have different cultures, different training. They often speak different languages. Environmentalists talk about ecosystems and biodiversity; businesspeople speak of discounted cash flow and return on invested capital. They are divided by what the great British biologist C. P. Snow called a "gulf of mutual incomprehension."[3] And yet, bridging that gulf is exactly what we need to do.

Let me describe one example of conservation that can operate at the speed of business and achieve the scale needed to get the job done. According to the U.S. Forest Service, the United States is projected to lose nearly 40 million acres of privately held working forests to non-forest uses by 2040. This loss is the direct result of an unprecedented consolidation of working forests into institutional investor ownership that has short-term, financially driven business models. The transition of these forests from integrated pulp and paper companies to investment entities began in the 1980s, and since then more than 20 million acres have been lost to development, and more than 13 million acres have been significantly fragmented. Unchecked, these trends will continue.

The loss of these forests does irreparable harm to our nation's efforts to address climate change, protect biodiversity, enhance water quality, and expand rural prosperity. These forests provide clean air to breathe and clean water to drink, sequester millions of tons of carbon, and support more than one million jobs—jobs that cannot be exported overseas. Yet, for lack of capital and a business model that can deploy it efficiently, we are losing these forests at an accelerating rate. In response, the Conservation Fund and other organizations are working to protect these privately held forests. At the Conservation Fund, we have launched an approach that would allow charitable money to be aggregated with low-cost loans so that we can move faster, conserve large blocks of land, and revolve the capital from one acquisition to the next. Here's how it works.

Working with foundations, individual donors, and state agencies, we have capitalized a working forest fund that allows us to buy critical forests when they come up for sale. Under this model, the first step after purchasing a forest is to develop a sustainable harvest plan; timber may be removed only at the rate at which the forest naturally replaces it. Harvesting timber keeps existing jobs in place and allows forest owners to cover their expenses. The revenue generated by sustainably harvesting timber allows owners to hold the forest long enough to put in place a conservation easement that permanently protects the forest but allows for sustainable logging in the future.

This model calls for the sale of a conservation easement to the state resources agency or a land conservation organization so that the protections are enforced in perpetuity. (In the case of state agencies as easement holders, reversionary clauses or co-hold positions can be implemented to add an additional layer of certainty, allowing for additional state action if conservation restrictions are violated.) The amount paid to retire the development rights allows the owners to recoup a portion of their investment in the forest. Finally, after the conservation easement is secure, owners can resell the land to someone who wants to own a sustainable forest, allowing them to recover all their invested capital. To date, the Conservation Fund has invested in more than 650,000 acres of high-conservation-value working forests across 15 states. Under this model of ownership, the lands are kept on the tax rolls, the forest-related jobs are kept in place, and the forests are sustainably harvested. The model is scalable and financially self-sustaining.

## LOOKING FORWARD

What have we learned in developing and implementing this model? To paraphrase the title of the leadership coach Marshall Goldsmith's terrific book, what got you here won't get you there. The tools that have made the environmental movement successful in the past will not be sufficient to address issues such as climate change, rural economic distress, and forest loss. Some years ago, the president of the Surdna Foundation, Ed Skloot, said about environmental nonprofits and those who fund them: "We need to peel back our fear of and contempt for the marketplace and recognize that the United States is a commercial republic by our Founding Fathers' design."[4] If conservation is to succeed in the future, especially for large intact private lands such as working forests, we must integrate the best of the marketplace into our work. In other words, we need to behave more like for-profit organizations so that we can better fulfill our missions.

It was not that long ago that the idea of working forests as conservation was unacceptable to a majority of environmental organizations and those who funded them. I know this because in 1999 we went under contract with Champion International to acquire nearly 300,000 acres of forestland—145,000 acres in New York, 133,000 acres in Vermont, and 18,000 acres in New Hampshire. Our vision was to purchase the land, sell one-third of the acreage to federal and state public agencies to be included in the Adirondack Park and the Silvio Conte National Wildlife Refuge, then sell conservation easements on the remaining two-thirds of the land, after which we would resell the land with the timber rights intact back into the private market as permanently conserved working forest. No fragmentation, no development, no conversion to non-timber uses, and with sustainable forestry standards codified in the easement.

This outcome protected the forests and kept the jobs and tax base intact for those rural communities that depended on the forest products industry for their livelihoods. Yet, we were criticized severely by funders and other nonprofits because at that time economic development (that is, cutting trees) was not viewed as conservation, even if done sustainably. Their fear of and contempt for the marketplace would not allow them to see a third way. Not a park and not an industrial forest; rather, a permanently conserved working forest. They fell into the trap articulated by Albert Ruesga, vice president of the Eugene and Agnes Meyer Foundation: "In [philanthropy] . . . we tend to affirm and recreate the world rather than challenge and remake it."[5]

Conserving private lands at a large scale will require the environmental movement to challenge and remake the status quo. Nonprofits must be willing to emulate the business world's innovation, sophistication, and financial leverage. Philanthropies need to be more open to new approaches to financial support, including using their own funds to leverage public, corporate, and other foundation support. In addition, by emphasizing easements on large tracts of private lands instead of direct purchases, charitable investments will get two or three times as much permanent conservation accomplished, and they will get the additional leverage embedded in protecting the forest products, jobs, and local communities that depend on conserved land. Conservation without local community endorsement rarely lasts, and we need to make sure that rural communities benefit from our conservation actions.

Government agencies can play an equally powerful role by providing significantly more money to help acquire conservation easements on working lands. In addition to the Land and Water Conservation Fund, other funding mechanisms such as the U.S. Department of Agriculture's Forest Legacy Program and the Regional Conservation Partnership Program are especially well positioned to work at landscape scale and allow for private ownership with public environmental interests protected through permanent easements. They should be funded at much higher levels in future Congresses.

States too can play a leading role. Georgia, for example, recently passed its first dedicated funding for conservation and is expressly targeting its large, private working forests for conservation easements. The forest products industry is the second-largest industry in the state, injecting $35 billion and almost 145,000 jobs into the state's economy.[6] Investing in the conservation of these private lands is just good business.

Finally, companies also have a role to play. As companies increasingly seek to minimize their impact on our natural resources, they are taking steps to reduce their footprints—energy, water, land, fiber—and offset the rest through various credit programs such as the California cap-and-trade program for carbon emissions. As the carbon and climate value of forests is better understood, and as deforestation in many parts of the developing world continues unabated, permanently protecting America's large, private working forests is an increasingly attractive business option.

Today, working forest conservation has become a mainstream strategy. This breakthrough in the use of market-based tools to conserve private lands and promote public conservation goals offers valuable insights into the future of large-scale private land conservation. Applying similar approaches to working farms and ranches would accelerate private land conservation across the United States in unprecedented and exciting ways, and yield a much more resilient landscape for wildlife, water quality, carbon sequestration, outdoor recreation, and traditional economic uses.

## NOTES

1. "National Survey Results," Public Policy Polling, National Wildlife Federation, November 26–27, 2018, https://www.nwf.org/-/media/Documents/PDFs/Press-Releases /LWCF-Results/National-LWCF-Results.ashx?la=en&hash=A8B3AB2D7B60EBBD 6814E67EBD61A02082F88A65.

2. This description of the history of the environmental movement draws on and builds on the author's previously published article "Environmental Sustainability and Economic Vitality: We Can Have Both," *The Conservation Fund* (blog), January 4, 2016, https://www.conservationfund.org/blog/1200-environmental-sustainability-and -economic-vitality-we-can-have-both.

3. C. P. Snow, *The Two Cultures and the Scientific Revolution* (New York: Cambridge University Press, 1959), 4.

4. Edward Skloot, "The Second Gilded Age: Time for a New Bargain," *The Chronicle of Philanthropy* (blog), May 4, 2000, https://www.philanthropy.com/article/The-Second -Gilded-Age-Time/185953.

5. Mitch Nauffts, "A Conversation with Ed Skloot (and Friends)," *Philanthropy News Digest* (blog), November 7, 2007, https://pndblog.typepad.com/pndblog/2007/11/a -conversation-.html.

6. Jessica Saunders, "How Much Money Does Forestry Contribute to Georgia's Economy?," *Atlanta Business Chronicle*, January 10, 2018, https://www.bizjournals.com /atlanta/news/2018/01/10/how-much-money-does-forestry-contribute-to.html.

# Stewards of the Land

## HARNESSING AMERICAN AGRICULTURE FOR A SUSTAINABLE FUTURE

Erin Fitzgerald and Greg Gershuny

FOR MORE THAN TEN THOUSAND YEARS, agriculture has been the foundation on which civilizations are built, empires rise and fall, and humans raise themselves out of poverty. Food is the foundation of family and communities, the thing that brings us together, and, in some cases, the thing that can drive us to war.

If humans are going to continue to prosper and feed our ever-growing population, we need to understand agriculture's role in our society and maximize its potential to promote sustainability and to address climate change. To achieve true sustainable agriculture, the farming community and food supply chain must be *stewards* not just of the land but also of sustainable nutrition and climate change action. On the farm, this principle has long required not just that farmers plant for this season's harvest or raise a herd of animals, but that they equally maintain a far deeper sense of commitment to the land, their children, and their grandchildren. This stewardship obligation should be seen as a commitment by the farming community and the food supply chain as a whole to simultaneously provide for the current population while also preserving and enhancing the land for the next generation. Farmers and ranchers look to the horizon, making decisions now based on what is best for today and the future. With the help of established practices, newer technologies, and renewed commitments, American farmers and ranchers—who care for almost half of all U.S. land—can continue to adopt new solutions that will help create a better, more sustainable future.

## CHALLENGES—NUTRITION AND CLIMATE CHANGE

Agriculture has provided nourishment to people and has allowed us to flourish as a society. However, as agricultural productivity has grown over past decades and centuries, many have been left behind. In 2016, the United Nations launched the Decade of Nutrition to put special emphasis on Zero Hunger, the second of seventeen Sustainable Development Goals meant to guide human progress. The triple burden of malnutrition (that is, undernutrition, micronutrient deficiency, and overweight and obesity) is recognized globally as a universal challenge. Malnutrition affects nearly one in three people worldwide and can have negative long-term consequences.[1] Undernutrition increases the risk of disease and death, drives up health care costs, burdens families and communities, limits educational potential, and impedes economic progress.[2] On a societal level, proper nutrition and basic food security underpin peace and prosperity. Adding to these challenges, between 2009 and 2050, the global population is projected to grow by one-third, requiring around a 70 percent increase in food production from 2005–2007 levels.[3]

In addition to nutrition challenges, we face the growing threat of climate change, which could destabilize the current food system and undermine efforts to achieve nutrition for all. In 2016, agriculture accounted for about 9 percent of total U.S. greenhouse gas emissions.[4] Practices in both animal and crop agriculture release greenhouse gases, primarily methane, nitrous oxide, and carbon dioxide. Of all climate-warming greenhouse gas emissions associated with the U.S. agricultural sector, most come from livestock production, with crop production accounting for the next largest amount.[5] Embedded in all these source emissions is food waste, which is the largest source, and accounts for 30 to 40 percent of the carbon impact from the food and agriculture sector.

While farming and ranching contribute to warming the planet, climate change also greatly affects the sector. Increases in average temperature can cause major impacts on crop production, spread pests and diseases to new environments, increase soil evaporation rates, and threaten the health of field workers. More extreme heat may also cause more heat stress for livestock and greater risk of heat exhaustion, heatstroke, and heart attack for humans. Increased occurrences of heavy rainfall could lead to excessive runoff, flooding, and soil erosion, as well as degraded water quality in nearby bodies of water and loss of the carbon important for soil health. Increased droughts and other changes in precipitation could lead to reduced availability of water for rain-fed and irrigated agriculture. Changes in the frequency and severity of extreme weather events (for example, floods, heat waves, storms) and wildfires (for example, on rangelands) could cause devastation to agricultural lands.

Keeping farming resilient in the face of a changing climate requires significant adaptation. With increased carbon dioxide in the air, plants will garner increased yields, but episodic weather patterns, droughts, and extreme rainfalls could affect growing and stability in this sector. Adaptation of production methods, input use, new genetic varieties for drought and water adaptation, climate smart precision agriculture, and sensing could enable better management and predictability. For instance, biotechnological plant breeding of corn, cotton, soybeans, and several other crops offers an extremely precise strategy to help with our evolving climate. Other adaptation measures could include changing crop mixes, irrigation methods, fertilization practices, tillage practices, pesticides (and pesticide uses), and land management. All of these measures, however, while helpful, have limits as climate change impacts grow more severe.[6]

Nourishing a growing world population while reducing environmental impacts will require food and agriculture systems to integrate their conservation and efficiency efforts. These sectors will also need to collaborate closely to document environmental impacts while working to continually improve their environmental footprint. Advancements in precision agriculture, data sensing for carbon, soil, and water that helps manage outcomes and predictive capabilities, and other new technologies are essential. Working together, farmers, ranchers, and food makers across the food supply chain can explore new ways to produce nutrient-rich foods that are affordable and accessible and help pave the way to sustainable nutrition for all—today and for future generations. While the challenges will be hard to overcome, food and agriculture around the world can co-create the sustainable food systems of the future.

## TOOLS AND OPPORTUNITIES

From changing the composition of livestock feed to reduce methane emissions from digestion[7] to continuing to improve agricultural yields, thereby avoiding conversions of native landscapes to cropland,[8] many pathways exist for the U.S. agricultural community to reduce its impacts on climate change, increase resiliency, and promote sustainability more broadly. Two of the most important and fundamental opportunity areas are soil and water resource management.

*Soil Health and Carbon Cycle Management.* The carbon cycle is at the heart of agriculture. Through photosynthesis, plants take carbon from the air, use some for growth, and put the rest into the soil through their roots. Carbon from the air is thus stored both aboveground (for example, in leaves and stems) and belowground (for example, in roots, soils, and rocks). Globally, soil contains more carbon dioxide than the atmosphere, and the more carbon that remains in the soil, the better for the soil, crop yields, and the planet.[9] In addition to storing carbon, however, agricultural and forestry processes can also produce it, including through land use conversion and land management practices. The net carbon flux between the land and the atmosphere depends on the balance between sequestration gains and carbon losses.[10]

While agriculture contributes to greenhouse gas production, it can also be part of the solution to climate change. Advances in soil sciences and soil management can be tools in the fight against malnutrition and climate change, helping to sequester carbon while also improving yields. According to the United States Department of Agriculture, sustainable soil practices involve minimizing soil disturbance, cultivating a variety of species, not uprooting living plants, and maintaining soil cover.[11] Soil disturbance through tillage, improper input use, or overgrazing can destroy soil microbes, interfere with the symbiotic relationships among soil microorganisms, damage roots, and increase soil temperature. Likewise, failing to keep soil covered can cause a loss of soil moisture, raise soil temperatures, and expose soil to the impacts of rainfall. Accordingly, practices to improve soil carbon include conservation tillage practices that reduce disturbance to soil structure; returning crop residues to the soil; using cover crops; rotating planting with perennial crops and those with greater root mass; addition of manure, compost, and digestate; and rotational grazing on grasslands. In addition, advanced nutrient management techniques and precision agriculture can more precisely allow for fertilizer inputs.[12]

Many practices to improve soil health have multiple benefits. For instance, windbreaks and riparian forest buffers integrate trees and shrubs into agricultural landscapes, thereby not only reducing soil erosion and surface water pollution but also adding important carbon sinks. Increasing the carbon stored in topsoil worldwide by just 0.4 percent per year would both improve soil fertility and halt the annual increases in atmospheric carbon dioxide.[13] Some practices that sequester more carbon in soils, though, can also impact the fluxes of methane and nitrous oxide—two other powerful greenhouse gases—so we have to consider the net impacts of various management strategies on all greenhouse gases.[14] All practices require place-based solutions through adaptation and attention to detail on farms, given that there are over twenty thousand soil types. Enabling precision application on each acre can drive improved outcomes related to soil health and carbon management.

*Water Use, Quality, and Scarcity.*   Every corner of the globe is now experiencing the effects of water scarcity.[15] This new reality has a big impact on agriculture, which of course depends on water. As global population growth and economic development increase competition for water, access to adequate clean water has become a growing concern for agriculture stakeholders around the world.[16]

American agriculture accounts for about 80 percent of the country's consumptive water use, although much of that cycles back through the water cycle for eventual reuse. Over time, the source of water used for irrigation purposes in the United States has shifted, with growing reliance on groundwater compared with surface water. As of 2008, the most depleted U.S. aquifers were the High Plains, Mississippi Embayment, and Central Valley, which all serve as the primary source of irrigation in major agricultural regions.[17] Water uses for industrial purposes, drinking, and food consumption risk becoming increasingly at odds.

Efficient irrigation systems and water management practices can reduce agricultural water use. The most common type of irrigation has "shifted over time," from gravity and flood irrigation to more efficient pressurized sprinkler and drip irrigation.[18] Precision technologies (for example, soil moisture sensor networks) are also becoming more typical in irrigation systems, given their ability to increase efficiency and reduce costs. Improving water use efficiency can improve crop yields and reduce water costs while also freeing up more water for other uses (for example, habitat).[19] Improvements in irrigation efficiency, however, can sometimes lead to greater water usage, such as when farmers expand their irrigated acreage or start growing more water-intensive crops as a result.[20]

For livestock agriculture, water conservation practices have to focus on how feed is grown, which consumes a huge portion of the water livestock systems use. In dairy, for instance, feed production makes up more than 90 percent of water use.[21] To address water scarcity, farmers can use less water-intensive crops as feed. They can also reuse water (where safe and appropriate) on the farm.[22] One example of this is dairy farmers using a plate cooler to chill their milk. They then use the same sanitary water for the cows to drink. Water usage has long been a challenge for our food supply chain. However, reducing water usage is particularly important in arid geographies and will only grow in importance as climate change impacts affect future water availability.

In the United States the vast majority of precipitation falls first on private lands, almost half of which are devoted to farming and ranching. Water quality depends on nutrient management, precise application of fertilizers, and integrated pest management. Increasingly, we are seeing community-based solutions for urban and rural management of water quality, such as with the Chesapeake Bay watershed. Agriculture can uniquely make strides in water quality through buffer strips, precision agriculture practices, soil management, and wetland conservation. As urban environments expand, nutrient pollution of waters increases; agriculture can act as a solution. One key consideration to keep in mind is that best practices in hydrology and water systems vary in different regions and therefore have to be tailored to local conditions. Equally, an urban and rural approach to integrated water management solutions can take into account agriculture's unique ability to contribute to and manage for water quality in urban environments.

## AGRICULTURE FOR THE FUTURE

The work of American farmers and ranchers depends on the environment, and the environment is dependent on their work. Effective resource management, like optimized soil management and water usage, can enhance opportunities for farmers and ranchers to be more sustainable while producing more food that's also more nutritious. Recognition of agriculture's role in providing ecosystem services that support human well-being, encouraging innovation, and providing information to enable more precise decisions on carbon, soil, and water management can unlock solutions for climate change adaptation in the future. Guided by the values of stewardship embraced by farmers and ranchers for generations, today's agriculture can be the foundation of prosperity, environmental resilience, and food security.

Five pathways, in particular, will be critical for a more sustainable future:[23]

- **Collaboration**: Encourage farmers, agricultural experts, researchers, and investors to collaborate with the food value chain to find shared solutions to the full spectrum of environmental and social challenges—and create much-needed research on sustainable food systems.

- **Emphasis on nutrition**: Ensure that agriculture meets the nutritional needs of a diverse and growing population. Plant and animal agriculture play important and complementary roles, not only in human health but also in supporting cultural, social, and economic well-being and enjoyment, improving our quality of life.

- **Focus on reducing food waste**: Food should always be put to its best use, which means we must reduce the amount of food wasted every year. Encouraging consumption patterns focused on lifestyles, including not taking or buying too much, and reducing food waste and food loss across the value chain from farm to consumer can have a large impact on sustainable food consumption.

- **Technology innovation**: Investments should be focused on enabling mitigation and adaptation to natural resource constraints while improving production efficiencies for yield and quality, including nutrient content, food safety, environmental outcomes, and resistance to pestilence and climate shocks. These investments should not underestimate the place-based complexity of solutions for farmers. Further, advancements in economic modeling to look at return on investment for both production and environmental services would provide valuable insights for farmers and policymakers.

- **Carbon sequestration as a solution**: Collaboration across our food systems and an outcome-based approach should elevate the ability for agriculture to create climate-smart solutions and provide vital ecosystem services in the emerging Anthropocene era characterized by human impacts on the planet. Current trajectories predict the ability for U.S. agriculture's soil to continue to improve and store more carbon. With the right policies and practices in place, agriculture has the potential to completely offset its greenhouse gas emissions and sequester carbon.

**NOTES**

Dave Grossman, Anna Giorgi, Nick Goesser, and Paul Spooner contributed to writing this essay.

1. International Food Policy Research Institute, *Global Nutrition Report 2016: From Promise to Impact: Ending Malnutrition by 2030* (Washington, DC: International Food Policy Research Institute, 2016), http://ebrary.ifpri.org/cdm/ref/collection /p15738coll2/id/130354; Food and Agriculture Organization of the United Nations, International Fund for Agricultural Development, United Nations International Children's Emergency Fund, World Food Program and World Health Organization, *The State of Food Security and Nutrition in the World 2017* (Rome: Food and Agriculture Organization of the United Nations, 2017), http://www.fao.org/3/a-I7695e.pdf;

High-Level Panel of Experts, *Nutrition and Food Systems: A Report by the High-Level Panel of Experts on Food Security and Nutrition* (Rome: Committee on World Food Security, 2017), http://www.fao.org/fileadmin/user_upload/hlpe/hlpe_documents /HLPE_Reports/HLPE-Report-12_EN.pdf.

2. Monika Blössner and Mercedes de Onis, *Malnutrition: Quantifying the Health Impact at National and Local Levels*, No. 12 of *WHO Environmental Burden of Disease Series* (Geneva: World Health Organization, 2005), http://www.who.int/quantifying _ehimpacts/publications/eb12/en/; Global Panel, *The Cost of Malnutrition: Why Policy Action Is Urgent* (London: Global Panel on Agriculture and Food Systems for Nutrition, 2016), https://www.glopan.org/sites/default/files/pictures/CostOf Malnutrition.pdf.

3. High Level Expert Forum: How to Feed the World in 2050, *Global Agriculture towards 2050* (Rome: Food and Agriculture Organization of the United Nations, 2009), http:// www.fao.org/fileadmin/templates/wsfs/docs/Issues_papers/HLEF2050_Global _Agriculture.pdf.

4. "Sources of Greenhouse Gas Emissions," U.S. Environmental Protection Agency, accessed December 5, 2018, https://www.epa.gov/ghgemissions/sources-greenhouse -gas-emissions.

5. U.S. Department of Agriculture, *U.S. Agriculture and Forestry Greenhouse Gas Inventory: 1990–2013* (Washington, DC: U.S. Department of Agriculture, 2016), https://www.usda.gov/oce/climate_change/AFGG_Inventory/USDA_GHG _Inventory_1990-2013_9_19_16_reduced.pdf.

6. U.S. Global Change Research Program, *Fourth National Climate Assessment, Volume II: Impacts, Risks, and Adaptation in the United States, Summary Findings* (Washington, DC: U.S. Global Change Research Program, 2018).

7. U.S. Department of Agriculture, *U.S. Agriculture and Forestry Greenhouse Gas Inventory*; Jeff Mulhollem, "Feed Supplement Greatly Reduces Dairy Cow Methane Emissions," *Penn State News*, August 4, 2015, https://news.psu.edu/story/364787 /2015/08/04/research/feed-supplement-greatly-reduces-dairy-cow-methane -emissions; Terence Chea, "Study Tests Whether Seaweed in Cattle Feed Reduces Emissions," *Associated Press*, August 31, 2018, https://www.apnews.com/835789442 443441baab77a3077870634.

8. Jennifer A. Burney, Steven J. Davis, and David B. Lobell, "Greenhouse Gas Mitigation by Agricultural Intensification," *Proceedings of the National Academy of Sciences* 107, no. 26 (June 29, 2010): 12052–57, https://doi.org/10.1073/pnas.0914216107.

9. "The Carbon Cycle and Soil Organic Carbon," Agronomy Fact Sheet Series, Cornell University Cooperative Extension, last modified July 1, 2016, http://nmsp.cals .cornell.edu/publications/factsheets/factsheet91.pdf.

10. U.S. Department of Agriculture, *U.S. Agriculture and Forestry Greenhouse Gas Inventory*.

11. "Soil Health Management," Soils, U.S. Department of Agriculture Natural Resources Conservation Service, accessed December 5, 2018, https://www.nrcs.usda .gov/wps/portal/nrcs/main/soils/health/mgmt/.

12. "Soil Health FAQs," Soil Health Partnership, National Corn Growers Association, accessed December 5, 2018, https://www.soilhealthpartnership.org/faq/.

13. "Welcome to the '4 Per 1000' Initiative," 4 Per 1000 Initiative, accessed December 5, 2018, https://www.4p1000.org/.

14. U.S. Department of Agriculture, *U.S. Agriculture and Forestry Greenhouse Gas Inventory*.

15. "Water Scarcity," U.N. Water, United Nations, accessed January 14, 2019, http://www.unwater.org/water-facts/scarcity/.

16. Food and Agriculture Organization of the United Nations, *Coping with Water Scarcity: An Action Framework for Agriculture and Food Security* (Rome: Food and Agriculture Organization of the United Nations, 2012), http://www.fao.org/docrep/016/i3015e/i3015e.pdf.

17. Leonard F. Konikow, *Groundwater Depletion in the United States (1900–2008)* (Washington, DC: U.S. Geological Survey, 2013), http://pubs.usgs.gov/sir/2013/5079.

18. Megan Stubbs, *Irrigation in U.S. Agriculture: On-Farm Technologies and Best Management Practices*, CRS Report No. R44158 (Washington, DC: Congressional Research Service, 2016), https://fas.org/sgp/crs/misc/R44158.pdf.

19. "Irrigation & Water Use," Economic Research Service, U.S. Department of Agriculture, last modified December 14, 2018, https://www.ers.usda.gov/topics/farm-practices-management/irrigation-water-use/.

20. Stubbs, *Irrigation in U.S. Agriculture*.

21. Innovation Center for U.S. Dairy, *U.S. Dairy's Environmental Footprint: A Summary of Findings, 2008-2012* (2013) https://www.usdairy.com/~/media/usd/public/dairysenvironmentalfootprintbrochure-july.pdf.

22. Innovation Center for U.S. Dairy, *U.S. Dairy's Environmental Footprint*.

23. The description of these pathways draws on and builds on Erin Fitzgerald's previously published essay "Cultivating Collaboration for Sustainable Food Systems," KTIC Radio, January 31, 2019, http://kticradio.com/agricultural/cultivating-collaboration-for-sustainable-food-systems/.

# Toward an Evergreen Revolution

SUSTAINABLE INTENSIFICATION IN
SMALLHOLDER FARMING

Meha Jain and Balwinder Singh

FOOD PRODUCTION MUST INCREASE by around 70 percent by 2050 to ensure everyone across the world has access to sufficient, safe, and nutritious food. The demand for food will increase substantially as the world's population grows to over nine billion and diets shift to include more dairy and meat. In the past, food production increases largely came from the introduction of new technologies, but often with substantial environmental costs. We argue that this pattern must not be repeated and that further increases in food production must now come from *sustainable intensification,* where crop yields are increased with limited negative impacts on the environment. This essay sheds light on what it will take to successfully promote sustainable intensification technologies and make them on-farm realities.

## THE PAST AND FUTURE OF AGRICULTURAL ADVANCEMENT

While food production must grow rapidly to meet rising demand, warming temperatures and the degradation of the natural resources on which agriculture depends threaten to reduce farm productivity across the globe. These problems will be especially acute for smallholder farmers, households that depend on agriculture for their livelihoods and farm on less than two hectares of land. Smallholder farming systems—found largely in the tropics in Asia, Africa, and Latin America—will be under great stress given that these regions are projected to face some of the world's largest population gains and

worst impacts of climate change. Such damage could upend global food systems, negatively impacting food security in both developing and developed
nations, since smallholder agriculture produces about one-third of the global
food supply. Yield losses in smallholder systems are not only a matter of global
food security but also of household welfare given that smallholder farming
employs approximately one-sixth of the world's population.

In the past, technological advances in seed varieties, irrigation infrastructure, and fertilizers drove increased agricultural production. This pattern was
particularly evident in Asia and Latin America throughout the *Green Revolution* (1940s to 1970s), based on the wide promotion and transfer of such inputs by governmental and nongovernmental agencies. But these interventions
also polluted waterways because of excess nitrogen runoff from the overuse of
fertilizers, drained freshwater resources because of overextraction of ground
and surface water for irrigation, and depleted soil stocks as farms moved
toward increasingly intensive practices.

Because of these damages, sustainable intensification must deliver on an
*Evergreen Revolution* that transforms the next generation of improved agricultural production. The concept of sustainable intensification does not prescribe
how yield gains should be achieved, and instead considers a wide range of
strategies, including green technologies that help conserve agricultural inputs, new seed varieties that are higher yielding or respond better to stress,
and real-time weather information to improve farm management decisions.

We examine ways that smallholder yields can be increased through technology transfer and the adoption of sustainable intensification technologies,
and what it takes to promote these solutions at the regional and national
scales. We focus on the promotion and adoption of a set of improved soil management technologies across the Indo-Gangetic Plains, which is India's main
grain belt and where farmers typically plant rotations of rice followed by
wheat. These case studies shed light on how to successfully transfer and promote a given technology at large spatial and temporal scales, and inform how
future policies can sustainably increase smallholder yields. We focus on India
because it is home to over half of the world's one billion smallholder farmers
and is the second-largest producer of rice and wheat worldwide. Yield growth
has also stalled in parts of the country since the 1990s, demanding novel
ways to increase production. Identifying entry points for sustainable intensification, and ways to make it self-sustaining and scalable, presents a formidable
challenge. But to feed a growing number of people in India and across the
world, it is one that we will have to tackle head-on.

## THE ADOPTION OF ZERO-TILLAGE

*Conservation agriculture* offers "a set of soil management practices that mini-mize the disruption of soil structure, composition, and natural biodiversity."[1] These practices increase crop yields while simultaneously improving the long-term quality of soil. In turn, because soil fertility is improved, farmers use less fertilizer and irrigation than they would otherwise, which reduces harmful excess nitrogen runoff and freshwater depletion.

Conservation agriculture embodies three major practices. The first is minimum mechanical soil disturbance; farmers use zero-tillage technologies to directly plant seeds into fields without having to first soften it by tilling. The second is maintaining permanent organic soil cover—covering at least 30 percent of the field at all times with either crop residues that are left after a crop is harvested or cover crops. The final practice is diversifying crop rota-tions, where at least three different crops are planted in succession. Adopting one or more of these practices offers a multitude of benefits, including re-duced soil erosion, increased organic matter, and soil moisture conservation.[2]

Conservation agriculture practices, particularly zero-tillage, were first de-veloped and adopted in the United States in the 1960s in response to the vast soil erosion that occurred during the Dust Bowl, and spread exponentially in the 1990s to both industrialized and developing countries across the world. We turn now to a case study on the adoption of zero-tillage across the Indo-Gangetic Plains, and then to a second on the adoption of technologies that maintain soil organic cover.

In India, the promotion of zero-tillage began in the 1990s when a new, low-cost zero-tillage machine was introduced by the International Maize and Wheat Improvement Center from Australia. Through on-farm field experi-ments, zero-tillage was found to increase wheat yields by approximately 15 percent while simultaneously reducing irrigation and fertilizer inputs com-pared with those of conventional tilling practices.[3] Production increased because zero-tillage reduced the amount of time and inputs needed for field preparation, allowed for earlier planting of wheat, and reduced the growth of a common weed. However, despite being manufactured locally at relatively low cost, there was little demand for the new technology since the imported technology was not well adapted to Indian farming conditions.

In response, a consortium of academics and policymakers worked with farmers, zero-tillage manufacturers, and agricultural research scientists to further adapt the machinery to better suit Indian farms and their unique needs. Once the design was improved, manufacturers produced the machinery for large-scale use. Simultaneously, state agricultural research centers and the International Maize and Wheat Improvement Center spread awareness about the machinery and its benefits through on-farm field trials. Finally, the state government offered a 25 percent subsidy for the machinery. These multiple factors worked in confluence to increase zero-tillage adoption across the western Indo-Gangetic Plains, primarily in the states of Punjab and Haryana. To date, the use of zero- and reduced tillage is the most widely adopted conservation agriculture strategy across India, with approximately one-fifth of the wheat area in the western Indo-Gangetic Plains under this practice.[4]

It is important to note that zero-tillage was not widely adopted across the whole of the Indo-Gangetic Plains. Specifically, the level of adoption was very low in the eastern Indo-Gangetic Plains, in the states of Uttar Pradesh and Bihar. Through participatory research with farmers, the reasons for the lack of adoption became clear. The technology was too expensive for the average farmer to purchase as farmers were generally poorer than in the western Indo-Gangetic Plains, it required farmers to have access to a tractor (most farmers did not own tractors in this region and instead hired tractors as needed), and smaller field sizes made zero-tillage less cost-effective.[5] The model that led to widespread adoption of improved practices in the west was not universally applicable.

In response, the International Maize and Wheat Improvement Center developed a *service provider* model, where one or two farmers who owned tractors within a village purchased the zero-tillage machinery and provided it as a rented service to other farmers in the community. Staff from the center traveled across villages in the eastern Indo-Gangetic Plains spreading awareness about zero-tillage and identifying key farmers who could possibly become service providers. The center helped these farmers purchase machinery and develop a business to provide zero-tillage service to other farmers in the community. The service provider model has been successful in the eastern Indo-Gangetic Plains, leading to up to 30 percent adoption of zero-tillage in the regions where service providers reside.[6]

Despite the overall successes of zero-tillage adoption across the Indo-Gangetic Plains, there is still significant room for improvement. To date, only one-sixth of the wheat area and less than 5 percent of the rice area is under zero-tillage. Even though farmers may be using zero-tillage for wheat in the winter season, these same farmers till their soil when planting rice in the monsoon season, reducing the long-term benefits of zero-tillage on soil quality. In addition, there are relatively low rates of zero-tillage adoption in the eastern Indo-Gangetic Plains compared with the west. This disparity likely persists because farmers with less land are unlikely to adopt zero-tillage even with the service provider model since the fixed rental cost reduces profits for those with little land.

Moving forward, there are several ways to enhance the effectiveness of zero-tillage practices. Given that there are still low rates of awareness of zero-tillage technology, particularly in the eastern part of the region, agricultural extension agencies that have a large and broad presence across rural India should spread awareness about the technology. This is particularly important given that farmers in this region typically receive information about new technologies through word of mouth; smartphones and the internet have reached less than 2 percent of the population. Furthermore, service provider models should be adapted to become more cost-effective for farmers with smaller landholdings. For example, service providers can offer demand aggregation, which would allow neighboring farmers to coordinate and hire the service provider at the same time for a lower per capita cost.

## THE ADOPTION OF SOIL ORGANIC COVER

Maintaining soil organic cover to improve soil quality is uncommon across the Indo-Gangetic Plains. Instead, the majority of farmers remove residues once crops are harvested, in part because current seeding machinery, including zero-tillage machinery, is not effective for planting seeds in fields with heavy residues. The fastest and easiest way to clear these residues is by burning, which contributes to extremely high air pollution levels across northern India. To overcome these challenges, a new zero-tillage machine was developed in collaboration with Indian and Australian scientists called the Happy Seeder, which removes rice residues mechanically, turns them into mulch, and plants wheat seeds directly into these mulch-covered fields. Experiments have shown that the Happy Seeder increases profits by reducing field preparation costs, improves soil health by maintaining soil organic cover, and increases wheat yields compared with conventional residue burning practices. As a means to improve air quality across northern India, the Indian government has heavily subsidized the Happy Seeder, with up to an 80 percent subsidy in the western Indo-Gangetic Plains.

Yet, only a small percentage of farmers (less than 1 percent) have adopted the technology. The main reason for low adoption is lack of awareness of the technology and its benefits; Happy Seeder awareness remains much lower than that of zero-tillage in its initial years. In addition, many farmers do not believe that the Happy Seeder is profitable. To overcome these constraints, a consortium of academic, governmental, and nongovernmental organizations working to reduce residue burning in northern India suggests that a multi-pronged approach is needed to enhance Happy Seeder adoption.[7] Awareness of the technology and its benefits must increase through agricultural extension agencies and demonstration farms, which can facilitate peer-to-peer learning about the technology. In addition, the business case for Happy Seeder versus other residue management strategies must be clarified and promoted. As of now, few farmers see the financial value of using, purchasing, or becoming a service provider for Happy Seeder technologies.

## A NEW APPROACH TO TECHNOLOGY PROMOTION

As these two case studies highlight, sustainable intensification technologies can increase cereal yields in smallholder systems while improving stewardship of the land. However, current rates of adoption remain far too low to meet growing food demand, suggesting that we need new approaches for developing and promoting these technologies. We offer several key recommendations for increasing the effectiveness and adoption of such technologies in smallholder systems:

- Technologies have to be developed to meet the needs and circumstances of farmers. This is particularly important given that desired technologies are often transferred from other countries where the technology was first developed and shown to be successful. For example, in the case of zero-tillage technologies, machinery was imported from Australia, where the technology had resulted in yield gains and improved soil fertility. Yet, farmers in India did not use the imported machinery at first because it was not adapted to meet the unique needs of smallholder farmers. Through participatory research with farmers and on-farm experiments, agricultural scientists and manufacturers were able to redesign the zero-tillage equipment to better match local farming conditions, meet farmer demands, and increase the efficiency of the technology in the Indian context. Once the technology was adapted, farmers were willing to use it. Before promoting sustainable intensification technologies, it is critical for researchers and manufacturers to conduct on-farm experiments and research with farmers to understand the technology's effectiveness and how it should be adapted to better match local needs.

- Policies must consider the socioeconomic, market, and institutional context of farming communities when promoting and marketing any agricultural technology. While manufacturers may develop a technology that performs well in experimental conditions, the technology may never be adopted if it is not accessible, affordable, and profitable for smallholder farmers. Policies must consider the local context in which smallholder farmers may access the technology. Given the diversity among smallholder farmers, it is unlikely that there will be one universal policy that enhances adoption in every location. For example, in the eastern Indo-Gangetic Plains, zero-tillage technologies were used only after the International Maize and Wheat Improvement Center developed a service provider business model that matched the local markets for tilling. Simply developing and promoting a technology through awareness campaigns and subsidies may not lead to widespread use. Participatory research with farmers and surveys that identify barriers to adoption can help inform policies that are better targeted to a given locale's constraints.
- Our case studies show that one of the keys to adoption of any sustainable intensification technology is awareness. Yet, typical methods of spreading awareness, such as advertisements, may be challenging in smallholder systems given limited information flows. Our case studies have shown that word of mouth and peer-to-peer learning are the most effective ways to spread information about a given technology and increase its use. In smallholder systems, awareness campaigns that target peer-to-peer learning—such as demonstration farms and visits from agricultural extension agents—may be the most effective ways to increase awareness and adoption of a given technology.
- As seen in our case studies, there is often *scale bias* in the adoption of new technologies, with richer and larger-landholding farmers more likely to try them. Agricultural policymakers should identify ways to target poorer and smaller-scale farmers to ensure that the benefits of a given technology do not accrue only to the wealthiest few. Some ideas include a tiered subsidy system with larger subsidies for poorer farmers, targeting demonstration farms and peer-to-peer learning to the social networks of poorer and smaller-scale farmers, and increasing competition among manufacturers and service providers to lower costs of the technology.

It is a critical time to identify the most effective ways to promote sustainable intensification. Smallholder systems will face some of the greatest food security challenges as populations rapidly increase, the natural resources on which agriculture depends continue to degrade, and climate change threatens staple crops. Technologies to sustainably increase yields exist. If we can transfer and promote them more effectively, we can improve on-farm practices, increase food production, and reduce environmental degradation over the coming decades.

**NOTES**

1. "Conservation Agriculture: Global Research & Resources," Cornell University College of Agriculture and Life Sciences, accessed April 17, 2019, http://conservationagriculture .mannlib.cornell.edu/pages/aboutca/whatisca.html.

2. Peter Hobbs, Ken Sayre, and Raj Gupta, "The Role of Conservation Agriculture in Sustainable Agriculture," *Philosophical Transactions of the Royal Society B* 363 (July 2007): 543–55, https://doi.org/10.1098/rstb.2007.2169.

3. Olaf Erenstein and Vijay Laxmi, "Zero Tillage Impacts in India's Rice–Wheat Systems: A Review," *Soil and Tillage Research* 100 (July 2008): 1–14, https://doi.org/10 .1016/j.still.2008.05.001.

4. Olaf Erenstein, *Zero Tillage in the Rice-Wheat System of the Indo-Gangetic Plains* (Washington, DC: International Food Policy Research Institute, November 2009), http://www.ifpri.org/publication/zero-tillage-rice-wheat-systems-indo-gangetic -plains.

5. Alwin Keil, Alwin D'souza, and Andrew McDonald, "Zero-Tillage Is a Proven Technology for Sustainable Wheat Intensification in the Eastern Indo-Gangetic Plains: What Determines Farmer Awareness and Adoption?," *Food Security* 9, no. 4 (July 2017): 723–43, https://doi.org/10.1007/s12571-017-0707-x.

6. Erenstein, *Zero Tillage in the Rice-Wheat System*.

7. Heather Tallis et al., *The Evergreen Revolution: Six Ways to Empower India's No-Burn Agricultural Future* (Jaipur, India: University of Minnesota, The Nature Conservancy, International Maize and Wheat Improvement Center, and Borlaug Institute for South Asia, November 2017), https://repository.cimmyt.org/handle/10883/19483.

# Found Water

## REUSE AND THE DECONSTRUCTION OF "WASTEWATER"

G. Tracy Mehan, III

IN THE CLASSIC 1942 film *Casablanca,* Rick, played by Humphrey Bogart, is asked by the world-weary Vichy French captain Renault, played by Claude Rains, "What in heaven's name brought you to Casablanca?"

"I came to Casablanca for the waters," replies Rick.

Captain Renault responds, "The waters? What waters? We're in a desert."

"I was misinformed," deadpans Rick.

So what, in heaven's name, has brought so many Americans to live in the desert or arid regions—say, drought-plagued California or the Colorado River basin? Arizona increased its population by 40 percent between 1990 and 2018, Colorado by 30 percent. Clark County, Nevada, home to Las Vegas, doubled its water consumption between 1985 and 2000.[1] Water levels in nearby Lakes Mead and Powell are dropping precipitously. California will grow to 44.1 million people by 2030 from 38.7 million in 2015. Add the risk of drought, climate variability, loss of snowpack, and groundwater depletion to this growth as aggravating water supply challenges. Were all the Americans moving west misinformed?

The Paris-based Organisation for Economic Co-operation and Development notes that global water demand is projected to increase 55 percent due to growing demand from manufacturing, thermal electricity generation, and domestic use—largely from emerging economies and developing countries.[2]

Western states have made solid progress in reducing water consumption over the past few years. But the question remains: can water utilities keep up with growing populations, expanding economies, drought, and climate variability?

A set of new practices and technologies, collectively referred to as *water reuse,* provides new opportunities to discover "found water" in a community's own wastewater stream and convert it into a valuable resource.[3] These new approaches deconstruct the very idea of "wastewater." No longer is there such a thing. There is only water that is wasted.

## THE FUTURE OF WATER

Like Rick in *Casablanca,* many are misinformed as to what water reuse entails. A primer published by the American Water Works Association in 2016 provides some useful definitions. *Water reuse* "involves using water more than once to expand a community's available water supply." *Nonpotable reuse* refers to water that is not used for drinking but is safe to use for its intended purpose, such as irrigation (including golf courses and lawns) or industrial processes. *Potable reuse* "refers to recycled or reclaimed water that is safe for drinking." *Indirect potable reuse* "introduces purified water into an environmental buffer" (like a groundwater aquifer, reservoir, or lake) "before the blended water is introduced into a water supply system." Finally, *direct potable reuse* "introduces purified water directly into an existing water supply system." Direct potable reuse is the final frontier of water reuse and is just beginning to come into its own in the United States.[4]

Water reuse is local, sustainable, and cost-effective because wastewater is available even during drought conditions and causes less damage to the environment than other water-supply solutions like dams, reservoirs, and canals. It is an interesting question whether, because of cost advantages, reuse may in the long run outdistance desalination of ocean water. The competition, though, is healthy; and both are needed.[5]

In 2012 the board of the Water Environment Federation, the primary organization for wastewater utilities in the United States, formally replaced the traditional term "water treatment plant" with "water resource recovery facility," to reflect the facilities' expanded functions—recovering and reusing water, nutrients, and energy.[6] This shift represents what the Berkeley professor David Sedlak has described as *Water 4.0* in his 2014 book of the same name. In the beginning Water 4.0 will look like upgraded versions of current centralized systems in which "imported water will be supplemented or replaced by desalination and potable water recycling," according to Sedlak, along with a vast array of incentives for conservation. Sewage treatment plants "will evolve from a means of protecting surface waters from pollution to systems that recover water, energy, and nutrients from the sewage."[7]

Ancient Romans perfected our current *linear* model of moving water from a source, often distant, through a treatment train and then distributing it to water users. That model will now be complemented, not necessarily replaced, by an integrated portfolio that includes a circular model of reuse.

## THE RISE OF WATER REUSE

Wastewater is treated for release to nearby rivers or other surface waters by a combination of biological treatment and clarification that allows solids to settle. But for potable reuse, plants must also take additional treatment steps, including membrane filtration to remove particles and microorganisms, reverse osmosis to remove salts and contaminants, advanced oxidation with UV disinfection, and disinfection with chlorine and potentially granular activated carbon as well.

One of the early pioneers of indirect potable reuse in the United States was not in the arid west but in northern Virginia. Beginning in the mid-twentieth century, suburban development led to the profusion of wastewater pollution into a drinking water source, the Occoquan Reservoir, one of the area's two primary sources of water that today serve nearly two million residents just outside Washington, DC. By the early 1970s, eleven wastewater plants were all discharging into tributaries of the reservoir, thereby polluting an important source of drinking water.

As a solution, all wastewater was rerouted to a single wastewater treatment plant equipped with technologies that, according to Dr. Sedlak, were "a water engineer's dream." Observes Sedlak, "The plant's designers threw everything they could come up with at the wastewater: activated sludge, filtration, activated carbon treatment, ion exchange, chlorination, and lime clarification."[8]

After this expanded treatment, "the water in the Occoquan Reservoir was probably better than water flowing in rivers and reservoirs downstream of many cities," writes Sedlak.

There was resistance in the water sector to reuse based on the standards of source water protection or the "multiple-barrier approach" to drinking water protection. According to the American Water Works Association's G300 standard, this approach requires selecting the highest-quality source water possible and protecting that source, among other steps.[9] Observers asked: is reused water the highest quality? Time, experience, and necessity have substantially reduced concerns, but care must be taken in the design and operation of any system given that public health is at stake, most especially for direct potable reuse. Pathogens, say, require careful attention.

Out of concern for public health impacts, the WateReuse Association, American Water Works Association, and the Water Environment Federation contracted with the National Water Research Institute to convene an expert panel and develop a risk management strategy for direct potable reuse based on the available research. In 2015, the panel released its *Framework for Direct Potable Reuse: A Path Forward*, the first of its kind in the United States.[10] It provides a systems approach to developing direct potable reuse through modern technology, control systems, governance structures, and personnel training for the protection of public health.

Presently, there is no direct federal regulation of potable reuse other than the baseline water quality statutes of the Safe Drinking Water and Clean Water Acts, the fundamental regulations with which all projects must comply. Nevertheless, the Environmental Protection Agency published nonbinding guidelines for reuse in 2012 and followed with a 2017 *Potable Reuse Compendium*, both very useful resources.

Many states are moving forward with their own regulatory regimes for direct potable reuse.[11] According to HDR, an international engineering firm, no states have yet promulgated regulations for direct drinking water reuse (although they do regulate other kinds of reuse). North Carolina is moving in that direction, though, and "approved legislation in 2014 allowing limited [direct potable reuse] with engineered storage buffering and blending with other sources. . . . In 2016 the California State Water Resource Control Board concluded that it is feasible to develop uniform water quality criteria" for direct potable reuse, a big first step toward regulation.[12] Thus, the 2015 *Framework* will help utilities and communities navigate such regulatory requirements.

Las Vegas may be associated in the popular mind with wretched excess, but it suffers from no excess supplies of water. The Las Vegas strip is home to many of the world's largest hotels, with fountains, a lake, and even pirate ship battles in the middle of a scorching desert. Water reuse and recycling make all this possible. When the political pundit George Will visited the city in 2009, he was impressed that the average hotel room used 300 gallons per day, almost all of it recycled. The strip uses between 1 and 3 percent of Nevada's water but accounts for close to 60 percent of its economic output. Statewide, agriculture accounts for 75 percent of water use.[13]

Water reuse is a new source of supply for California's Orange County Water District, which provides drinking water to 2.5 million people in a region with less than 15 inches of precipitation annually. The district wholesales groundwater to retail water agencies serving the county. In 2018 the utility celebrated the tenth anniversary of its Groundwater Replenishment System, the world's largest potable reuse project. Orange County now has diverse sources of water, including the Santa Anna River, rainfall, and imported water from the State Water Project and the Colorado River, as well as potable reuse. According to Mike Markus, general manager of the Orange County Water District, the Groundwater Replenishment System takes treated wastewater that would otherwise flow to the sea and puts it through advanced purification utilizing microfiltration, reverse osmosis, and ultraviolet light with hydrogen peroxide.[14] Approximately one-third of this water is injected into a seawater barrier along the coast, and the remainder is pumped to recharge basins seventeen miles away. This is a new source of supply for the groundwater basin and produces 100 million gallons per day. Potable reuse provides 30 percent of the basin's supply. The district operates under very strict California standards.

Orange County's project is cutting-edge. It starts with treated wastewater and serves up purified water. It pumps this water into a groundwater basin, taking a year to move through sand, gravel, and clay before consumption as drinking water.[15] The advanced treated water is cleaner than the groundwater into which it is injected.[16]

More reuse is coming in California. The City of San Diego is pursuing its Pure Water project, a $1.4 billion investment in a new advanced facility to produce 30 million gallons of high-quality drinking water per day.[17] And the Metropolitan Water District of Southern California, in partnership with the Sanitation Districts of Los Angeles County, is commencing a $13.9 million pilot, a first step toward what will be the Regional Recycled Water Program, one of the world's largest water recycling projects. The pilot's advanced water treatment demonstration facility will take treated wastewater and purify it with a view to replenishing the region's groundwater basin. The complete project will cost $2.7 billion.[18]

In Texas, El Paso is pursuing potable reuse given concerns with decreasing flows in the Rio Grande. According to a 2018 story from CNN Health's Nadia Kounang, "Now, El Paso is on track to become the first large city in the United States to treat its sewage and send it directly back into its taps."[19]

Technology, necessity, and familiarity may be swinging public perceptions in favor of reused water. In 2017 the global water technology company Xylem commissioned a survey of California residents regarding attitudes on recycled water.[20] Three-quarters "supported using recycled water as an additional local water supply, regardless of water shortages." Eighty-seven percent "were willing to use recycled water in their daily lives." Seventy-five percent indicated that they "felt more willing to use recycled water for personal household purposes after learning more about the treatment process used to purify recycled water." And 90 percent said they would be supportive if it reduced monthly bills.

Back in Virginia the Hampton Roads Sanitation District (HRSD), serving 1.7 million people over 3,087 square miles, established its Sustainable Water Initiative for Tomorrow (SWIFT) with the opening of the SWIFT Research Center.[21] Hampton Roads is home to the world's largest naval base. As we will see, the initiative delivers multiple benefits. The center replenishes the Potomac Aquifer with one million gallons per day of effluent from the nearby treatment plant, adding advanced treatment (ozone biofiltration with granular activated carbon adsorption) meeting safe drinking water standards for public health as opposed to just ambient water quality standards under the Clean Water Act. The research center will provide data to inform permitting and design of full-scale implementation at five facilities throughout the region. These new reuse-ready facilities will have a combined capacity in excess of 100 million gallons per day by 2030.

Of no small consequence for the Chesapeake Bay and its tributaries, at full scale the initiative will reduce nutrient discharge by approximately 90 percent below current requirements of the applicable total maximum daily limit, the relevant pollution budget. That is nearly three million pounds of nitrogen and 300,000 pounds of phosphorus for the James River alone. These reductions have made the HRSD a nutrient credit supplier in the trading market for 11 localities holding "MS4" stormwater permits, supplying 95 percent of the reductions the municipalities together required.

The Hampton Roads project also has the potential to reduce the rate of land subsidence, the harmful sinking of land due to aquifer withdrawal. In this region it accounts for roughly 25 percent of net sea level rise, and early modeling data indicate that aquifer recharge may actually slow, stop, or reverse subsidence.[22]

**THE WAY FORWARD**

Policy recommendations for water reuse and recycling usually involve a mix of subsidies, mandates, educational and recognition programs, and the elimination of regulatory barriers.[23] For instance, California's Water Code Section 13551 states, "A person or public agency, including a state agency, city, county, city and county district, or any other political subdivision of the state, shall not use water from any source of quality suitable for potable domestic use for nonpotable uses."[24] Florida's "Ocean Outfall" bill of 2008 requires all facilities discharging domestic wastewater through outfall pipes into the ocean to meet higher treatment requirements and achieve at least 60 percent reuse of the wastewater by 2025.

Presently, reuse is eligible for funding under the new federal Water Infrastructure and Finance Innovation Act as well as state revolving loan programs under the Clean Water and Safe Drinking Water Acts. The Bureau of Reclamation also funds projects under its Title XVI program. The WateReuse Association recommends the establishment of "a federal tax credit for retrofitting industrial facilities to use municipal recycled water or to recycle water onsite."[25] The group also believes that federal procurement mandates, such as Buy America requirements that limit purchase of imported goods, impair the development of critical infrastructure including water reuse and recycling.

The question of federal regulation of this evolving practice is often raised. Yet, this may be an instance where the concept of state laboratories or "laboratories of democracy," as articulated by Justice Louis D. Brandeis's famous 1932 dissent in *New State Ice Co. v. Liebmann,* makes sense for testing new laws and regulations.[26] Brandeis suggested state jurisdictions should be allowed "to try novel social and economic experiments without risk to the rest of the country." There is constant research and technological innovation under way in the water reuse space, and there may be a real danger of locking in, by way of national regulation, what may become obsolete technology given the ponderous pace of federal regulating and the near impossibility of changing existing environmental laws post-factum. Also, private voluntary associations and international bodies have been effectively working to develop practices, standards, frameworks, and manuals for all aspects of reuse projects.

According to Bluefield Research, current reuse capacity of reclaimed flows in the United States is expected to increase 37 percent by 2027.[27] Industrial applications will grow 31 percent by the same year. The United States is already the largest reuse market by volume with further future growth projected. The development of water reuse is a sustained, organic process of measured growth and evolution and should be allowed to proceed at its own pace and continue to prove its effectiveness over time.

**NOTES**

1. G. Tracy Mehan, III, "They Came for the Water, But Were They Misinformed?," *Growing Blue* (blog), May 21, 2013, https://web.archive.org/web/20131121051637 /http://growingblue.com/blog/economics/they-came-for-the-water-but-were-they -misinformed/.

2. Organisation for Economic Co-operation and Development, *OECD Environmental Outlook to 2050: The Consequences of Inaction* (Paris: OECD Publishing, 2012), https://doi.org/10.1787/9789264122246-en.

3. American Water Works Association, "Potable Reuse 101: An Innovative and Sustain-able Water Supply Solution," 2016, https://www.awwa.org/Portals/0/AWWA/ETS /Resources/Potable%20Reuse%20101.pdf?ver=2018-12-12-182505-710.

4. Alex Gerling, "Water Reuse: Reclaim Water for Public Water Supplies," *Opflow* 44, no. 1 (January 2018): 10–14.

5. Jennifer Duffy, PE, "Potable Reuse—Not a Dirty Word Anymore," HDR, *SDWA Newsletter,* No. 1, 2018, 5.

6. Water Environment Federation, "Changing the Terms," *WEF News/WEF High-lights,* May 22, 2014, https://news.wef.org/changing-the-terms/.

7. David Sedlak, *Water 4.0: The Past, Present, and Future of the World's Most Vital Re-source* (New Haven, CT: Yale University Press, 2014), 278.

8. Sedlak, *Water 4.0,* 202.

9. American Water Works Association, "Source Water Protection," *AWWA Manage-ment Standard,* 2014, ANSI/AWWA G300-14, vii.

10. Steve Via and George Tobanoglous, "Introducing the Framework for Direct Potable Reuse," *Journal - American Water Works Association,* November 2016, 28–33; WateRe-use Research Foundation, American Water Works Association, Water Environment Federation, and National Water Research Institute, *Framework for Direct Potable Re-use* (Alexandria, VA: WateReuse Research Foundation: 2015).

11. U.S. Environmental Protection Agency, *Guidelines for Water Reuse,* EPA/600/ R-12/618 (Washington, DC: U.S. Environmental Protection Agency, 2012).

12. U.S. Environmental Protection Agency, *Potable Reuse Compendium,* EPA/810/ R-17/002 (Washington, DC: U.S. Environmental Protection Agency, 2017).

13. G. Tracy Mehan, III, "Coping with Water Scarcity, Risk and Uncertainty: Resilience and Hope," *Texas A&M Journal of Property Law* 1, no. 1 (2013): 2, https://scholarship .law.tamu.edu/cgi/viewcontent.cgi?article=1000&context=journal-of-property-law.

14. Kris Polly, "Replenishing Infrastructure Investment: Mike Markus of the Orange County Water District" (interview), *Municipal Water Leader* 4, no. 2 (February 2018): 6–11.

15. Mehan, "Coping with Water Scarcity," 12.

16. Sedlak, "The Toilet-to-Tap Solution," in *Water 4.0,* 187–216.

17. "San Diego Gets WIFIA Loan for Pure Water Project," *Water Finance & Management,* December 2018, 17.

18. "Contract Worth $13.9M Awarded for Recycled Water Demonstration Facility in CA," *Water World,* July 13, 2017, https://www.waterworld.com/articles/2017/07/contract-worth-13-9m-awarded-for-recycled-water-demonstration-facility-in-ca.html.

19. Nadia Kounang, "El Paso to Drink Treated Sewage Water Due to Climate Change Drought," *CNN Health,* December 1, 2018, https://www-m.cnn.com/2018/11/30/health/water-climate-change-el-paso/index.html?r=https%3A%2F%2Ft.co%2FpxDkMNyM3mf.

20. For information on the 2017 Xylem survey, see Ron Askin, "Making the Case for Recycled Water," *Water Finance & Management,* August 2018, 22–23.

21. Hampton Roads Sanitation District (HRSD), "HRSD Begins Replenishing Potomac Aquifer, Celebrates Opening of SWIFT Research Center in Suffolk," *HRSD,* May 18, 2018, https://www.hrsd.com/news-release-may-18-2018; regarding HRSD's SWIFT Research Center, see "Finished Water," *Opflow* 44, no. 8 (August 2018): 36.

22. Ted Henifin, general manager, HRSD, emails to author, November 21 and 26, 2018.

23. Jon Freedman and Colin Enssle, "Addressing Water Scarcity through Recycling and Reuse: A Menu for Policymakers," *General Electric Ecomagination,* 2015.

24. CA Water Code § 13551 (through 2012 Leg Sess).

25. "Investment Tax Credit for Industrial Reuse," WateReuse Association, accessed April 18, 2019, https://watereuse.org/advocacy/federal-priorities/investment-tax-credit-for-industrial-reuse/.

26. New State Ice Co. v. Liebmann, 285 U.S. 262 (1932).

27. Bluefield Research, "U.S. Municipal Water Reuse: Opportunities, Outlook, & Competitive Landscape 2017–2027," *Bluefield Research Focus Report,* September 2017.

# People and the Ocean 3.0

## A NEW NARRATIVE WITH TRANSFORMATIVE BENEFITS

Jane Lubchenco

NARRATIVES ABOUT OUR WORLD help frame our thinking and bring order to chaos. The most powerful narratives focus on universal questions: Who are we? Where did we come from? Where are we going? They help us navigate, set expectations, influence values. How we treat other human beings and nature reflects our values and our narratives about each other and the natural world. Indeed, narratives can blind, constrain, inspire, or liberate us.

To be sure, a new narrative does not automatically change the status quo, but if widely adopted, it can alter people's sense of what is possible. It can create space for new ideas, new solutions. It can liberate ingenuity and reset expectations of what could be, not what is. In this essay, I articulate three narratives that trace the history of people's attitudes toward the ocean and conclude with an open invitation to help create a new collective wisdom and reality.

*People and the Ocean 1.0: The ocean is so vast, bountiful, and endlessly resilient, it is simply too big to fail.*

For most of human history, and well into the late twentieth century, the ocean's immense size, productivity, and resilience made it impossible for people to ever imagine depleting or disrupting it. In many places, fish were so abundant they sometimes leaped into fishing boats.[1] The 1960s mantra

"Dilution is the solution to pollution" reinforced the notion that anything we put into the ocean could not possibly affect such a vast place. We took for granted the beauty and the bounty of the ocean and assumed these were intrinsic features of the ocean that would continue forever. And we acted accordingly. The ocean was a seemingly endless source of food, minerals, oil and gas, salt, and more. The ocean was also a convenient repository for wastes: sewage, vehicles, garbage, toxins, military debris, or nuclear wastes. The list is endless. Because the ocean represents approximately 99 percent of the living space on Earth, it became a convenient source of materials and a dumping ground for wastes. These practices were enabled by the overarching narrative "The ocean is so vast, it is simply too big to fail."

*People and the Ocean 2.0: The ocean is doomed. Massively and fatally polluted, depleted and disrupted, the ocean is too big to fix.*

Over the past few decades, the attitude that the ocean represented an endless bounty and bottomless dump was gradually questioned. It is now overwhelmingly obvious that the previous mind-set—along with a broad suite of human actions—has inadvertently caused widespread depletion and disruption. Scientists tell us we have fundamentally altered its very chemistry, biology, and physical structure—something once thought impossible. Now we see daily graphic images of widespread coral bleaching, unimaginable plastic pollution, and tumor-riddled sea turtles. We hear that fishery collapses and illegal fishing threaten the health and livelihoods of millions of people today and their food security tomorrow. We see vivid evidence that climate change is making the ocean warmer, higher, stormier, sicker, more acidic, oxygen-depleted, less resilient, and less predictable. And we witness the all-too-real consequences of these changes. Every day, somewhere on Earth, communities, governments, and disaster responders are overwhelmed with new or more extreme disasters. Scientists warn that time is running out.

And, as if that were not sufficiently bad, all of this comes at a time when we need more—much more—from the ocean, not less. Because we have nearly exhausted the land, because there are more mouths to feed, and because economic development is urgently needed for many, we look to the sea for new opportunities for job creation, poverty alleviation, food security, minerals, energy, and more.

These changes altogether mean big problems for people and the planet. They threaten the future of the most vulnerable people among us, the economic prosperity, quality of life, and opportunities for everyone, and the well-being of the ocean's amazing life forms. The situation appears impossibly complex, the drivers too ingrained, the vested interests too powerful, and the available options too limited to make a difference. How could we possibly feed more people when fisheries are already so depleted? It is all too easy to conclude that the situation is not only dire but hopeless. In short, the common perception is that problems in the ocean are now so overwhelming, so massive, and so complex that they are impossible to fix. Today's ocean narrative has quickly become "The ocean is impossibly broken and it's simply too big to fix."

*People and the Ocean 3.0: The ocean is so central to our future, it is too big and too important to ignore. If we heal the ocean, we can solve multiple global problems and heal ourselves. It is our path forward.*

Like a phoenix rising from the ashes, hope is beginning to emerge and steer us away from the current dismal ocean narrative. The challenges *are* unprecedented, complex, and wicked. The future *is* unpredictable and likely to harbor hidden challenges. But, the challenges facing the ocean are not insurmountable. New science, awareness, leadership, and thinking are giving way to innovative technologies, nontraditional partnerships, creative financing, fresh champions, and timely institutions and agreements. We are gaining a better understanding of how much we depend on a healthy ocean. Myriad examples of proven or promising solutions exist. That they are not yet deployed at the scale or pace needed for real transformation and healing presents a golden opportunity. It *is* possible to use the ocean without using it up. It *is* possible to restore the bounty and the resilience of ocean ecosystems. It *is* possible to look to the ocean for sustained sustenance and opportunity. And, indeed, our very survival depends on our doing just that.

Despite the obvious problems in the ocean, many nations that have exhausted their resources on land are looking to the ocean for new opportunities for poverty alleviation, job creation, and food security. The new, in-vogue term "Blue Economy" encapsulates the enthusiasm for resources from the ocean. But if pursued blindly, without the benefit of current scientific understanding or attention to lessons learned from past mistakes, this new interest could result in even greater disaster: short-term economic benefit for a few and long-term disaster for the planet. The renewed interest in the ocean thus provides a stark choice: we can plunder, or we can prosper. The latter requires a new mind-set—being smarter about our uses of the ocean versus just accelerating more of the same uses.

The United Nations' Sustainable Development Goals, which lay out environmental and social targets for humanity to reach by 2030, encapsulate the big challenges facing society. Many of them relate directly to the ocean and coastal margins—food, energy, health, waste disposal, housing, development, equity, loss of biodiversity, climate change, and ocean acidification. Our new ocean narrative can address many of these.

Two examples of potentially transformative solutions already under way are fisheries reform and creation of Marine Protected Areas. Each has potential to scale up and form the basis of a new transition to sustainable, equitable, and smart ocean stewardship. They are interconnected to each other and to other big challenges such as climate change and human health. Neither is sufficient alone, but together they provide core elements for a new awakening and a new future.

Reforming fisheries is essential to food security, livelihoods, and human health and produces collateral benefits: it can help avert some of the worst ravages of climate change, relieve pressure on ocean wildlife, and help restore ocean health.

The situation is dire: fully one-third of ocean fisheries are overfished; another one-third is fished to capacity. Poor fishery management costs the world's fisheries $83 billion annually, wastes vast amounts of seafood, and kills other ocean wildlife in the process. Because fisheries provide livelihoods to 10 percent of the global population and over 20 percent of the protein for over three billion people, this is an urgent problem. Moreover, some fisheries inadvertently kill countless sea turtles, albatrosses, and marine mammals, rendering many of them in danger of extinction.

The good news is that fishery reform *is* possible, and the enabling conditions for success are *finally* becoming clear.[2] One key condition—long overlooked until recently—is to align the long-term interests of sustainable fisheries with the short-term needs of fishers. In other words, pay attention to the incentives for the primary actors. A proven way to do so is through secure fishery rights.[3] Conventional fishery management unintentionally incentivizes fishers to catch as much as possible, as quickly as possible, without regard to long-term impacts to their fishery, the environment, or safety—often called the "race to fish"—with the all-too-frequent result of a collapsed fishery. In contrast, *secure rights* fishery management incentivizes fishers to be good stewards of the resource and the ocean. Although secure rights are not a panacea for all fisheries or all cultures, and they must be well designed to avoid unintended consequences, multiple examples from developed and developing countries alike suggest that flipping the incentives for fishers by using secure fishery rights can reverse overfishing and rebuild fisheries.[4]

Recent U.S. fishery reforms demonstrate the potential for ocean recovery. After many decades of overfishing, the United States recently ended overfishing for most of its fisheries and is recovering dozens of depleted stocks to much greater abundance than before. Keys to success were mandated in landmark legislation passed in 2006: science-based quotas, a mandate to end overfishing within a specified time, accountability, and the option of using either conventional fishery management or secure rights management (in the United States this practice is called catch shares[5]).

These reforms, plus leadership from fishers, scientists, and environmental groups, resulted in impressive turnarounds of fisheries[6]: in 2000, there were 92 overfished stocks; by 2018, that number had been slashed to 41 (out of 199 stocks assessed[7]). Even more impressive is that many previously depleted stocks recovered quickly and can again be fished—this time sustainably. There were zero stocks in 2000 that had been depleted and then recovered. But by 2018, an astounding 45 stocks had been recovered. Some stocks recovered decades earlier than predicted. This impressive turnaround suggests that it *is* possible to reform fisheries successfully. Moreover, doing so can return fisheries to both sustainability and profitability while benefiting ocean ecosystems. In these fisheries, catches are on the rise, fishery value is increasing, and impacts to the environment are minimized—a win-win-win for the ocean and people. Currently around two-thirds of the fish caught in U.S. federal waters by volume are now under a secure rights (catch shares) program. In short, by using good science, smart economic policy, and strong engagement of fishers and civil society, we have learned to fish smarter, not harder.

Many nations have explored similar reforms, especially the powerful use of secure access to flip incentives and thereby align economic and conservation goals. Australia, Canada, Chile, the European Union, Fiji, Indonesia, Japan, Mexico, Namibia, Norway, Peru, the Philippines, and Portugal are a few of the over 40 countries with secure fishery rights programs that globally total over 200 programs and over 500 species. It is clear there is an appetite for fishery reform, even though it is notoriously difficult. Moreover, there are excellent models for success for those fisheries that are not on a sustainable path. The availability of finance to help transition to more sustainable fisheries could unleash a bounty of seafood, healthier ocean ecosystems, good jobs, and fishers and communities that are more prosperous.

Two recent scientific analyses provide powerful motivation to tackle the tough work of fishery reform and create the enabling conditions. A global analysis of the potential benefits of fisheries recovery suggests that the global abundance of fish could increase by approximately 5 percent, seafood yields by about 40 percent, and enhanced revenues by nearly 30 percent.[8] A parallel study suggests that reforming fisheries could prevent the most devastating impacts of climate change on fisheries.[9] This is because climate change is altering both the productivity of the ocean and the location of many stocks. Fisheries could be reformed to jointly fix current problems and make fisheries more resilient to climate changes.

The seafood industry is beginning to respond to the many threats to its businesses, from climate change to overfishing, from consumer and supply-chain demands for traceability and transparency to increased scrutiny over slave labor and illegal practices. The 10 largest seafood companies, in partnership with scientists led by the Stockholm Resilience Center, recently announced the creation of Seafood Businesses for Ocean Stewardship with the goal of making seafood production more sustainable.[10] Time will tell how successful this unusual approach will be, but engagement by industry is essential for fisheries to be sustainable.

For decades, illegal, unregulated, and unreported fishing has been a scourge on the ocean—employing slave labor, facilitating human, drug, and arms trafficking, depriving law-abiding fishers of their livelihoods, endangering fishers and others in nearby waters, pillaging ocean ecosystems, and empowering dysfunctional governments. Such fishing is big business, accounting for at least 20 percent of all wild caught fish and worth $23 billion.[11] Until recently, the idea of dealing with illegal, unregulated, or unreported fishing or policing the ocean seemed preposterous. The ocean was simply too big. There were too many places to hide. The *New York Times* reporter Ian Urbina calls this the "Outlaw Ocean"; I call it the "Wild, Wild Wet."

Today, thanks to intersecting interests, strong political and civil society leadership, new policies, technology, and public attention, illicit fishing itself is under assault. Ocean conservation organizations helped put illegal, unregulated, and unreported fishing on the radar screen. Interpol recognized it as an international crime and created a dedicated unit to address it. High-profile heads of state, foreign ministers, and fishery management heads made it an international diplomacy issue. The United States and the European

Union—both significant importers of seafood—began warning countries whose vessels had been identified as fishing illegally that unless they corrected the situation, their seafood would no longer be imported. Three international treaties were created to help stamp out clandestine and pirate fishing. Mainstream journalists uncovered links between illegal or unregulated fishing and slave labor,[12] entraining human rights attention to the issue. International conferences such as the Our Ocean Conference provide annual visibility. But the big game-changer was technology that combines satellite remote sensing with artificial intelligence, machine learning, and Big Data to track activities on the water—in near real time.[13] With this capability, it is harder for illegal fishing actors to hide, and easier for governments to enforce their new policies. Multiple agendas—political, economic, humanitarian, and conservation—are now aligned and are making a dent in the problem. As with all of the fishery topics, the problem is not solved, but progress is real and the pathway ahead is clear.

A Marine Protected Area (MPA) is an area of the ocean that is managed to achieve conservation objectives.[14] From a biological standpoint, the most effective MPAs are fully or highly protected from any extractive activity. In a Fully Protected MPA, no fishing, mining, drilling, or extraction is allowed, and destructive activities are limited to the greatest extent possible. (This is the equivalent of a wilderness area on land.) In a Highly Protected MPA, only very minimal extraction is allowed (for example, for subsistence purposes).

In truth, most of the ocean used to be a de facto Fully or Highly Protected MPA: it was simply too remote, too deep, or too rocky to access for routine extraction of natural resources. Although many Polynesian, Melanesian, and Micronesian peoples routinely used "tapu" protected areas for conservation and fishery management, elsewhere the general idea of protecting places from extraction seemed unnecessary, if not preposterous. Then, in the 1940s and 1950s, new technology revolutionized extraction of ocean resources. As a consequence, today we fish, mine, and drill almost everywhere. Many of the benefits that the ocean provides to people began to decline.

Concerns about damage to local habitats and threats to certain species resulted in small protected areas being established on shorelines and nearby coastal waters. Conservation groups such as the International Union for the Conservation of Nature actively promoted MPAs. By the 1990s there were thousands of mostly tiny MPAs, but they totaled less than 0.1 percent of the ocean, and Fully or Highly Protected MPAs totaled less than 0.01 percent.

More recent depletion and disruption have triggered increased recognition of the importance of protecting intact ecosystems so that they can continue to provide the benefits we want and need. Thus, we now look to MPAs to protect both iconic places, habitats, and species and the functioning of ocean ecosystems. Of course, MPAs cannot protect against all threats. Parallel actions will also be needed to address climate change, ocean acidification, and pollution, for example. But by reserving some areas as "off limits" to extractive activities, we can control some of the major threats and thus protect many species and the functioning of their ecosystems as much as possible.

Even if all fisheries were sustainable, protected areas would still be needed to provide safe havens for wildlife and natural processes. This is because even the most sustainable fisheries still affect ocean ecosystems. The most common impacts result from the removal of biomass, apex predators, and the large-bodied individuals in a population. Each of those impacts can affect the functioning of the ecosystem; the abundance, distribution, diversity, and behavior of other species; the genetic diversity, social dynamics, and behavior of the fished species; and more. More often than not, fishing gear also has significant impacts, inadvertently "catching" nontarget species like marine mammals, birds, sea turtles, fish, and invertebrates. Some gear, such as bottom trawls, often destroy sea floor habitat. In short, as we work toward making fisheries sustainable, we must also create, manage, and fund Fully and Highly Protected MPAs. We need wilderness areas in the ocean as much as we need them on land.

Fortunately, extensive scientific studies of MPAs shed light on what they can achieve.[15] If they are large, well designed, and enforced, Fully and Highly Protected MPAs do indeed provide safe havens for wildlife and protect habitats. They can also capture and store carbon, restore ecological balance, and preserve genetic diversity that is essential for adaptation. By protecting coastal ecosystems such as coral reefs, mangroves, oyster reefs, and kelp forests, MPAs can protect coastal areas from storm surge and coastal erosion. Fully and Highly Protected MPAs can help recover many depleted fisheries and enhance other fisheries by providing spillover to adjacent fished areas outside the MPA and protecting the large-bodied individual fishes whose reproduction is key to healthy future populations. But that is not all! They bring new economic opportunities and protect culturally important resources, places, and practices. And they can serve as a buffer against mistakes and uncertainty and provide valuable reference areas. Finally, recent evidence suggests that Fully and Highly Protected MPAs are among the strongest tools we have to protect and enhance the resilience of ocean ecosystems.[16]

The good news is that, after examining the evidence about the merits of MPAs, countries of the world have agreed on a target of protecting 10 percent of the ocean by 2020 in MPAs and other types of sites that have conservation benefit. Indeed, the number and size of MPAs have increased dramatically—from 0.3 percent to about 5 percent in just the past decade.[17] The bad news is that only about 5 percent of the ocean is currently protected in implemented MPAs, and only a little over 2 percent is implemented in Highly or Fully Protected MPAs. For comparison, consider that 15 percent of the land is currently protected.

Make no mistake, the actual percentages are less important than the actual protection afforded by well-designed, adequately funded, and well-managed Fully and Highly Protected MPAs. But the numbers do reveal that despite being a powerful tool, MPAs are seriously underutilized. Scientists tell us that to achieve meaningful conservation benefits, we should be targeting at least 30 percent of the ocean in Highly and Fully Protected MPAs by 2030. A key point here is that only Fully and Highly Protected MPAs provide the biodiversity and climate adaptation outcomes we need. Lightly and Minimally Protected MPAs simply do not. In summary, in light of the wealth of benefits provided by Fully and Highly Protected MPAs, there is strong reason to be hopeful that establishing more and more effective MPAs could help reverse some of the current depletion and degradation and provide greater resilience in the years to come.

Innovative leaders are exploring combinations of the fishery and conservation tools mentioned above and using them to enhance ocean resilience to climate change, human health, and other big challenges.

For example, where spatially explicit secure access rights are feasible for fishery management, they can be combined with Fully Protected MPAs to protect both biodiversity and ecosystem functioning as well as reap the benefits of spillover and export of larvae from the MPA to the managed fishery area outside. Thus the fishers who agree to protect the MPA benefit directly from the bounty produced by the MPA, enhancing fisheries in their fished areas. Instead of MPAs and good fishery management as alternatives, they can be combined in ways that enhance the effectiveness of both.

Fishery and conservation tools can also help build the ocean's resilience to climate change and ocean acidification. Recent analyses suggest that reforming fisheries is one of the most powerful actions available to make fisheries more resilient to climate change impacts. Large, enforced Fully Protected Areas can also enhance resilience by protecting the ecological balance, genetic diversity, and viability of the large-bodied individuals that contribute disproportionately to future generations.

The benefit of protection of genetic diversity in Fully and Highly Protected MPAs may become especially important in a warmer, more acidic, and deoxygenated ocean. Researchers are discovering that some genotypes of corals can withstand water temperatures that bleach most of the others. It makes sense that protecting as much genetic variation as possible today in large Fully or Highly Protected MPAs is a smart bet-hedging strategy that could enhance the likelihood that genotypes will be able to survive in future ocean conditions.

Both fisheries and Fully or Highly Protected MPAs contribute meaningfully to human and planetary health. Seafood is well known to be healthful food. Less well known but important to our future is the fact that, overall, animal protein produced in the sea (from both wild capture fisheries and aquaculture) has a much lower environmental footprint than animal protein produced on land.[18] Moreover, as we learn more about the health benefits of spending time in nature, we come to appreciate the personal and psychological benefits of ocean wildlife and habitats—opportunities for renewal, inspiration, reflection, and learning.

So how do we "Seas the Day" or make Ocean 3.0 a reality? Fishery reform and Fully and Highly Protected MPAs are proven tools to yield big economic, social, and environmental benefits. Both have huge potential to achieve much more than is currently being realized. And they can be used in tandem to achieve even greater benefits. Moreover, both can help provide insurance against other serious problems such as the effects of climate change and ocean acidification. Neither is being deployed at the scale needed for restoring ocean health, but they could be by removing barriers to that scaling.

Moreover, successes with fisheries and MPAs bring co-benefits for food security, human health, jobs, human rights, poverty alleviation, and climate change adaptation. Both sustainable fisheries and MPAs are enabled or strengthened through judicious use of artificial intelligence, machine learning, Big Data, and new technologies. For example, the website Global Fishing Watch helps patrol the seas remotely and identifies illegal fishing activities while simultaneously patrolling MPAs. The right economic and social incentives can transform a vicious cycle of unsustainable practices into a virtuous cycle of sustainable practices. Market and supply-chain incentives can be particularly powerful.

There are comparable advances and encouraging models in other arenas ranging from aquaculture (fish farming) to energy generation. Similar advances are needed to deal with plastics, nutrient pollution, and coastal development—approaches that seek regenerative solutions, work with nature, and understand that people and nature are intimately interconnected in complex adaptive systems.

We do not yet have all the answers to realize this new vision for the ocean. The examples cited are seeds for a new awakening. We are beginning to understand that the ocean is the key to a thriving future—both underwater and on land. The ocean is essential to mitigating and adapting to climate change and addressing global sustainability challenges, and has immense potential to provide food for billions through healthy fisheries and especially from smart aquaculture. Furthermore, the ocean can refresh our bodies, renew our souls, and touch our hearts. For, as the Chilean Nobel laureate Pablo Neruda noted in his poem "El Mar" (The Sea): Necesito del mar porque me enseña[19] (I need the sea because it teaches me). We need to act on this new knowledge and embrace a new, hopeful narrative, then work to realize that vision.

We are beginning to understand how interconnected the ocean is with our food system, climate system, health, and well-being. In creating a new vision, we could address a range of broader, interconnected global problems. In short, we have already moved beyond the narrative "The ocean is too big to fail"; now it is time to jettison the current idea "The ocean is too big to fix." We must pursue a more enlightened, humbler, more holistic path and acknowledge "The ocean is too important and too big to ignore." It is time to heal the ocean, and in the process heal ourselves. Will you help?

**NOTES**

I greatly appreciate the assistance of H. Fulton-Bennett; comments on earlier drafts by M. Caldwell, K. Grorud-Colvert, S. Gaines, J. Leape, E. Sala, and A. Steer; discussions with S. Bachhuber, V. Constant, B. Menge, and J. Sullivan; assistance from G. HaBarad and C. Kent; and funding from the Ocean Science Innovation Fund at Oregon State University.

1. Callum Roberts, *The Unnatural History of the Sea* (London: Island Press/Shearwater Books, 2007).

2. Jane Lubchenco et al., "The Right Incentives Enable Ocean Sustainability Successes and Provide Hope for the Future," *Proceedings of the National Academy of Sciences* 113 (December 20, 2016): 14507–15, https://doi.org/10.1073/pnas.1604982113.

3. Christopher Costello, Steven D. Gaines, and John Lynham, "Can Catch Shares Prevent Fisheries Collapse?," *Science* 321 (September 19, 2008), 1678–81, https://doi.org /10.1126/science.1159478; Environmental Defense Fund, "Fishery Solutions Center," accessed May 6, 2019, http://fisherysolutionscenter.edf.org/.

4. Michael C. Melnychuk et al., "Can Catch Share Fisheries Better Track Management Targets?," *Fish and Fisheries* 13 (July 18, 2011): 267–90, https://doi.org/10.1111/j.1467 -2979.2011.00429.x; Costello, Gaines, and Lynham, "Catch Shares"; Dietmar Grimm et al., "Assessing Catch Shares' Effects Evidence from Federal United States and Associated British Columbian Fisheries," *Marine Policy* 36 (May 2012): 644–57, https://doi.org/10.1016/j.marpol.2011.10.014; Environmental Defense Fund, "Fishery Solutions Center."

5. "How Catch Shares Work," Environmental Defense Fund, accessed March 15, 2019, https://www.edf.org/oceans/how-catch-shares-work-promising-solution.

6. "Fishery Stock Status Updates," NOAA Fisheries, accessed March 15, 2019, https://www.fisheries.noaa.gov/national/population-assessments/fishery-stock -status-updates; Allison K. Barner et al., "Solutions for Recovering and Sustaining the Bounty of the Ocean: Combining Fishery Reforms, Rights-Based Fisheries Management, and Marine Reserves," *Oceanography* 28, no. 2 (June 2015): 252–63, https://doi.org/10.5670/oceanog.2015.51; Lubchenco et al., "The Right Incentives."

7. "Stock Status Updates."

8. Christopher Costello et al., "Global Fishery Prospects under Contrasting Management Regimes," *Proceedings of the National Academy of Sciences* 113, no. 18 (May 3, 2016): 5125–29, https://doi.org/10.1073/pnas.1520420113.

9. Steven D. Gaines et al., "Improved Fisheries Management Could Offset Many Negative Effects of Climate Change," *Science Advances* 4 (2018), doi:10.1126/sciadv.aao1378.

10. "Seafood Business for Ocean Stewardship (SeaBOS)," Keystone Dialogues, accessed March 15, 2019, http://keystonedialogues.earth/.

11. Reg A. Watson and A. Tidd, "Mapping Nearly a Century and a Half of Global Marine Fishing: 1869-2015," *Marine Policy* 93 (July 2018): 171–77, https://doi.org/10.1016 /j.marpol.2018.04.023.

12. "AP Wins Pulitzer Prize for 'Seafood from Slaves' Investigation," *Associated Press*, April 18, 2016, https://www.ap.org/press-releases/2016/ap-wins-pulitzer-prize-for -seafood-from-slaves-investigation; Ian Urbina, "The Outlaw Ocean," *New York Times* (2015–2016), https://www.nytimes.com/interactive/2015/07/24/world/the -outlaw-ocean.html.

13. Global Fishing Watch, accessed May 6, 2019, https://globalfishingwatch.org/.

14. "An Introduction to the MPA Guide," The MPA Guide, accessed June 4, 2019, http://wcmc.io/8408.

15. Jane Lubchenco et al., "The Science of Marine Protected Areas—Mediterranean Sea," Partnership for Interdisciplinary Studies of Coastal Oceans (PISCO), 2016, http://www.piscoweb.org/science-marine-protected-area-med.

16. Callum M. Roberts et al., "Marine Reserves Can Mitigate and Promote Adaptation to Climate Change," *Proceedings of the National Academy of Sciences* 114 (June 13, 2017): 6167–75, https://doi.org/10.1073/pnas.1701262114.

17. Jane Lubchenco and Kirsten Grorud-Colvert, "Making Waves: The Science and Politics of Ocean Protection," *Science* 350 (October 23, 2015): 382–83, https://doi.org/10.1126/science.aad5443.

18. Steven D. Gaines, "The Future of Food: The Rise of the Sea," *TedX Talks*, December 18, 2017, https://www.youtube.com/watch?v=0KDsIa6-NVA.

19. Pablo Neruda, "El Mar," in *A la Orilla Azul Del Silencio* [On the blue shore of silence] (New York: Harper Collins, 2004), 1–3.

**PART TWO**   INNOVATION AND TECHNOLOGY

# Red Lights to Green Lights

## TOWARD AN INNOVATION-ORIENTED SUSTAINABILITY STRATEGY

Daniel C. Esty

ENVIRONMENTAL LAW AND POLICY as framed in the 1970s and 1980s focused on "command and control" regulatory strategies under which the government told businesses (and to some extent individuals) what they should *not* do. It was a world of stop signs and *red lights* for polluters.[1] But this framework has proven to be incomplete. It has failed to offer signals as to what society needs businesses *to do,* including what problems to solve, what research and development to undertake, and what investments to make. So years have gone by and many environmental problems persist, including our dependence on polluting fossil fuels and reliance on the same costly and inefficient electrical system that was put in place more than 100 years ago, with electricity flowing across wires on poles.[2] To address these enduring problems, we need to reframe our approach to environmental protection—offering a systematically designed structure of incentives to encourage innovation and problem solving. In short, we need to complement our system of red lights with an expanded set of *green lights.*

## PROGRESS, AT A PRICE

The *red lights* approach made sense five decades ago as the need to stop harm-causing behavior seemed obvious. From Cleveland's Cuyahoga River catching fire to the thick smog that often hung over Los Angeles to the toxic waste and human health crisis of Love Canal, the problems seemed obvious.[3] The public demanded action. With a primitive base of environmental knowledge and limited theory about how to respond to pollution threats, government-defined regulatory mandates offered a path forward. And they worked—to some extent. Our air and water are much cleaner today. Chemicals are regulated, and waste disposal occurs under a regime of careful controls.

But this progress has come at a price. The command and control framework is now widely recognized as slow and inefficient insofar as the government does almost all of the environmental work—spotting problems, analyzing the causes of various harms, identifying safe pollution thresholds, spelling out standards, and sometimes even requiring specific "best available technologies" to be adopted by particular industries. This over-reliance on government as the central (and often sole) actor also leads to high costs, avoidable inefficiencies, constant litigation over standards, and disincentives for innovation.

Today, we know, moreover, that red lights are not enough. Limiting or even forbidding pollution is not the same as solving environmental problems. Just as a traffic intersection needs green lights as well as red ones to optimize the flow of vehicles, we need a policy framework that highlights for businesses and individuals across the nation and around the world where problems exist that require solutions—and thus where their innovative thinking would be particularly welcome. Fundamentally, while the red lights framework of the past helped us curb pollution, reduce waste, and limit chemical exposures, it did not spur transformative change in response to critical challenges such as the need for breakthroughs in clean energy or expanded funding for safe drinking water. It did not engage the business community and the financial markets as potential problem solvers. It did not harness their capacity for out-of-the-box thinking and the delivery of solutions. To put a sharp point on the limitations of the red lights approach, note that entrepreneurs do not get up early and stay at the office until very late in pursuit of their dreams of delivering a marketplace breakthrough because the government told them what *not* to do.

So while regulatory rules and prohibitions have a place in controlling pollution, our present environmental law and policy framework must be seen as incomplete. It should be rethought with an eye on creating incentives for problem solving and rewards for innovation—based on a structure of *green lights* as well as red ones.

Of course, we have had some policy efforts that fit the green lights model of providing incentives for innovation and signaling where entrepreneurial activity would be welcome. The 1990 Clean Air Act, for example, set up an emissions allowance trading system to control sulfur dioxide emissions and reduce acid rain. This "cap and trade" approach spurred creative thinking about how best to reduce power plant emissions and led to a 50 percent reduction in acid-rain precursors. Likewise, the 33/50 toxic emissions reduction strategy of the Environmental Protection Agency (EPA), building on the mandated reporting of the Toxics Release Inventory, helped highlight opportunities to cut chemical release and rewarded companies that met ambitious pollution reduction goals. And the Department of Energy's Advanced Research Projects Agency–Energy (ARPA-E) program has helped induce and leverage investments of private capital in energy efficiency and renewable power.

But more could be—and should be—done to promote innovation as a centerpiece of America's energy and environmental strategies. The push for fresh thinking and new ideas should, of course, include technology development, but it should also promote innovation in policy approaches, public engagement, conservation, and finance for environmental infrastructure (including expanded funding for renewable power, electricity storage, drinking water systems, sewage treatment, clean technologies for industry, and low-emissions mobility). Law and policy should ensure that the work of environmental protection is not seen as solely the purview of the public sector. Rather, incentives should be in place to encourage broad engagement in environmental problem-solving that draws companies, inventors and creative spirits of all kinds, think tanks, research centers, universities, and other nongovernmental entities into the pursuit of a sustainable future.

### INCENTIVES TO INNOVATE

The expanded framework of green lights that I envision would take many forms. Perhaps the greatest spur to innovation and a transformed future would be a commitment to adopt the *polluter pays principle* and to insist on an "end to *externalities*"—meaning that those who inflict environmental harms on society must pay for them. Implementation of this principle would require that those who cause air or water pollution or chemical exposures and spill harms beyond their own property lines—or who consume natural resources without paying for their full value—be charged for their emissions or other negative impacts. These *harm charges* would establish a very substantial incentive (or green light) that would signal where efforts to remake products or production processes would find a payoff.

The expectation that harm causers should stop the activities that burden society or pay for these impacts is as American as apple pie. It derives from one of the fundamentals of law: the constitutional principle of protecting property rights, which my Yale colleague Carol Rose has described as the "keystone" right for building a fair and prosperous society.[4] Indeed, the concept of protecting property rights, including against environmental infringements, goes back at least four centuries in the Anglo-American legal tradition. Specifically, the polluter pays principle can be traced to a 1611 court decision (*Aldred's* case) in which an English pig farmer was required to get rid of his smelly animals or compensate his neighbors for the nuisance. Reinvigorating this principle through adoption of a broad-based rule that puts a price on causing environmental harms would sharply focus those facing these charges on the need to rethink their activities with an eye toward reducing their impacts. Such price signals would also induce innovation and encourage problem solvers to find ways to reduce these harms with the hope that they might sell their solutions to those paying harm charges.

The success of this approach to environmental problems has been demonstrated many times over. As noted above, the 1990 Clean Air Act required electric utilities to buy "emissions allowances" for the acid-rain-causing sulfur dioxide they were sending up their power plant smokestacks. The prospect of having to pay for their emissions induced these companies to rethink their activities and led most to switch to low-sulfur coal as a way to cut their pollution and their costs.

Likewise, when a class of "miracle chemicals" called chlorofluorocarbons, or CFCs—used to blow Styrofoam, clean semiconductors, produce spray deodorants, and cool refrigerators—was found to be causing the Earth's protective ozone layer to thin, the U.S. government put in place an escalating per-pound CFC charge. This economic incentive—another green-light-signaling opportunity to inventors—induced such significant process and product innovation that ozone-layer-damaging CFCs were driven out of the market in under a decade.

Green lights can take other forms and spur innovation in other domains. For example, one of the biggest mistakes in our current environmental protection regime has been the assumption that once pollution control requirements were in place, the money to implement them would follow. And while big industries have spent millions of dollars on smokestack scrubbers and effluent controls, much less investment in pollution control technologies has been made by small businesses, households, and other entities with limited access to capital. But in recent years, innovative financing tools, such as Green Banks and Green Bonds, have created new incentives that encourage investment in environmental infrastructure.[5] These "sustainable finance" green lights make capital available at attractive rates for borrowers—a model that could easily be expanded.

Another green light that could be scaled up centers on incentives that steer the flow of private capital toward businesses and projects that contribute to a sustainable future—and away from enterprises with business models that cause environmental degradation.[6] Specifically, a growing number of mainstream investors want to align their stock holdings with their issue interests and values. For many people, this alignment means that they want to be sure that the companies in their investment portfolios have good track records on critical sustainability issues. The rise of *sustainable investing* has driven up demand for corporate performance metrics on a range of environmental/social/governance (ESG) issues.[7] The strength of this signal and therefore the scale of capital flows could be enhanced if the government were to require mandatory ESG reporting on a structured basis—just as the Securities and Exchange Commission requires corporate accounting according to a specified framework and methodology. By ensuring comparability across companies and strengthening investor confidence and trust in the data, an ESG framework could emerge as a powerful green light. These stronger ESG requirements would induce business leaders to pay attention to their environmental results so as to make their companies attractive to sustainability-minded investors.

### CAREFUL POLICY DESIGN

As discussed earlier, our existing environmental policy framework includes some green lights, but their success as incentives has been muted by poor design and uneven implementation. Notably, the Department of Energy offers Investment Tax Credits and Production Tax Credits for projects generating electricity from renewable sources. But the strength of these tax credits as green lights for innovation and investment in renewable energy has been dulled by ongoing uncertainty over whether Congress will continue to fund these programs.[8] It turns out that unpredictability and unreliability severely undermine business confidence in the value of incentives. So just as drivers will act with caution on a road where the traffic lights are intermittently failing, clean energy investors have tended to pull back in the face of uncertainty over the future of the government's clean energy incentives.

Similarly, many states have adopted Renewable Portfolio Standards (RPSs) setting out targets and timetables for expanded wind and solar power. For example, when I became commissioner of Connecticut's Department of Energy and Environmental Protection, the state had a goal of 20 percent renewable power by 2020. But little progress had been made toward this goal. And when I pressed as to the reasons for the ineffectiveness of the millions of ratepayer dollars being devoted to driving clean energy innovation, I learned not only that Connecticut was falling way short of its RPS targets but also that the bulk of the money was funding biomass projects. Thus, the precious ratepayer innovation-inducing dollars were being spent on burning wood—an energy source that has been around for 20,000 years.

It became clear that Connecticut needed more carefully crafted incentives (green lights) to drive funding into truly innovative projects. This gap led us to launch the first-in-the-nation Green Bank, with a commitment to use limited public money to leverage private capital and scale up clean energy innovation and project deployment. Connecticut thus moved to the use of "reverse auctions" (in which the project developer that promises the *lowest* electricity prices wins) to select renewable energy projects with the promise of a Power Purchase Agreement (a commitment to buy the electricity generated for 15 years) for winning bidders. By harnessing the power of competition—including a requirement that wind, solar, fuel cells, and other clean energy options compete against each other—renewable energy prices were driven down. Moreover, while the promise that Connecticut would someday receive 20 percent of its electricity from renewable sources had provided insufficient certainty to past projects to enable them to get bank financing, the presence of a 15-year electricity supply contract made the projects "bankable."

To be fair, some states have backed their RPS goals with a structure of "feed-in tariffs" or Renewable Energy Credits that has induced a ramp-up in solar and wind power, but often at very high costs. So once again, the lesson is that the presence of incentives is not enough. The green lights framework must be carefully considered and sharply focused on driving innovation and scaling up the engagement of private capital to deliver on public policy goals. Simply put, the goal cannot be "clean power." It needs to be cheaper, cleaner, and more reliable energy supplies.

Some might ask why certain activities—such as clean energy development—deserve government attention and green lights prioritization while others do not. The answer is straightforward: these projects offer public benefits alongside the private gains of the project developers. Indeed, insofar as a commitment to the "end of externalities" and the polluter pays principle means that those causing harms to society should pay for their *negative* externalities, it also implies that those delivering *positive* externalities—benefits to society—should be compensated. This logic means that not only should clean energy get government help but so too should private landowners whose property provides habitat for endangered species.

## CONTINUOUS IMPROVEMENT

I recognize that my call for much greater attention to incentives for action and innovation inescapably requires political decisions about what issues get tagged for *green light* focus and prioritization. Given this reality, there will be disputes over the framework of incentives created and the sorts of signals that get sent out. But I hope the broader point about needing to refresh America's approach to sustainability—and to bring an emphasis on innovation to the energy and environmental arenas—does not get lost.

Change is never easy, especially within a fraught political context. But whether we call it continuous improvement or regular revitalization, the importance of *innovation* leading to new and better ways of doing essential activities—including our approaches to energy strategy and environmental protection—needs to be highlighted.[9] Indeed, one of the most significant findings in social science of recent decades centers on the importance of *innovation* to healthy organizations.[10]

Baseball teams pick players today in a very different way than they did in the 1970s. Rather than tobacco-chewing scouts making recommendations based on intuition and their "gut," teams now rely on data geeks such as Theo Epstein, whose pioneering approach to baseball data analytics has delivered world championships for the long-denied Boston Red Sox and Chicago Cubs. Epstein's fresh thinking about the underpinnings of success in pitching, hitting, and fielding—built on advanced data analytics and new metrics (such as a focus on on-base percentage rather than batting average)—has now been adopted by all the major league teams.

Likewise, corporate leaders in every industry have come to learn that they must constantly reinvent their business models and corporate strategies to stay competitive and profitable.[11] As a result, companies today market their products and target their customers in very different ways from a generation ago. They rely on new data science, microtargeting of potential buyers, and constant testing, tracking, and refining of sales pitches to stay ahead of the market.

Other institutions, including government entities, have similarly learned to remake themselves to stay vibrant. Some parts of our administrative state have been fundamentally re-engineered for the twenty-first century. In fact, recast telecommunications regulations helped usher in the smartphone era.[12] Major regulatory reforms have also transformed the airline industry, railroads, and other sectors of society.[13]

But the foundations of energy and environmental policy have remained largely static for decades—and this must not continue.[14] So even if there will be disputes over the structure of green lights and the direction of change, that conversation will be important. We cannot possibly meet the demands of the emerging "sustainability imperative"[15] with a twentieth-century policy framework that has failed to capitalize on recent breakthroughs in mapping pollution flows, tracing ecological and epidemiological effects, and understanding chemical exposure thresholds and so many of the other advances in knowledge that have emerged in the past four decades. It is time to put Big Data, the internet, advanced sensors, omnipresent telecommunications links, and other tools of our Digital Age to work on energy and environmental challenges. A commitment to incentives—green lights—that facilitate innovation needs to be at the heart of a remade sustainability policy framework.

## NOTES

This essay builds on the author's prior published article, "Red Lights to Green Lights: From 20th Century Environmental Regulation to 21st Century Sustainability," *Environmental Law* 47, no. 1 (2017): 1–80. In addition to his positions at Yale, the author is a principal of Constellation Research and Technology (www.constellationresearch.com), a New York–based financial technology firm that provides advanced ESG metrics and data analytics for investors.

1. Carol M. Rose, "Environmental Law Grows Up (More or Less), and What Science Can Do to Help," *Lewis & Clark Law Review* 9, no. 2 (2005): 276–77, https://law .lclark.edu/live/files/9701-rosepdf (describing the first wave of major environmental regulations as "behavior-based" regulations that "constrained the actions of resource-users"); Carol M. Rose, "Rethinking Environmental Controls: Management Strategies for Common Resources," *Duke Law Journal* 40, no. 1 (February 1991): 8–10, https://scholarship.law.duke.edu/dlj/vol40/iss1/1/ (laying out four core "controls" for managing shared resources).

2. David Crane, letter to NRG Energy shareholders, March 27, 2014.

3. Daniel A. Farber, "Politics and Procedure in Environmental Law," *Journal of Law, Economics & Organization* 8, no. 1 (March 1992): 59, 67, https://doi.org/10.1093 /oxfordjournals.jleo.a037032 (describing Love Canal, Three Mile Island, and other environmental disasters as catalyzing public support for environmental legislation in the 1970s); Richard J. Lazarus, "A Different Kind of 'Republican Moment' in En-

vironmental Law," *Minnesota Law Review* 87, no. 3 (2003): 999–1000, https://scholarship.law.georgetown.edu/facpub/165/ (noting legislative responses to the burning of the Cuyahoga River and the *Exxon Valdez* oil spill).

4. Carol M. Rose, "Property as the Keystone Right?," *Notre Dame Law Review* 71, no. 3 (January 1996): 329–65, https://scholarship.law.nd.edu/ndlr/vol71/iss3/1.

5. Whitney Angell Leonard, "Clean Is the New Green: Clean Energy Finance and Deployment through Green Banks," *Yale Law & Policy Review* 33, no. 1 (2014): 197–299, https://digitalcommons.law.yale.edu/ylpr/vol33/iss1/6; Hallie Kennan, "Working Paper: State Green Banks for Clean Energy," Energy Innovation, accessed January 2, 2019, https://energyinnovation.org/wp-content/uploads/2014/06/WorkingPaper _StateGreenBanks.pdf; Daniel C. Esty, "Regulatory Transformation: Lessons from Connecticut's Department of Energy and Environmental Protection," *Public Administration Review* 76, no. 3 (2016): 403–12.

6. Daniel C. Esty and Quentin Karpilow, "Harnessing Investor Interest in Sustainability: The Next Frontier in Environmental Information Regulation," *Yale Journal on Regulation* 36, no. 2 (2019): 1–68.

7. Daniel C. Esty and Todd Cort, "Corporate Sustainability Metrics: What Investors Need and Don't Get," *Journal of Environmental Investing* 8, no. 1 (2017): 11–53.

8. Merrill Jones Barradale, "Impact of Public Policy Uncertainty on Renewable Energy Investment: Wind Power and the Production Tax Credit," *Energy Policy* 38, no. 12 (December 2010): 7698–709, https://doi.org/10.1016/j.enpol.2010.08.021.

9. Beth Simone Noveck, *Smart Citizens, Smarter State: The Technologies of Expertise and the Future of Governing* (Cambridge, MA: Harvard University Press, 2015), 32–33.

10. Clayton M. Christensen, *The Innovator's Dilemma: When New Technologies Cause Great Firms to Fail* (Boston: Harvard Business Review Press, 1997); Clayton M. Christensen and Michael Overdorf, "Meeting the Challenge of Disruptive Change," *Harvard Business Review*, March–April 2000, https://hbr.org/2000/03/meeting-the -challenge-of-disruptive-change; John P. Kotter, "Accelerate!," *Harvard Business Review*, November 2012, https://hbr.org/2012/11/accelerate; Gary P. Pisano, "You Need an Innovation Strategy," *Harvard Business Review*, June 2015, https://hbr.org/2015 /06/you-need-an-innovation-strategy.

11. Mark W. Johnson, Clayton M. Christensen, and Henning Kagermann, "Reinventing Your Business Model," *Harvard Business Review*, December 2008, https://hbr .org/2008/12/reinventing-your-business-model; Michael E. Porter, "How Competitive Forces Shape Strategy," *Harvard Business Review*, March 1979, https://hbr.org /1979/03/how-competitive-forces-shape-strategy.

12. Reed Hundt, "Wireless: The Common Medium of Conversation," *Media Law & Policy* 20, no. 1 (Fall 2011): 95, 97, http://www.nyls.edu/documents/media_center /archives/20-1-article-3-by-reed-hundt.pdf (describing Federal Communications Commission regulations that helped create a robust competitive market for wireless).

13. Clifford Winston, "U.S. Industry Adjustment to Economic Deregulation," *Journal of Economic Perspectives* 12, no. 3 (Summer 1998): 89, 101, https://DOI.org/10.1257/jep .12.3.89 (showing improvements in consumer welfare as a result of deregulation in the airlines, trucking, railroad, banking, and natural gas industries).

14. David W. Case, "The Lost Generation: Environmental Regulatory Reform in the Era of Congressional Abdication," *Duke Environmental Law & Policy Forum* 25, no. 1 (Fall 2014): 49–51, https://scholarship.law.duke.edu/cgi/viewcontent.cgi?article =1307&context=delpf; Jody Freeman and David B. Spence, "Old Statutes, New Problems," *University of Pennsylvania Law Review* 163, no. 1 (December 2014): 10, https:// www.pennlawreview.com/print/163-U-Pa-L-Rev-1.pdf ("Since the mid-1990s, EPA and [the Federal Energy Regulatory Commission] have continued to confront new and important environmental and energy challenges, but Congress has been largely absent from the policy response").

15. David A. Lubin and Daniel C. Esty, "The Sustainability Imperative," *Harvard Business Review,* May 2010, https://hbr.org/2010/05/the-sustainability-imperative.

# Environmental Protection through Systems Design, Decision-Making, and Thinking

Paul T. Anastas and Julie B. Zimmerman

FOR THE PAST HALF CENTURY, our understanding of the environment has been built on the scientific reliance on reductionism: obtaining understanding through observation of what changes take place when modifying a single factor while holding all other factors constant. Environmental laws, organizational structures, budgeting mechanisms, analytical tools, metrics, and decision-making processes all depend on it. While this reductionist approach has brought about truly astounding progress and discoveries, it has profound limitations when applied to complex systems such as environmental protection.[1]

Although many of these examples are historical, we continue to carry this reductionist framework forward to address current sustainability challenges. That is, new solutions are implemented with the necessary—but not sufficient—knowledge generated through the reductionist framework. When the scientific community mobilizes to protect human health and the environment—to do the right things—we have too often found that we are doing the right things wrong. To do the right things right, we need to couple reductionism with *systems thinking;* to address complex environmental problems, we need to simultaneously consider multiple variables and moving parts.

## MISTAKES OF THE PAST AND PRESENT

What are some examples of doing the right things wrong?

*Biofuels from Food Crops.*   Environmental managers and innovators around the world are trying to alleviate dependence on fossil fuels by producing fuel energy from agricultural products. One of the clearest examples of this effort is the emphasis in the United States on producing ethanol fuel from corn. There are a couple of ways the economics of this approach can be measured: by calculating the total cost of all emissions generated during biofuel production and use, or by measuring direct environmental impacts, including water, fertilizer, and pesticide use.[2] Either way, corn-based ethanol requires, per unit of fuel produced, more fossil fuel and carbon-intensive, air-polluting fertilizer than current petroleum-based fuels.

This is not to suggest that producing energy from bio-based resources is not an appropriate or ultimately sustainable strategy. It is rather to suggest that pursuing renewable energy in a way that uses an intensive monoculture food crop and addresses only the singular goal of reducing use of finite petroleum supplies can lead to increased environmental and human health impacts and even greater stress on the Earth's systems.

*Water Purification by Hazardous Chemicals.*   The consumption of untreated water contributes to significant human health risks ranging from cholera to stunted child development.[3] The most prevalent approach to water treatment for municipal systems in much of the developed world has been the use of chlorine.

There has been recent attention given to both the potential health and security risks posed by the use of chlorine for water treatment. Scientists have identified chloroform and other toxic halogenated organic compounds in chlorinated drinking water supplies, leading to numerous studies on their health risks. In general, these studies support the notion that by-products of chlorination are associated with increased cancer risk, among other health risks.[4]

Due to the major terrorist attacks of the twenty-first century, municipal water systems are giving greater attention to the security of their facilities. Many systems are conducting comprehensive "vulnerability assessments" on the storage, handling, and protection of chlorine supplies.

Again, this is not to suggest that providing safe, reliable drinking water is not critically important to improved quality of life and human development. It is. The point is, however, to question the approach being taken to achieve this crucial goal. Must we achieve clean drinking water through the use of potentially lethal and toxic chemicals? There are many more considerations to this sustainability challenge beyond the immediate goal of clean drinking water, highlighting the need to systematically consider multiple sustainability criteria simultaneously.

*Solar Panels Using Rare, Toxic Metals.*    The need to harness the sun's energy to meet current energy demand is becoming increasingly clear given concerns over the use of fossil fuels from a societal, political, and environmental perspective. The current class of photovoltaic solar cells relies on toxic chemicals, explosive gases, corrosive liquids, and solid forms of suspected carcinogens. These risks occur throughout the solar panel life cycle with particular concern for worker safety during manufacturing and environmental exposure during disposal.

While the operation of photovoltaic systems significantly reduces the emissions of sulfur oxide, nitrogen oxide, harmful particulate matter, and carbon dioxide, these critical advances are being realized through the use and generation of hazardous chemicals. There are many emerging pathways to photovoltaic cell synthesis, demonstrating that there is not an inherent trade-off between solar energy and increased risk to human health and the environment. Through innovation and green design, solar energy can be realized sustainably. This will only occur if the pursuit of solar energy is not singularly focused on efficiency but rather considers human health and environmental factors in identifying which technological pathways to pursue.

*Energy-Saving Lighting Technology Based on Neurotoxins.*    As a final example of addressing sustainability challenges in a manner that leads to further impacts on human health and the environment, we highlight the recent push toward compact fluorescent lamps. While the amount of mercury contained in each bulb is relatively small, the large market for lighting means that, in total, fluorescent bulbs represent a significant source of mercury-containing wastes in many mercury emissions inventories. Mercury is an element that is known to persist, bioaccumulate, and biomagnify in the environment, with known and well-documented toxicity concerns. While reducing demand through more efficient lighting technology is an important component of the sustainable energy challenge, this approach can lead to increased environmental mercury emissions and subsequent human exposures in certain states and countries.[5]

Recognizing that the optimal way to reduce energy demand is not through the use, generation, and emission of toxic chemicals, industry leaders are working to reduce the mercury content in lamps. Similarly, the U.S. Department of Energy's Vision 2020 project brought together researchers, manufacturers, and policy makers to push for the elimination of mercury from the bulbs by 2020.[6]

Given the goal of energy conservation, we must question the push toward the use of a technology reliant on a known toxin with significant potential to adversely impact human health and the environment. By systematically considering the sustainable energy demand question, the likely solution would not be fluorescent lights. Once again, we are attempting an unsustainable solution to a sustainability challenge.

In each of these examples and many others, scientists, engineers, and policy makers, with the best of intentions to take on the greatest challenges of our generation, were pursuing the noblest of goals. But they pursued the goals in an unsustainable way due to the lack of integrative systems thinking. While reductionism is necessary, integrative systems thinking is also necessary. Both will be required to address the sustainability challenges facing our world—challenges that lie at the nexus of climate, energy, water, chemicals, waste, health, agriculture, technology, policy, and society.

## THINKING SYSTEMATICALLY

The type of problems created as a result of human activity on the natural environment have changed over past decades. In the twentieth century, our focus was on environmental problems that were local, acute, obvious, immediate, and discrete.[7] That is, issues such as unhealthy air in Los Angeles, rivers on fire in Ohio, and entire communities evacuated because of toxics in New York and Missouri. In response, our environmental laws and technologies focused on such direct impacts—realizing significant benefits to the environment, human health, and quality of life. However, the nature of environmental challenges has evolved in the twenty-first century. We now face issues that are global, chronic, subtle, multigenerational, complex, and interconnected. That is, our understanding of environmental challenges must now extend beyond treating direct impacts to discrete environmental compartments, and consider the movement of contaminants among air, water, and land; the value we can realize from recovery of materials rather than "safe" disposal; and the socioeconomic drivers that can inadvertently encourage behaviors that are harmful to the environment.

This expanded understanding suggests the need to enhance our current skills, capabilities, and perspectives. We need to more effectively address the challenges we face rather than the symptoms we experience.[8] This shift requires new knowledge, perspectives, and awareness, as well as expanding our purview to a more holistic, systems-based view of environmental challenges. While this does not, as some would suggest, require generating *more* information, it does require generating different kinds of information. Such information should allow insight into the interconnections and linkages of the environment as a system, in order to generate more robust and effective solutions.

Thought leaders in environmental protection could then consider a broader array of issues, allowing for more innovative and appropriate solutions. This includes recognizing the vital role of ecological systems and services, acknowledging who has been disadvantaged through the lens of environmental justice, using life cycle analysis to consider the impacts of a manufacturing system from acquiring the raw materials to end of life, and leveraging economic incentives and policy instruments to align socioeconomic choices with environmental goals, to name just a few examples. That is, the systems in which environmental decision makers work are integrated and complex. They include technical aspects as well as social, environmental, and economic facets. The historical approaches that did not consider these broader systems resulted in unintended consequences.

Of course, this important evolution of environmental decision makers to a broader systems view is challenging. It had long been recognized that these complex systems are very difficult to predict in that they are non-linear, have feedback mechanisms, are adaptive, are difficult to predict from constitutive components, and have emergent behavior.[9] Only recently has our computing power increased enough to model both technological advances and changes to underlying social and economic systems.[10] In this way, we can design solutions to environmental challenges that realize our goals while minimizing unintended consequences.

There are many discrete recommendations that could begin to put a systems-thinking framework into practice. A few of the most essential recommendations are the following:

- Break down the walls in the U.S. Environmental Protection Agency (EPA). The current organizational structure of *media-based* offices for air, water, solid waste, and so forth, can be counterproductive when trying to solve systems problems. While many U.S. environmental laws have media-specific orientation, they usually do not require that the corresponding organizational or budget structure be oriented that way as well. Ideally, statutes would be adjusted to allow for cross-media approaches, but in the meantime, there is much that can be done to ensure that environmental problem-solving strategies use systems approaches instead of the historical fragmented organizational framework.

- Establish a solutions orientation. While the precise budgetary percentage would be difficult to attain, it is known that an inordinate amount of funding for environmental issues is spent observing, measuring, monitoring, assessing, and characterizing the *problem*. While it is true that understanding a problem is necessary, *the only reason to deeply understand a problem is to inform and empower its solution.* A solutions orientation can help avoid the trap of endless study, often referred to as "paralysis by analysis" in many regulatory agencies like EPA. By consciously setting solutions as the goal, we require only the level of analysis necessary to identify and justify what action to take to implement the solution.

- Use a new toolbox. The decision-making tools for justifying actions at EPA and other agencies are largely relics of the past. The flaws in and need for evolution of current "risk assessment" paradigms were well documented in the so-called Silver Book put out by the National Academies of Science, Engineering, and Medicine[11] nearly a decade ago. The book lays out the need for systems considerations in EPA decision-making. In 2012, the so-called Green Book by the National Academy of Sciences[12] outlined the tools needed to move from acceptable risks to inherently sustainable design and win-win solutions. The models and tools of the past will perpetuate the ineffectiveness and frustrations of status quo approaches. This new approach calls for a repository of shared data and models as well as new metrics that capture system objectives beyond economic costs and direct emissions.

- Collaborate across agencies. The environment cuts across the missions of virtually every government agency, not just EPA. Fragmented, piecemeal mission statements for federal agencies that reflect their founding statutes have often proven an impediment to genuine systems approaches. Climate is inextricably linked to energy, energy to water, water to health and agriculture and defense and . . . There have been important interagency processes that have recognized this linkage. Yet they are the exception rather than the rule, and they face tremendous hurdles to effectiveness—the budget process being one of the larger ones. For environmental issues (and many others), we must recognize that trans-governmental approaches are required. A thoughtful, strategic, and well-staffed White House Council on Environmental Quality and Office of Science and Technology Policy could be very effective in advancing these processes across the government.

Although the past fifty years have been marked by extraordinary environmental improvements in many parts of the industrial world, there have also been equally extraordinary unintended consequences, oversights, and inequities. Through a systems framework that more adequately reflects the world we are striving toward, we can expect progress while minimizing negative trade-offs. That is, we can realize environmental protection in ways that enhance competitiveness, align values with economic profits, and equitably improve quality of life.

**NOTES**

This essay includes and builds on several paragraphs in an abstract for a presentation, Julie B. Zimmerman, "Design of Sustainable, Resilient Infrastructure Systems" (presented at U.S.-Japan Workshop on Life Cycle Assessment of Sustainable Infrastructure Materials, Sapporo, Japan, October 21–22, 2009).

1. Philip W. Anderson, "More Is Different," *Science* 177, no. 4047 (1972): 393–96.
2. Jason Hill et al., "Environmental, Economic, and Energetic Costs and Benefits of Biodiesel and Ethanol Biofuels," *Proceedings of National Academy of Sciences* 103, no. 30 (2006): 11206–10; Rosa Dominguez-Faus et al., "The Water Footprint of Biofuels: A Drink or Drive Issue?," *Environmental Science & Technology* 43, no. 9 (2009): 3005–10.
3. Mark D. Sobsey et al., "Point of Use Household Drinking Water Filtration: A Practical, Effective Solution for Providing Sustained Access to Safe Drinking Water in the Developing World," *Environmental Science & Technology* 42, no. 12 (2008): 4261–67.
4. Gary A. Boorman et al., "Drinking Water Disinfection Byproducts: Review and Approach to Toxicity Evaluation," *Environmental Health Perspectives, The National Institute of Environmental Health Sciences (NIEHS), Reviews in Environmental Health* 107 (1999): 207–17.
5. Matthew J. Eckelman, Paul T. Anastas, and Julie B. Zimmerman, "Spatial Assessment of Net Mercury Emissions from the Use of Fluorescent Bulbs," *Environmental Science & Technology* 42, no. 22 (2008): 8564–70.
6. U.S. Department of Energy, NREL, *Vision 2020: The Lighting Technology Roadmap* (Golden, CO: National Renewable Energy Laboratory, 2000).
7. James R. Mihelcic, Julie B. Zimmerman, and Martin T. Auer, *Environmental Engineering: Fundamentals, Sustainability, Design* (New York: John Wiley and Sons, 2009), 720.
8. Donella Meadows, *Leverage Points: Places to Intervene in a System* (Hartland, VT: Sustainability Institute, 1999).
9. John D. Sterman, "Learning in and about Complex Systems," *System Dynamics Review* 10, nos. 2–3 (1994): 291–330.

10. National Academy of Engineering and National Academies of Sciences, *Environmental Engineering for the 21st Century: Addressing Grand Challenges* (Washington, DC: National Academies Press, 2018), 120.

11. National Research Council, *Science and Decisions: Advancing Risk Assessment* (Washington, DC: National Academies Press, 2009), 422.

12. National Research Council, *Sustainability Concepts in Decision-Making: Tools and Approaches for the US Environmental Protection Agency* (Washington, DC: National Academies Press, 2014), 155.

# Genomics as a Driving Force for Climate Change Response and Community Health

Vasilis Vasiliou and Alexia Akbay

SOCIETIES ACROSS THE WORLD will face extraordinary challenges in the years ahead, including the need to provide healthy food for a global population that may reach nine billion, avoid health-threatening pollution exposures even while industrial development expands in many nations,[1] and address a growing list of diseases that may be caused by the use of chemicals. We therefore face a critical question: how do we avoid crisis in the face of these stresses? The answer in part may come from *genomics*—the study of the mapping, function, evolution, and editing of genomes.

New technologies almost certainly will have a major role to play. In this regard, genomics has the potential to reshape our food systems, industrial processes, forest management strategies, and much more. The field is already changing industries like health care and agriculture. Although its environmental applications are still nascent, incorporating genomics into ecosystem protection efforts has already proven to be valuable. Detailed genomic study of the biodiversity and interactions within ecosystems is opening new frontiers and creating new solutions for pressing environmental challenges. Here, we profile a few areas of genomic study that we believe to be of high potential in the coming decade: human health–environment interactions, plant-based mitigation of climate change, improving food production, and using model organisms to consume pollutants.

## BIG DATA AND THE IDENTIFICATION OF
## GENOME-ENVIRONMENT INTERACTIONS

Diseases in humans come from a combination of inherited ancestral DNA and environmental exposures; genetics predispose an individual, while exposures lead to the manifestation of disease.[2] With today's air pollution, ubiquitous use of harmful chemicals, and profound changes in nutrition and lifestyle, discovering novel genome-environment interactions could drastically change our understanding of adverse birth outcomes, deficits in human neurological development, increased cancer risks, and chronic diseases such as diabetes and asthma. Modern genomic research has demonstrated the potential of combining full *genotyping*—the cataloging of an entire set of DNA— with extensive fine-scale environmental exposure data. This meshing of data can show how our changing environment shapes disease risk. For example, pollution exposure, such as that from nitrogen and sulfur dioxides, has been shown to inhibit tumor-suppressing genes and promote inflammation that can lead to cardiorespiratory dysfunction.[3] In other words, our environment can change the way our genes react to health threats. Understanding the human body through the sum of these interactions will require not only massive datasets but also the ability to actively improve on scientific conclusions— to learn through genomics.

Using machine-learning techniques to measure indicators of environmental quality, such as air quality, lifestyle, and dietary habits, is currently opening the door to improved environmental health understandings. Systems approaches allow the quantification of layers of proteins, metabolites, bacterial communities, and genomic material; however, there is a lack of consensus on how to deduce meaning from these large and entirely unique findings—this gap provides a solvable challenge for machine learning, an active vision for those studying environmental health. Wider adoption of this approach would help identify how communities, especially women and children, are susceptible to health risks from specific environmental conditions, and further direct preventive health efforts. We do not currently use predictive data when establishing allowable exposure levels for pollutants. Methodologies have yet to change despite the availability of more consistently accurate machine-learning-based data sources.

## IMPROVING THE CAPACITY OF CARBON SINKS

Genomics can improve not only human health but also the health of the planet. In recent years, integrating genomics into forest conservation "has made it possible to develop forward-looking strategies" for improving tree growth and promoting forest health.[4] Forests provide important ecosystem services, such as water cycling, biodiversity conservation, and soil protection. In addition, scientists estimate that over the past few decades, the world's terrestrial ecosystems—much of which are forested—have absorbed between 15 and 30 percent of all the climate-change-causing carbon dioxide emitted by humans.[5] The health of these ecosystems will be highly influential in the speed and magnitude of climate change impacts.

Unfortunately, extreme weather conditions can prevent forests from sequestering carbon. For example, recent fires in Northern California have destroyed more than tens of thousands of acres of forest land. Not only do forest fires pose a threat, but pests have also taken a toll. While these are a few domestic examples, the trend is global. Accordingly, conservation could use a genomic boost; genomic studies may allow the discovery of genes involved in the adaptation of trees to current and future climate changes. For example, sequencing the genomes of economically important trees, such as white spruce (*Picea glauca*)[6] and Norway spruce (*Picea abies*),[7] "has contributed to the design of strategies to improve tree breeding and forest management."[8] Such works explore favorable traits like insect resistance, wood quality, growth rates, and adaptive potential. Once the genetic drivers of these traits are understood, tree breeders can select for them and give ecosystems an advantage in survival and growth potential.[9] Additionally, more in-depth knowledge of tree species' genetic makeup has the potential to boost the impact and economic viability of strategies like agroforestry, an increasingly important way to adapt to the effects of climate change by combining agricultural and forest systems. Policies should seek to maximize the impact of genomics in forest-based climate change mitigation. Similarly, policy makers can implement ways to both prevent climate change and *adapt* to its effects through genomic crop-breeding tools.

## HARNESSING NATURAL EVOLUTION FOR SUSTAINABLE AGRICULTURE

In the future, agriculture will have to confront a number of stresses, including drought, extreme temperatures, soil salinity, nutrient deficiency, and toxic metals, all of which can damage crop production in a changing climate. Just as breeding adaptable trees can help protect forests, developing stress-resistant crops will help bolster food systems against the effects of climate change. This genomic work will be particularly important in the face of threatened increases in plant disease outbreaks and reduced grain quality due to climate change. Improving the genetic composition of crop species will also help reduce the expansion of crops into virgin land and the huge ecological costs involved in that expansion.

Most of the focus of genomic crop study to date has been on a few major crops (rice, wheat, corn, soybean, and potato) that now occupy a hefty amount of human nutritional intake. Future research needs to embrace the natural tendencies of these crops. "Evolution has created thousands of species of naturally stress-resistant plants," according to the researchers Heng Zhang, Yu-anyuan Li, and Jian-Kang Zhu.[10] Some of them are currently domesticated but seen only as minor crops. Prioritizing these resistant features will naturally diversify the human diet and provide greater consumption of superior food sources—for example, produce with higher nutrient and antioxidant levels. Understanding naturally climate-resilient plants through genomics could be crucial to global food security and health. Investigation of naturally stress-resistant plants should focus on increasing their agricultural productivity without compromising their stress tolerance and nutritional quality. These possibilities may also be critical to sustaining the livelihoods of smallholder farmers across the world, as their operations are at greater risk in the face of climate change.

Genetic study of one plant—seaweed—has shown particularly strong sustainability potential. While not used extensively in Western countries, seaweed is one of the fastest-growing sources of biomass on the planet.[11] Today, 99 percent of global seaweed production takes place in Asia, where it is processed for food. Unlike crops whose genetic diversity has been damaged by industrialized production, seaweed is a diverse group of organisms; there are thousands of different species with the ability to grow in a multitude of environments. Importantly, cultivating seaweed requires no arable land, no fertilizer, and no fresh water. As a newcomer to the global economy and scientific community alike, seaweed is both a promising food source and answer to climate change. Further exploration into its genetic diversity and value could prove increasingly relevant in the coming years and decades.

## DEVELOPING MODEL ORGANISMS TO CONSUME POLLUTANTS

In addition to fighting climate change, genomic techniques have the potential to address industrial pollution. Industrial spills often pose dangers to ecosystems. Genomics has shown that harmful pollutants in soils and water can be cleaned up by plants (*phytoremediation*) or bacteria (*bioremediation*) selected for their ability to consume a pollutant. Such bioremediation approaches have been used on large oil spills, such as the 1989 *Exxon Valdez* oil tanker crash in Alaska and the 2010 *Deepwater Horizon* disaster in the Gulf of Mexico.

New discoveries can improve these strategies as well. Studying natural oil and gas contamination, as well as surrounding microbial populations in marine environments, has been groundbreaking in the quest for enhanced bioremediation techniques.[12] Researchers have sequenced the genomes of entire marine habitats and discovered which bacteria are most efficient in breaking down hydrocarbons, such as methane, and other pollutants, such as sulfates. In Canada, researchers are seeking to apply this knowledge by studying how groups of bacteria consume oil and other fossil fuels.[13] This creates possibilities to make oil and gas extraction more environmentally friendly. In China, research is focused on how microorganisms interact with the local geology that surrounds them, with the goal of improving bioremediation techniques.[14]

Models for natural remediation can also be brought indoors. There is evidence that air in homes is more densely polluted than air in offices or schools, elevating children and homeworkers' exposures.[15] Among home air carcinogens, the most common are *volatile organic carcinogens*, which include benzene, formaldehyde, chloroform, and many other chemicals. These cancer-causing compounds are found in cleaning agents and by-products of cooking. But some plants have the capacity to filter these chemicals and therefore decrease indoor exposure levels. A number of companies are already taking advantage of this concept in the marketing of currently available plants. However, the service these plants provide can be improved through genomic research. Emerging work has shown that a detoxifying gene from rabbits can be successfully transferred to and expressed in houseplants, allowing for the removal of volatile organic carcinogens at substantial rates.

## DEEPENING GENOMIC DISCOVERIES

Genomic applications for environmental research and discovery are far and wide. A number of targeted efforts could catalyze further creativity within the field, including expanding work on environmental genomic sequencing in target priority areas like oil spill remediation; developing integrative approaches for building personalized genomic profiles to improve individuals' understanding of human disease vulnerability and precision environmental health; conducting high-throughput DNA sequencing of stress-resistant plants to further develop nutritious crops able to sustain people in a changing climate; and funding research that drives down the price of products in competition with the fossil-fuel industry. The genome is the foundation of all life, and it is clear that our deepened understanding of it will be a key part of building a sustainable future. As is the case with the bulk of current emerging technologies, policy discussion about the use of genomics is critical—and policy action is overdue to begin to harness a solution of massive potential.

## NOTES

Alexia Akbay is a co-founder of Symbrosia, a Yale-based, genomics-inspired start-up enterprise focused on seaweed.

1. Philip J. Landrigan et al., "The Lancet Commission on Pollution and Health," *Lancet* 391, no. 10119 (2018): 462–512, https://doi.org/10.1016/S0140-6736(17)32345-0.
2. Juan Enriquez and Steve Gullans, *Evolving Ourselves: How Unnatural Selection and Nonrandom Mutation Are Changing Life on Earth* (London: Current-Penguin Group, 2015).
3. Marie-Julie Favé et al., "Gene-by-Environment Interactions in Urban Populations Modulate Risk Phenotypes," *Nature Communications* 9, no. 1 (2018), https://doi.org/10.1038/s41467-018-03202-2.
4. Gerardo Jimenez-Sanchez, "Genomics Innovation: Transforming Healthcare, Business, and the Global Economy," *Genome* 58, no. 12 (2015): 514.
5. Marcos Fernández-Martínez et al., "Global Trends in Carbon Sinks and Their Relationships with $CO_2$ and Temperature," *Nature Climate Change* 9 (January 2018): 73–79, https://doi.org/10.1038/s41558-018-0367-7.
6. Jill L. Wegrzyn et al., "Unique Features of the Loblolly Pine (*Pinus Taeda* L.) Megagenome Revealed through Sequence Annotation," *Genetics* 196 (2014): 891–909.
7. Björn Nystedt et al., "The Norway Spruce Genome Sequence and Conifer Genome Evolution," *Nature* 497 (2013): 579–84.
8. Jimenez-Sanchez, "Genomics Innovation," 514.
9. National Academies of Sciences, Engineering, and Medicine, *Forest Health and Biotechnology: Possibilities and Considerations* (Washington, DC: National Academies Press, 2019), https://doi.org/10.17226/25221.
10. Heng Zhang, Yuanyuan Li, and Jian-Kang Zhu, "Developing Naturally Stress-Resistant Crops for a Sustainable Agriculture," *Nature Plants* 4, no. 12 (2018): 989, https://doi.org/10.1038/s41477-018-0309-4.
11. "Biofuel Production from Kelp," ARPA-E, accessed March 14, 2019, https://arpa-e.energy.gov/?q=slick-sheet-project/biofuel-production-kelp.

12. Adrien Vigneron et al., "Comparative Metagenomics of Hydrocarbon and Methane Seeps of the Gulf of Mexico," *Scientific Reports* 7, no. 1 (2017): 1–12, https://doi.org/10.1038/s41598-017-16375-5.

13. Dongshan An et al., "Metagenomics of Hydrocarbon Resource Environments Indicates Aerobic Taxa and Genes to Be Unexpectedly Common," *Environmental Science and Technology* 47, no. 18 (2013): 10708–17, https://doi.org/10.1021/es4020184.

14. Jimenez-Sanchez, "Genomics Innovation"; Weimin Sun et al., "Microbial Communities Inhabiting Oil-Contaminated Soils from Two Major Oilfields in Northern China: Implications for Active Petroleum-Degrading Capacity," *Journal of Microbiology* 53, no. 6 (2015): 371–78, https://doi.org/10.1007/s12275-015-5023-6.

15. Long Zhang, Ryan Routsong, and Stuart E. Strand, "Greatly Enhanced Removal of Volatile Organic Carcinogens by a Genetically Modified Houseplant, Pothos Ivy (Epipremnum aureum) Expressing the Mammalian Cytochrome P450 2e1 Gene," *Environmental Science & Technology* 53 (2018): 325–31, https://doi.org/10.1021/acs.est.8b04811.

# There's an App for That

## CAN TECHNOLOGY SAVE THE PLANET?

David Rejeski

ACCORDING TO RESEARCHERS at the Stockholm Resilience Center, humanity has begun to push up against what they call "planetary boundaries." Think of Earth system limits as guardrails for the planet. Staying inside these boundaries, in areas such as climate change, nitrogen pollution, water consumption, and genetic diversity, increases the Earth's chances to flourish.[1] These guidelines have significant consequences for human activities, aspirations, and our quality of life. For instance, a team of scientists studying the global food system's impact on the environment found that the average American citizen will need to eat 75 percent less beef and 90 percent less pork to reduce climate change and other impacts over the next thirty years. One of the researchers commented that in order to live within the planet's boundaries, "we would need a combination of very ambitious options . . . pushed to the edge of what is possible."[2]

In such situations, there is a natural tendency to fall into the "solutionism" trap and assume that human problems will be solved by technology. *There must be an app for that.* The hope for a technological solution naturally intensifies if other options (like a carbon tax) appear impractical or politically untenable. Can technology generate carbon-free energy or deliver ample fresh water and sufficient protein for a human population of nine billion people by 2050? Should we pin our hopes on technology at all?

The short answer is "maybe, but . . ." Technology cannot solve all of our environmental problems. But, guided by a set of fundamental principles, a technology innovation initiative could help promote breakthroughs that move society toward a more sustainable future.

## THE LONG PATH TO INNOVATION

The tech world has convinced us that innovation moves at exponential rates. Much of this thinking goes back to Moore's Law—the 1965 assertion that the performance of integrated computer circuits would double every eighteen to twenty-four months—and an implicit understanding that it drives today's rapid innovation tempo. But technologists have a habit of underestimating scaling costs and time requirements while overestimating consumer demand. It has been jokingly said that computer scientists, looking at new markets, count "1, 2, 3, . . . a million."[3] Technologies often take decades to develop and commercialize, and the path to success is littered with failed ideas and start-ups. The public seldom sees, or appreciates, the twenty to thirty years of investment (often by the government) in basic research that occurs before these technological marvels appear. The recent rise of hydraulic fracturing, or "fracking," of natural gas, for instance, depended on over two decades of basic research supported by the U.S. Department of Energy. The first components for the Global Positioning System (GPS) were put into orbit by the Defense Department in the late 1960s, with preliminary operations of GPS beginning in 1977. Over forty years later, we now take it for granted. Photovoltaic solar cells, now competitive with fossil-fuel-generated electricity, were commercially produced in the mid-1950s and first used in the NASA space program—a seventy-year time lag.

This typical development timetable suggests that some of the technologies needed to address future energy and environmental challenges may already be in existence or under development, but largely out of view and potentially not receiving attention from policymakers. For instance, compressed air can be used to store energy and has been successfully used for many years in megawatt-scale renewable energy installations in McIntosh, Alabama, and Huntorf, Germany, but has received little attention. Meanwhile, recent advances in nanoscale science and engineering have resulted in the development of more efficient thermoelectric devices capable of converting excess heat generated by power plants, cars, or even cooking stoves directly into electricity. It is estimated that 70 percent of all energy loss is through heat. Generating more electricity from that wasted heat could result in significant reductions in power demand and associated carbon emissions, as well as other pollutants.

Regardless of their current status, it will take time to develop and deploy sustainable technologies, especially if they have to compete with existing ones, which can stick around for decades or longer. The English historian David Edgerton describes this phenomenon in his book *The Shock of the Old.* The U.S. strategic arsenal still relies on the B-52 bomber (in service since 1955), machetes and small arms kill most people in conflicts (not high-tech armed drones we marvel at in YouTube videos), and our environmental policies still focus on mitigating impacts from technologies invented during past industrial revolutions, such as the internal combustion engine (from the 1860s), steam-powered electricity generation (1880s), and chemical synthesis (1910–1920).[4] Not all older technologies should be dismissed as environmental liabilities. For instance, it makes little sense to retire nuclear power plants—a zero-carbon electricity source—years before their licensed end dates.

Looking toward 2050, we face two challenges simultaneously: (1) increasing the efficiency of existing technologies (if and where possible) and (2) disrupting them and replacing them with environmentally friendly alternatives while avoiding negative unintended consequences. Thirty years may be enough time to accomplish these goals, but the greatest challenge may be organizational: which organizations can think, plan, and implement that far out? In a study covering the period from 2001 to 2015, the McKinsey Global Institute found a notable increase in corporate *short-termism,* as more businesses focus on delivering immediate results to stockholders.[5] The pressures placed on new businesses for quick financial returns are well known. As one venture capital investor put it: "We don't fund science experiments."[6] The U.S. government has traditionally had a role in supporting long-term research, but a report by the National Research Council has highlighted the declining funding for our research universities over the past decades.[7]

To complicate matters, disruptive technologies are difficult to see. When game-changing technologies appear, they often perform worse than their existing competitors.[8] In any given industry, existing technologies are supported and reinforced by long-term beliefs and notions of customer preferences, regulation, cost drivers, and the role of technology itself in creating competitive advantage. Moving off well-established technological pathways in search of disruptive alternatives is risky. Aversion to such risk can perpetuate not only aging technologies themselves but also entire systems, including feedstocks, supply chains, waste streams, regulatory frameworks, an established consumer base, and political support. Our technologies become habits, if not addictions, that are hard to break. So, how do we break the habits and find more sustainable innovations? There are a few key principles.

*Disrupt.*   The telegraph dramatically changed the way humans communicate; the railroad, the way we travel; the microprocessor, the way we store and process information. These are examples of what have been termed *disruptive* innovations, which enable the emergence of entirely new capabilities, functions, markets, services, and businesses and often upend existing technologies—think of the impact of digital photography on the use of film.

In trying to address future environmental challenges, one logical first step is to develop technology road maps and an overarching strategy (including transition management) to radically improve or disrupt the most energy- and environmentally intensive production processes on the planet. Energy-intensive ammonia fertilizer production is an obvious choice. Another is cement production, one of the most energy-intensive manufacturing sectors, accounting for over 5 percent of global greenhouse gas emissions. Despite recent closings of coal plants in the United States, sectors such as cement, steel, and chemicals have resulted in emissions increases of over 5 percent in 2018. These production processes may be difficult to decarbonize and have received too little attention to date.[9] Existing efforts to replace carbon-based manufacturing have shown some promise. For instance, a small spinout company from the Massachusetts Institute of Technology, Boston Metal, is developing a method to produce steel (which accounts for about 5 percent of global carbon dioxide emissions) that uses an electrolytic cell rather than carbon-based fuel to process raw iron ore.[10] There may also be technological interventions, such as better process control with machine learning, which could benefit multiple production systems.

In disrupting unsustainable technologies, we should seek to design technological pathways that could, within a thirty- to forty-year time frame, allow us to produce more of what we need, in terms of food, shelter, and energy, with a dramatically reduced environmental footprint. We must also accomplish this by 2030, when around three billion consumers from the developing world will have entered the middle class. Unfortunately, nobody is in charge of an endeavor like this. As James Schlesinger, the first secretary of energy, stated, "The basic problem" is that "there is no constituency for an energy program. There are many constituencies opposed."[11] In a more complex and globalized world, this problem has only become worse.

*Find Carbon-Plus Solutions.*   As we approach this task, we should be searching for synergies across sectors—win-win strategies. There is an old adage that in complex systems you cannot do just one thing—a habit we have a hard time breaking. A singular and obsessive focus on just carbon or nitrogen or biodiversity may prevent us from seeing opportunities to address multiple interconnected environmental and societal challenges.

For instance, we could move away from the energy and carbon impacts associated with ammonia production by genetically engineering plants like maize to "fix" their own nitrogen, a strategy that also addresses the urgent need to reduce nitrate runoff into water bodies while addressing food security. Global models run at the International Institute for Applied Systems Analysis have indicated that global temperature rise could be slowed considerably by 2100 using engineered microalgae to create protein for livestock and free up land for fast-growing biofuel crops that replace fossil fuels. Additionally, the co-location of microalgae facilities near power plants could allow growers to fertilize the algae using techniques that capture carbon dioxide emissions from the plants. This approach would avoid the pitfalls of past interventions, where the production of biofuels (from palm oil, for instance) resulted in diverting high-grade protein away from human consumption and demanded more land for fuel-related crops, often resulting in the clearing of virgin forests and the loss of carbon sinks.[12] This nexus of energy, food, and land use is in urgent need of more crosscutting solutions. As Janet Ranganathan of the World Resources Institute has noted, "Food is the mother of all sustainability challenges.... We can't get below 2 degrees without major changes to this system."[13]

*Innovate Faster.*   If we are facing urgent challenges, there should be some focus on investments and strategies that speed up the innovation process itself, especially for enabling technologies that could underpin advances across multiple sectors. One strategy to reduce both cost and time to market focuses on shortening what is commonly known as the *design-build-test-learn* cycle, allowing researchers to run, evaluate, and learn lessons from more experiments, then use them to inform future designs. Making things faster has historically been identified as the single most important determinant of manufacturing productivity.

Over the past decade, investments by the U.S. Department of Energy, the Defense Advanced Research Projects Agency (DARPA), and others have reduced the time and cost to engineer new biological organisms by orders of magnitude, from hundreds of millions of dollars and fifteen years in the mid-2000s to under $50 million and ten years a decade later and under $10 million and one year in 2018.[14] The reductions continue, driven by the application of so-called bio-foundries, which use large libraries of gene sequences combined with computer-aided design tools and artificial intelligence to run millions of experiments searching for the optimal molecular design. Biology as a manufacturing platform could create a wide variety of alternative ways to produce chemicals and materials while simultaneously shifting inputs from greenhouse-gas-emitting hydrocarbons to more climate-friendly carbohydrates.

Rapidly improving *design-build-test-learn* cycles in areas like biotechnology can offer opportunities to create new disruption pathways, but this task requires early and proactive strategies for path creation.[15] Biotechnology development uses simulation, machine learning, rapid prototyping, and computer modeling to speed up the innovation cycle. These techniques are not unique to biology, however. Researchers are also using them to "reduce the cost and development time of materials discovery, optimization, and deployment" as part of the U.S. government's Materials Genome Initiative.[16] Novel materials could have large impacts on the performance of photovoltaic solar cells, wind turbines, battery storage, and thermoelectric devices.

*Avoid Mistakes: The Department of Unintended Consequences.*   There are downsides of accelerating the pace of technological innovation and focusing on disruptive change that we need to proactively address through policy and institutional innovation, such as the creation of a unit with a mandate to focus on unintended consequences. As former secretary of defense Ash Carter recently noted, "We [need to] make disruption more good than bad."[17] This is a non-trivial problem since many disruptive technologies cut both ways. For instance, gene editing, the same disruptive technology that can allow us to create new strains of drought-resistant crops as a hedge against climate change, can also be used to edit the germ line of humans, which set off global alarm bells when scientists in China did it in 2018. In many cases we are facing what have been termed "predictable surprises," in which organizations and individuals have all the information necessary to anticipate events and their consequences but fail to act or to act in time.[18] An extensive study of dozens of environmental problems by the European Environmental

Agency—from lead in gasoline to invasive species and climate change—found that in most cases early warnings did exist, in some cases for decades, but no action was taken.[19]

To avoid mistakes, increase flexibility, and generally underpin greater policy innovation, we could begin to apply *design-build-test-learn* approaches to public policy and administration—what some are calling a shift to more "entrepreneurial administration" designed to facilitate "policy experimentation and trial-and-error problem-solving."[20] Governments around the world also need to expand their technology assessment infrastructure, which has been systematically dismantled over the past three decades, starting with the elimination of the U.S. Office of Technology Assessment in 1995 and, more recently, the Danish Technology Board in 2011. In an op-ed in the *Washington Post*, New Jersey congressman Bill Pascrell bemoaned the lack of technical expertise in the U.S. Congress, observing that "the federal government spends $94 billion on information technology, while Congress spends $0 on independent assessments of technology issues."[21] There are hopeful moves afoot to expand the technology foresight and assessment capacities of the U.S. Congress, beginning with legislation that creates a Science, Technology Assessment, and Analytics unit at the Government Accountability Office and efforts by the National Academy of Public Administration to explore possible designs for a new type of technology assessment office.[22]

## FROM PRINCIPLES TO PRACTICE

At a more general level, we must address the fact that the U.S. government is not optimally designed to drive the technological changes required for a sustainable future. This institutional handicap is hardly a new situation. During the industrial revolution of the late nineteenth century, the sociologist Lester Ward wrote about the "failure of government to keep pace with the changes which civilization [had] wrought."[23] Few agencies today combine the fiscal resources and long-term perspective necessary to both drive significant efficiency gains and promote disruptive change at scale. Our best hope may be the Department of Energy, which has programs in energy efficiency along with ARPA-E, the Advanced Research Projects Agency–Energy, modeled after DARPA at the Defense Department. The Defense Department created DARPA to take on problems often referred to as "DARPA hard"—challenges that are so difficult and complicated that only a Pentagon agency with expansive funding could solve them. The environmental problems we face today are just as "hard," but no environmental DARPA exists. To complicate matters, the private sector lacks institutions like the former Bell Labs, which had the "immense and complete institutional capabilities to . . . solve the biggest of problems."[24]

Even if such organizations existed, that still leaves the issue of finding real multi-sector solutions, including ways to avoid the commonly occurring problem of a solution in one area creating negative impacts in another. In theory, the National Environmental Policy Act provides a framework to work across institutional silos to address energy, food, land use, and other environmental challenges, but the White House office largely responsible for its implementation, the Council on Environmental Quality, has atrophied in size and influence over the past three decades. The White House Office of Science and Technology Policy (OSTP), along with the National Science and Technology Council, could provide leadership in this area, provided lawmakers gave it the mandate and staff. Indeed, OSTP created and implemented the National Environmental Technology Strategy in the 1990s, but that development occurred during a time of far less partisan bickering and significant federal budget surpluses. That was two decades ago. Today, technologies are affecting not just the environment but our institutions and their potential to deliver timely environmental solutions. As the computer pioneer Danny Hillis recently noted, we have moved beyond the enlightenment, with its reverence for the rule of law and scientific reason, and entered a world of entanglements, a hyper-interconnected world where the institutions we created have evolved to a point where their complexity defies our control and our machines will soon develop the ability to learn, adapt, create, and evolve without us.[25]

We face global environmental challenges with a set of governance tools that are outdated and in flux. If environmental conditions deteriorate quickly over the next decades, there may be social and political pressure to reach for relatively cheap, quick technological fixes, such as geo-engineering the Earth's climate with solar radiation management techniques or using gene editing to create climate-adapted species. These interventions could be advanced without adequate technological assessments or public discussion of their social, ethical, and economic implications and global governance mechanisms. This is not inevitable, but it will be difficult to avoid. Technology has tricked us into believing it can solve humanity's problems, but there is no app for that.

**NOTES**

This essay draws on and builds on the author's prior published work on technology innovation, including "Public Policy on the Technological Frontier," in *The Growing Gap between Emerging Technologies and Legal-Ethical Oversight: The Pacing Problem*, ed. Gary E. Marchant, Braden R. Allenby, and Joseph R. Herkert (New York: Springer, 2011), 47–59.

1. Johan Rockström et al., "Planetary Boundaries: Exploring the Safe Operating Space for Humanity," *Ecology and Society* 14, no. 2 (2009).

2. Damian Carrington, "Huge Reduction in Meat-Eating 'Essential' to Avoid Climate Breakdown," *The Guardian*, October 10, 2018, https://www.theguardian.com /environment/2018/oct/10/huge-reduction-in-meat-eating-essential-to-avoid -climate-breakdown.

3. John Seely Brown and Paul Duguid, *The Social Life of Information* (Cambridge, MA: Harvard Business School Press, 2000), 57.

4. Historians often distinguish among four industrial revolutions that have transformed our social, cultural, and economic conditions, beginning in the nineteenth century with such advances as steam power and railroads, followed by electricity and mass production, the rise of digital technologies, and, today, the emergence of areas like robotics, artificial intelligence, and biotechnology—the so-called Fourth Industrial Revolution, or what the Organisation for Economic Co-operation and Development terms the Next Production Revolution.

5. Dominic Barton et al., *Measuring the Economic Impact of Short-Termism* (New York: McKinsey Global Institute, 2017).

6. Jon Gertner, *The Idea Factory: Bell Labs and the Great Age of American Innovation* (New York: Penguin Press, 2012), 348.

7. National Research Council, *Research Universities and the Future of America: Ten Breakthrough Actions Vital to Our Nation's Prosperity and Security* (Washington, DC: National Academies Press, 2012).

8. Clayton Christensen, *The Innovator's Dilemma* (Cambridge, MA: Harvard Business School Press, 1997).

9. Steven J. Davis et al., "Net-Zero Emissions Energy Systems," *Science* 360, no. 6396 (2018): eaas9793, https://doi.org/10.1126/science.aas9793.

10. James Temple, "A New Way to Make Steel Could Cut 5% of $CO_2$ Emissions at a Stroke," *MIT Technology Review*, September 24, 2018, https://www.technologyreview .com/s/611961/this-mit-spinout-could-finally-clean-up-steel-one-of-the-globes -biggest-climate-polluters/.

11. James Everett Katz, ed., *Congress and National Energy Policy* (New Brunswick, NJ: Transaction Publishers, 1984), 117.

12. Abrahm Lustgarten, "Palm Oil Was Supposed to Help Save the Planet. Instead It Unleashed a Catastrophe," *New York Times*, November 20, 2018, https://www .nytimes.com/2018/11/20/magazine/palm-oil-borneo-climate-catastrophe.html.

13. Brad Plumer, "Can We Grow More Food on Less Land? We'll Have to, a New Study Finds," *New York Times*, December 5, 2018, https://www.nytimes.com/2018/12/05 /climate/agriculture-food-global-warming.html.

14. Jay Keasling, conversation with author, University of California, Berkeley, December 7, 2018.

15. Maj Munch Andersen, "Path Creation in the Making—The Case of Nanotechnology," proceedings (online), in *DRUID 10. Anniversary Summer Conference 2005 on Dynamics of Industry and Innovation: Organizations, Networks and Systems* (Copenhagen: Danish Research Unit for Industrial Dynamics, 2005).

16. "Materials Genome Initiative," National Institute of Standards and Technology, accessed April 22, 2019, https://www.nist.gov/mgi.

17. Ash Carter, "Shaping Disruptive Technological Change for Public Good," Harvard Belfer Center for Science and International Affairs, August 2018, https://www.belfercenter.org/publication/shaping-disruptive-technological-change-public-good.

18. Max H. Bazerman and Michael Watkins, *Predictable Surprises: The Disasters You Should Have Seen Coming, and How to Prevent Them* (Cambridge, MA: Harvard Business Press, 2004).

19. European Environmental Agency, *Late Lessons from Early Warnings: The Precautionary Principle 1896–2000*, EEA, Report No. 22/2001 (Copenhagen, Denmark: European Environmental Agency, 2001), https://www.eea.europa.eu/publications/environmental_issue_report_2001_22.

20. Philip Weiser, "Entrepreneurial Administration," *Boston University Law Review* 97 (2017), 2012.

21. Bill Pascrell, Jr., "Why Is Congress So Dumb?," *Washington Post*, January 11, 2019, http://www.washingtonpost.com/news/posteverything/wp/2019/01/11/feature/why-is-congress-so-dumb/.

22. Details of these efforts can be found in H. R. Rep. No. 115-929—Energy and Water Development and Related Agencies for the Fiscal Year Ending September 30, 2019, and for Other Purposes, at 211-12; and "Science and Technology Policy Assessment for the U.S. Congress," National Academy of Public Administration, accessed March 14, 2019, https://www.napawash.org/studies/academy-studies/science-and-technology-policy-assessment-for-the-us-congress.

23. Lester F. Ward, "Plutocracy and Paternalism," *The Forum* 20 (November 1895): 304.

24. Gertner, *The Idea Factory*, 358.

25. Danny Hillis, "The Enlightenment Is Dead, Long Live the Entanglement," *Journal of Design and Science*, February 22, 2016, https://jods.mitpress.mit.edu/pub/enlightenment-to-entanglement.

# Reimagining Solar Fuels to Power the Planet with Renewable Energy

Gary W. Brudvig

NOBEL LAUREATE RICHARD SMALLEY (Nobel Prize for Chemistry, 1996) identified energy as the most significant problem facing humanity in the next fifty years. An abundant supply of clean energy would solve many of the major problems facing humanity, in addition to mitigating the environmental impacts of our current use of fossil fuels to power our planet. With enough energy, we could desalinate seawater to solve the problem of clean water for drinking and irrigation. With more affordable water for irrigation, increased food production would be possible. Conflicts due to energy supplies would end if we had an abundant supply of energy. And the list of solutions to critical problems goes on.

Where will we obtain such an abundant supply of clean energy? Solar energy has the capacity to provide for all of our energy needs. Enough solar energy strikes the Earth's surface each hour to provide for all of our current worldwide energy needs for an entire year.[1] Together with other sources of renewable energy, such as wind and hydroelectric power, clean, renewable energy could power the planet—except that these power sources provide electricity intermittently. What do we do when the sun is not shining or the wind is not blowing? For renewable energy to provide for all of our energy needs, we must find economical methods for storing solar and wind energy.

Currently, we rely on the burning of fossil fuels for more than 75 percent of our energy, but this is not sustainable, owing to the rising level of carbon dioxide in the atmosphere that is produced from the combustion of coal, oil, and natural gas and that threatens major damage from climate change. We therefore need to switch to carbon-neutral energy sources. We do have one carbon-free source—nuclear—but security and safety concerns have significantly dampened interest, and it seems unlikely that nuclear energy will be expanded to meet our energy needs. Various other options are being considered and discussed, ranging from continued burning of fossil fuels coupled with carbon capture and sequestration schemes to a transition to completely carbon-free renewable energy. It is not clear that carbon capture is technically feasible on the scale necessary or with the widespread distribution of our current carbon emissions. It is also not clear that carbon sequestration schemes, such as pumping carbon dioxide underground, will provide a long-term solution.

On the other hand, renewable power sources such as wind and solar can provide carbon-neutral sources of energy—but not twenty-four hours a day, seven days a week as required for baseload electricity. Despite tremendous growth in the installation of photovoltaic solar panels and wind turbines, renewable energy sources provide only about 10 percent of our total energy usage. And at present, most of this renewable energy comes from traditional sources such as hydroelectric power and biomass burning. The major impediment to increased usage of solar and wind energy centers on our current lack of viable methods for storage.

## NATURE'S BATTERIES

We can, however, look to nature to find a solution to the storage problem. In natural photosynthesis, plants use solar energy to fix carbon dioxide from the atmosphere. The end result provides storage of the sun's energy in the chemical bonds of high-energy chemicals such as carbohydrate, fat, and protein molecules. We think of these molecules as food, but they also are the components of all biomass. Over the Earth's history, photosynthesis has produced an excess of biomass that has been buried in the ground to form the fossil fuels—coal, oil, and natural gas:

$$\text{carbon dioxide} + \text{water} + \text{sunlight} \rightarrow \text{biomass (fossil fuel)} \\ + \text{oxygen (21\% of atmosphere)}$$

We are now extracting these fossil fuels to power our planet, thus harvesting solar energy that was stored eons ago. The process of photosynthesis also produced oxygen that was released into the atmosphere, transforming the early Earth from an anaerobic atmosphere to our current aerobic atmosphere, which contains 21 percent oxygen and sustains all aerobic life on the planet. The overall process, shown in this equation, is a balanced chemical equation in which reactants, carbon dioxide and water, are used up and fossil fuel and oxygen are produced. We hear concerns raised about running out of fossil fuels. However, we have been burning fossil fuels for centuries (the reverse direction of the equation), and at an increasing rate, but have not significantly changed the amount of oxygen in the atmosphere. Because fossil fuels and oxygen are consumed simultaneously in the burning process, this means we have not significantly depleted the amount of fossil fuels buried in the ground. The problem in the foreseeable future is not running out of fossil fuels, but rather the environmental impacts of the rising level of carbon dioxide in the atmosphere produced from the combustion of fossil fuels.

Storage of solar energy in chemical bonds has many great advantages, as nature learned billions of years ago when photosynthesis first evolved. One advantage is that high-energy molecules can be very stable, thus enabling the energy to be stored for very long periods of time without loss. Another advantage is that the energy density can be very high; a tank of gasoline provides a car with a range of hundreds of miles and weighs much less than an equivalent amount of energy stored in batteries. By mimicking natural photosynthesis using artificial processes, it could be possible to store solar energy in the form of high-energy molecules such as alcohols or even hydrocarbons like those in gasoline. A major advantage of producing such "solar" fuels is that the energy storage product would be equivalent to what we already use for transportation and home heating fuel, and thus it could utilize our existing infrastructure for transport and delivery of fossil fuels. This would enable a complete transition away from fossil fuels to an energy economy based on renewables.

## SOLAR FUEL TECHNOLOGIES

There are still huge barriers that impede the development of "solar" fuels, both economic and technological.[2] On the economic side, the low price of fossil fuels is a major impediment for development of an economy based on "solar" fuels. This is unlikely to change until we put a price on carbon emissions and adopt supportive policies.[3] In addition, we need to develop innovative and cost-effective technologies to produce "solar" fuels so that it is possible to implement the new technology on a global scale.

Several technologies are already being used to produce "solar" fuel. The largest is the bioethanol industry, whereby the liquid fuel ethanol is produced by fermentation of corn starch. Approximately 40 percent of U.S. corn crop-land is used for ethanol production. However, the process to produce bioetha-nol uses a significant amount of fossil fuels in the growing and transportation of corn, and in the distillation of ethanol after the fermentation process. The net energy gain from the production of bioethanol is minimal because only the corn starch is currently used; it could be improved by the implementation of processes for production of bioethanol from cellulose. There are also sig-nificant concerns about competition of the bioethanol industry with food production. Although bioethanol currently contributes significantly as a transportation fuel, it is unlikely that biofuel production could be scaled up much, or that cellulosic ethanol could provide a major source of biofuel to displace the current use of fossil fuels, owing to the low efficiency of plant photosynthesis for solar energy conversion and the competition of biofuels with food production.[4]

There are emerging "solar" fuel technologies that use excess solar photo-voltaic electricity to generate renewable fuels by using an *electrolysis* process that utilizes an electric current to create a chemical reaction. Processes for solar thermal and photochemical conversion—to create fuels through heat transfer or chemical reactions—are also being developed. These provide al-ternatives to pumped hydropower to solve the storage problem of excess solar and wind electricity. One example used by the company Electrochaea GmbH involves a biohybrid approach to convert low-cost, excess solar photovoltaic electricity and carbon dioxide into pipeline-grade natural gas. In this process, hydrogen gas is produced by water electrolysis and used together with a car-bon dioxide waste stream to form methane gas using a bacterial methane generation process. The methane produced in this way can be injected di-rectly into a natural gas pipeline. This enables utility-scale energy storage, electrical grid balancing, and carbon reuse.

While these technologies are important for storage of excess solar and wind electricity, we do not yet have cost-effective technologies to produce "so-lar" fuels on a scale that could replace fossil fuels. To do this, we need innova-tion and new technologies to store solar and wind energy in chemical bonds. Researchers are exploring a number of pathways to produce renewable "solar" fuels.[5] These include biofuels (discussed above), solar thermal conversion, electrochemical conversion, and photochemical conversion.

The thermal conversion process uses concentrated solar energy to gener-ate heat that promotes a thermochemical reaction such as the splitting of carbon dioxide and water to form high-energy chemicals. Challenges for development of these processes include the need for new catalysts that are stable and work efficiently at the high temperatures needed for the thermo-chemical reactions.

Electrochemical and photochemical conversion involve related chemical processes. The difference is that the processes are indirect in the electro-chemical process, whereby solar (or wind) energy is used to generate electric-ity followed by an electrolysis reaction, and the processes are direct in the photochemical process, whereby light directly promotes the formation of a high-energy chemical.

An advantage of the electrochemical (indirect) process is that it meshes well with our existing technologies for solar panels and wind turbines that generate electricity. The electricity generated can be used to drive an electro-chemical process such as the production of hydrogen gas by water electroly-sis. Water electrolyzers are already commercially available with good efficiency, so no new technology is needed to implement the electrochemical process of renewable fuel production. The main impediment is the high cost of the "so-lar" fuel produced by the electrochemical process relative to the cost of fossil fuels.

The photochemical (direct) process most closely mimics natural photo-synthesis. This process also can yield the highest efficiency because interme-diate steps, which can lead to losses, are avoided. However, we do not currently have viable systems for direct, photochemical "solar" fuel production that meet the requirements of low cost, high stability, and high efficiency.

There is also the question of the choice of "solar" fuel. Splitting water to produce hydrogen gas offers a much simpler chemical process than the pro-duction of liquid fuels such as alcohols or hydrocarbons. Hydrogen gas itself could be used as a fuel, although there are challenges. Being a gas, hydro-gen lacks the energy density of liquid fuel. It thus requires high-pressure storage. In addition, we lack an infrastructure for the distribution of hydro-gen gas. Distribution is also problematic because it embrittles steel pipes. Nonetheless, as noted above, there are emerging technologies that use ex-cess solar photovoltaic electricity to produce hydrogen for renewable fuel processes.

The problems of using hydrogen as a renewable fuel could be avoided by converting hydrogen gas into a liquid fuel. There is already a well-developed method, called the Fischer-Tropsch process, by which hydrogen and carbon monoxide can be converted into gasoline. A mixture of hydrogen and carbon monoxide is often called syngas and has been used to produce gasoline to be used as a transportation fuel by countries lacking a source of petroleum—for example, by the company Sasol in South Africa.

## NEXT STEPS

Photosynthesis in plants and bacteria, the original source of the energy embodied in fossil fuels, stores energy in chemical bonds. To power the planet completely with renewable energy, we need to develop innovative and cost-effective technologies to store energy in chemical bonds using artificial photosynthesis, thus mimicking nature's production of "solar" power. The direct photochemical production of "solar" fuels, which most closely mimics the processes of natural photosynthesis, could emerge as a particularly attractive option because of its potential for the highest efficiency. This technology does not currently exist. A combination of sustained funding for basic research and economic incentives is needed to deliver the breakthrough in solar power storage that could transform our energy future.

## NOTES

1. Nathan S. Lewis and Daniel G. Nocera, "Powering the Planet: Chemical Challenges in Solar Energy Utilization," *Proceedings of the National Academy of Sciences of the United States of America* 103, no. 43 (October 2006): 15729–35, https://doi.org/10.1073/pnas.0603395103.
2. Remko J. Detz, Joost N. H. Reek, and Bob C. C. van der Zwaan, "The Future of Solar Fuels: When Could They Become Competitive?," *Energy and Environmental Science* 11, no. 7 (July 2018): 1653–69, http://doi.org/10.1039/C8EE00111A.
3. Thomas Faunce et al., "Artificial Photosynthesis as a Frontier Technology for Energy Sustainability," *Energy and Environmental Science* 6, no. 4 (April 2013): 1074–76, https://doi.org/10.1039/C3ee40534f.
4. Robert E. Blankenship et al., "Comparing Photosynthetic and Photovoltaic Efficiencies and Recognizing the Potential for Improvement," *Science* 332, no. 6031 (May 2011): 805–9, http://science.sciencemag.org/content/332/6031/805.
5. Detz, Reek, and van der Zwaan, "The Future of Solar Fuels," 1653–69.

# Fostering Energy Innovation for a Sustainable Twenty-First Century

Kenneth Gillingham

GLOBAL CLIMATE CHANGE has emerged as one of the most pressing policy challenges of our time. Without deep decarbonization over the next few decades, we are rolling the dice and risking consequential environmental damages around the world. From the shorelines of North Carolina to the glaciers of the Andes and the docks of New York City, the science has become increasingly clear: our communities, our people, and our economy will be affected in potentially devastating ways.[1]

Deep decarbonization requires changing the energy underpinnings of our economy to replace fossil fuels with clean and renewable energy sources. Executing this transformation will not be a trivial task. While the cost of renewable energy has declined rapidly over the past decade, making the shift from fossil fuels to renewable power sources remains daunting. The transition to a clean energy future will require not just new infrastructure but also coordination between many disparate stakeholders. The key to deep decarbonization is further innovation—both technological innovation and policy innovation—that clears the path for a low-carbon economy.

Recasting our nation's energy policy to create incentives to spur innovation, drive investments at the vast scale required to meet clean energy infrastructure needs, and encourage policy coordination will be essential to the transition to a low-carbon economy. This essay presents a new approach, building on an already-proven policy tool to repair our nation's aging infrastructure: competitively awarded grants for innovative projects delivering long-term benefits. The approach is not a substitute for other policies, such as carbon pricing, but is intended to complement them by providing the connective tissue to facilitate deeper decarbonization.

## THE RATIONALE FOR CLEAN ENERGY INNOVATION POLICY

The motivation for a competitive federal energy innovation grant program stems from multiple *market failures* that afflict the process of innovation and the diffusion of new technologies. The economic concept of market failures refers to cases where the privately optimal decision for an individual is not the same as the optimal decision for society. It is based on the idea that markets lead to the efficient allocation of scarce resources unless there is a deviation between the incentives for private individuals and society as a whole.

The first market failure that influences clean energy innovation derives from research and development spillovers that cannot be captured by those putting up the research and development funds. When companies decide how much to invest in clean energy, they weigh the cost of the investment against the potential returns from the investment that they can profitably obtain. Most research and development investments are, however, not fully *appropriable,* which means some of the benefits from the innovation flow to other firms, which can profit from the research and development undertaken. Similarly, for many new technologies, as economy-wide experience with the technology increases, firms learn how to lower costs through trial and error. For example, research into new solar energy technologies may spread, benefiting the entire industry rather than just the company that made the investment. Along the same lines, deployment of new solar technologies can lead to firms learning how to reduce their costs; but because they emulate each other and hire successful employees from each other, some of the profits that could come from reduced costs also spill over to benefit other firms.[2] Because they have to cover all costs but receive only some benefits, businesses tend to under-invest in research and development and deploy too little of new technologies.[3]

Patent protection for new technologies can help address this under-investment incentive. The idea is that if companies own the rights to technologies they develop, they will have more incentive to invest since they do not have to share the returns on that investment. But patents do not offer a complete solution. Intellectual property rules represent an especially imperfect solution for early-stage research that is difficult to monetize. Such rules also cannot protect innovations that are difficult to patent or help firms that choose to keep their breakthroughs secret (recall that the recipe for Coca-Cola has never been patented!).

The research and development spillovers described here loom especially large for early-stage research on pathbreaking new technologies.[4] Indeed, funding for early-stage research is a widely accepted response to this market failure. For example, the U.S. government funds the National Science Foundation, National Institutes of Health, and for clean energy, programs such as the well-known Advanced Research Projects Agency–Energy (ARPA-E) program. While we have seen vast improvements in renewable power generation, achieving deep decarbonization would be much less expensive and likely more politically palatable with further technology advances that cost less and include all aspects necessary for widespread low-carbon technology adoption.

The second market failure stems from the environmental consequences of burning fossil fuels, leading to global climate change (and local air pollution). When consumers or firms make decisions about how much fuel to consume, and thus how much carbon to emit, they rarely take into account the full (global) costs of their actions. For climate change, these full costs include costs from damages both today and well into the future.

These market failures interact, creating a further obstacle to investment in clean energy innovation. This interaction has been mapped out in a set of recent papers in economics.[5] The basic idea centers on the fact that, because climate change is a long-run problem, investments in new technologies that have a limited short-run payoff may have substantial long-run payoffs. Thus, the lowest-cost long-term approach to addressing climate change in many cases may seem expensive in the short run, but it relies on investments in new technologies that provide benefits well into the future.[6] For example, investments in electric vehicles may seem like a very expensive way to reduce emissions in the short term because the technology is expensive and much of our electricity is still generated by fossil fuels. In the long run, however, as the electric sector decarbonizes and the cost of batteries declines, electric vehicles may provide a key pathway to reduced greenhouse gas emissions from transportation at a reasonable cost.[7]

A third market failure gets much less attention but may turn out to be incredibly important to a smooth transition to a low-carbon economy. This market failure is commonly known through the classic question: what came first, the chicken or the egg? Chicken-and-egg problems, also known as "coordination issues," or in economics, "network externalities," occur when an activity is much more valuable if everyone agrees to the same approach and also implements all complementary technologies.[8] For example, widespread adoption of electric vehicles will be more challenging without widespread accessibility of fast-charging electric charging stations. But it is difficult to justify investing in the charging stations without the electric vehicles to use them. Hence, the chicken-and-egg issue: do the charging stations come first, or the electric vehicles?

Occasionally the private sector can overcome such coordination issues, but it often takes time, and in many cases private firms have their own interests in mind. For example, Tesla's supercharging stations are available only for customers driving a Tesla electric vehicle, which is beneficial to Tesla, but may be slowing the adoption of electric vehicles more generally by requiring the creation of two separate charging station networks. Such coordination issues may also slow the siting of renewable electricity generation and the most efficient integration of small-scale "distributed" electricity generation into the electricity grid.

Correcting these three market failures can bring economic benefits through improved economic efficiency while at the same time smoothing the path to a large-scale transition to a deeply decarbonized economy. I turn now to a proven policy approach that has the potential to at least partly address these failures.

## TIGER GRANTS

In 2009, with the economy in the depths of a recession, President Barack Obama signed into law an economic stimulus bill. The American Recovery and Reinvestment Act contained many components to try to kick-start the economy, including the Transportation Investment Generating Economic Recovery (TIGER) grant program. The stimulus package initially provided $1.5 billion (less than 2 percent of its total funding) through September 30, 2011, to the U.S. Department of Transportation to be "awarded on a competitive basis for projects that will have a significant impact on the Nation, a metropolitan area or a region."[9]

The TIGER funding was intended for "shovel-ready" projects that result in "desirable, long-term outcomes" for some area of the United States. These projects included road, rail, transit, port, and multimodal transport projects, and the Department of Transportation expected applicants to demonstrate that the projects were "innovative." While of course simply fixing a bridge is not usually considered innovative (although important!), all grant proposals were expected to demonstrate how the project fits into comprehensive transportation plans that included all modes of transportation and considered long-run effects. The goal was to push for deep-thinking, innovative proposals that likely would not have otherwise been funded. The grants could be used for up to 80 percent of total project costs in urban areas and 100 percent in rural areas.[10]

In the initial round, dubbed TIGER I, 51 projects were awarded from nearly 1,400 applications. Eligible applicants included state and local governments, transit agencies, port authorities, and metropolitan planning organizations, as well as consortia of these groups. After TIGER I, Congress continued to fund the program annually. Table 14.1 shows the rounds of funding in each year.

There are a few notable observations we can make from Table 14.1. Perhaps most importantly, the consistent annual funding of the program indicates that TIGER grants are broadly politically popular. Regardless of the political composition of Congress or the White House, and regardless of whether the country is in a recession or upswing, this transportation infra-

**Table 14.1**

TIGER/BUILD grant funding rounds

| FUNDING ROUND | TOTAL FUNDING (MILLIONS $) | RECIPIENTS |
| --- | --- | --- |
| TIGER I (2009) | 1,498 | 51 |
| TIGER II (2010) | 557 | 42 |
| TIGER III (2011) | 511 | 46 |
| TIGER IV (2012) | 485 | 47 |
| TIGER V (2013) | 458 | 52 |
| TIGER VI (2014) | 547 | 41 |
| TIGER VII (2015) | 485 | 39 |
| TIGER VIII (2016) | 485 | 40 |
| TIGER IX (2017) | 487 | 41 |
| BUILD (2018) | 1,500 | 91 |

*Sources*: "BUILD-TIGER Discretionary Grants," U.S. Department of Transportation, last modified January 7, 2019, https://ops.fhwa.dot.gov/freight/infrastructure/tiger/; Jake Varn and Andy Winkler, "TIGER Changes Its Stripes," *Bipartisan Policy Center* (blog), May 3, 2018, https://bipartisanpolicy.org /blog/tiger-changes-its-stripes/; Tom Ichniowski, "U.S. DOT Awards $1.5B in 'BUILD' Infrastructure Grants," *Engineering News-Record*, December 11, 2018, https://www.enr.com/articles/46035-us-dot-awards -15b-in-build-infrastructure-grants.

structure investment continues to be renewed. Indeed, in 2018 the Republican-dominated Congress tripled the size of the program, renaming it the Better Utilizing Investments to Leverage Development (BUILD) grant program.[11] The 2017 TIGER IX program and the BUILD program administered by the Trump administration are in many respects the same as previous TIGER programs, although the Trump administration has focused much less on finding innovative projects and has steered much more of the investment into roads and bridges in rural areas. Some may critique this change in 2018 as a pork-barrel reinvention of the program, but the fact that the program survived at all (despite attempts by the White House to defund it in the president's annual budget) indicates clear bipartisan support for *competitive* grants focused on infrastructure investment.[12]

The continued renewal of the TIGER program attests to its success in bringing funding to infrastructure priorities spread around the country. This dispersion of the funding perhaps may reduce the cost-effectiveness of the program somewhat, but it is decisive for political support for the program. Organizations across the ideological spectrum have written about the program, ranging from the libertarian Reason Foundation to the centrist Bipartisan Policy Center and progressive Smart Growth Online.[13] And by and large, nearly all agree that investment in infrastructure has long-run benefits and, more importantly, that there is a place for a TIGER-style program that competitively awards high-priority grants. From an economic perspective, the TIGER program reflects the fact that infrastructure investment is a public good that has benefits to society as a whole—much in the same way that our climate is a public good.

## APPLYING THE TIGER GRANT MODEL TO CLEAN ENERGY INVESTMENT

The goal of the TIGER grant model is to follow three principles: competitively awarded grants, long-term benefits, and innovative projects. I propose applying these principles to a new grant program that facilitates clean energy investment. The market failures in clean energy innovation discussed above can shape the structure of such grants. They should focus on high-priority areas that remain unfunded or deeply underfunded by other government programs or the private sector. In particular, these are areas where a modest amount of funding can go a long way toward accelerating a transition to clean energy by bringing down barriers to private sector investment. They can provide the connective tissue to spur further investment.

Projects could fund investments in clean energy infrastructure, including efforts to:

- Enable early-stage research for both firms and universities in promising clean energy technologies, focusing on connective technologies that might be neglected otherwise
- Speed adoption of technologies that allow for a smoother transition to renewables—especially projects focused on upgrading to a "smarter" electric grid
- Strategically locate battery storage to help smooth the intermittency from renewable energies that generate power only when there is ample sunlight or wind
- Support new electric transmission capacity that will make greater penetration of renewables even more viable
- Set nation-wide technical standards for new technologies to encourage a single, most efficient standard
- Enable consortiums of states to set regulations that simplify the paperwork required to site new technologies, including renewables (such as offshore wind), batteries, and smart grid technologies
- Develop new clean transportation technologies, such as underground electric charging stations at bus stops that automatically charge buses when they are stopped to pick up passengers.

What is critical is that all investments that the program funds have long-run innovative potential and be projects that simply would not happen (or would take a very long time to happen) without government support. The logical agency to house this type of innovation program would be the U.S. Department of Energy, but the U.S. Department of Transportation could also help facilitate clean transportation innovation projects.

Awards should emphasize spurring innovation efforts all around the country, in all states and regions, rural and urban. This breadth of focus should help with the goal of building broad-based bipartisan political support by spreading the investments widely. There may be some resistance from fossil-fuel-extracting states, but the program can be designed to ensure that these states receive benefits from it as well. The investments should also be focused on building and enabling the infrastructure we need for reliable low-carbon energy, to allow for deeper decarbonization in the next few decades that may even be less expensive than the energy system we have today. This proposal is not a replacement for broader efforts to incentivize decarbonization, such as carbon pricing, but rather is a complementary policy. The key is to develop the connective tissue, enabling infrastructure, and technologies that facilitate a smooth and rapid transition to a low-carbon economy.

**NOTES**

The author would like to acknowledge an especially insightful conversation with Ali Zaidi of Kirkland & Ellis LLP that helped inspire this piece, as well as terrific conversations at the Yale Environmental Dialogue workshop on February 8–9, 2019.

1. U.S. Global Change Research Program, *Fourth National Climate Assessment, Volume II: Impacts, Risks, and Adaptation in the United States* (Washington, DC: U.S. Global Change Research Program, 2018), https://nca2018.globalchange.gov/.

2. Arthur van Benthem et al., "Learning-by-Doing and the Optimal Solar Policy in California," *Energy Journal* 29, no. 3 (2008): 131–51, https://ideas.repec.org/a/aen/journl/2008v29-03-a07.html; Bryan Bollinger and Kenneth Gillingham, "Learning-by-Doing in Solar Photovoltaic Installations" (working paper, Yale University, 2014) http://environment.yale.edu/gillingham/BollingerGillingham_SolarLBD.pdf.

3. Kenneth Gillingham and Jim Stock, "The Cost of Reducing Greenhouse Gas Emissions," *Journal of Economic Perspectives* 32, no. 5 (2018): 1–20, https://pubs.aeaweb.org/doi/pdfplus/10.1257/jep.32.4.53.

4. William Nordhaus, "Designing a Friendly Space for Technological Change to Slow Global Warming," *Energy Economics* 33, no. 4 (2011): 665–73, https://doi.org/10.1016/j.eneco.2010.08.005.

5. Daron Acemoglu et al., "The Environment and Directed Technical Change," *American Economic Review* 102, no. 1 (2012): 131–66; Daron Acemoglu et al., "Transition to Clean Technology," *Journal of Political Economy* 124, no. 1 (2016): 52–104; Adrien Vogt-Schilb, Guy Meunier, and Stéphane Hallegatte, "When Starting with the Most Expensive Option Makes Sense: Optimal Timing, Cost and Sectoral Allocation of Abatement Investment," *Journal of Environmental Economics and Management* 88 (2018): 210–33, https://doi.org/10.1016/j.jeem.2017.12.001.

6. Gillingham and Stock, "The Cost of Reducing Greenhouse Gas Emissions," 1–20.

7. Gillingham and Stock, "The Cost of Reducing Greenhouse Gas Emissions," 1–20; Jing Li, "Compatibility and Investment in the U.S. Electric Vehicle Market" (working paper, Massachusetts Institute of Technology, 2018); Katalin Springel, "Network Externality and Subsidy Structure in Two-Sided Markets: Evidence from Electric Vehicle Incentives," Resources for the Future discussion paper, 2017, http://econweb.umd.edu/~sweeting/kspringel_ev.pdf.

8. Kenneth Gillingham and James Sweeney, "Barriers to Implementing Low-Carbon Technologies," *Climate Change Economics* 3, no. 4 (2012): 1–25, https://doi.org/10.1142/S2010007812500194.

9. "BUILD-TIGER Discretionary Grants," U.S. Department of Transportation, last modified January 7, 2019, https://ops.fhwa.dot.gov/freight/infrastructure/tiger/.

10. Jake Varn and Andy Winkler, "TIGER Changes Its Stripes," *Bipartisan Policy Center* (blog), May 3, 2018, https://bipartisanpolicy.org/blog/tiger-changes-its-stripes/.

11. Tom Ichniowski, "U.S. DOT Awards $1.5B in 'BUILD' Infrastructure Grants," *Engineering News-Record*, December 11, 2018, https://www.enr.com/articles/46035-us-dot-awards-15b-in-build-infrastructure-grants.

12. Two key Senate appropriators, Senators Susan Collins and Jack Reed, wrote a letter of displeasure in 2018 at the lack of transparency under the BUILD program and concern about the new criteria being used to award the projects. For example, one new criterion is non-federal revenues, which is intended to encourage public-private partnerships but also may encourage awarding funds to projects that will bring in the highest profit to firms, rather than promote the greatest public good.

13. Baruch Feigenbaum, *Evaluating and Improving TIGER Grants*, Policy Brief 99 (Washington, DC: Reason Foundation, 2012), https://reason.org/wp-content/uploads/files/improving_transportation_tiger_grants.pdf; Varn and Winkler, "TIGER"; Lisa Prevost, "Highway Conversion to Reconnect New Haven Neighborhoods," *Next City*, January 20, 2017, https://nextcity.org/daily/entry/highway-urban-renewal-new-haven-neighborhoods.

# Building Climate Change Resilience by Design

Amanda Brown-Stevens

CLIMATE CHANGE HAS BEGUN to alter our nation. In recent years, the increase in number and intensity of weather events from hurricanes to wildfires is bringing these challenges to the forefront of public consciousness. Despite this emerging reality, the conversation around climate change often still focuses on *mitigation*—on how we change course to prevent a build-up of greenhouse gases in the atmosphere. Some feel that talking about *adaptation* to the effects of climate change would be to admit defeat and to give ourselves a pass to continue polluting at the scale we are today.

But when it comes to our "built environment," it is time to begin preparing. Climate change puts a huge stress on existing infrastructure and will continue to do so, exacerbating already-urgent problems. While we still lack a concerted, coordinated effort to adapt to a changing climate, a growing understanding of the challenges we face offers us an opportunity. We can make investments that improve our communities today while reducing future risk, which if we do not address will lead to much greater costs over time. Instead of waiting for a disaster, we can proactively plan for and invest in a more resilient future.

## RESILIENT INFRASTRUCTURE FOR A RESILIENT FUTURE

Our cities are already facing ongoing stresses due to a systematic lack of investment in infrastructure. Even places that once enjoyed great public transit service are suffering from insufficient funding for maintenance and upgrades, and climate change will only make these problems worse.[1] While the two major American political parties offer different infrastructure policy prescriptions, the agreed-upon need for greater investment persists as one of the few remaining bipartisan political issues. This consensus can provide the basis for reimagining how we build and adapt for the future.

So what is resilient infrastructure? Resilience is often discussed in the context of individual action—the ability to bounce back in the face of challenges. Resilient infrastructure imparts a built environment with the capacity to withstand and bounce back—from challenges like severe storms, fires, increased flooding, severe heat impacts, and more. A community can have a strong social fabric—can be resilient in the face of many challenges—and yet without resilient infrastructure, increasingly severe weather events can cause widespread devastation.

While as a nation we are not making nearly the investments we need, hundreds of billions of dollars are spent on infrastructure every year throughout the country. Much of that spending is increasingly vulnerable to climate change impacts, including flooding and fires, meaning that the lifespan of these investments may be severely shortened.

Creating the political consensus to break the cycle of years of disinvestment and expand infrastructure investments to make our communities more resilient can seem daunting in a polarized political climate. Investment in infrastructure can be appealing, however, to political leaders across the ideological spectrum. A more resilient built environment can create jobs and on-the-ground impact, help communities weather economic downturns, and protect against climate-change-related threats. Additionally, increasingly severe and destructive weather events are creating a growing constituency and momentum for action.

State and local elected officials in areas recovering from disasters can be powerful leaders to spur this effort, as their constituents demand action. One of the moments when we do invest in infrastructure is rebuilding after a natural disaster. Yet various forces, including the political climate and a need to rebuild quickly, often lead us to miss the opportunity to rebuild in a way that will reduce economic risk and keep people safer in the future. We can change this with education and planning before disaster strikes to help connect the dots, so that when the inevitable storm hits, affected communities can band together to demand solutions that do not just build back existing structures. We have done this in the past. After devastating earthquakes, new policies and building codes that increase protections have been put in place.

We can use this model to address climate-change-related challenges and ensure we build for a more resilient future.

## A SHIFT IN PERSPECTIVE

The implementation of this vision means facing tough choices. Take, for example, the way we have built around water. Throughout the history of the United States, cities have been built on waterways, along coasts, around rivers and lakes. These areas were built in a different era, when the focus of the design professionals like architects and engineers was to "conquer" nature—to fill in wetlands and marshes, to reroute creeks through culverts or underground, and to keep the sea at bay through walls, barriers, and gates. But nature can never be truly conquered. The successful effort to build around water means that our economy and our lives now depend on homes, jobs, and infrastructure at severe and increasing risk of flooding.

What we have made, however, we can unmake. We can harness the same creative energy that envisioned cities on swamps and bluffs and imagine new cities. We can learn to live with water and nature in a new way—ensuring all of our investments in homes, job centers, and public infrastructure bring us back toward a new ecological balance. We must begin building our communities in a way that reduces the severe risks we are facing, provides social benefit, and maintains ecological stability today and in the future.

Across the nation, we need to accelerate action significantly to adapt to climate change. Partnering with leaders in the design field can help local governments imagine greater possibilities, connect with a broader audience, and motivate a movement to advocate for this investment. Some examples of innovative ideas from the San Francisco Bay Area show how local jurisdictions can lead the way in developing resilient infrastructure ideas and creating on-the-ground impact. These ideas were developed through the Resilient by Design Bay Area Challenge—a year-long design challenge that brought together internationally renowned design professionals with local community leaders to develop innovative, inspiring visions for reimagining the region's approach to flooding in a way that reduces risk in the future and benefits communities today.

*Back to Nature—Using History to Guide Future Development.*   Much of the land at risk for severe flooding in the Bay Area was taken from nature—areas where we filled in wetlands, and built on marshes and in the path of creeks and streams. Currently, land use restrictions and private property rights limit our ability to make short-term wholesale change in these areas. Most coastal communities are hesitant to even broach conversations around "managed retreat" from rising sea levels. Some areas, however, may be ripe for tools like land swaps, which would allow increased density along main urban corridors in exchange for converting some shoreline land to parks and wetlands. These voluntary programs shift residents and businesses away from vulnerable areas through incentives, such as density bonuses, that allow developers to build more densely than local law would otherwise permit.

In an area with high land values, low density, and increasing flood risk, such as on the San Francisco Peninsula in and around Silicon Valley, a land use swap could provide a model for significant restoration of what was previously marshland. This model could serve dual goals. First, "to densify, to enable and encourage more dense and mixed forms of development in suitable sites and [second] to de-densify, to release the lowest-lying areas to provide space to support the region's flood management strategy."[2] Land swaps in this area could also provide a number of other benefits. The changes could offer traffic relief through more transit-oriented development, much-needed housing close to job centers, increased flood protections for homes and businesses, and a significant increase in natural habitat for wildlife. While these programs have been used in the past for conservation goals, the need for climate change adaptation in dense areas could make this model viable at a much larger scale.

*Imagining Green Schools—a Built-In Resilience Network.* Even in cities working to proactively prepare for disaster and plan for recovery, those functions tend to be siloed—with planning departments focused on resilience schemes, and emergency services managed separately. Integrating these efforts can leverage existing work and create opportunities for collaboration. For example, some cities designate schools as emergency response locations, since they tend to be spread out throughout the city with playgrounds and open areas for gathering. Along with disaster response, this natural network within a city can be expanded to proactively reduce risk and build resilience as well.

Currently, many urban school districts have primarily concrete play areas with little natural vegetation. This lack of green space can exacerbate the *heat islands* of higher temperature often found in cities and create more rainwater runoff—intensifying the negative effects of climate change. Efforts in the Bay Area and throughout the country to "green" schoolyards are starting to combat these effects, installing natural spaces with permeable pavement and other features that provide shade, capture stormwater, and create a more natural educational environment for students. These efforts should be expanded and amplified—leveraging investments to multiply the benefits. Pairing green schoolyards with the installation of stormwater detention basins at all schools within a community could provide an essential escape valve for water in a severe storm event, and could even be developed to capture, treat, and reuse water on-site, an important benefit in increasingly drought-stricken areas.

*Public Access, Public Protection: Building Floodgates into Everyday Infrastructure.* Regional leaders in the San Francisco Bay Area have a grand vision for a connected "Bay Trail" network circling San Francisco Bay, and the area has made significant progress in developing large stretches of this well-used pathway. Gaps exist, however, particularly in more urban areas, where existing development makes the investment more complicated and costly. These urban waterfront areas can be great sites for community amenities and trail connections, but they are currently at severe flood risk. As the Bay Trail continues to be developed, ideas have emerged such as creating a bike lane levee—a multi-use path along the shoreline that doubles as flood protection for adjacent homes and businesses. This innovation could also house upgraded stormwater infrastructure, future-proofing our aging sewage and stormwater systems.[3] In the Bay Area and beyond, waterfront trails combined with levees can also protect a bigger investment in recreational infrastructure, increasing flood protection and generating habitat for wildlife.

*Living with Water—Integrating Water into the Urban Form.* With the combination of sea levels and groundwater rising due to climate change, there are places where no amount of protection, whether through green or conventional infrastructure, will keep the water out of residential and commercial areas. To reduce the need for wholesale retreat from urban areas we love, in many places we will literally need to learn to live with water. Cities like Venice are currently anomalies, but proactively planning communities that integrate water can create new, safe, and adaptable neighborhoods.

Unlike some of the urban resilience ideas that take existing infrastructure efforts and layer on climate change adaptation components, "floating cities" represent a totally new way of thinking about how we build. They would need experimentation and pilot projects to be tested and refined. A multidisciplinary design team working as part of the Resilient by Design Bay Area

Challenge in San Leandro Bay (in the cities of Oakland and Alameda) developed a "Tidal City" pilot vision for this purpose. As the design team explains, "Tidal Cities combine tidal lagoons with floating structures to live with rising tides and rising groundwater. These dynamic landscapes interweave built and natural environments to create new communities that can adapt in place and are resilient to various environmental vulnerabilities."[4] These landscapes can be constructed through a *cut and fill* process, in which earth dug out to form lagoons is then added to build a higher-elevation structure around them. Then, "tide gates would maintain a stable water table within the lagoons and facilitate periodic hydraulic flows in and out to keep water from becoming stagnant. Building units would be placed on shared decking floated with pontoons." This idea could be tested or modeled in other parts of the country with similar sea-level-rise challenges.

### HOW TO MAKE IT HAPPEN

Resilient infrastructure, like that being envisioned in the Bay Area, cannot be made in one fell swoop—no single overarching legislative fix will transform our country's infrastructure. The country needs a policy, communications, and advocacy agenda to make this happen on a large scale.

*Investment for Change.*   The country must prioritize public investment that increases resilience—by design—by collaborating more, integrating natural systems with the built environment, highlighting social equity, and bringing innovative design thinking to the forefront to help us solve some of our nation's biggest challenges to build a resilient future for all. Building public support and experimenting with adaptation solutions should lead to policies that ensure all infrastructure investment is climate-change-resilient, similar to building standards that ensure all structures are designed to withstand earthquakes. These principles can be incorporated into general plans, building codes, and guidelines for public investment.

Additionally, significant increases in investment in public infrastructure will provide benefits to communities today and risk reduction in the future. We need to:

- Build climate change adaptation protections into infrastructure while shoring up our crumbling roads, bridges, transit, and public spaces to improve quality of life today and create good jobs and stronger communities.

- Shift our perspective. New thinking should look to rebalance the natural and urban environments, reduce our environmental impact, rebuild natural areas, and look toward a future where we develop in a way that protects and enhances our waterways, forests, and ourselves as well.
- Leverage rebuilding efforts after disasters to reduce the risk of disasters in the future.

*Public Engagement and Participation.*   Public participation is essential to drive leaders to make the many policy changes we need for resilience, and to sustain a significant effort over time. At the same time, it is very difficult to convey the urgency of an impending disaster of the scale of climate change, because it is both slow-moving and overwhelmingly daunting. We need creative communications that show the urgency of the climate problem and that we can come together to make a difference. Collaborations between designers and local leaders can help raise awareness among the public and broaden support for policies that build resilience. These educational efforts need to be tied to political pressure for increased investment in adaptation and increased participation in planning for communities' resilience—to prepare for and recover from disasters.

*The Need for Collaboration.*   Addressing these resilience challenges will require an unprecedented level of collaboration among governments, businesses, and citizens, which means few models exist showing the path forward. While our need for investment in infrastructure is not new, we are facing new challenges. Coastal cities were built to accommodate people and jobs over time, but not to adapt to a significantly changing shoreline. Recent hurricanes have shown us that trillions of dollars' worth of assets in cities such as New York and Houston are much more vulnerable than previously understood. This means that sectors not always known for flexibility and innovation—such as transportation agencies, utilities, and other government sectors—will need to experiment and encourage innovation in both public and private investment.

Throughout the country, however, local communities are starting to realize the extent of climate change challenges and develop creative pilot projects to bring the experimentation and innovation needed to address them. A growing cohort of leaders at the local, state, and national levels are raising awareness around the need to reduce carbon emissions, including developing and implementing policy and advocacy agendas. These leaders can provide a strong base of support for adaptation measures as well, as we must shift toward a dual approach, with climate change mitigation and adaptation seen by all as two sides of the same coin.

*Communicating Risk.*    To make this shift—and create the willingness to invest and experiment within government—a broad coalition of constituencies needs to advocate for taking action. It is crucial to both raise awareness about climate change risks and highlight the path forward toward more investment in risk-reducing infrastructure.

Creative ways to visualize both risks and solutions are essential to connect with that broader audience and build support. Beyond traditional community meetings and online platforms, cities and advocates can get creative about bringing the issue out to where people are. Showing a floodplain on a map might help some people understand the risk of sea level rise, but painting potential flood lines on telephone poles can connect on a more visceral level. Lectures and panels on the benefits of green infrastructure help cultivate an informed audience, but interactive models displayed at parks, schools, and community events can build a new generation of advocates. Creative communications, along with innovative designs, experimentation, and bold actions, can create a viable path forward.

In the past, we have come together as a nation to invest in our future. We literally moved mountains to create cities and transportation networks. It is time to come together again. We can invest in our communities, create models for the rest of the world, and protect our nation's future.

**NOTES**

1.  World Bank, *Financing a Resilient Urban Future: A Policy Brief on World Bank and Global Experience on Financing Climate-Resilient Urban Infrastructure* (Washington, DC: World Bank Group, 2018).
2.  Field Operations Team, *Final Report* (San Francisco, CA: Resilient by Design | Bay Area Challenge, 2018), 94, http://www.resilientbayarea.org/south-bay-sponge.
3.  Bionic Team, *Elevate San Rafael* (San Francisco, CA: Resilient by Design | Bay Area Challenge, 2018), http://www.resilientbayarea.org/elevate-san-rafael.
4.  All Bay Collective, *The Estuary Commons: People, Place, and a Path Forward* (San Francisco, CA: Resilient by Design | Bay Area Challenge, 2018), 92, http://www.resilientbayarea.org/estuary-commons.

# Bracing for Impact

## TRANSFORMING THE NATIONAL WEATHER SERVICE FOR THE CLIMATE CHANGE CHALLENGES AHEAD

Monica Medina

WEATHER FORECASTING MIGHT seem to be the most mundane of governmental services, and yet nearly every American relies nearly every day on the forecasts issued by the National Weather Service. In the face of rising risk from climate change—leading to more hurricanes, wildfires, floods, droughts, and other extreme weather events—we need an expanded set of forecasts and a National Weather Service that has been remade for the twenty-first century. Indeed, understanding the weather has been important to our nation since its birth, given our rich natural environment, expansive ocean territory (the largest in the world), and the weather hazards generated by our country's topography. For more than a century, we have responded to weather disasters with efforts to better warn the public to protect them from catastrophic events. Congress passed the law creating the original civilian Weather Bureau in 1890 after floods ruptured a Pennsylvania dam, killing more than two thousand people.[1] After the worst natural disaster in U.S. history, the hurricane that made landfall in Galveston, Texas, in 1900—killing between six and twelve thousand surprised and unprepared Americans—the new bureau began to issue warnings for floods and hurricanes from its national headquarters in order to ensure they were based on the best science.

Today, the modern National Weather Service has as its mission to "provide weather, water, and climate data, forecasts and warnings for the protection of life and property and enhancement of the national economy."[2]

According to the United Nations, even under the best-case scenario, "limiting global warming to 1.5°C would require 'rapid and far-reaching' transitions in land, energy, industry, buildings, transport, and cities."[3] As part of such transitions, it is again time to upgrade our weather, warning, and watch systems in the United States in order to best adapt to the dangers that lie ahead due to the changing global climate.

## THE UNITED STATES IS WEATHER-READY

Most consumers of weather information in the United States are now accustomed to on-demand information—freely available from the government and from private weather services—about current conditions and up to fourteen-day advance forecasts on smartphones and computers, as well as localized weather news replete in traditional and social media outlets. But behind all those public and private weather products and communications there is a weather infrastructure composed of satellites, balloons and buoys, radars, weather stations on land, observatories, supercomputers, and models and algorithms, not to mention tens of thousands of dedicated meteorologists and scientists.

Dealing with the uncertainties of forecasts and predictions beyond the two-week time frame goes beyond the boundaries of modern meteorology (the science of forecasting the weather) and is currently the domain of climate science, though the gap between the two is closing. To the weather-consuming public, this distinction is not readily apparent. "Weather" refers to local conditions on the scale of minutes, hours, and days. "Climate" is an average of weather conditions over thirty years or more and can be assessed for a single location, a large area, or even globally. In recent years, the Weather Service's ability to provide precise (for the most part) daily weather forecasts, warnings, and watches has only improved. The daily weather forecasts are now 90 percent reliable within five days, as are the storm tracks for hurricanes. However, weather forecasts even today are only about 50 percent accurate beyond ten days, which prompts the question: are we as a nation sufficiently climate-change-ready? Do we have the systems in place to deal with the increasingly stressful impacts of climate change?

## THE UNITED STATES IS NOT CLIMATE-CHANGE-READY

Even though the Weather Service's mission includes compiling data about climate, this role falls short of what is needed to deal with climate change going forward. The Weather Service's current climate work is limited to data gathering and science, and does not go as far as its weather role to create more robust information products such as forecasts, warnings, and watches out beyond the ten-day horizon or specialized products for new climate-change-related challenges. Since these are two distinct functions employing different data, models, and time scales, the Weather Service does not currently have the capacity to provide the full suite of climate services that are needed now and into the future. However, the federal government's United States Global Change Research Program has stated unequivocally that climate change is already impacting the United States, and with expected temperature increases ahead, the impacts will worsen. As a result, neither "global efforts to mitigate the causes of climate change nor regional efforts to adapt to the impacts currently approach the scales needed to avoid substantial damages to the U.S. economy, environment, and human health and well-being over the coming decades."[4] The Global Change Research Program works exceedingly well as an inter-agency committee to coordinate climate research and will be essential to closing the gap between today's forecasts and the ones we need, but it is also not equipped to undertake the task of providing climate products as a routine service to the public.

Each year the Weather Service issues approximately 1.5 million forecasts and fifty thousand warnings, at a minimal cost to each American of about three dollars.[5] However, in recent years the Weather Service has been stretched thin, with some former Weather Service leaders arguing that this situation puts the public at risk given the additional demands from climate-change-related weather events.[6] Moreover, there are key limits on its authority; for example, the Weather Service does not currently have the authority to issue event-specific fire warnings, but only to say when drought conditions make fires more likely in a particular region. As a result, there were no Weather Service fire warnings for the 2018 fires in Paradise, California, which killed at least eighty-six people and were among the deadliest fires and most expensive natural disasters in American history. Currently, a local emergency manager must request a fire warning by the National Oceanic and Atmospheric Administration (NOAA).[7]

The Weather Service must contend with a tremendous number of weather threats each year—on average, 5,000 floods, 1,300 tornadoes, 2 Atlantic hurricanes, and widespread droughts, as well as hundreds of other events like wildfires. But these figures no longer match the current climate reality. Indeed, in 2017, the United States experienced a record-breaking year of weather and climate disasters with sixteen separate billion-dollar events causing

$306 billion in total damages. In 2018, fourteen weather events exceeded $1 billion in damage, as compared with the adjusted average from 1980 to 2018, which was roughly six events annually. Emergency managers, in the United States and globally, are now sounding the alarm that they need better infrastructure to deal with the events that loom in the future.[8]

Any significant infrastructure initiatives or climate change adaptation programs must take this information into account when prioritizing and planning investments. The case of Hurricane Sandy is instructive. When Hurricane Sandy slammed into lower Manhattan in 2012, it badly damaged two tunnels that connect Manhattan to Brooklyn and Queens. They both filled with water, damaging their electrical and lighting systems. Removing the water required quick and sophisticated engineering work—it was not simply a matter of pumping out the seawater, as that would have risked collapsing the tunnels completely. Re-opening the tunnels and reconnecting lower Manhattan to the neighboring boroughs was only possible thanks to the in-house expertise of the Army Corps of Engineers and numerous Situation Room sessions involving the secretaries of Defense and Homeland Security. At the time, engineers were "shocked" that New York City had not done far more to safeguard its tunnels given that city officials knew of the risks of rising seas and extreme weather associated with climate change.[9]

The Weather Service as currently constituted simply cannot take on the additional challenge of more robust climate assessments, predictions, and forecasts that will be needed going forward. There is a relatively small climate prediction office inside the Weather Service with a few dozen staff members at headquarters and spread around the country, which provides three- to four-week outlooks, one- and three-month seasonal outlooks that look at temperature and rainfall expectations (warmer or wetter than average, for example), and drought and hazard seasonal outlooks as well. But the climate prediction office staff is not large enough to take on the climate change demands that lie ahead. This is particularly true considering the types of extreme events that we anticipate in a changing climate, and that, according to NOAA, one-third of the U.S. economy (about $3 trillion worth of gross domestic product) is weather or climate sensitive.

## THE ANSWER: EXPAND THE WEATHER SERVICE TO BE THE NATIONAL WEATHER AND CLIMATE SERVICE

In 2009, Congress and NOAA leadership proposed creating a stand-alone climate service within NOAA; however, a different model might be less expensive and disruptive to build. The NOAA Science Advisory Board, in a 2009 report entitled *Options for Creating a National Climate Service,* argued that a combined weather and climate service would provide a single, authoritative government voice on climate, which could be built quickly from existing components of the National Weather Service, and provide users "one-stop shopping" for a full spectrum of weather and climate products.[10]

Some might argue that the private sector should expand weather forecasts to create more robust and comprehensive climate-specific products than exist today. However, forecasting climate events is an "inherently governmental function" because, similar to issuing warnings and watches by the Weather Service, it fundamentally involves the protection of the lives and property of private citizens.[11] These services should be available to the entire public, not just those who can afford to pay a private company for this type of information. Private services may also be unwilling or unable to provide sufficiently accurate climate information to protect the public. The expense of the complex and extensive system required for gathering, analyzing, and maintaining the necessary climate data is prohibitive for most private enterprises, and much of it is already done by the government's various climate science programs.

Plus, if the government performs the basic climate functions we need, the data must be publicly available for private companies and researchers. Private entities can then further refine the data into commercial products and services that are even more targeted and user-friendly, just as private weather companies do now, but their work would be built on top of the government's climate science infrastructure. Finally, a single, authoritative government voice on climate products is needed. The National Weather and Climate Service would have the benefit of the expertise and reputation of the current Weather Service to build on, plus the support of the entire federal government enterprise. And once established, it would not have to worry about liability questions, profitability to keep it afloat, or risk of public confusion caused by "dueling" private forecasts.

## THE BENEFITS OF A NATIONAL WEATHER AND CLIMATE SERVICE FOR THE TWENTY-FIRST CENTURY

The expanded weather and climate service would not only provide the country with essential protection of life and property within the mission of the Weather Service; it would also enhance the economic vitality of the nation and improve ecological stewardship. This service would be used on a daily basis by public and private decision makers, multinational corporations, nonprofits, small businesses, and individuals. All of them could then better safeguard lives and property, ensure our nation's economic growth and vitality, and bolster our environmental sustainability. The service would also help our nation and its people avoid costly mistakes as we attempt to mitigate climate change whether through a Green New Deal or any other broad overhaul of the energy and infrastructure foundations of our economy.

In fact, it will likely achieve societal benefits that we do not even foresee today. For example, a climate service could help save lives by allowing us to focus on preventing illnesses and diseases that are likely to increase with warming (such as Zika and Lyme disease) by using climate and weather prediction capabilities to anticipate health threats. Similarly, our national defenses could be strengthened based on climate information since there are numerous active coastal military installations in the United States that are at a significant and increasing risk due to flooding. The weather and climate service could enhance and expand the United States' growing green economy by optimizing the site selection, infrastructure design, and operations for solar and wind energy systems contemplated by proposals for a Green New Deal or other new government policies and spending. Finally, with a better understanding of climate change, we could limit its impacts on natural resources and agriculture through crop rotation or other response strategies that enable farmers and foresters to respond to existing invasive species and prepare for new invasions. We could also better predict toxic algal bloom events—such as those in Lake Erie and off the coast of Florida—that negatively impact drinking water supplies, tourism, and fishing.

One other significant benefit of building on the existing framework of the Weather Service is that once these services exist, they can be easily made available to the public through both the existing data.gov portal for raw data and the Weather Service's communications network for the forecast products themselves. It is essential that this information be disseminated widely, and the National Weather and Climate Service is best equipped to ensure that all of the public will be able to receive the information they need to plan for today, next year, and the years ahead.

## NEXT STEPS TOWARD U.S. CLIMATE CHANGE PREPAREDNESS
To be most effective, a detailed plan for how to expand the Weather Service needs to be developed, perhaps by the NOAA Science Advisory Board, just as

it did when it first envisioned a national climate service in 2009. Any plan to expand the Weather Service should begin with full funding for its current functions and with expanded capabilities in forecast offices, which in 2017 and 2018 were subject to $65 million in proposed budget cuts. This improved capacity will allow services to begin immediately in key areas of the country and for important sectors of the economy.

Upgrades in at least three areas will likely be needed: more supercomputers for modeling and data analysis, more people to take in observations and create products, and more observations equipment and systems. We will need drones, buoys, and sensors on anything we can get to embed or carry them—such as private fishing vessels, roads, buildings, and even people. The current climate data center would need to be expanded to house, sort, and validate all the additional data taken in by the government. The new services would also benefit from an extensive public process to understand how to best support the country in creating the new products and services.

The cost of the expanded National Weather and Climate Service would likely be multiple billions to plan and establish, and could increase the current yearly costs of the Weather Service by two times—perhaps to as much as $2.5 billion annually. But this cost is a drop in the bucket compared with the costs of the green infrastructure investments that need to be made in the coming decades at the municipal, state, and federal levels. And it will likely save thousands of lives and billions of dollars in wasteful or ineffective expenditures that would be made without the benefit of this climate information. The climate service also has the potential to create jobs and economic benefits. Workers who are not saddled with illnesses or inefficiencies caused by climate-change-related disease and disruptions will be more productive, and expanded private sector climate services and technologies will generate business. The cost is also a pittance as compared with what we spend on post-disaster funding to deal with the effects of the hurricanes, wildfires, droughts, and floods.

Looking back, the United States has sustained 241 weather and climate disasters between 1980 and 2018 in which the overall damage reached or exceeded $1 billion in 2018 dollars, at a cumulative cost of $1.6 trillion.[12] It is safe to assume that what our country will face because of climate change in the next forty years will be more damaging and costly. We must rise to meet the challenge. We should expand the Weather Service to include much greater

climate services so that we can adapt to climate change and be a truly weather-
*and* climate-change-ready nation.

**NOTES**

1. "History of the National Weather Service," National Oceanic and Atmospheric Ad-ministration, accessed January 11, 2019, https://www.weather.gov/timeline.
2. "About the NWS," National Weather Service, accessed March 2, 2019, https://www.weather.gov/about/.
3. "Special Climate Report: 1.5°C Is Possible but Requires Unprecedented and Urgent Action," *Sustainable Development Goals* (blog), United Nations, October 8, 2018, https://www.un.org/sustainabledevelopment/blog/2018/10/special-climate-report-1-5oc-is-possible-but-requires-unprecedented-and-urgent-action/.
4. Alexa Jay et al., "Overview," in *Fourth National Climate Assessment, Volume II: Impacts, Risks, and Adaptation in the United States* (Washington, DC: U.S. Global Change Research Program, 2018), 34, https://nca2018.globalchange.gov/downloads/NCA4_Ch01_Overview.pdf.
5. *National Weather Service: Actions Have Been Taken to Fill Increasing Vacancies, but Opportunities Exist to Improve and Evaluate Hiring*, GAO-17-364 (Washington, DC: Government Accountability Office, 2017), 8, https://www.gao.gov/assets/690/684905.pdf.
6. Scott Friedman, "Former National Weather Service Official Says Low Staffing at Forecasting Offices Creates Risky Situation," NBC5 Dallas, June 24, 2015, https://www.nbcdfw.com/investigations/Former-National-Weather-Service-Official-Says-Low-Staffing-at-Forecasting-Offices-Creates-Risky-Situation-309644671.html.
7. Andrew Friedman, "Why It's So Hard to Issue a Fire Warning," Axios Newsletter, November 15, 2018, https://www.axios.com/california-camp-fire-why-no-warning-cb62b3a0-4820-4289-8be0-4ac9cebe2519.html.
8. Katherine Bagley, "Climate Data Now Key to Disaster Preparedness, First Responders Say," Inside Climate News, February 2, 2016, https://insideclimatenews.org/news/02022016/extreme-weathers-first-responders-use-climate-forecasts-guide.
9. Elisabeth Rosenthal, "Hurricane Exposed Flaws in Protection of Tunnels," *New York Times*, November 10, 2012, https://www.nytimes.com/2012/11/10/nyregion/hurricane-sandy-showed-vulnerability-of-citys-tunnels.html.
10. NOAA Science Advisory Board, *Options for Developing a National Climate Service*, May 18, 2009, ftp://ftp.oar.noaa.gov/SAB/sab/members/2010/november/pdf/OptionsforDevelopingaNCS_FinaltoNOAA_5_18_09.pdf.
11. Federal Activities Inventory Reform Act of 1998, Pub. L. No. 105-270, 112 STAT. 2382 § 5(b). 1998.
12. "Billion Dollar Weather and Climate Disasters: Overview," NOAA National Centers for Environmental Information, accessed March 2, 2019, https://www.ncdc.noaa.gov/billions/.

# PART THREE    LAW AND POLICY

# Building Public and Political Will for Climate Change Action

Anthony Leiserowitz

GLOBAL CLIMATE CHANGE is a "massive collective action problem."[1] While changes in individual behavior (for example, energy conservation) can help reduce emissions, system-level changes to the way human societies use energy and natural resources are necessary to limit global warming to "safe" levels. Government policy is one important means of system change—including laws, rules, regulations, standards, and incentives. But many climate change policies, from the local level to the global level, founder on the lack of "political will"—the unwillingness or inability of government officials to enact policies that will reduce carbon pollution at the scale and speed required. Public will, especially as expressed through citizen activism, is an important influence on the policymaking process. Strong public demand increases the likelihood that governments will prioritize climate change action.[2]

*Public will* refers to a "social system's shared recognition of a particular problem and resolve to address the situation in a particular way through sustained collective action."[3] Indicators of public will can include public support for mitigation policies, contacting government officials, and pro-climate consumer behavior. Importantly, however, there is no single, homogenous "public"—there are many diverse "publics" within any society.[4]

One key set of citizens is an *issue public*—a relatively small proportion of a population that is passionate about a specific issue.[5] Issue publics are highly attentive to and seek out information about their issue, have relatively high levels of knowledge, have developed strong and stable attitudes, and are more likely than other citizens to take action on the issue. Some issue publics are diffuse, with few and weak connective ties between individual members. Others are highly organized through social, institutional, or advocacy groups and networks, which can make them powerful political actors. One example of the latter is the National Rifle Association—an organized issue public of approximately four to five million members (in a country of more than 250 million adults) who wield political clout far beyond their numbers on the issues they care about. *Public will* can thus include at least three levels of citizen engagement: (1) general public support for an issue or policy, (2) an issue public focused on that issue or policy, and (3) an organized issue public mobilized to exert influence on policymakers. In turn, a mobilized issue public can include diverse groups, organized into a coordinated "advocacy coalition" of partners working together to achieve a common goal.[6]

Separately, there is always "limited space available on the political or decision-making agenda, that is the continually evolving, brief list of issues that command policy makers' attention at a given time."[7] "Windows of Opportunity" theory says an issue is "most likely to reach the political agenda when three things occur at the same time: a problem is perceived as important and urgent by the public and elites [public will]; viable policy solutions are available; and political commitment to adopt a solution is high [political will]."[8] When these three elements converge, a "policy window" opens during which significant change is possible. All three elements are necessary for policy change, but even then, change is not inevitable. Advocates have to be ready and able to take advantage of a policy window when it opens. After it closes, only incremental progress is likely until the next window opens.

### GLOBAL WARMING'S SIX AMERICAS

Building *public will* for climate change action must start with an understanding of the different publics within a population. Since 2008, the Yale Program on Climate Change Communication, in partnership with the George Mason University Center for Climate Change Communication, has conducted a twice-a-year nationally representative survey called *Climate Change in the American Mind.* One key insight has been the identification of "Global Warming's Six Americas"—six distinct segments of the American public that each respond to the issue in a different way.[9]

As of 2018, 21 percent of Americans were alarmed about climate change.[10] The Alarmed are convinced that global warming is happening, human-caused, and an urgent threat, and they strongly support climate change action. Most, however, do not know what they can do to solve the problem. Next are the Concerned (30 percent), who also think human-caused global warming is happening and is a serious threat. However, they believe that it is still a distant problem—distant in time, with impacts a generation or more away, and distant in space—a problem that will primarily impact plants, penguins, or polar bears but not the United States, their communities, or the people and places they care about. The Concerned support policy action but do not see the issue as an urgent priority.

Next are the Cautious (21 percent), who still question: Is global warming happening? Is it human-caused or natural? Is it serious or overblown? The Cautious have not yet made up their minds. Then come the Disengaged (7 percent), who know little about global warming. They rarely or never hear about it in the media or from their own friends or family members. Next are the Doubtful (12 percent), who do not think global warming is happening, but if it is, it is just a natural cycle. They do not think about climate change much or consider it a serious risk. The final group are the Dismissive (9 percent), who are convinced global warming is not happening, human-caused, or a threat. Most endorse conspiracy theories: global warming is a hoax, scientists are making up the data, or it is just a get-rich scheme by Al Gore. The Dismissive are just a small percentage of the American public. But they are very vocal, and their views have had an outsize influence in Congress, the White House, and many state governments.

### ENGAGEMENT STRATEGIES

A first priority is to organize the Alarmed, who are currently a latent issue public. There are approximately 53 million Americans alarmed about climate change. Of this group, 7 percent (about 3.7 million) say they are already part of "a campaign to convince elected officials to take action to reduce global warming," 28 percent (about 14.8 million) say they "definitely would join" a campaign, and 37 percent (about 19.6 million) say they "probably would join" such a campaign. This represents an enormous *potential* social movement—if they were recruited, organized, and deployed. But unlike other issue publics, the citizen activist wing of the climate movement remains relatively small and disorganized.

Second, the diverse organizations advocating for climate change action need to be organized into an *advocacy coalition* with the political muscle to sway elections, influence policymakers, and overcome the concerted opposition of climate change action opponents.[11] Advocacy coalitions can include nongovernment organizations, social movements, governments, political parties, research institutions, companies, and media outlets. On the issue of climate change, opponents of climate change policy, such as the fossil fuel industry billionaires Charles Koch and David H. Koch, have constructed a larger, better organized, and better financed coalition, sustained over decades, than have proponents, who—despite having majority public support for many policies, a larger issue public, and a larger number of organizations working on climate change—continue to pursue relatively diverse agendas, with less coordination and focus.[12] The balance of power and influence between these different coalitions can have very significant effects on the policy-making process.

A third priority is to build the "silent permission" for action among the 70 percent of Americans in the middle four groups of the Six Americas. These audiences are unlikely to become active members of the climate change issue public (for example, the Alarmed), but critically, they do represent the majority of voters. They are unlikely to ever lobby a public official, call their members of Congress, march in the streets, or donate money to a climate change organization. But most elected officials need their silent permission to pass climate policies—their tacit support and willingness to not punish political leaders at the ballot box for taking action. A slightly more ambitious goal for this silent majority is to persuade them to prefer political candidate X over candidate Y, because candidate X favors stronger climate change action.

A fourth priority is to build a *diverse* issue public among the Alarmed. Many Americans currently associate climate change with three main messengers: scientists, environmentalists, and liberal politicians. For most Americans, however, these are relatively abstract others. Most people trust scientists and hold them in high esteem; however, for most Americans, scientists remain a distant abstraction. Few Americans personally know a scientist, let alone a climate scientist, and rarely identify with science or scientists themselves. Likewise, many Americans do not consider themselves "environmentalists," who are often stereotyped as "others," with different values, attitudes, and behaviors than mainstream Americans. Finally, most Americans do not identify as strong liberals. Likewise, pre-existing political identities shape attitudes toward climate champions like former vice president Gore. Gore successfully engaged the liberal Democratic base and elites in the issue of climate change, but he also activated strong opposition from those Americans who dislike him and his politics—intensifying the partisan divide on climate change. All three of these messengers reinforce the perception for many Americans that climate change is "their" issue, not "my" issue. Most Americans have not yet seen people like themselves demanding climate change action.

But climate change threatens the life-support systems all human beings, human societies, and other species depend on. This recognition has led to the emergence of diverse new voices also demanding action, including business, faith, and military leaders, media organizations, artists, minority groups, doctors, lawyers, children, parents, grandparents, and every other sector of society.

It is critical to organize and amplify these new voices. Beyond their own political, social, and cultural power, their participation communicates to the silent majority that people other than scientists, environmentalists, and liberals care about climate change. Diverse Americans are starting to see and hear from people who look like them, dress like them, talk like them, and share their values, who are now saying climate change is "our" issue too. This mental shift—from perceiving climate change as "their" issue to "our" and ultimately "my" issue—helps build public will for policy action. That public will can then be mobilized when policy windows open at the local, state, national, or international levels.

## MOTIVATIONS TO REDUCE GLOBAL WARMING

Research has also found that different groups are motivated to reduce global warming for different reasons. Building public will among different audiences can thus benefit from tailored engagement strategies. Another *Climate Change in the American Mind* survey conducted by Yale and George Mason Universities asked respondents to identify their three most important reasons for reducing global warming.[13] The Alarmed, Concerned, and Cautious were all most likely to cite providing a better life for our children and grandchildren, saving many plant and animal species from extinction, and preventing the destruction of most life on the planet. The Disengaged and Doubtful also prioritized providing a better life for our children and grandchildren, but then diverged. The Disengaged prioritized protecting God's creation and improving people's health. The Doubtful prioritized protecting God's creation and freeing the United States from dependence on foreign oil. Finally, the Dismissive did not support any reason strongly but most frequently cited freeing the United States from dependence on foreign oil, protecting God's creation, and improving national security as reasons to reduce global warming.

## BARRIERS TO CONTACTING ELECTED OFFICIALS

The Six Americas each face a different set of barriers to contacting elected officials—one critical expression of public will for climate change action (among others). Most people say that the primary reason why they have never contacted an elected official is because no one has ever asked them to. Alarmed Americans are already very worried and motivated to act, but many feel relatively isolated and alone, and have never been contacted by a group working on climate change and asked to express their concerns to their elected officials.

Political fatalism is another important barrier—the belief that elected officials do not listen to their constituents. This perception highlights the importance of building a shared sense of collective efficacy, especially among the Alarmed. Climate change organizers must help the Alarmed understand that they can contact elected officials, that it is easy to do, especially with other people, and most importantly, that taking action can make a difference.[14] Individuals need to understand that working together, as part of an organization or movement, greatly increases their impact on the policymaking process.

Not knowing which elected officials to contact also constrains political engagement. This simple informational barrier is easily overcome when people join grassroots organizations. Grassroots organizations can also help activists overcome another common barrier: not knowing what to say to elected officials. In addition, many people do not self-identify as activists, so contacting elected officials can seem out of character. Membership in an advocacy organization helps overcome this barrier as well. Individuals join a group of people united in a common cause, where members teach and support each other to take actions that may feel uncomfortable at first but soon become part of a new group norm and shared identity as activists.[15]

## DISCUSSION

Engaged citizens, organized issue publics, and advocacy coalitions can build public and political will for climate change action. These groups will be vital to the achievement of strong and sustained climate change policies. While many organizations with professional staff advocate for such policies, relatively few find, recruit, train, and deploy active citizens as a means of political power. Instead, many environmental groups focus on legal challenges, policy development, economic analysis, or professional lobbying of elected officials. These are all critical functions of a robust climate movement, but relatively few environmental or other groups focus on developing citizen activists. Citizen's Climate Lobby, the Sierra Club's Beyond Coal campaign, 350.org, the Sunrise Movement, and some state and local-based organizations are a few examples of groups that have made citizen organizing a core part of their DNA.

Building a powerful issue public, with political muscle, requires a different kind of organization. It necessitates different strategies and tactics: taking advantage of twenty-first-century data-driven tools to find Alarmed citizens; connecting them to organizations devoted to developing and amplifying citizen voices and power (not just fund-raising or petition-signing), also known as "deep organizing"[16]; building a shared sense of collective efficacy through wins big and small; and investing in sustained power building so the movement is ready to act when policy windows open.

Ultimately, advocates must shift the political climate of climate change. Climate change itself provides an analogy—as the planet warms, extreme events become more frequent and severe. Similarly, as the climate movement shifts the political climate of climate change in a positive direction, the movement will win more frequently and the policy wins will go further and be less vulnerable to electoral swings. As the climate itself shifts in an ever-more dangerous direction, it will become ever more imperative that advocates build public and political will—shifting the political climate toward more ambitious climate change action.

## NOTES

1. Connie Roser-Renouf et al., "The Consumer as Climate Activist," *International Journal of Communication* 10 (2016): 4760.
2. David Ockwell, Lorraine Whitmarsh, and Saffron O'Neill, "Reorienting Climate Change Communication for Effective Mitigation: Forcing People to Be Green or Fostering Grass-Roots Engagement?," *Science Communication* 30, no. 3 (2009): 305–27.
3. Eric D. Raile et al., "Defining Public Will," *Politics and Policy* 42, no. 1 (2014): 105.
4. Lori Ann Post, Amber N. W. Raile, and Eric D. Raile, "Defining Political Will," *Politics and Policy* 38, no. 4 (2010): 653–76.
5. Jon A. Krosnick, "Government Policy and Citizen Passion: A Study of Issue Publics in Contemporary America," *Political Behavior* 12, no. 1 (1990): 59–92.
6. Hank Jenkins-Smith and Paul Sabatier, "Evaluating the Advocacy Coalition Framework," *Journal of Public Policy* 14, no. 2 (1994): 175–203.
7. Roger Karapin, *Political Opportunities for Climate Policy: California, New York, and the Federal Government* (Cambridge: Cambridge University Press, 2016), 62.
8. Karapin, *Political Opportunities*, 62.

9. Edward W. Maibach et al., "Identifying Like-Minded Audiences for Global Warming Public Engagement Campaigns: An Audience Segmentation Analysis and Tool Development," *PloS One* 6, no. 3 (2011): e17571.
10. Anthony Leiserowitz et al., *Climate Change in the American Mind* (New Haven, CT: Yale Program on Climate Change Communication, March 2018).
11. Paul Cairney, "Paul A. Sabatier, 'An Advocacy Coalition Framework of Policy Change and the Role of Policy-Oriented Learning Therein,'" in *The Oxford Handbook of Classics in Public Policy and Administration*, ed. Martin Lodge, Edward C. Page, and Steven J, Balla (Oxford: Oxford University Press, 2015), 484–97.
12. Robert J. Brulle, "Institutionalizing Delay: Foundation Funding and the Creation of U.S. Climate Change Counter-Movement Organizations," *Climatic Change* 122, no. 4 (2013): 681–94, https://doi.org/10.1007/s10584-013-1018-7.
13. Anthony Leiserowitz et al., *Climate Change in the American Mind* (New Haven, CT: Yale Program on Climate Change Communication, May 2017).
14. Connie Roser-Renouf et al., "The Genesis of Climate Change Activism: From Key Beliefs to Political Action," *Climatic Change* 125, no. 2 (2014): 163–78.
15. Hahrie Han, *How Organizations Develop Activists* (Oxford: Oxford University Press, 2014).
16. Jane F. McAlevey, *No Shortcuts: Organizing for Power in the New Gilded Age* (Oxford: Oxford University Press, 2018).

# Broadening Action on Climate Change

## THE PARIS AGREEMENT CANNOT DO IT ALONE

Susan Biniaz

THE 2015 PARIS AGREEMENT on climate change represents a significant milestone in the world's attempts to address the build-up of greenhouse gases in the atmosphere.[1] However, the Agreement cannot meet the enormity of the challenge on its own. It needs the help of other international agreements and institutions, both to remove potential obstacles to climate change action and to take affirmative steps to promote it.

To date, the help has been uneven. In this regard, we need a "climate change SWAT team" composed of practitioners, academics, and others with broad international law expertise. It could be convened by a national government, a think tank, an academic institution, or a U.N. body, or operate as an independent ad hoc group. It should conduct a full evaluation of international agreements and institutions, analyzing what is needed from each in order to better align international law and policy with the Paris Agreement's goals, as well as the challenges to achieving it.

### WHAT IS THE CLIMATE CHANGE CHALLENGE, IN BRIEF?

The Intergovernmental Panel on Climate Change's Special Report "Global Warming of 1.5° C," released in 2018, makes even clearer what was already clear: emissions from human activities are contributing to climate change and, even if warming could be limited to 1.5 degrees Celsius above pre-industrial levels (a daunting task), there would be significant negative impacts.[2] At higher degrees of warming, such as 2 degrees Celsius, the impacts related to human health, food, water, sea level rise, and species loss could be devastating.

If global emissions were on track to limit warming to either of these temperature goals, there would still be ample cause for alarm. However, emissions are currently not even close to such a trajectory; current policies put the predicted warming above 3 degrees Celsius. Avoiding the worst impacts will require, among other things, a massive transition from fossil to non-fossil energy, as well as the large-scale removal of carbon from the atmosphere.[3]

## WON'T THE PARIS AGREEMENT TAKE CARE OF IT?

The Paris Agreement can make a substantial contribution to addressing the climate change challenge. It aims to hold the global average temperature increase to "well below" 2 degrees Celsius, while pursuing efforts to limit it to 1.5 degrees Celsius. It also sets forth various means of promoting the achievement of that goal. These include requiring Parties (those countries that have joined the Agreement) to regularly communicate their self-determined emissions targets (so-called "nationally determined contributions"); providing for a "global stocktake" of collective progress every five years; creating an expectation that nationally determined contributions will increase in ambition over time; and building a strong "transparency" process that includes reporting and review of emissions, as well as progress toward meeting nationally determined contributions. The Agreement also includes two other goals: increasing the ability of Parties to adapt to adverse climate change impacts and bringing finance flows into line with low-emissions and climate-resilient development.

Theoretically, the Paris Agreement alone, through its combination of regular stocktakes, progressively ambitious nationally determined contributions, and reporting/review process, could keep us within the designated temperature goal. However, there are several reasons why this is not likely to be the case.

As a threshold matter, the *very design* of the Paris Agreement—emissions limitations that are "nationally determined," rather than negotiated or derived from a cap on global emissions—means that adequate emissions reductions depend on the will of individual Parties. In other words, there is nothing automatic about Parties' nationally determined contributions getting more ambitious over time. Parties will need to be in a position to feel confident— economically, technologically, and politically—that they can put forward, as well as implement, progressively stronger emissions targets and other measures.

The jury is still out on the viability of the Paris experiment. The first official global stocktake does not take place until 2023, with updated nationally determined contributions to follow. Thus, the extent to which nationally determined contributions will reflect greater stringency over time is unknown. Although there will be a preview of sorts in 2020 (as Parties are invited at that point to increase their ambition), it may or may not be indicative of things to come. In any event, even if Parties' nationally determined contributions were to leap progressively upward, there are several reasons why the Paris Agreement will need the help of other international agreements and institutions (also called "regimes").

First, many developing countries will need *financial assistance and capacity-building* to carry out their nationally determined contributions and, more broadly, to move toward low–greenhouse gas emissions development. Part of this funding will come from the Paris-related Green Climate Fund. But the transition cannot be achieved unless, in addition to increased levels of funding, climate change concerns are mainstreamed into all forms of assistance and investment so as to promote alignment with nationally determined contributions and climate-friendly development. The Paris Agreement recognizes this imperative and includes, as a core objective, making finance flows "consistent with a pathway towards low greenhouse gas emissions and climate-resilient development."[4] However, much of this work will need to be carried out by multilateral development banks, including the World Bank, and other institutions outside the Paris Agreement.

Second, there may be *external impediments* to implementation of the Paris Agreement. Particularly if Parties take on increasingly ambitious targets, at least some of the measures taken to achieve them are likely to be challenged under other regimes that regulate trade or investment. The Paris Agreement is not like many other environmental agreements, under which Parties' measures are multilaterally agreed. In such cases, while it might hypothetically be possible to challenge the measures in another forum (such as the World Trade Organization), most countries are unlikely to challenge a globally agreed measure. In the case of the Paris Agreement, however, measures are nationally determined—not agreed—and therefore potentially more vulnerable to challenge under the rules of other agreements. Further, unless there is greater certainty in other legal venues concerning the legality of climate-change-related measures, there may be a chilling effect on their adoption in the first place.

Third, for certain issues, where specialized expertise is required or where the issue lends itself to consideration by a sub-set of Parties, *other international fora may be more appropriate*. For example, the Paris Agreement calls for the strengthening of cooperative action on technology development and transfer. However, no one would expect an agreement to reduce or eliminate tariffs on climate-friendly goods to be negotiated under the auspices of the Paris Agreement.

Fourth, with respect to certain sectors, *other international regimes have been specifically designated* as the fora for addressing greenhouse gas emissions. In part because of the difficulty in reaching agreement on attributing aviation and maritime emissions from international bunker fuels to particular countries, the 1997 Kyoto Protocol on climate change sought the help of the International Civil Aviation Organization and the International Maritime Organization. While the Paris Agreement does not explicitly exclude such emissions from the scope of nationally determined contributions, it is generally considered that these organizations, rather than the Paris Agreement, have the responsibility to deliver on curbing those emissions.

Fifth, certain issues are so *cross-cutting* that they cry out for treatment across multiple international fora.[5] A prime example is the ocean, which is a major mitigator of climate change (for example, by absorbing heat) and also its victim (for example, by absorbing carbon dioxide, which leads to ocean acidification). The Paris process has not yet paid sufficient attention to the ocean in either regard. However, even if it were to do so, there would be a need to look to other ocean-related regimes. For example, climate change impacts on the ocean cannot be fully addressed without also addressing other stressors, such as overfishing and marine pollution. Another cross-cutting issue is "carbon removals," which the Intergovernmental Panel on Climate Change's 1.5 degree report highlights as a significant component of any pathway to a safe temperature increase. Both natural removals (for example, forests) and artificial removals (for example, direct carbon capture), if implemented at sufficient scale, are bound to implicate other international regimes. The prospect of solar radiation management by humans would do so in the extreme.

Beyond the temperature goal, the Paris Agreement's goal regarding *adaptation and resilience* to adverse climate change impacts is difficult to carry out in a Paris vacuum, as so many other international fields are affected. For example, climate change impacts on human populations raise migration and security issues. The Paris outcome specifically calls for involving outside organizations in making recommendations regarding climate-change-related displacement. Further, sea level rise raises both legal and policy issues regarding the law of the sea, including the implications for previously established maritime zones and maritime boundaries.[6]

Thus, while the Paris Agreement is an indispensable tool in the arsenal, it cannot be the only one. It requires the help of other international regimes, which brings us to our SWAT team's first task.

> SWAT Team Task #1: Complete an inventory of the ways in which the Paris Agreement needs assistance from other international agreements and institutions.

## SO, ARE OTHER REGIMES HELPING OUT?

Not surprisingly, other environmental agreements have been most responsive to the climate change challenge. Most significantly, Parties to the Montreal Protocol, which generally addresses substances that deplete the ozone layer, adopted an amendment to control the production and consumption of hydrofluorocarbons. Hydrofluorocarbons are substitutes for ozone-depleting substances but are also potent greenhouse gases. The 2016 Kigali Amendment to the Protocol, on hydrofluorocarbons, is said to have the potential to spare the world up to half a degree Celsius of warming by the end of the century.

Parties to the London Protocol have also responded, specifically in relation to ways in which the ocean might be used to mitigate climate change. The Protocol prohibits ocean dumping of a substance unless it is specifically allowed. Because of the potential to store carbon dioxide in geological formations below the ocean floor to prevent its release into the atmosphere, the Parties adopted an amendment in 2006 to permit such storage, while addressing the risk of possible carbon dioxide leakage into the marine environment.

Parties to the Convention on Biological Diversity have adopted numerous decisions reflecting their awareness of climate-biodiversity links. Like the ocean, biodiversity has a two-way relationship with climate change. Climate change impacts drive biodiversity loss; at the same time, biodiversity conservation can reduce carbon emissions (such as from deforestation) and reduce climate change impacts (such as conserved mangroves impeding flooding). Thus, certain conservation actions pursuant to the Convention, even if taken for other reasons, can further the Paris goals. At the same time, the Parties have urged a broad ban on climate-change-related geo-engineering activities that may affect biodiversity unless and until numerous conditions have been met; in so doing, they have arguably helped delegitimize geo-engineering as a potential means of addressing climate change.

Other groups have helped as well. The United Nations Environment Programme engages in extensive climate-change-related work—for example, capacity-building to help developing countries address climate change issues and periodic reports analyzing the "gap" between current efforts and what is needed. The Climate and Clean Air Coalition has a particular emphasis on short-lived climate forcers. Other groups have a broader mandate but include climate change issues within their cooperation, such as the Arctic Council (whose members include the eight countries with land territory above the Arctic Circle) and its activities relating to the warming effects of black carbon.

The international organizations focused on aviation and shipping have taken some steps toward addressing greenhouse gas emissions from their respective sectors:

- Within a year after the adoption of the Paris Agreement, the International Civil Aviation Organization adopted a global market-based scheme to address greenhouse gas emissions from international aviation. The Carbon Offsetting and Reduction Scheme for International Aviation (also called CORSIA) provides for the aviation sector to offset its international carbon dioxide emissions above 2020 levels by acquiring credits from outside the aviation sector. The scheme complements a larger basket of measures designed to achieve the goal of carbon-neutral growth from 2020.

- In the case of shipping, the International Maritime Organization had previously adopted regulations on emissions of air pollutants from ships, as well as mandatory energy-efficiency measures to reduce emissions of greenhouse gases. In 2018, the Organization issued an "initial strategy" on the reduction—and ultimate phasing out—of greenhouse gases from ships. Expressly citing "a pathway of carbon dioxide emissions reductions consistent with the Paris Agreement temperature goals," it aims for peaking of total greenhouse gases as soon as possible and at least a 50 percent cut below 2008 levels by 2050.[7] The overall goal has not been allocated to individual countries.

From a more surprising sector, the Universal Postal Union has developed best practices for a "greener postal sector," which, among other types of sustainability, encourages postal services around the world to reduce their carbon footprints.

In terms of financial assistance to developing countries, the picture is mixed. The Green Climate Fund has had a somewhat rocky start but is starting to deliver on funding for mitigation and adaptation. However, that type of funding is a drop in the bucket compared to the overall financial flows that need to be "greened." There the progress has been slower, with high-level climate-friendly policies not always reflected in project-level decisions. It is a hopeful sign that the multilateral development banks are starting to take into account in their development strategies recipient countries' nationally determined contributions under the Paris Agreement.[8] (It should be noted that, even if all multilateral institutions fully reflected the climate change dimension in their funding decisions, it would not necessarily affect the ability of individual donor countries to fund carbon-intensive investment, such as through China's Belt and Road Initiative; other international initiatives may need to be brought to bear on these development activities.)

In short, while there has been some responsiveness to the challenge beyond the climate change regime itself (and this is not an exhaustive list), it has been welcome but limited, particularly in the economic realm.

> SWAT Team Task #2: Assess the steps being taken under other international agreements and institutions to support the Paris Agreement and climate change action more generally.

### WHAT COULD OTHER INTERNATIONAL REGIMES BE DOING?

Ideally, each regime would be identifying ways it can make a contribution to the climate change cause, including by scrutinizing its rules, etc., for both negatives (potential impediments to climate change action) and positives (affirmative ways to help):

- In the case of international trade, the World Trade Organization might examine potential impediments, such as rules that could limit border carbon adjustments, subsidies for renewable energy, or standards based on process and production methods. On the affirmative side, interested countries could consider how to revive the stalled negotiations on an agreement to reduce tariffs on "green" goods, as well as undertake further efforts to reduce fossil fuel subsidies.[9]
- Parties to existing and future bilateral and regional trade agreements could consider the inclusion of climate-change-related provisions (akin to

the way many free trade agreements between the United States and other countries contain a multitude of provisions related to environmental concerns).

- Other economic agreements, including those related to investment and commodities, could be reviewed to consider the extent to which they are taking appropriate account of the need to transition to low-emissions and climate-resilient economies.
- Ocean-related regimes, including the instrument on biodiversity beyond national jurisdiction currently being negotiated at the United Nations, could consider ways in which they might promote the ocean's role in mitigating or adapting to climate change.
- Given the significant greenhouse gas emissions associated with food production, farming, and ranching, the U.N. Food and Agriculture Organization, in addition to addressing potential climate change impacts on food security, could develop sustainable agriculture strategies that offer ways to reduce emissions in various segments of the industry.
- Consistent with its mandate, the U.N. Security Council could consider potentially destabilizing impacts of climate change, including in the form of humanitarian disasters and political violence.[10]

Some of this work is happening, such as ongoing efforts of the so-called Friends of Fossil Fuel Subsidy Reform and the inclusion of Paris-specific provisions in the 2018 European Union–Japan trade agreement. To the extent it is not happening, it is important to consider the root causes. They may be informational (for example, insufficient awareness of the climate change challenge), substantive (for example, conflicts between various imperatives), political (for example, lack of will to take difficult steps), or even bureaucratic (for example, lack of coordination within individual governments between specialists in climate and other international fields).

> SWAT Team Task #3: Identify the range of steps not yet taken that could be taken under various international agreements and institutions to support the Paris Agreement and climate change action, as well as to consider, in each case, the best means of promoting such steps in light of the underlying reasons for insufficient action to date.

## WHAT ABOUT NON-STATE ACTORS?

No inventory of support for the Paris Agreement's goals would be complete without acknowledging the active engagement of actors beyond countries.

Cities, states, companies, and others are making a surprisingly strong contribution to climate change efforts.

The Paris Agreement, while traditional in restricting formal adherence to States and regional economic integration organizations like the European Union, broke new ground in its emphasis on the engagement of what it calls "non-Party stakeholders." Beyond the "NAZCA portal," which provides a platform for the reflection of non-Party stakeholder commitments and other preexisting efforts (such as the Global Covenant of Mayors), the Paris Conference launched various initiatives to broaden the nature of stakeholder interaction with the process.

In the United States, cities, states, and companies were already undertaking climate change commitments before President Trump's 2017 announcement of intended U.S. withdrawal from the Paris Agreement.[11] However, that announcement created an explosion in U.S. non-State actor engagement. Almost instantly, a group of U.S. states mobilized to create the United States Climate Alliance, committed to the Agreement and the U.S. emissions target.[12] The "We Are Still In" coalition also erupted, comprising a wide range of pro–Paris Agreement stakeholders. In 2018, California hosted the Global Climate Action Summit, which galvanized an impressive array of commitments from states, regions, cities, businesses, investors, and others from around the world.

In some realms, non-Party stakeholders are arguably ahead of international agreements and institutions (for example, some private investors are applying greener standards than multilateral development banks, and some shipping companies are moving beyond International Maritime Organization emissions standards). Given the likely challenges associated with prompting additional action from many of the regimes mentioned above, particularly at a time when U.S. climate change leadership is lacking, it will be important to encourage as much supportive stakeholder action as possible.

> SWAT Team Task #4: Identify ways in which stakeholders can be supportive of the Paris Agreement goals, whether through engagement under the Paris Agreement or through support for the climate-change-related action of other international agreements and institutions.

It is important that we prepare now for what a future full court press on climate change would look like, should greater political will emerge to maximize the use of international agreements and institutions in all relevant fields. In some cases, this preparation may involve assessing what is needed and, in others, assessing how to mobilize support for what we already know must be done.

**NOTES**

1. "Paris Agreement," United Nations Framework Convention on Climate Change, accessed January 15, 2019, https://unfccc.int/files/meetings/paris_nov_2015/application/pdf/paris_agreement_english_.pdf.
2. "Special Report: Global Warming of 1.5°C," Intergovernmental Panel on Climate Change, accessed January 15, 2019, http://www.ipcc.ch/report/sr15/.
3. Elizabeth Kolbert, "Can Carbon-Dioxide Removal Save the World?," *New Yorker*, November 13, 2017, https://www.newyorker.com/magazine/2017/11/20/can-carbon-dioxide-removal-save-the-world.
4. "Paris Agreement," Article 2.1(c).
5. "Climate Change and the Ocean," Ocean Conservancy, accessed January 3, 2019, https://oceanconservancy.org/climate/.
6. "Sea-Level Rise in Relation to International Law," United Nations, accessed January 15, 2019, http://legal.un.org/ilc/reports/2018/english/annex_B.pdf.
7. "Initial IMO Strategy on Reduction of GHG Emissions from Ships," Resolution MEPC. 304 (72), April 13, 2018, ¶3.1.3.
8. "Toward Paris Alignment: How the Multilateral Development Banks Can Better Support the Paris Agreement," World Resources Institute, accessed January 15, 2019, https://www.wri.org/publication/toward-paris-alignment.
9. "Making the International Trade System Work for Climate Change," Climate Strategies, accessed January 15, 2019, https://climatestrategies.org/projects/making-the-international-trading-system-work-for-climate-change/.
10. Shirley V. Scott and Charlotte Ku, eds., *Climate Change and the UN Security Council* (Cheltenham, UK: Edward Elgar Publishing, 2018).
11. "We Mean Business," We Mean Business Coalition, accessed January 3, 2019, http://www.wemeanbusinesscoalition.org/.
12. "States United for Climate Action," U.S. Climate Alliance, accessed January 3, 2019, https://www.usclimatealliance.org/.

# Helping Kids Stand Up for Their Rights

## THE ROLE OF CLIMATE CHANGE LITIGATION

Paul Rink

GLOBAL FOCUS ON THE NEED for action to address climate change has emerged as a critical sustainability imperative, but long-established environmental strategies seem incapable of delivering change at the scale and pace required. Luckily, the modern environmental movement has proven itself adaptable, evolving over time to accommodate various social, political, and economic contexts. In keeping with this tradition of change, now is the time for climate change advocacy to take a hard *rights* turn,[1] emphasizing novel, rights-based strategies that can reinforce traditional environmental approaches. In particular, climate change litigation centered on the rights of young people can focus the climate change debate on those who have the most to lose: future generations.

### FUNDAMENTAL RIGHTS AND CLIMATE CHANGE LITIGATION
Significant precedent already exists for rights-based environmental advocacy worldwide. Over 75 percent of national constitutions contain some reference to environmental rights or responsibilities, although the extent of these provisions varies.[2] The Belizean Constitution, for instance, briefly lists the environment as one of many things that require policy protection, whereas the Brazilian Constitution waxes poetic about each major biome within the country.[3]

In addition to constitutional rights, recognition of the connection between human rights and climate change continues to grow globally. The 2015

Paris Agreement on climate change specifically refers to human rights in the preamble, albeit briefly.[4] The U.N. Special Rapporteur on Human Rights and the Environment has more emphatically stated that "climate change clearly and adversely impacts the right to life."[5] National governments are also beginning to officially acknowledge that climate change will "have negative effects across the spectrum of recognized international human rights norms," as the Canadian government puts it.[6]

In response, citizens around the world have pursued climate change litigation to uphold their fundamental rights. The Urgenda Foundation filed a climate change case in 2015 claiming that the Dutch government's existing greenhouse gas emissions reduction target was not sufficient to comply with constitutional or international human rights law. The Hague Court of Appeals ultimately ruled in favor of the Urgenda Foundation, determining that the Dutch national government failed to comply with European Court of Human Rights Article 2 (the right to life) and Article 8 (the right to private life, family life, home, and correspondence).[7] Similarly, a Pakistan appellate court determined that "the delay and lethargy of [Pakistan] in implementing the [National Climate Policy and Framework] offend the fundamental rights of the citizens."[8] Comparable claims have been filed recently in both Ireland and Germany.

Citizen responses have expanded beyond litigation as well. For example, the Philippines Human Rights Commission is currently conducting an inquiry into the responsibility of oil and gas companies for violations of human rights that have resulted from climate change impacts. The Northern Institute for Environmental and Minority Law also released a report about how climate change has impacted the human rights of indigenous people and women throughout the Arctic region.[9]

## PROPERTY RIGHTS AND CLIMATE CHANGE LITIGATION

Such constitutional and human-rights-based advocacy often focuses on "positive" rights (those rights that a government is obligated to actively ensure for its citizens). Yet, although positive-rights-based environmental litigation has seen some success (most notably in the Urgenda case), courts are often reluctant to impose government requirements to uphold positive rights. Some judges believe that such rulings violate separation of powers doctrine by asserting judicial control over executive action. For this reason, positive rights advocacy may be more effective outside the court system in certain contexts.

The U.S. legal system is arguably one of those contexts. There are relatively limited ways to pursue positive-rights-based environmental advocacy in U.S. courtrooms. Notably, the U.S. Constitution does not contain any provisions explicitly protecting environmental rights. In addition, recent judicial decisions in the United States have cut back on pathways to file international human-rights-based claims.[10]

These restrictions do not mean that the United States has been left out of the environmental rights conversation completely, however. In particular, some U.S. citizens have used their property rights to push back against the negative impacts they have experienced due to climate change. Most notably, the native village of Kivalina in Alaska filed a lawsuit in 2008 against Exxon-Mobil, attempting to hold the fossil fuel company liable for monetary damages. Kivalina claimed that ExxonMobil was directly responsible for causing climate-change-related losses stemming from flooding damages to their coastal property.[11]

Lawyers in such cases have historically struggled to convince judges that fossil-fuel-intensive companies should be held liable for environmental and property damages that result from climate change. As the environmental law professor Douglas Kysar points out, the U.S. system of *tort law*—in which someone harmed sues his or her alleged "harmer" for monetary compensation—is ill equipped to handle "the magnitude and the complexity of the climate change conundrum."[12] Kysar outlines many reasons why tort law has trouble accommodating climate change claims, including the difficulty in pinning down any one harmer as the cause of climate change, as well as the difficulty in determining how much climate change contributes to harms like a once-in-a-lifetime flood.

Thus, it is not surprising that the Ninth Circuit Court of Appeals ultimately ruled in favor of the fossil fuel company in *Kivalina v. ExxonMobil*. Nevertheless, the novel nature of Kivalina's claim has fostered other creative property-rights-based climate claims around the world. Perhaps most famously, a Peruvian farmer is suing German energy company RWE (Europe's largest carbon emitter) for its part in causing the glaciers on which he lives to recede.[13]

Such cases may seem far-fetched, but similar arguments have seen some success. In the United States, claims of coastal property damage were crucial in establishing Massachusetts's standing to sue the U.S. government in 2007 for failing to regulate carbon dioxide emissions that contributed to climate change.[14] In addition, more recent property-rights-based climate change claims have incorporated lessons from the experiences of *Kivalina* and other suits when tailoring their litigation strategy (for example, by filing cases in state courts rather than federal court so as to potentially have fifty bites at the same apple).[15] Such claims have also been able to capitalize on recent developments in climate change science, including an increasing ability to attribute greenhouse gas emissions to particular companies[16] and to attribute the probability and severity of certain extreme weather events directly to climate change.[17]

## YOUTH AND CLIMATE CHANGE LITIGATION

Whether asserting property-rights-based claims (as has been common in the United States) or human-rights-based claims and constitutional environmental-rights-based claims (as has been common in other countries), climate change cases with youth plaintiffs have been able to harness the advantage of a compelling ethical narrative. It is hard to deny that all people alive today have a moral obligation to respect the rights of young people and unborn generations to an atmosphere that can support their future existence. Incorporating this ethical duty into climate change lawsuits can bolster legal claims that fossil fuel companies and governments are denying the fundamental rights of both current and future people. In fact, many countries have explicit legal mandates, in their respective constitutions or otherwise, to respect the rights of future generations. Based on these mandates, a global initiative of youth-versus-government climate change litigation has emerged in recent years. Lawsuits brought by young plaintiffs in Colombia, Pakistan, India, and Canada have demanded climate change justice, taking advantage of their respective countries' intergenerational legal provisions.

Although the U.S. Constitution does not have any explicit intergenerational ethics provision, youth plaintiffs can and have filed creative constitutional-rights-based climate change cases. For example, in *Juliana v. U.S.*, twenty-one youth plaintiffs filed a lawsuit against the U.S. government claiming that they have a right to resources that are shared by all U.S. citizens—such as fresh water—and that the federal government is responsible for maintaining these resources under a legal doctrine called "the public trust." The *Juliana* plaintiffs assert that current and past government officials have failed to uphold their responsibility to ensure the public trust resource of a clean atmosphere for the youngest citizens who will live to see increasingly severe impacts from climate change.[18]

The youth plaintiffs also argue that the federal government violated their constitutional rights to life, liberty, and property by actively perpetuating a fossil-fuel-based energy system that causes climate change. More specifically, the youth allege that the U.S. government knew about the connection between fossil fuels and the severe negative effects of climate change as far back as the 1970s, but it nevertheless continues to allow and promote oil and gas extraction to this day. Because those negative effects are already restricting their liberties and damaging their property and may eventually shorten their lives, the youth plaintiffs argue that the U.S. government's affirmative actions have detrimentally affected their fundamental constitutional rights.[19]

It is important to note that the *Juliana* plaintiffs' constitutional claims reference "negative rights" rather than the previously mentioned "positive rights." Negative rights are those that the government is not permitted to disrupt (for example, a right to free speech). Enforcing negative rights involves mandating that the government *stop* doing something rather than start doing something. Thus, negative rights are often more manageable within the judiciary.

Perhaps this strategy to focus on negative rights contributed to the *Juliana* plaintiffs' preliminary success even before officially going to trial. In her denial of the government's pre-trial motion to dismiss the case, District Court Judge Ann Aiken made it clear that she had "no doubt that the right to a climate system capable of sustaining human life is fundamental to a free and ordered society."[20] In other words, Aiken asserted that the U.S. Constitution implicitly contains a right to a stable climate system even though it does not mention climate or the environment once. By guaranteeing other rights that can be upheld only in the presence of a healthy climate regime, the Constitution prevents the U.S. government from taking actions that unduly disrupt that regime. Regardless of the eventual outcome of the case, injecting the idea that constitutional rights indirectly protect environmental rights into legal discourse represents an immense victory for the *Juliana* plaintiffs.

Similarly, "youth-versus-government" plaintiffs such as those in *Juliana v. U.S.* arguably present compelling arguments regarding "standing," that is, the right to have their day in court. In comparison, traditional claims against private entities for climate-change-based damages have struggled to argue the three elements of standing: (1) injury, (2) causation, and (3) redressability. Such private injury-based claims often have difficulty demonstrating a private entity is specifically responsible for past climate-change-based injuries or that those injuries can be adequately addressed by any remedy that a court can provide.

Youth-versus-government cases, on the other hand, better match the scale of the injury to the behavior of the defendant. In particular, because these youth plaintiffs are suing the federal government for its affirmative actions in supporting the fossil fuel industry, they present a causation argument that is system-wide rather than focused on a particular polluter. In other words, these youth plaintiffs are attempting to hold the federal government responsible as the "gatekeeper" for the injuries caused by the stampede of fossil fuel "bulls" it has unleashed, rather than seeking liability against any particular bull or group of bulls.

Additionally, the federal government as a defendant is much more likely to be able to meaningfully address climate change than any particular fossil fuel company if commanded to do so as a remedy by a judge. Granted, such remedies may raise objections regarding whether it is the judicial branch's proper role to impose system-wide changes to national energy policy. Yet, significant precedent exists for such broad remedial action, most famously in *Brown v. Board of Education*, the civil rights case that deemed school segregation unconstitutional.[21] In addition, strategic youth plaintiffs, including those in *Juliana v. U.S.*, often incorporate more narrow remedies along with their far-reaching requests for relief in case they find themselves before a judge heavily resistant to imposing massive, economy-wide disruption.

In relation to the injury element of standing, such youth-driven climate cases are able to capitalize on the fact that young people generally present compelling rights-based, moral claims in the context of climate change. In addition to experiencing current impacts, youth will continue to endure harm from climate change long into the future. Connecting young people's present-day injuries with those that they will feel throughout their lives paints a fuller picture for courtroom judges of the damage caused by climate change and how the resulting injuries undermine intergenerational climate change justice. In contrast, past climate change cases focused on property damage have typically been limited to considerations of negative impacts that have already occurred. As a result, courts have often ruled against such claims because, in addition to the previously discussed climate change attribution difficulties, the requested financial remedies do not match the global scale of the climate change problem.[22] Youth-based claims can get around this problem by emphasizing the immense scale of climate change impacts both in terms of increasing severity over time and in terms of the fundamental nature of the rights under threat. In so doing, cases like *Juliana v. U.S.* are transforming climate change advocacy from a cost-benefit consideration of environmental damage to a constitutional question of fundamental rights.

## PUBLIC OPINION AND YOUTH-BASED CLIMATE CHANGE LITIGATION

Such a shift toward fundamental climate rights for youth not only provides better framing for climate change litigation but also helps reframe climate change in the court of public opinion. Just like judges, U.S. citizens are more likely to grasp the scale of the climate change problem when considering far-reaching intergenerational impacts that will affect their own loved ones for decades to come. By developing a public-facing campaign that focuses more on impacted children and less on polar bears or present-day natural disasters, litigation can make climate change less abstract for many people. As the legal scholar Grace Nosek points out, climate change litigation that highlights the "vivid, gripping" risks to the future livelihoods of children can help overcome the tendency of people to "underestimate the risks of less visceral or emotionally charged dangers, like climate change."[23] Thus, not only can youth-based climate change litigation make the threat of climate change more legally tractable, but it can also potentially lead to increased public understanding of the issue. The power of such youth-centered litigation is especially potent in conjunction with recent youth-led climate activism ranging from student strikes in Sweden and France to the work of youth-run organizations such as the Sunrise Movement, Zero Hour, and the fossil fuel divestment campaigns that have swept college campuses.

Of course, given the partisan nature of the climate change issue in the United States, there are many people who may be resistant to climate change action no matter how the threat is framed. At the same time, even die-hard deniers of anthropogenic climate change may be more open to learning about and acting on climate change if they see it as a threat to their children's future. Moreover, because climate rights are not easily pigeonholed into a particular ideological frame, they may help break through deadlocked U.S. environmental debates. Unlike regulatory or business-minded environmental strategies, rights-based strategies are not easily segmented into a pro- or anti-business agenda. Solutions of all sorts are possible and encouraged as long as they respect each person's legally recognized rights.

Regardless, the fact that climate change litigation is increasing in the United States and across the globe sends a broader signal to decision makers throughout society. According to the Quartz reporter Ephrat Levni, youth-based climate change lawsuits have the power to "creat[e] new precedents that bolster activism—and may . . . alter the way governments think about their responsibility to protect citizens against climate change."[24] Such shifts in thinking can lead to stronger climate change regulations and better business practices from forward-thinking companies.

At a more basic level, youth-oriented rights-based litigation focuses the climate change conversation on fundamental first principles. Why do we, as humans, care about the environment? Primarily because it provides us with services that are essential for the daily comportment of our lives—benefits that deserve respect and deference, according to legal systems around the world. Pointing to the importance of preserving rights to these life-giving benefits (whether such rights are based on property ownership, national constitutions, or internationally recognized human rights) can offer a line of environmental advocacy that may be more convincing than traditional appeals to Mother Nature. Similarly, rights-based arguments can be com-pelling when forcing nations to answer to their greenhouse gas emissions reduction commitments, as demonstrated in the previously mentioned Urgenda case.

In the same manner, rights-based advocacy can be used in conjunction with business-friendly environmental policies that aim to incentivize sustain-ability within the marketplace. By emphasizing rights-based arguments, en-vironmentalists can frame business-environment win-win scenarios as triple wins for business, the environment, and rights preservation. For example, encouraging companies to increase their operational energy efficiency can be marketed as a strategy that saves costs, protects the environment through pol-lution reduction, and helps ensure people's right to a clean, stable atmosphere. In situations where such triple wins are not possible, an emphasis on people's rights will ensure that they remain a top priority and are not side-stepped for the sake of profit margins. Of course, whether businesses are helping or harming human rights in any given scenario is typically a complex, context-dependent question. Nevertheless, if wielded effectively, rights-based climate advocacy tools can be leveraged to achieve improvements in corporate social responsibility even in circumstances where the full extent and gravity of human rights impacts remains unclear.

Climate change has had and will continue to have a negative impact on human rights, constitutional rights, and property rights around the world. It is important to remind everyone of this reality when promoting climate change action. Framing climate change in terms of the rights it threatens can help sharpen public focus on the problem and, particularly, the intergenerational equity considerations at issue. On the other hand, if we neglect to keep these climate change threats at the forefront of our minds, we will almost certainly fail to rise to the challenge with the required urgency and dedication. Young people standing up in court for their right to a viable future may be our best chance to ensure that we do not fall into this trap and instead fight hard to avoid the worst climate change impacts.

## NOTES

The author has conducted legal research and writing for *Juliana v. U.S.* for academic credit at the Yale Law School and as a summer legal fellow for Our Children's Trust, an organization representing the plaintiffs.

1. Jacqueline Peel and Hari M. Osofsky, "A Rights Turn in Climate Change Litigation?," *Transnational Environmental Law* 7, no. 1 (March 2018): 37.
2. David R. Boyd, "The Status of Constitutional Protection for the Environment in Other Nations," *David Suzuki Foundation*, November 2013, 6.
3. Belizean Constitution preamble (e), "Belize's Constitution of 1981 with Amendments through 2011," 2011, https://www.constituteproject.org/constitution/Belize_2011.pdf ?lang=en; Brazilian Constitution, "Chapter VI: The Environment," Article 225 §4, 2014, https://www.constituteproject.org/constitution/Brazil_2014.pdf.
4. Paris Agreement, "Preamble," United Nations, 2015, https://unfccc.int/sites/default /files/english_paris_agreement.pdf.
5. David R. Boyd, "Mandate of the Special Rapporteur on Human Rights and the Environment," *United Nations Human Rights Special Procedures*, October 25, 2018, 13.
6. Government of Canada, Global Affairs Canada, "Climate Change and Human Rights," GAC, June 5, 2017, https://international.gc.ca/world-monde/issues _development-enjeux_developpement/human_rights-droits_homme/climate _rights-droits_climat.aspx?lang=eng.
7. Gerechtshof Den Haag, ECLI:NL:GHDHA:2018:2610 (Urgenda Foundation/Netherlands) (Neth.) ¶76, September 10, 2018, https://www.urgenda.nl/wp-content/uploads /ECLI_NL_GHDHA_2018_2610.pdf.
8. Ashgar Leghari v. Federation of Pakistan, Case No. W.P. No. 25501/2015 p. 3 (Pakistan Lahore High Court, September 4, 2015), https://elaw.org/PK_AshgarLeghari_v _Pakistan_2015.
9. Tahnee Prior et al., "Addressing Climate Vulnerability: Promoting the Participatory Rights of Indigenous Peoples and Women through Finnish Foreign Policy," *Juridica Lapponica* 38 (2013).
10. Kiobel v. Royal Dutch Petroleum Co., 621 F.3d 111, 118 (C.A.2 (N.Y.), 2010); Medellin v. Texas, 128 S.Ct. 1346, 1351 (U.S.Tex., 2008).
11. Kivalina v. ExxonMobil, 11649–50, United States Court of Appeals for the Ninth Circuit, http://cdn.ca9.uscourts.gov/datastore/opinions/2012/09/25/09-17490.pdf.
12. Douglas A. Kysar, "What Climate Change Can Do about Tort Law," *Environmental Law* 41, no. 1 (2011): 3.

13. Agence France-Presse, "Peruvian Farmer Sues German Energy Giant for Contributing to Climate Change," *The Guardian*, November 13, 2017, https://www.theguardian.com/world/2017/nov/14/peruvian-farmer-sues-german-energy-giant-rwe-climate-change.

14. Massachusetts v. EPA, 549 U.S. 497 (United States Supreme Court, 2007).

15. John O'Brien, "Others 0 for 2, but Rhode Island Joining Climate Change Litigation Anyway," *Forbes*, July 3, 2018, https://www.forbes.com/sites/legalnewsline/2018/07/03/others-0-for-2-but-rhode-island-joining-climate-change-litigation-anyway/.

16. Richard Heede, "Tracing Anthropogenic Carbon Dioxide and Methane Emissions to Fossil Fuel and Cement Producers, 1854–2010," *Climate Change* 122, nos. 1–2 (January 2014): 229 (attributing 63 percent of worldwide carbon dioxide and methane emissions between 1751 and 2010 to only ninety companies).

17. National Academies of Sciences, Engineering, and Medicine, *Attribution of Extreme Weather Events in the Context of Climate Change* (Washington, DC: National Academies Press, 2016), https://doi.org/10.17226/21852.

18. First Amended Complaint for Declaratory and Injunctive Relief at 97-98, Juliana v. U.S., 217 F. Supp. 3d 1224 (D. Or. 2016) (No. 7).

19. First Amended Complaint, *Juliana*, 217 F. Supp. 3d at 90.

20. Juliana v. United States, No. 6:15-cv-01517 (Aiken, J.), 46 ELR 20175, (D.OR., 10 Nov. 2016).

21. See Brown v. Board of Education, 347 U.S. 483 (1954).

22. City of Oakland v. BP P.L.C., 2018 WL 3609055 1, 15 (N.D. Cal., 2018).

23. Grace Nosek, "Climate Change Litigation and Narrative: How to Use Litigation to Tell Compelling Climate Stories," *William & Mary Environmental Law & Policy Review* 42, no. 3 (2018): 733, 788.

24. Ephrat Levni, "Kids around the World Are Suing Governments over Climate Change—and It's Working," *Quartz*, July 24, 2018, https://qz.com/1334102/kids-around-the-world-are-suing-governments-over-climate-change-and-its-working/.

# Environmental Justice for All Must Be a Human Right Enforceable in U.S. State Constitutions

Barry E. Hill

IN 1969, THE UNITED STATES CONGRESS articulated the nation's environmental policy in the National Environmental Policy Act, and the federal government steadily established, implemented, and enforced standards for the protection of human health and the environment through extensive legislation and regulations. In 1970, the U.S. Environmental Protection Agency (EPA) was established as the federal agency responsible for administering protective environmental laws and their implementing regulations related to enforcement, standard setting, monitoring, and research for the protection of human health and the environment. According to the EPA website, its primary purpose is to ensure that "all Americans are protected from significant risks to human health and the environment where they live, learn and work."[1]

But this comprehensive regulatory framework has not adequately addressed the concerns of all communities because EPA has not enforced equally the federal laws protecting human health and the environment for all communities. Indeed, the unevenness of enforcement of protective environmental laws and policies across the nation raises a salient question about how best to ensure environmental justice, which EPA defines as "the fair treatment and meaningful involvement of all people regardless of race, color, national origin, or income with respect to the development, implementation, and enforcement of environmental laws, regulations, and policies."[2] According to EPA, environmental justice, as a public policy issue, seeks to ensure that all Americans have clean water, clean land, and clean air where they live, learn, and work. As the environmental activist and author of *The Green Amendment: Securing Our Right to a Healthy Environment* Maya van Rossum observes, when it comes to protecting human health and the environment, existing environmental laws have failed us. In response, van Rossum argues for "environmental constitutionalism," which is centered on placing an environmental rights amendment in the bill of rights sections of our 50 state constitutions.[3]

## WHY ENVIRONMENTAL JUSTICE REQUIRES A CONSTITUTIONAL RIGHT TO ENVIRONMENTAL PROTECTION

In many respects, Flint, Michigan, currently serves as the poster child for environmental injustice in the United States. This predominantly African-American city continues to struggle today with the decisions made by state and local government officials that resulted in dangerous levels of lead in the drinking water of tens of thousands of children.

According to a 2016 report, EPA's inspector general concluded that inadequate drinking water treatment exposed many of Flint's residents to lead ingestion.[4] The report recounts how the problem came about: Flint had formerly bought drinking water from Detroit Water and Sewerage but turned to the Flint River as its water source in 2014. "Treated water from Detroit Water and Sewerage included a corrosion-inhibiting additive, which lined pipes to minimize the level of lead leaching into drinking water," the report said. Flint's new water treatment process did not involve this addition. Soon after, residents, whose initial concerns had been either ignored or dismissed by state officials, began informing EPA of water color and odor issues.[5] Lead was found in the water in February 2015, and in April, EPA determined that the new Flint water system was not using the additive that protected against lead leaching. Signs of lead contamination began to appear in the community, and in children's blood lead levels. Flint once again began using water from Detroit Water and Sewerage in October 2015.

Representative Dan Kildee (D), who represents Flint, said: "Drinking water is a fundamental human right. It's something that's necessary to sustain human life, and so it's hard to think of a more important priority for every level of government."[6]

The United Nations would agree with Congressman Kildee's statement. In 2010, the U.N. General Assembly declared, through a historic vote, that clean water was a fundamental human right. Resolution 64/292 states that the United Nations "recognizes the right to safe and clean drinking water and sanitation as a human right that is essential for the full enjoyment of life and all human rights."[7] The measure passed with a vote of 122 in favor to none against, with 41 abstentions. The U.S. representative was concerned, however, whether this human right was an enforceable right under international law. The United States, consequently, abstained from voting in favor of the resolution.

Access to safe and clean drinking water and sanitation has been recognized as a critical link to human health throughout the passage of time.[8] Marcus Vitruvius Pollio, a famous Roman architect and engineer, recognized this relationship as far back as the first century BC in his seminal work, *The Ten Books on Architecture*. He wrote that "water from clay pipes is much more wholesome than that which is conducted through lead pipes, because lead is found to be harmful for the reason that white lead is derived from it, and this is said to be harmful to the human system. . . . This we can exemplify from plumbers, since in them the natural colour of the body is replaced by a deep pallor. For when lead is smelted in casting, the fumes from it settle upon members, and day after day burn out and take away all the virtues of the blood from their limbs. Hence, water ought by no means to be conducted in lead pipes, if we want to have it wholesome."[9]

Thus, more than 2,000 years ago, Vitruvius realized that lead was highly toxic, and therefore poisonous, because it interfered with some of the body's basic functions. Without the benefit of modern medical technology, he was able to observe the adverse health effects of lead ingestion.

Lead can adversely affect the health of anyone, but children under age six face special hazards because their brains and nervous systems are still developing. The scientific community and public health professionals generally agree that, in low levels, lead can cause permanent harm to children, including injuries to the nervous system and kidneys, learning disabilities, attention deficit disorder, reduced intelligence, speech and behavior issues, muscle coordination problems, diminished muscle and bone growth, hearing damage, and many other issues.[10] There is chelation therapy treatment for high blood levels of lead, but there is no medical cure.

In response to the Flint water crisis, federal and state class action civil lawsuits were filed against Michigan, the state's governor, its Department of Health and Human Services, its Department of Environmental Quality, and others since, according to one complaint, the state government "made the final decision that deliberately created, increased and prolonged the hazards, threats and dangers that arose by replacing of safe drinking, washing and bathing water with a highly toxic alternative."[11] The Michigan attorney general also filed criminal charges against some state and local government officials.

But all of these civil suits and criminal charges may not be enough to address the simple fact that access to safe and clean drinking water and sanitation is not a human right protected by the U.S. federal government. It is clearly not an expressed right in the U.S. Constitution and its Bill of Rights. According to the University of Virginia professor Jonathan Z. Cannon, the U.S. Constitution is "pre-ecological."[12] Nor is there a Supreme Court decision declaring that it falls within a *penumbral right*—a right that could be derived from other rights explicitly protected in the Bill of Rights—as the Supreme Court has declared for the right to privacy or the right for same-sex couples to marry.

Moreover, in spite of Congressman Kildee's bold assertion, environmental justice is not a recognized human right in Michigan. There is no environmental rights amendment in the Michigan Constitution to help Michiganders defend their human right to safe and clean drinking water and sanitation.

## HOW ENVIRONMENTAL CONSTITUTIONALISM WORKS

The residents of Flint are not alone in facing what should be viewed as environment-related human rights violations.

The residents of rural Franklin Forks (a small, low-income, white rural community in Susquehanna County, Pennsylvania) began to notice in 2013 that the water coming out of their private household wells had turned gray. Tests found dangerous levels of methane in the water—forcing many residents to buy bottled water to drink and leaving them at the mercy of WPX Energy (the natural gas company that was fracking in pursuit of gas in the area from the Marcellus Shale formation) for non-potable water for showers and washing clothes. But the citizens of Franklin Forks had leverage that the citizens of Flint did not have: Pennsylvania citizens benefited from the protections afforded by Article I, Section 27, of the Declaration of Rights in the Pennsylvania Constitution. Section 27 reads: "The people have a right to clean air, pure water, and to the preservation of the natural, scenic, historic and esthetic values of the environment. Pennsylvania's public natural resources are the common property of all the people, including generations to come. As trustee of these resources, the Commonwealth shall conserve and maintain them for the benefit of all the people."[13]

Ultimately, WPX Energy provided water tanks for impacted residents of Franklin Forks, and the company was incentivized to take a greater level of precaution and avoid potential civil and criminal liability. Although a constitutional case did not end up being litigated, the company's recognition of Pennsylvania's constitutional environmental rights amendment undoubtedly shaped the dynamic.

In some Pennsylvania cases, the constitutional environmental rights provision has been front and center. In 2013, in the *Robinson Township v. Commonwealth of Pennsylvania* case, numerous municipalities were outraged by the speed and environmental impact of natural gas development of the nearby Marcellus Shale formation. The political subdivisions were concerned that the new state oil and gas law (Act 13) not only impacted the enforceable right to the environment for individual citizens, or "individual environmental right," that is found in the state constitution but also impacted their governmental duty to protect the environment. The environmental activist and author Maya van Rossum—as the "Delaware Riverkeeper" tasked with protecting the watershed—was one of the citizen plaintiffs in this lawsuit challenging the constitutionality of Act 13. The towns and the citizens successfully sued the state to overturn key portions of the state oil and gas law, which were found to be inconsistent with Pennsylvania's constitutionally protected individual environmental right.

In that case, the Pennsylvania Supreme Court succinctly declared: "The right to 'clean air' and 'pure water' sets plain conditions by which government must abide. We recognize that, as a practical matter, air and water quality have relative rather than absolute attributes. . . . Courts are equipped and obliged to weigh parties' competing evidence and arguments, and to issue reasoned decisions regarding constitutional compliance by the other branches of government. The benchmark for decision is the express purpose of the Environmental Rights Amendment to be a bulwark against actual or likely degradation of, *inter alia*, our air and water quality."[14]

In this moment, the Pennsylvania Supreme Court vindicated the individual citizen's environmental rights amendment that had been added to the state constitution in 1971. For more than 40 years, this constitutional provision had played a relatively minor role in the state and local governments' environmental decision-making processes. But, as a result of the *Robinson Township* decision, lower courts and appellate courts throughout the Commonwealth must now be prepared to enforce the provision. In addition to determining whether proposed state and local government actions comply with state and federal environmental laws and regulations, Pennsylvania courts may also have to determine whether those entities have complied with the individual citizen's environmental rights amendment. Again, the Pennsylvania Supreme Court determined in *Robinson Township* that "courts are equipped and obliged to weigh parties' competing evidence and arguments, and to issue reasoned decisions regarding constitutional compliance by the other branches of government."

The Pennsylvania Environmental Defense Foundation, an environmental advocacy organization, also sued the Commonwealth of Pennsylvania, challenging the constitutionality of laws that removed conservation restrictions on the use of revenue from oil and gas exploration on state forests and park lands. In 2017, in *Pennsylvania Environmental Defense Foundation v. Commonwealth of Pennsylvania,* the Pennsylvania Supreme Court held that the state government's responsibility as a trustee of the land was governed by the environmental rights amendment, and, therefore, the legislation that allowed the monies received to be used for activities beyond conservation and care for public natural resources was unconstitutional on its face.

This is environmental constitutionalism at work. Pennsylvania residents can now seek to ensure that their right to a clean, safe, and healthy environment is given the highest level of legal protection in the Commonwealth. An environmental rights amendment is an additional strategy that can be utilized to ensure environmental justice for all—not only by affected individuals and communities but also by state and local environmental regulatory agencies in their decision-making processes.

Much like in Pennsylvania, two landmark state supreme court decisions have paved the way for a broader understanding of environmental rights in Montana. In 1972, the state constitution was amended with Article II, Section 3, which reads: "All persons are born free and have certain inalienable rights. They include the right to a clean and healthy environment."[15] In 1999, in *Montana Environmental Information Center v. Department of Environmental Quality,* the Montana Supreme Court recognized a challenge to a state law by Montanan environmental activists. In accordance with an exemption in state environmental law, the Department of Environmental Quality had declined to perform a review of mining activities near the Blackfoot and Landers Fork Rivers, leading to a dangerous build-up of arsenic levels in the water. The Montana Supreme Court determined that the state law violated the environmental rights amendment providing for a clean and healthy environment, and decided in favor of the activists. The Montana Supreme Court stated:

"Our constitution does not require that dead fish float on the surface of our state's rivers and streams before its farsighted environmental protections can be invoked."[16] Two years later, the Montana Supreme Court extended this logic to include limitations on private actors by ruling, in *Cape-France Enterprises v. In re Estate of Peed,* that a private landowner could not drill a well on their own land if it would cause significant pollution of uncontaminated aquifers and risk serious public health issues.[17]

These Pennsylvania and Montana cases indicate that the inclusion of an environmental rights amendment in the state constitution allows the judiciary to protect the environment and human health from harms caused by the state government or private individuals.

## BROADENING ENFORCEMENT

Perhaps Pennsylvania and Montana can serve as models for environmental constitutionalism across the United States. In 2018, the New Jersey legislature began considering concurrent resolutions (ACR85 and SCR134) that would embed an environmental rights amendment in the state constitution—based on Article I, Section 27, of the Pennsylvania Constitution. The proposed amendment states:

(a)  Every person has a right to a clean and healthy environment, including pure water, clean air, and ecologically healthy habitats, and to the preservation of the natural, scenic, historic, and esthetic qualities of the environment. The State shall not infringe upon these rights, by action or inaction.

(b)  The State's public natural resources, among them its waters, air, flora, fauna, climate, and public lands, are the common property of all the people, including both present and future generations. The State shall serve as trustee of these resources, and shall conserve and maintain them for the benefit of all people.

(c)  This paragraph and the rights stated herein are: (1) self-executing, and (2) shall be in addition to any rights conferred by the public trust doctrine or common law.[18]

To become a law, a New Jersey constitutional amendment needs either approval by three-fifths of the Senate and Assembly or majorities in both chambers in two consecutive years, followed by a citizen referendum in which New Jersey residents must approve the amendment by a majority vote. The intensely democratic process through which most states enact constitutional amendments gives a constitutional right a certain democratic legitimacy, which gives it strength that is distinct from a private right-of-action or legislative provision.

Several other states are also serving as "laboratories of democracy"[19] with regard to constitutional environmental rights. Hawaii, Illinois, Massachusetts, New York, and Rhode Island all have constitutional provisions for a right to a clean, safe, and healthy environment.[20] The environmental rights set forth in these state constitutions function as enforceable human rights, in stark contrast to the lack of any enforceable environmental right in a state such as Michigan that I discussed above.

### LESSONS LEARNED

In sum, there must be a concerted effort to amend state constitutions to include the environmental rights of individual citizens if environmental justice is to be secured for all communities. Otherwise, environmentally overburdened communities like Flint and Franklin Forks will continue to be exposed disproportionately to environmental harms and risks.

Achieving environmental justice for all communities should not be based on the race or the socioeconomic status of the residents of any community, and those factors should not dictate the environmental risks that any American faces. Securing environmental justice for all should not be conditional. Every American is entitled to clean land, clean air, and clean water to improve their lives, protect their families, and strengthen their communities. Arguably, the best way to protect and enforce the human right to a clean, safe, and healthy environment is through the addition of an enforceable individual citizen's environmental rights amendment to the bill of rights section of every state constitution. As cases in Pennsylvania, Montana, and elsewhere have demonstrated, environmental constitutionalism works.

### NOTES

This essay draws on and builds on the author's body of other scholarship on environmental justice and the importance of state constitutions, including "Time for a New Age of Enlightenment for U.S. Environmental Law and Policy: Where Do We Go from Here?," *Environmental Law Reporter* 49, no. 4 (April 2019): 10362–84.

1. "Our Mission and What We Do," United States Environmental Protection Agency, accessed March 8, 2019, https://19january2017snapshot.epa.gov/aboutepa/our -mission-and-what-we-do_.html.

2. "Toolkit for Assessing Potential Allegations of Environmental Injustice," United States Environmental Protection Agency, accessed March 8, 2019, https://www.epa .gov/sites/production/files/2015-04/documents/toolkitej.pdf.

3. Maya van Rossum, *The Green Amendment: Securing Our Right to a Healthy Environment* (Austin, TX: Disruption Books, 2017).

4. "Management Alert: Drinking Water Contamination in Flint, Michigan, Demonstrates a Need to Clarify EPA Authority to Issue Emergency Orders to Protect the Public," U.S. Environmental Protection Agency Office of Inspector General, October 20, 2016, https://www.epa.gov/sites/production/files/2016-10/documents/_epaoig_20161020-17-p-0004.pdf.

5. For a comprehensive discussion of the important grassroots community organizing role played by Flint residents, see Derrick Z. Jackson, "Environmental Justice? Unjust Coverage of the Flint Water Crisis," Harvard Kennedy School, Shorenstein Center on Media, Politics and Public Policy (2017), https://shorensteincenter.org/environmental-justice-unjust-coverage-of-the-flint-water-crisis/.

6. "Louisiana Town Is Like Thousands That Are Vulnerable to Contaminated Water, with No Fix in Sight," CNN Wires, November 28, 2018, https://edition.cnn.com/2018/11/28/health/enterprise-louisiana-water/index.html.

7. "International Decade for Action 'Water for Life' 2005-2015," United Nations, accessed February 22, 2019, http://www.un.org/waterforlifedecade/human_right_to_water.shtml.

8. Barry E. Hill, Steve Wolfson, and Nicholas Targ, "Human Rights and the Environment: A Synopsis and Some Predictions," *Georgetown International Environmental Law Review* 16, no. 3 (2004): 359–402.

9. Vitruvius, *The Ten Books on Architecture,* trans. Morris Hicky Morgan (Cambridge, MA: Harvard University Press, 1914), 246–47, http://academics.triton.edu/faculty/fheitzman/Vitruvius__the_Ten_Books_on_Architecture.pdf.

10. Barry E. Hill, *Environmental Justice: Legal Theory and Practice* (Washington, DC: Environmental Law Institute, 2009), 435; Agency for Toxic Substances & Disease Registry, "Lead Toxicity: What Are Possible Health Effects from Lead Exposure?," Environmental Health and Medicine Education: Case Studies in Environmental Medicine, 2017, https://www.atsdr.cdc.gov/csem/csem.asp?csem=34&po=10.

11. Mays et al. v. Snyder et al., No. 15-14002 (E.D. Mich. 2015).

12. Jonathan Z. Cannon, *Environment in the Balance: The Green Movement and the Supreme Court* (Cambridge, MA: Harvard University Press), 29.

13. Pennsylvania Constitution, art. I, sec. 27.

14. Robinson Township v. Commonwealth of Pennsylvania, 83 A.3d 901 (Pa. 2013).

15. Montana Constitution, art. II, sec. 3.

16. Montana Environmental Information Center v. Department of Environmental Quality, 988 P.2d 1236 (Mont. 2012).

17. Cape-France Enters. v. In re Estate of Peed, 2001 MT 139.

18. New Jersey Office of Legislative Services, "Bills 2018-2019: SCR134," accessed February 18, 2019, https://www.njleg.state.nj.us/bills/BillView.asp?BillNumber=SCR134.

19. New State Ice Co. v. Liebmann, 285 U.S. 262 (1932).

20. Hawaii Constitution, art. XI, sec. 9; Illinois Constitution, art. XI, sec. 1 & 2; Massachusetts Constitution, amend. art. XLIX; New York Constitution, art. XIV, sec. 4 & 5; and Rhode Island Constitution, art. I, sec. 17.

# Reinventing Political Borders for Environmental and Social Harmony

Saleem H. Ali

POLITICAL BORDERS HAVE BECOME a fraught area for ecological engagement as global inequality leads to greater human migration.[1] Calls for harder physical barriers across frontiers are gaining traction worldwide and particularly within the United States. Even those borders that had until recently been dissolving, such as those within the European Union, are now being more acutely demarcated as manifest in Brexit as well as calls for changes to the Schengen Treaty, which provides visa-free borders in many parts of Europe. Such developments have major implications not only for ecosystem fragmentation but also for environmentally efficient trade flows.

Growing food, mining minerals, or manufacturing products with both ecological and economic efficiency is only possible through green-smart trade policy. At the same time, some border restrictions on immigration are also important in considering how best to globally harness the *demographic dividend* to the economy that comes from a large working-age population. Political borders also serve as an important safeguard to contain the spread of pathogens, as they did during the Ebola epidemic of 2014. This essay looks at how pragmatic consideration of political borders might be advanced by using smart technologies and migration flow analysis based on ecological and social carrying capacity. The integrated social and ecological approach to borders management proposed in this essay considers the dynamic nature of carrying capacity and a policy for making decisions on migration and border protection accordingly.

The Russian researcher Anton Kireev, in his important work on border-land studies, developed a typology of how one might consider borders in social science as zones of regulation (a modified version of this is shown in table 21.1).[2] This framework offers an important starting point for our analysis as regulatory jurisdictions are often the most palpable and consequential aspect of borders.[3] The original typology omitted ecological regulation, which I have added, as it is where the key innovations are most necessary to ensure positive environmental outcomes.

## BIOPHYSICAL BORDERS POLICY IN THE AGE OF WALLS

The North American conservation movement has recognized the importance of ecosystem connectivity across political borders ever since the first transboundary international park was established between Montana and Alberta in 1932. Through grassroots efforts by Rotary International chapters on both sides of the border, Waterton-Glacier International Peace Park was established by an Act of Congress in the United States and a parallel Act of Parliament in Canada. To this day, park service officials on both sides of the border manage the area jointly. The park is now also a designated United Nations Educational, Scientific, and Cultural Organization (UNESCO) World Heritage Site (despite the United States' withdrawal from UNESCO in January 2019). The border within the park has an intriguing landscape. Instead of a wall or fence, the U.S. Department of Homeland Security has defoliated a stretch of woodland to be able to more visibly monitor any illegal border crossing activity within the park. Yet even in the highly securitized political climate after 9/11, someone in Canada without a valid U.S. visa can still get on a boat, cross Waterton Lake, and touch U.S. soil on the Montanan shore; walk around under the watchful eye of rangers; and then return to Canada.

This flexible approach highlights how biological and physical porosity across such frontiers can be managed. The International Boundaries Commission, which manages the U.S.-Canadian border, was established in 1907 and thus has over a hundred years of experience in collective management of the world's longest continuous border (over 5,500 miles). No doubt the softer enforcement along this border owes to the greater economic congruence between the United States and Canada in comparison with Mexico. There are, however, opportunities to ensure ecological connectivity while having a harder border in areas where conservation zones are less salient. For example, a similar transboundary conservation area has been proposed near Big Bend

**Table 21.1**

Border functionalism following the Kireev typology

| FUNCTION OF THE BORDER | OBJECTS OF REGULATION | EXAMPLES OF REGULATION |
|---|---|---|
| Political regulation | Relations of political powers, their influence on their participants, means and resources | Fighting international terrorism or conducting intelligence activities |
| Economic regulation | Movements of material goods, factors of production, objects of exchange and consumption, actors, means and resources | Customs taxation of goods; quotas for the import of foreign labor; national sanitary and technical standards |
| Social regulation | Transborder processes of production and reproduction of social capital, their participants, means and resources | Rules for obtaining residence; marriage to foreigners; measures to encourage educational migration |
| Cultural regulation | Ethnic consciousness, information, knowledge, values, behavioral patterns, their actors, means and resources | Censorship of imported foreign literature; registration of foreign media; cultural exchange and assimilation programs |
| Ecological regulation | Flow of natural resources in the form of water, wildlife, and biotic resources | Water impoundments/dams; fencing/walls; quarantine mechanisms |

*Source*: Saleem H. Ali, "Extracting at the Borders: Negotiating Political and Ecological Geographies of Movement in Mineral Frontiers," *Sustainable Development* 26, no. 5 (2018): 482. Adapted by permission from Anton A. Kireev, "State Border," in *Introduction to Border Studies,* ed. Sergei V. Sevastianov, Jussi P. Laine, and Anton A. Kireev (Vladivostok: Dalnauka, 2015), 98–117.

National Park in Texas. This designation would allow for better transboundary management but has stalled, even though no border wall exists in that region and the Trump administration's latest proposals do not call for one. A formidable mountain range forms enough of a deterrent for any itinerant illegal migrants in this region. Indeed, ecological boundaries such as mountains or rivers have traditionally formed political borders as well, and should compose the primary means of demarcating borders where possible. Policy makers should manage border zones through more technically advanced mapping of ecosystem functioning in terms of water flows and wildlife migration corridors.

Nations also should not consider political borders completely indelible on maps. History is replete with examples of borders being renegotiated based on changing circumstances and also hybrid border governance mechanisms evolving based on the needs of the time. Just as borders such as the Iron Curtain disintegrated while new borders in the Balkans formed, countries can indeed renegotiate borders where necessary to consider ecological norms. The International Union for Conservation of Nature has a long-standing task force on transboundary conservation that deserves to be further engaged in such conversations. Ultimately, border management should consider ecosystem viability and the sustainability of important natural resources for jurisdictions on either side of the boundary.

## GREENING TRADE POLICY TO ACCOUNT FOR NATURAL COMPARATIVE ADVANTAGE

In addition to physical borders, nationalism has also led to a wide swath of economic regulations that could have serious ecological implications. Although there has been a rich literature on the greening of the World Trade Organization,[4] it has mostly emphasized how environmental regulations can fit better within the mandate of fair competition.[5] Less attention has been paid to ensuring countries' *comparative advantage*—their ability to perform certain economic functions more efficiently—for certain products based on their geography. Such an approach would favor mining in areas where deposits are more accessible and less environmentally harmful to extract, engaging in agriculture and forestry where water is more accessible and soil is more conducive to growth without intervention, or siting manufacturing infrastructure where renewable energy supply is easily harnessed. Yet the world can mobilize such comparative advantage only if countries feel secure about the supply of important goods through international accords. Without such surety, security narratives that focus on economic self-reliance will dominate, no matter how ecologically inefficient that might be.

In addition to the production cycle, waste management and a move toward a *circular economy* that recycles its own by-products also require us to consider borders quite differently. Excessive risk aversion around waste materials can prevent a transition to a circular economy if countries are not willing to accept wastes for reprocessing across borders. International agreements such as the Basel Convention on Transboundary Movement of Hazardous Wastes and Their Disposal (1989) need reform to better align with opportunities for reprocessing while containing pollution exposure. Where reprocessing is not possible, countries need to also choose disposal sites through a confluence of technical and social criteria involving the U.N.'s principles of Free, Prior, and Informed Consent.

To follow such a wide-ranging approach to the true "greening of trade," nations must better coordinate comparative advantage through evaluating and valuing their natural resources and the goods and services that they provide to us all. The United States, Canada, and Mexico have a long history of partnership through the Commission on Environmental Cooperation established under the North American Free Trade Agreement. The role of this commission should be expanded to consider such "green comparative advantage" and take a more long-term view of sustainable development for the region. Other trade agreements can advance similar arrangements, as can the eventual incorporation of metrics for ecological efficiency into the World Trade Organization.

Comparative advantage does not have to be confined to natural resources alone. It could also reflect research and knowledge clusters, including traditional ecological knowledge. The global system of intellectual property rights can also better allow for more universal sharing of green innovation. In 2008, the World Business Council on Sustainable Development established the first Eco-Patent Commons, where major member companies pledged to make patents for green technologies they develop anywhere in the world downloadable and available for use in manufacturing without any charge. The World Intellectual Property Organization (WIPO) has also recognized the importance of broader dissemination of green technologies and launched WIPO GREEN in 2013, an online marketplace for green technologies that allows donors to assist with licensing arrangements.

Thus, a broad set of mechanisms can allow for natural comparative advantage to emerge, and more ecologically efficient sharing of resources across borders.

## GLOBAL PUBLIC HEALTH THREATS AND THE IMPORTANCE OF BORDERS

Political borders may seem a hindrance to trade and migration in a globalized world, but we should not neglect the very significant safeguards that they provide in containing the spread of pathogens, invasive species, and other noxious agents. Even in cases where borders have been an unfortunate result of colonialism, such as in Africa, they have now acquired a functionality that we cannot discount in times of crisis. For example, hard frontiers between Guinea and its neighbors Mali, Senegal, and Côte d'Ivoire prevented the Ebola epidemic of 2013–14 from becoming a far greater tragedy across Africa. The case raises the challenging question of how to balance positive movement toward economic deregulation of borders with the very important social regulation borders provide during crises.[6] Côte d'Ivoire did not have any Ebola outbreak in part because of its ability to close its border more effectively due to a better security environment, coupled with better preparedness of its medical staff.[7]

Quarantine procedures are also commonplace at borders to prevent the spread of invasive species. Countries with high levels of indigenous wildlife species—such as Australia and New Zealand—often strictly enforce these laws with major fines and potential for imprisonment. Countries even practice border control for such biotic agents internally. For example, domestic flights to Hawaii from the U.S. mainland, and vice versa, have additional screening for biological materials. "Living modified organisms" that have been altered genetically or through other biotechnological mechanisms have also come under scrutiny within the international Convention on Biological Diversity through the Cartagena Protocol on Biosafety. While the United States is the only nonparty country to the convention, it has regular contact with the signatories and could consider ways of incorporating some of the key insights on how to better regulate such agents at its borders as well.

The real challenge lies in balancing the ease of human travel for commerce and cross-cultural exchange with the exercise of caution to prevent maladies from crossing frontiers. The only plausible win-win solution in this regard is more refined technology to detect unwanted biotic agents while allowing for ease of human movement. Fortunately, optical recognition technology coupled with artificial intelligence algorithms is now advancing to the point where airports can rapidly identify biological security threats with high levels of accuracy. Australia will spend over US$250 million between 2019 and 2024 on biological security, a substantial portion of which will go toward smart technologies, which could provide some greater win-win strategies in this regard. Ultimately, countries need to coordinate the adoption of such technologies in the least intrusive ways that maintain border functionality for biological security.

## A SMART SOCIAL AND ENVIRONMENTAL APPROACH TO BORDERS MANAGEMENT

Political borders derive from historical events that have largely ignored planetary health.[8] They are nevertheless unavoidable and in some cases have the potential for protecting ecosystems from harm. As human migration flows cause greater anxiety in a world of structural economic inequality, we need a more reasoned approach to border functions that balances the needs of the environment with those of society. Such an approach follows the six-step framework researchers have developed at the University of California, Irvine:

- Identify a phenomenon as a social problem
- View the problem from multiple levels and methods of analysis
- Apply diverse theoretical perspectives
- Recognize human-environment interactions as dynamic and active processes
- Consider the social, historical, cultural, and institutional contexts of people-environment relations
- Understand people's lives in an everyday sense.[9]

This six-step process may seem fairly straightforward and intuitively reasonable, but decisions are often made on borders with an urgency that neglects such a structured, multifaceted approach. Countries often manage borders through commissions; the United States has the International Boundary Commission on the Canadian side and more topically specific commissions on the Mexican side—such as the United States–Mexico Border Health Commission or the International Boundary and Water Commission. These commissions have the potential to operationalize an integrated social and ecological approach to border policy through a confluence of science and social metrics. Although win-win opportunities might not exist in all cases of border delineation and enforcement, reason is more likely to prevail over rhetoric through such an incremental and considered path.

## NOTES

1. Robert D. Kaplan, *The Revenge of Geography: What the Map Tells Us about Coming Conflicts and the Battle against Fate* (New York: Random House, 2012).

2. Anton A. Kireev, "State Border," in *Introduction to Border Studies*, ed. Sergei V. Sevastianov, Jussi P. Laine, and Anton A. Kireev (Vladivostok: Dalnauka, 2015), 98–117.

3. Saleem H. Ali, "Extracting at the Borders: Negotiating Political and Ecological Geographies of Movement in Mineral Frontiers," *Sustainable Development* 26, no. 5 (October 2018): 482.

4. Daniel C. Esty, *Greening the GATT: Trade, Environment, and the Future* (Washington, DC: Institute for International Economics, 1994); World Trade Organization, *Harnessing Trade for Sustainable Development and a Green Economy*, 2011, https://www.wto .org/english/res_e/publications_e/brochure_rio_20_e.pdf; Gary Clyde Hufbauer and Jisun Kim, "The World Trade Organization and Climate Change: Challenges and Options," Peterson Institute Working Paper 09-9, 2009, https://piie.com /publications/working-papers/world-trade-organization-and-climate-change -challenges-and-options.

5. Linda Allen, *The Greening of US Free Trade Agreements: From NAFTA to the Present Day* (New York: Routledge, 2018).

6. Ali, "Extracting at the Borders," 487.

7. Lucy Breakwell et al., "Early Identification and Prevention of the Spread of Ebola in High-Risk African Countries," *MMWR Supplements* 65, no. 3 (2016): 21–27.

8. David Newman, "The Lines That Continue to Separate Us: Borders in Our 'Borderless' World," *Progress in Human Geography* 30, no. 2 (2006): 143–61.

9. "Conceptual Social Ecology," University of California Irvine School of Social Ecology, accessed February 15, 2019, https://socialecology.uci.edu/pages/conceptual-social -ecology.

# Deploying Machine Learning for a Sustainable Future

Cary Coglianese

IN THE FACE of extraordinary environmental challenges created by a warming planet and an increasingly complex, high-tech global economy, government needs to become smarter about how it makes and implements environmental policy. Specifically, government needs to build a robust capacity to analyze large volumes of environmental and economic data using machine-learning algorithms. It needs, in other words, to move toward algorithmic environmental governance.

Businesses have already demonstrated how algorithms can lead to more accurate and more optimal decisions across a wide range of functions, including medical treatments, fraud identification, and self-driving cars.[1] To meet the demands of a sustainable future, government will need to use these same kinds of algorithmic tools for improving environmental management. In the hands of responsible environmental officials, machine-learning algorithms can promote more efficient use of scarce resources and the design of more cost-effective solutions to persistent and new environmental challenges.

## WHAT IS ALGORITHMIC ENVIRONMENTAL GOVERNANCE?

An algorithm is simply a series of computational steps. In this most basic sense, algorithms have long helped environmental decision makers. But machine-learning algorithms—sometimes referred to as artificial intelligence or predictive analytics—are different. They take advantage of modern digital computing power to analyze vast quantities of data—Big Data—to produce highly accurate predictions. In contrast to conventional statistical analysis, they work by a process of "learning" on their own. With enough computing power, machine-learning algorithms can do their work at lightning speed.

To appreciate more fully how machine-learning algorithms work, it helps to contrast them with standard statistical techniques for making predictions, such as regression analysis. With conventional techniques, a human analyst selects both the variables to include in a mathematical model and the model's functional form. Machine-learning algorithms, by contrast, do the selecting of variables and functional forms on their own. Humans establish an objective that a learning algorithm is supposed to meet—namely, what it should predict—and the algorithm essentially takes things from there.[2]

Although machine-learning algorithms can be structured in different ways, the most intuitive way to understand how they work is by visualizing a computational process that rapidly tries out all possible combinations of variables from a large dataset using a host of different functional forms until it finds the best match—that is, the function and variables that yield the most accurate predictions.[3] Machine-learning algorithms "train" on existing data but then are tested and applied with new data.[4] Through this basic process, machine-learning robots help navigate self-driving cars, identify spam in email inboxes, and play difficult games, such as chess and go.

Government officials are beginning to see the value of machine-learning algorithms.[5] When addressing environmental problems, government leaders must rely on accurate predictions to inform their decisions. They could benefit from the superior predictive power and speed of machine learning. To see how algorithms could improve environmental governance, consider a few examples:

- *Identifying toxic chemicals.* The U.S. Environmental Protection Agency (EPA) faces the daunting challenge of determining which chemicals out of tens of thousands could cause cancer and should be banned. Conducting animal tests or even in vitro analysis on every chemical is simply not feasible. To select which chemicals to study further, EPA and other government agencies have built a massive dataset on toxic chemicals. EPA analysts have shown that they can use machine-learning tools to analyze those data and make predictions about whether any particular new chemical is likely to have toxic effects, saving the agency substantial time and resources while also protecting the public.

- *Targeting facilities for environmental inspections.* In any given year, EPA has the resources to inspect no more than about 10 percent of all facilities in the United States that operate with a water discharge permit.[6] Machine-learning tools can dramatically increase the efficiency of inspection targeting, enabling regulatory agencies to direct their limited number of inspectors toward facilities more likely to have compliance and environmental problems. After all, sending inspectors to facilities that are faithfully complying with the law is not a smart use of limited inspection resources. Researchers at Stanford have shown that EPA could improve the efficiency of its Clean Water Act inspection targeting by as much as 600 percent with machine-learning algorithms.[7]
- *Predicting areas with climate-related flood risks.* As climate change unfolds, coastal areas face heightened flood risks. Deciding where to undertake climate resilience actions, such as constructing levees or reforming building codes in coastal cities, will be greatly aided by accurate predictions of the areas facing the greatest risk. Cities can make more accurate infrastructure plans and better resource allocation decisions with machine learning.[8]

In these and other ways, algorithmic tools can become an essential component in a policy strategy for a sustainable future. Algorithmic tools not only can help better inform traditional regulatory functions, but they can also go further to support fully automated environmental compliance monitoring systems that integrate remote-sensing technology or infrared cameras to provide real-time information about emissions of pollutants. Over the longer term, real-time monitoring combined with machine-learning analysis could potentially support a type of automated performance-based regulatory system that would afford polluting facilities greater flexibility in the management of their environmental operations.[9]

## WHY SOCIETY NEEDS ALGORITHMIC ENVIRONMENTAL GOVERNANCE

Algorithmic tools are needed because environmental agencies face increasing demands due to changing technologies and a changing climate. Government will most likely need to meet its additional demands with the same or even fewer resources. By investing in computing technology and the right kind of human analytic capacity to support machine learning, government agencies should be able to save money and improve performance by better allocating

scarce human resources and facilitating more flexible and refined environmental policies—even perhaps to the point of regulating by robot.[10]

Three factors can be expected to drive the need for algorithmic environmental governance: more problems, less funding, and growing demands.

*More Problems.* The number and volume of potentially hazardous chemicals
and technologies will only continue to grow, at rates beyond environmental
regulators' capacities for testing and monitoring all possible risks. The sheer
number of pollution sources will also likely expand. For example, although
the United States' growing reliance on natural gas for energy will help reduce
planet-warming carbon dioxide emissions, it also will bring with it the challenge of preventing fugitive methane emissions—small leaks of an even
more potent greenhouse gas from any point in the vast production and distribution chain for natural gas.[11] Similarly, the advent of 3-D printing will usher
in an era of distributed manufacturing that will increase the number of
smaller polluting sources throughout the country.

These and other technological and economic changes will occur at the
same time as climate change continues to wreak havoc. Society's future will
depend on smart climate change mitigation policies—and it will also need
smart climate change adaptation decisions. Machine learning can help improve decision-making about infrastructure planning, flood and storm response, public health monitoring, and natural resource and agricultural
management.

*Less Funding.* Budgetary resources devoted to environmental protection appear unlikely to increase significantly in the foreseeable future. If at least
some governmental enforcement and monitoring functions can be entirely
automated by combining algorithmic tools with advances in remote sensing,
the cost savings for government could be substantial.[12] According to one estimate, greater reliance on machine-learning forecasting to screen chemicals
for toxicity could save close to $1 million per toxic chemical identified.[13]

*Growing Demands.* As the private sector continues to innovate with optimizing algorithms and other technologies, it will likely increase public demands
for more precise but flexible environmental policies. Individuals are already
growing accustomed in their private lives to the precision that machine-
learning algorithms make possible, such as the customized recommendations from companies such as Amazon, Netflix, Google, and Apple. Why not

make regulatory obligations customized too? Many business leaders would undoubtedly prefer that government shift away from a reliance on crude, one-size-fits-all rules to more cost-effective regulatory systems that micro-target industrial facilities and impose customized performance targets on each.[14]

## BUILDING CAPACITY FOR ALGORITHMIC GOVERNANCE

Making the move to algorithmic environmental governance will not be easy. Four obstacles will need to be overcome if EPA and other governmental agencies are to take full advantage of the predictive potential of machine-learning algorithms. These obstacles can be overcome, making algorithmic governance fully realizable, but it will require making deliberate investments and responsible management choices.[15]

First, government must invest in its information infrastructure. Unfortunately, too many government agencies at present are woefully behind the curve when it comes to computing power. According to an analysis by the U.S. Government Accountability Office, three-quarters of current spending by the federal government on information technology goes to supporting "legacy systems"—that is, to "increasingly obsolete" systems that are dependent on "outdated software languages and hardware."[16] Although upgrading information technology obviously will require capital investments, relatively modest technology investments, if made wisely, could support the use of algorithmic tools that could yield substantial savings in other administrative costs.

Of course, the kind of infrastructure needed to support algorithmic environmental governance goes well beyond computing power: it also entails large quantities of data. Fortunately, EPA and various state agencies have undertaken substantial efforts in recent years to transfer many paper-based reporting systems to electronic filing systems, which means that facility-level data can increasingly be archived in digital form.[17] As agencies come to rely more on remote sensing instruments for monitoring pollution, those data could also be fed into digital archives. The government will, of course, need to manage all the information it amasses so that environmental data can be linked with other datasets and analyzed by machine-learning algorithms.[18] In a study conducted at the Penn Program on Regulation, we found that machine learning markedly improved the accuracy of inspection targeting when facilities' records in both EPA and Occupational Health and Safety Administration datasets could be combined with publicly available financial data.

Second, government will need to address emerging concerns about privacy, fairness, and transparency associated with its reliance on Big Data and algorithmic analyses.[19] Individuals worry, for example, that seemingly innocuous and totally uninformative bits of data can, with the aid of machine-learning tools, yield remarkably accurate predictions about private aspects of their lives, such as their sexual orientations. Concern also exists that biases already contained in human-generated data—say, racial biases in police arrest records—will become baked into the outputs of algorithmic analyses that rely on those data. Others worry that machine-learning algorithms are insufficiently transparent due to inherent difficulty in explaining exactly how they achieve their forecasts.

These varied concerns have arisen to date about machine learning in a variety of contexts outside of environmental governance—for example, social media companies or criminal courts. Yet government officials can expect similar questions to arise with respect to algorithmic environmental governance, and so they should design and deploy algorithms responsibly to avoid these concerns. Data access and security protocols can help address privacy concerns. Biases can be identified and addressed through an emerging array of statistical techniques.[20] The "black box" nature of machine-learning algorithms should also not prevent governments from providing sufficient transparency.[21] With thoughtful planning and responsible management, governments should be able to address any concerns that arise over the use of machine-learning tools to improve environmental sustainability.

Third, government will need to strengthen its human capital to ensure it has personnel who understand how to use machine learning responsibly. One problem is that the federal government is already facing a significant shortfall of talent, with more than a third of federal employees eligible to retire by 2020.[22] At EPA, a quarter of the workforce is currently eligible for retirement.[23] These demographic trends are creating major challenges for government agencies, providing yet another reason why these agencies should take advantage of algorithmic tools and Big Data in the future. It will allow them to do more with less.

The demographic shift occurring in the government's workforce provides an excellent opportunity to rebuild the government in an even more analytically sophisticated way. In the coming years, environmental agencies can bring on board new professionals with the skills or aptitudes to use machine-learning tools. Training government staff in quantitative analytic tools will need to become a priority too. Although algorithms can make possible considerable efficiencies in governmental policymaking and oversight, the responsible design and use of algorithms will depend on more than just technology. People and their effective management will still matter.[24]

Finally, to work well, algorithms will need clearly defined objectives. In environmental policymaking, certain questions about risk management—such as how safe is safe enough—remain only loosely defined. But if environmental officials seek to use machine-learning algorithms to optimize certain kinds of risks, they will need to define those risks with clarity and precision. They will also likely need to define how algorithms should make trade-offs between forecasting accuracy and other values, such as fairness.[25] Toward this end, environmental officials will need to continue to engage with elected officials, members of the public, environmental groups, and industry representatives to forge clarity and consistency over how various risk and regulatory objectives should be specified. At the same time that government officials will need to strengthen their analytic and technological skills, they will continue to need to strive for excellence in social engagement.[26]

## THE ALGORITHMIC IMPERATIVE

Although the obstacles in the way of algorithmic governance are not trivial, they can be overcome with sufficient planning and action. The time to take this action is now. Although algorithmic environmental governance offers no panacea, it does promise to support strikingly more accurate and efficient environmental stewardship. The need for smarter governance, driven by more complex problems, increased public demands, and perennially scarce resources, will make it imperative that environmental agencies make greater reliance on machine-learning tools in the coming years. If policy makers and the public recognize the need for smarter governance, they can then start to tackle obstacles that stand in their way and better position society for a more sustainable future.

## NOTES

The author gratefully acknowledges helpful comments on an earlier draft from Richard Berk, Dan Esty, and Chris Lewis, as well as from participants at a Vanderbilt University Law School workshop.

1. Darrell M. West and John R. Allen, "How Artificial Intelligence Is Transforming the World," Brookings Institution (April 24, 2018), https://www.brookings.edu/research/how-artificial-intelligence-is-transforming-the-world/.
2. Machine-learning algorithms are designed to yield predictions but not support causal explanations. For an excellent overview of how these algorithms work, see

David Lehr and Paul Ohm, "Playing with the Data: What Legal Scholars Should Learn about Machine Learning," *University of California Davis Law Review* 51, no. 2 (2017): 653–717.

3. For a more technical treatment of a common type of machine-learning algorithm, see Leo Breiman, "Random Forests," *Machine Learning* 45, no. 1 (2001): 5–32.

4. Lehr and Ohm, "Playing with the Data."

5. Susan Athey, "Beyond Prediction: Using Big Data for Policy Problems," *Science* 355, no. 6324 (February 3, 2017): 483–85.

6. Miyuki Hino, Elinor Benami, and Nina Brooks, "Machine Learning for Environmental Monitoring," *Nature Sustainability* 1 (October 2018): 583–88.

7. Hino, Benami, and Brooks, "Machine Learning." Additional research has shown that machine learning can improve the detection of noncompliance with natural resource regulations. Cleridy E. Lennert-Cody and Richard A. Berk, "Statistical Learning Procedures for Monitoring Regulatory Compliance: An Application to Fisheries Data," *Journal of the Royal Statistical Society*, series A, 170, no. 3 (2007): 671–89.

8. Amir Mosavi, Pinar Ozturk, and Kwok-wing Chau, "Flood Prediction Using Machine Learning Models: Literature Review," *Water* 10, no. 11 (October 2018): 1536–76.

9. Of course, performance-based regulation needs to be well designed and adequately monitored to prevent gaming by regulated entities. Cary Coglianese and Jennifer Nash, "The Law of the Test: Performance-Based Regulation and Diesel Emissions Control," *Yale Journal on Regulation* 34, no. 1 (2017): 33–90.

10. Cary Coglianese and David Lehr, "Regulating by Robot: Administrative Decision-Making in the Machine Learning Era," *Georgetown Law Journal* 105, no. 5 (2017): 1147–223.

11. James Bradbury et al., "Clearing the Air: Reducing Upstream Greenhouse Gas Emissions from U.S. Natural Gas Systems," working paper, World Resources Institute (2013), https://wriorg.s3.amazonaws.com/s3fs-public/clearing_the_air_full_version.pdf. On the role of remote sensing and machine learning for methane leak detection, see Levente Klein et al., "Distributed Wireless Sensing for Methane Leak Detection Technology," U.S. Department of Energy Office of Scientific and Technical Information (2017), https://www.osti.gov/servlets/purl/1435713.

12. Cynthia Giles, "Next Generation Compliance," *Environmental Forum* (September–October 2013): 22–26.

13. Matthew T. Martin et al., "Economic Benefits of Using Adaptive Predictive Models of Reproductive Toxicity in the Context of a Tiered Testing Program," *Systems Biology in Reproductive Medicine* 58, no. 3 (2012): 4–6.

14. For a related discussion, see Anthony Casey and Anthony Niblett, "Self-Driving Laws," *University of Toronto Law Journal* 66, no. 4 (2016): 429–42.

15. Cary Coglianese, "Optimizing Regulation for an Optimizing Economy," *University of Pennsylvania Journal of Law and Public Affairs* 4, no. 1 (2018): 1–13.

16. U.S. Government Accountability Office, *Federal Agencies Need to Address Aging Legacy Systems: Hearing Before the H. Comm. on Oversight and Gov't Reform*, 114th Cong. (2016) (statement of David A. Powner, Director, Information Technology Management Issues), https://www.gao.gov/assets/680/677454.pdf.

17. Giles, "Next Generation Compliance."

18. Robert L. Glicksman, David L. Markell, and Claire Monteleoni, "Technological Innovation, Data Analytics, and Environmental Enforcement," *Ecology Law Quarterly* 44, no. 1 (2017): 41–88.

19. Cathy O'Neil, *Weapons of Math Destruction: How Big Data Increases Inequality and Threatens Democracy* (New York: Crown, 2016).

20. The statistical remedies will vary depending on whether bias exists in the data or in the algorithm.

21. Cary Coglianese and David Lehr, "Transparency and Algorithmic Governance," *Administrative Law Review* 71, no. 1 (2019): 1–56.

22. U.S. Government Accountability Office, *Federal Workforce: Sustained Attention to Human Capital Leading Practices Can Help Improve Agency Performance: Hearing Before the H. Comm. on Oversight and Gov't Reform*, 115th Cong. 3-4 (2017) (statement of Robert Goldenkoff, Director of Strategic Issues), https://www.gao.gov/assets/690 /684709.pdf.

23. Brady Dennis, Juliet Eilperin, and Andrew Ba Tran, "With a Shrinking EPA, Trump Delivers on His Promise to Cut Government," *Washington Post* (September 8, 2018), https://www.washingtonpost.com/national/health-science/with-a-shrinking-epa -trump-delivers-on-his-promise-to-cut-government/2018/09/08/6b058f9e-b143 -11e8-a20b-5f4f84429666_story.html.

24. Daniel C. Esty, "Regulatory Excellence: Lessons from Theory and Practice," in Cary Coglianese, ed., *Achieving Regulatory Excellence* (Washington, DC: Brookings, 2017): 133–47.

25. Richard Berk, "Accuracy and Fairness for Juvenile Justice Risk Assessments," *Journal of Empirical Legal Studies* 16, no. 1 (2019): 175–94.

26. Cary Coglianese, "Regulatory Excellence as 'People Excellence,'" The Regulatory Review (October 23, 2015), https://www.theregreview.org/2015/10/23/coglianese -people-excellence/.

# Focusing the Environmental Protection Enterprise to Put Ideas and Policies into Action

Derry Allen and John Reeder

THE ONLY WAY TO MEET the goals of environmental protection and sustainability is to focus the cooperative energy and passion of thousands of public and private organizations and citizens. This network or system—the "environmental protection enterprise"[1]—is what actually puts ideas and policies into action.

The players and dynamic of this enterprise have changed over the years. A half century ago, new programs to protect the environment emerged from a partnership between the federal government—mainly the young U.S. Environmental Protection Agency (EPA) and a bipartisan coalition in Congress—and state pollution control agencies, with the help of local governments and a small but growing number of nongovernmental organizations (NGOs). This relatively simple enterprise worked effectively to put into action the big ideas in the 1970s, such as the Clean Air Act and the Clean Water Act. Where states did not have the political will or expertise to implement pollution controls, EPA would step in—by law—to make sure that industries and communities met minimum standards. By most measures, air and water quality in the United States have improved remarkably since the 1970s.

EPA and the states remain central players in the enterprise today, but many other public and private players have joined to promote environmental quality and sustainability. The present enterprise includes countless government agencies at all levels, private companies and alliances, and NGOs. Although this network has inherent capacity to deliver environmental results, it is not focused well enough to tackle some critically important current and future challenges, political issues notwithstanding.

Addressing climate change leads the list of challenges, but it is not the only challenge. Population and economic growth relentlessly stress the environment, driving up energy use and greenhouse gas emissions, and also imperiling environmental quality in other ways: more intensive agricultural production, water shortages, resource extraction, waste generation, ecosystem destruction from changing land use, reliance on toxic chemicals, and extreme natural and human-made events. The enterprise must navigate through the nation's increasing political polarization, debates about science, government budget uncertainty, and concerns over environmental justice.[2] Despite the enterprise's inherent capacity, the question increasingly is whether this network will be able to operate to its full capacity and deliver the needed results.

Many of these challenges are systems issues and are harder to address than the (comparatively) simple individual pollution control issues for which the enterprise was originally designed. Continued progress will require changes in the economy and society to avoid environmental threats in the first place. Fortunately, the new enterprise pulls on greater collective resources and more creative tools for achieving desired outcomes than it used to have. New ideas for protecting the environment that rally the collective energy of the enterprise around shared goals and attend to the viability of the system itself are more likely to succeed than those fashioned in the traditional mind-set of the federal government imposing mandates on states.

Success in this realm will require three major actions: developing shared goals among enterprise members, paying special attention to the focus, strength, and roles of the individual institutions that together form the enterprise, and guiding the evolving relationships among these institutions to make the best use of their comparative strengths.

The task of implementing policies may seem boring to some people, but without thinking systemically about the environmental protection enterprise's new order, innovative policies will not take flight and achieve their intended outcomes. The approach described here will not replace political policy-making, nor will it solve every problem. Moreover, the ideas here are not new to some observers. But the approach does highlight a perspective that can help reach solutions. Focusing the environmental protection enterprise is an essential task that will take much imagination and effort.

## ROOTS OF THE ENTERPRISE

The size and shape of the focusing task are best understood by engaging in a closer but still very cursory review of the roots of the enterprise. Whereas some of these roots go back to the establishment of the federal government, the modern enterprise dates to roughly fifty years ago, when Congress responded to public concern about the environment with a remarkable burst of bipartisan legislative activity (especially as seen in hindsight). Beginning in 1969 with the passage of the National Environmental Policy Act and extending over the next several years, Congress enacted a series of laws that defined a basic framework that endures today. President Richard Nixon created EPA in 1970 to be at the center of the framework.

The agency often relied on its most powerful tool: setting standards to limit pollution and punishing polluters that were often egregious and uncooperative. Even in its relatively modest initial scale, EPA was a major force. Although its creators always envisioned that the agency would hand off much of the day-to-day implementation and enforcement to states and tribes, EPA played a dominant role because these entities often had limited budgets and experience. As it turns out, EPA's regulatory role gave rise to many adversarial relationships and helped shape the wide range of attitudes about the agency that we see today, from enthusiastic support to deep distrust.

Since the 1970s, the nation has witnessed considerable regulatory activity as well as steady improvement in environmental quality. EPA's evolving partnerships with states and tribes have been marked by innovation, growth, and tension. The scientific understanding of environmental problems has made huge leaps, particularly relating to climate and sustainability, and it has become clear that the traditional regulatory toolbox cannot do everything that is needed. Unfortunately, at the same time, the bipartisan legislative coalition that shaped early environmental legislation dissolved, thwarting efforts to update most environmental statutes for over a generation.

Meanwhile, another remarkable tide was swelling. Many public and private groups as well as members of the public stepped up their support for the environment and sustainability. They did so for their own reasons, using their own tools in their own ways. Cities wanted to be livable, and companies wanted to ensure sources of supply, open new markets, and protect their public reputations. NGOs grew and set new priorities, with everything from local to global ambitions.

The tools they have used are as numerous and varied as the organizations themselves. Most of these tools are not entirely new but are being used in new ways to promote environmental progress: zoning and land use planning, transportation planning, natural resource planning, scientific research, new technologies to use resources more efficiently, trade agreements, consumer information about products, public information about facilities, development of new information technologies, new production methods, purchasing requirements, privately promulgated standards and certifications, investment and finance tools, philanthropy, and social justice initiatives, among others.

Concurrently, power relationships have changed. Investors, customers (both corporate and individual), and NGOs now exercise increased influence. Work on environmental science and information has moved from being centered at EPA to being widely diffused among many parties.

The issue of climate change has profoundly motivated and challenged the enterprise. The growing scientific and public understanding of this threat, the political acrimony that surrounds it, and the slow-motion response at the national and international levels have led many cities, companies, and others to move ahead as best they can on their own. Interestingly, some of the most important news from recent U.N. environmental conferences has come from companies and NGOs hosting what are somewhat ironically called "side events." The issue of climate change has also helped the public understand other aspects of sustainability and advance nongovernmental leadership in those areas.

A vast network or enterprise has thus grown up—often somewhat randomly, each piece usually for a good reason but without a common articulated vision or plan. As suggested by the climate change example, many forces have shaped this new enterprise. They include, in no particular order, a growing public appreciation of a clean environment, new environmental challenges or old challenges newly understood, evolving federal-state relationships, shifting priorities among societal goals, actual or perceived shortcomings in management of environmental institutions, and changes in technology. The enterprise did not grow up as quickly as some people would have liked or evenly across geographic areas or industries, and in some places, it has hardly taken hold at all, for various reasons. Filling gaps where the enterprise has not taken hold is one of the reasons we continue to need a strong, forward-looking regulatory program with vigorous enforcement.

In many ways the enterprise is messy, flawed, and not working to capacity, but it generally has the potential to deliver progress in ways that the original federal and state organizations could not do alone with the limited tools they had. EPA and the states have generally welcomed the growth of the enterprise, and some leaders have sought to encourage environmental stewardship, especially when regulatory controls have faced strong political headwinds.

For instance, in 2005, a group of EPA senior staff wrote a report that proposed a vision of environmental stewardship "where all parts of society actively take responsibility to improve environmental quality and achieve sustainable results."[3] The EPA administrator responded, "This report outlines what I believe is the next step in an ongoing evolution of policy goals from pollution control to pollution prevention and sustainability. It also reflects an important reality—that while the Environmental Protection Agency (EPA) and our state partners share responsibility for bringing about our nation's environmental progress to date, we have not done so alone."[4]

Some diverse but telling indicators of the dominant forces in the enterprise include the annual reviews of sustainability activities published by journalists and the agendas of conferences on the environment and sustainability. The private sector, cities, and the science and technology communities often dominate these reviews and agendas. EPA and its state counterparts are mentioned but are not the center of attention.[5] Those that encourage and open up new possibilities receive attention, rather than those (regulatory agencies) that prohibit "bad" activities.[6]

## THE TASK AHEAD

Moving forward, success will hinge on our ability to focus the work of many actors in the new enterprise. Three major actions would help.

The first action should be for a multi-stakeholder coalition representing all major parts of the enterprise to articulate shared principles and goals. The statement does not need to be perfect, but it does need to be compelling. There is no shortage of principles and goals developed by different groups, but in the process of random growth there has never been a system-wide consensus articulation. The U.N. Sustainable Development Goals for economic and environmental progress are one such attempt on a global scale. Ideas for a Green New Deal currently generate discussion in the United States, although unfortunately the discussion is partisan. To the extent that actors can reach such agreement, and it becomes a part of people's consciousness, it will be easier for the enterprise to become an integrated and higher-functioning system. Ultimately, of course, implementation only occurs with public support, and a discussion about a set of principles that have been well publicized can also help address the frayed social consensus on the environment and sustainability.

Gus Speth, a noted environmental advocate, has used the analogy of jazz, where the musicians agree on a general tune, key, and tempo and then play together with little central direction. A common set of principles would help with "taking jazz to scale" (to use his phrase) in implementing sustainability.[7]

For instance, building on what currently exists piecemeal, the enterprise should stress the outcomes that most people desire, such as public health, economic and energy security, and social justice. It should explicitly explain and encourage sustainability and resilience. The system should prioritize holistic and integrated approaches that consider all the impacts of full life cycles and chains of commerce. State-of-the-art science (including citizen science), advanced information technologies, and market-based approaches should predominate. The system should allocate roles, responsibilities, and accountability, along with flexible partnerships throughout the enterprise and multiple and diverse forms of investment. Trust, transparency, and scientific integrity should be represented as the keys to public confidence.[8] The perspective should reflect the global economy. To these principles one more that was popularized by the scientist and author René Dubos should be added: "Think globally, act locally,"[9] to take into account actual local conditions, both geographically and by industry.

The second action should be to pay close attention to the focus, strength, and roles of the individual institutions, both public and private, that together constitute the enterprise. These institutions are the building blocks of the system, and significant progress depends on them being strong. To illustrate, one can look at EPA, but the same ideas can be applied elsewhere.

This action begins with defining a discrete role and doing it well. For EPA, this can include three general activities:

- Provide certain basic environmental services: regulate and enforce conscientiously to ensure at least minimum performance, and do so with a focus on rapid technological change and multimedia (air, water, land) opportunities; encourage sustainability; respond to emergencies (for example, storms); clean up where no one else will (Superfund pollution sites); and make technical assistance available where appropriate. This task includes distributing federal money to states and others to operate programs and build capacity.

- Be a leader in environmental science and generating information—doing some itself but also helping to guide and oversee the larger activities of the environmental protection enterprise.[10]
- Guide the entire enterprise: encourage best practices, convene people, assess and report to the public on environmental progress, and promote new opportunities. EPA should look to states and others for innovations and encourage others to adopt them. Others should do important tasks that do not fall in these areas, especially when government budgets are constrained. In some cases, this means the enterprise inventing new institutions, such as Green Banks, rather than trying to use existing ones.

To carry out this role, EPA needs to attract and manage a talented workforce and build an organization that attends to science and public concerns, acts quickly, innovates, responds to changing needs, and is ready to collaborate with other organizations. A large budget is not a goal in itself, but there needs to be a budget sufficient for the job. The size and allocation of resources within the entire enterprise are also important when considering what EPA's budget should be. Given the roles described above, proposals that are often heard for major legislation or reorganization to fix the agency's "stovepipes" or other perceived organizational improvements should not be a priority, although modest fixes may be necessary.[11]

The agency should focus on carrying out its particular roles in the context of the enterprise's system objectives. This may not be as easy as it sounds. The agency should be able to use its regulatory and other tools to promote sustainability as well as traditional pollution control. In practice, however, legal restrictions, budget limitations, and agency culture often can make this task very hard.[12]

The third action should be to guide the evolving relationships that these institutions have with each other—the relationships that can make them into a high-functioning system that is diverse, robust, resilient, and capable of adapting to change. Having real impact here is as hard as it is critical.

Going back to EPA, the top-down model is hard to shake. The question of EPA-state relations is no less important than it ever was, but now the discussion must take place in a larger context. EPA can expand its shared strategies and agreements with states to include new participants (for example, local governments) and issues beyond the implementation of regulations. It can streamline processes and fully implement new processes, such as E-Enterprise for the Environment, a new approach for EPA, states, and tribes to share responsibilities.[13] EPA can reexamine its relationships with local govern-ments, the private sector, and NGOs.[14] EPA can also put new focus on roles such as being a strategic funder, a convener, a supporter of shared environ-mental progress measures, and a supporter of constant progress, asserting itself when leadership is needed.

One way to move in this direction is to encourage active thinking on *who* should implement new ideas as soon as they are suggested. These choices are key. Another approach, suggested by the National Research Council, is to se-lect some high-priority big ideas and use them as demonstrations of how agencies and others can collaborate.[15] Such collaboration has occurred where there has been political will, such as when large research expenditures are involved and instances such as the Partnership for Sustainable Communities between the Department of Housing and Urban Development, Department of Transportation, and EPA,[16] but these instances are not common.

Another idea to promote all of these actions would be to form a high-profile multi-stakeholder group to help develop broad consensus advice. Such a group could resemble the Enterprise for the Environment project, which thoughtfully examined many similar questions about what it called "The En-vironmental Protection System in Transition," in the late 1990s.[17]

With enough imagination and energy, the environmental protection en-terprise has the potential to meet the most daunting and complex challenges. Finding ways to focus the diverse strengths of enterprise participants is crit-ical for successfully implementing new ideas and achieving the goals of environmental protection and sustainability.

### NOTES

The views expressed in this essay are those of the authors and do not necessarily repre-sent those of the U.S. Environmental Protection Agency, the EPA Alumni Association, or American University, institutions with which the authors are or have been affiliated.

1. "The EPA of the Future," EPA Alumni Association, accessed June 14, 2019, https://www.epaalumni.org/future/. The authors borrowed the term "environmental pro-tection enterprise" from a group of individuals in the EPA Alumni Association. The association has a project titled "Future Directions for Environmental Progress and EPA's Role," which has involved several hundred former staff from EPA with vast collective experience, plus scholars from American University. This essay draws on and extends some of the ideas from that project. Both authors are actively involved and are grateful to their colleagues. Focus Group 2 from that project used the term "environmental protection enterprise" in a slightly different sense than used here, to mean "the national framework for protection established through laws passed in the 1970s."

2. Stan Laskowski et al., "Focus Group 1: Future Environmental Challenges," Environment 2045: Future Directions for Environmental Progress and EPA's Role, EPA Alumni Association and American University, Summer 2018, https://www.epaalumni.org/future/access.cfm.

3. U.S. EPA Innovation Action Council, *Everyday Choices: Opportunities for Environmental Stewardship* (with preface by the administrator) (Washington, DC: U.S. EPA, November 9, 2005), https://archive.epa.gov/stewardship/web/pdf/rpt2admin.pdf, 1.

4. U.S. EPA, *Everyday Choices,* iii.

5. "The 2019 State of Green Business Report," GreenBiz, accessed February 15, 2019, https://www.greenbiz.com/report/2019-state-green-business-report; Andrew Winston, "The Story of Sustainability in 2018: We Have about 12 Years Left," *Finding the Gold in Green* (blog), January 11, 2019, http://www.andrewwinston.com/blog/2019/01/the_story_of_sustainability_in.php.

6. See Daniel C. Esty's "Red Lights to Green Lights" essay in this volume.

7. James Gustave Speth, *Red Sky at Morning: America and the Crisis of the Global Environment* (New Haven, CT: Yale University Press, 2004), 173.

8. Bob Perciasepe et al., "Focus Group 2: The Environmental Protection Enterprise," Environment 2045: Future Directions for Environmental Progress and EPA's Role, EPA Alumni Association and American University, Summer 2018, https://www.epaalumni.org/future/access.cfm.

9. Andrew C. Revkin, "A 'Despairing Optimist' Considered Anew," *Dot Earth* (blog), *New York Times,* June 6, 2011, https://dotearth.blogs.nytimes.com/2011/06/06/a-despairing-optimist-considered-anew/.

10. Penelope Fenner-Crisp et al., "Focus Group 4: Science, Technology, and Information," Environment 2045: Future Directions for Environmental Progress and EPA's Role, EPA Alumni Association and American University, Summer 2018, https://www.epaalumni.org/future/access.cfm.

11. Stan Meiburg et al., "Focus Group 5: Tools, Processes, Culture, and Resources," Environment 2045: Future Directions for Environmental Progress and EPA's Role, EPA Alumni Association and American University, Summer 2018, https://www.epaalumni.org/future/access.cfm.

12. See, for instance, U.S. EPA, *Sustainable Materials Management: The Road Ahead* (Washington, DC: U.S. EPA, June 2009), https://www.epa.gov/smm/sustainable-materials-management-road-ahead; National Research Council, *Sustainability and the U.S. EPA* (Washington, DC: National Academies Press, 2011), https://www.epa.gov/sustainability/sustainability-and-us-epa.

13. E-Enterprise for the Environment (homepage), accessed February 20, 2019, https://e-enterprisefortheenvironment.net/.

14. David Ullrich et al., "Focus Group 3: EPA's Relationships with States and Other Public and Private Actors," Environment 2045: Future Directions for Environmental Progress and EPA's Role, EPA Alumni Association and American University, Summer 2018, https://www.epaalumni.org/future/access.cfm.

15. National Research Council, *Sustainability for the Nation: Resource Connections and Governance Linkages* (Washington, DC: National Academies Press, 2013), https://doi.org/10.17226/13471.

16. "HUD-DOT-EPA Partnership for Sustainable Communities," January 19, 2017, EPA website snapshot, U.S. EPA, accessed March 6, 2019, https://19january2017snapshot.epa.gov/smartgrowth/hud-dot-epa-partnership-sustainable-communities_.html.

17. Enterprise for the Environment, *The Environmental Protection System in Transition: Toward a More Desirable Future: Final Report of the Enterprise for the Environment* (Washington, DC: Center for Strategic and International Studies, 1998).

# Science as a Foundation for Policy

## THE CASE OF FRACKING

James Saiers

SOLAR POWER, WIND ENERGY, smart grids, and energy storage often command current discourse on energy innovation. Yet, none of these technologies has transformed the U.S. energy landscape to the degree of high-volume hydraulic fracturing ("fracking"). This energy extraction process is unlocking previously inaccessible crude oil and natural gas from underground reservoirs throughout the nation. Thanks to fracking, the forty-year decline in U.S. domestic crude oil production has reversed, and the United States pumped more crude oil in 2018 than ever before.[1] Natural gas production has similarly skyrocketed, and owing to a newfound surplus, the United States is on the verge of becoming a net exporter of natural gas for the first time in its history. For many, this record-setting pace of oil and gas production is no cause for celebration because it reflects a continued reliance on Earth-warming fossil fuels, when there are cleaner, carbon-free alternatives to light our homes, power our industries, and fuel our automobiles. Nevertheless, fracking has made oil and gas plentiful and cheap, making these energy resources hard to resist, even if infrastructural and political impediments to a transition to renewable energy were removed. Like it or not, we may be stuck with oil and gas—and the technologies that produce them—for the foreseeable future.

Public perceptions of fracking are shaped by controversies between an industry that has downplayed the risks of fracking and citizens alleging that fracking and attendant activities have polluted air, contaminated drinking water, and scarified landscapes. This tension was particularly apparent in Pennsylvania more than a decade ago, when fracking was catapulted to the national stage. Homeowners were videoed igniting their methane-laced tap water, and protesting citizens were photographed with jars of green well water, presumably polluted from nearby hydraulic fracturing operations. Industry rebutted, claiming that the contamination predated the arrival of fracking operations and that it was not responsible. People within communities hosting fracking were scared and looking to experts to make sense of this issue. While experts were easy to find, facts, data, and definitive answers were in short supply. Deployment of hydraulic fracturing and supporting technologies had raced ahead of the science needed to illuminate its potential impacts on water quality.

Now, more than a decade later, concern over hydraulic fracturing still simmers but is no longer a frequent subject of media reporting. Why did fracking slip from national attention? Did the environmental damage prophesized by some fail to materialize or did communities simply acclimate to the disruptions and risks posed by the practice? Did new science lead to decisions and policies that eliminated vulnerabilities people encountered in the early phases of the fracking boom? By drawing from the Pennsylvania experience, I explore these questions and use the lessons learned to prescribe a science-based approach to management of fracking activities as they continue to evolve into the twenty-first century.

## OUT OF THE OIL PATCH AND INTO THE APPALACHIANS

Fracking is just one of several stages involved in the extraction of hydrocarbons from unconventional bedrock reservoirs that require extra coaxing to release the oil and gas they contain. Fracking commences after a gas or oil well is drilled and involves injecting a mixture of water, sand, and chemical additives under high pressure. The high pressure causes the rock to fracture, while the sand keeps the fractures propped open once the injection ceases and the pressure drops. These fractures, which extend radially outward tens of meters, are key because they provide conduits for the oil and gas to flow from the rock and into the nearby wellbore. Modern-day hydraulic fracturing is typically conducted in boreholes that are drilled horizontally, in parallel with the rock layers that contain the oil or gas, and requires millions of gallons of water and thousands of tons of sand per job. With the support of government subsidies, fracking got its start in Texas's Barnett Shale, after more than a decade of trial and error.

Hydraulic fracturing remained below the public's radar until it moved out of the oil patch and into areas unaccustomed, at least in recent history, to intensive oil and gas development. The natural gas company Range Resources inaugurated Pennsylvania's shale gas rush in 2004, with a Barnett-fashioned frack of Renz #1, a vertical well penetrating two kilometers deep into the gas-rich Marcellus Shale that spans much of the northeastern United States. Dozens of other production companies followed suit, scampering along the arc of the Alleghany Plateau, before focusing most intensely on Marcellus Shale sweet spots discovered in the southwest and northwest corners of Pennsylvania. Gas production from the Marcellus Shale has increased every year since the Renz well was fracked, and the Marcellus now stands as North America's highest-producing shale gas play.

## PENNSYLVANIA'S EXPERIENCE: THE GOOD, THE BAD, AND THE UNPLEASANT

The shale gas boom revitalized many of Pennsylvania's small towns that had long been suffering from shrinking budgets and services, disappearing jobs, and falling populations. Still, not everyone was happy. Residents grew frustrated with traffic snarls caused by the surge in the number of slow-moving trucks that hauled freshwater and wastes to and from drilling sites, while those living near drilling sites were unprepared for the noise, bright lights, and dust. Tensions mounted between residents that held lucrative natural gas leases and those forced to endure inconveniences of natural gas development without benefiting from the financial windfall. And the public was becoming increasingly concerned about its water.

Hydraulic fracturing is thirsty. Anywhere from four to eight million gallons of water are jetted underground to frack a single horizontal gas well. In Pennsylvania, the lion's share of this water was pumped from rivers and streams, leading to concerns that these waterways—particularly smaller streams with lower flows—could be sucked dry in support of hydraulic fracturing. Fortunately, the Pennsylvania Department of Environmental Protection, together with inter-state basin commissions, had rules in place to protect streams against excessive withdrawals. According to independent scientific reviews, these regulations appear to be accomplishing their purpose.[2]

Although water withdrawals for hydraulic fracturing were not imposing undue stress on Pennsylvania's streams and rivers, problems arose when industry tried to put this used water back. Ten to eighty percent of the water injected during a frack job is quickly regurgitated from the well, whereupon the well will continue to produce water at a gentler pace throughout its operational lifetime. This wastewater is exceptionally salty, often three to five times more saline than seawater, and may contain naturally occurring radioactive materials, such as radium, in addition to various hydrocarbon compounds. Particularly in the early phases of Marcellus Shale development, much of this wastewater was trucked from drill sites and discharged to streams and rivers after processing at wastewater treatment facilities.[3]

The treatment plants were not equipped to handle these briny wastewaters. Trouble sprouted in 2008, when monitoring of the Monongahela River in southwestern Pennsylvania revealed that the waterway was growing saltier and carrying elevated loads of bromide, a precursor in the formation of cancer-causing brominated disinfection by-products (Br-DBPs).[4] This discovery was alarming. The Monongahela River hosts intakes for more than a dozen drinking water plants that serve one million people, and, at the time, several of these plants were reporting high levels of Br-DBPs in their finished water. The problem extended beyond the Monongahela and persisted. Two years later, the Pittsburgh Water and Sewer Authority observed dramatic increases in Br-DBPs in its distribution system's drinking water, which were linked to rising bromide levels caused by discharge of partially treated Marcellus Shale brines into the Allegheny River and its tributaries.[5]

Fears of contamination stemming from intentional discharges were compounded by uncontrolled releases of fracking fluids, drilling fluids, and wastewater into the environment. Leaks from flow lines, storage pits, and storage tanks were the most common causes of uncontrolled releases at drill sites. Trucking accidents and illegal dumping led to offsite releases of fracking fluids and wastewater. Nearly 1,300 spills, releasing more than one quarter of a million gallons of various fluids, were reported to the Pennsylvania Department of Environmental Protection between 2005 and 2014.[6] Evidence from forensic analyses, though not definitive, suggests that contaminants from some of these spills leached into groundwaters tapped for residential drinking water supply.[7] Moreover, a small fraction of unintentional releases resulted in the transmission of wastewater and hydraulic fracturing solutions to streams.[8]

Spills and stream salinization raised anxieties among regulators and the public alike, but what was happening underground was far more dramatic and, more than any other issue, galvanized antipathy to hydraulic fracturing. Methane, the primary component of the natural gas slurped up from the

Marcellus Shale, was detected in dangerously high levels in well waters of eighteen households in Dimock, a small town tucked into the Endless Mountains of northern Pennsylvania. The homeowners blamed nearby gas wells that were drilled and fracked by Cabot Oil and Gas. Methane is terrific for heating homes and for generating electricity, but its presence in drinking water has no upside. While not toxic, methane is flammable and its outgassing into the enclosed air space at the top of a water well can lead to explosion. Norma Fiorentino, a Dimock resident, experienced this phenomenon firsthand when her water well blew up in 2009. Luckily, her water supply was the only casualty. The calamity was carried widely by local and national media. Cabot Oil and Gas eventually reached a settlement with most of the eighteen homeowners but, as part of the settlement terms, was not required to acknowledge responsibility for the contamination.

The first scientific study published after the Dimock incident received considerable attention, even making its way into public discourse.[9] By leveraging chemical fingerprinting techniques, the scientists attributed the source of methane present in a subset of sixty groundwater samples collected in the region around Dimock to industry activities. Other scientists countered, demonstrating with data that methane occurred ubiquitously and naturally in freshwater aquifers of northern Pennsylvania long before hydraulic fracturing entered the picture.[10] The two sets of conclusions are not mutually exclusive. That there are natural sources of aquifer methane does not let industry off the hook. Groundwater contamination by methane has been traced unequivocally to shale gas development. A recent analysis of Pennsylvania environmental records revealed that thirty-nine wells drilled into the Marcellus Shale between 2004 and 2015 allowed methane migration that impacted 108 drinking water supplies.[11] But, contrary to popular belief, the hydraulic fracturing process itself was not to blame. Instead, the weak link was poorly constructed and sealed gas wells that allowed natural gas—either from the Marcellus Shale or from overlying bedrock formations—to seep upward along the outside of gas wells and into groundwater aquifers plumbed for drinking water.

## PENNSYLVANIA'S REGULATORY RESPONSE

The problems encountered at the outset of the shale gas boom did not arise, as its critics and media narratives sometimes portray, from an utter lack of regulation. Pennsylvania was not a wild west, where fracking companies operated at will and fossil fuel production proceeded unchecked in the absence of environmental protections. In fact, the state had a regulatory framework in place that was built around more than a century's experience with conventional oil and gas extraction, during which time hundreds of thousands of wells were drilled into hydrocarbon-bearing formations above and below the Marcellus Shale. And, though bad actors surely existed, most natural gas producers did not operate with careless disregard for the environment, but instituted practices expected to protect surface water and groundwater. Nevertheless, neither the state nor industry was fully prepared for the new management challenges posed by the rapid diffusion of hydraulic fracturing.

As awareness of fracking-related impacts grew, the regulatory community reacted by strengthening policies intended to safeguard freshwater and human health. To address rising surface water salinities, the state banned shipments of Marcellus wastewaters to municipal treatment plants unless the waste was pretreated to new, more restrictive standards. Regulations for storing and containing wastewaters, drilling fluids, and fracking solutions were updated to lower the likelihood of uncontrolled releases at drill sites. The state also issued new rules for well construction intended to reduce incidences of methane leakage and migration. Additionally, the state increased protective setback distances of gas wells from water supplies, established disclosure requirements for fracking chemicals, and expanded presumptions of operator liability for drinking water contamination.

These regulatory improvements have not put Pennsylvania in the clear. The frequency of private water supply impacts attributed to oil and gas activities has declined, yet remains stubbornly above zero. In the five years since regulations were strengthened, the Department of Environmental Protection has documented 132 new cases of water supply contamination caused by shale gas operations.[12] This figure may underestimate the real extent of the problem because settlements reached between industry and homeowners with impaired water supplies need not be disclosed.[13] To compound these present dangers, new threats to freshwater quality and supply may emerge as gas wells, pipelines, and supporting infrastructure age and as industry practices evolve to minimize costs and maximize fossil fuel recovery.

Pennsylvania's experience suggests that the challenge of safeguarding freshwater resources from hydraulic fracturing will persist in one form or another as long as fossil fuels continue to be pulled from the ground. Meeting this challenge will rely, at least in part, on management and policy approaches that better leverage data and science in decision-making.

## SMART MANAGEMENT NEEDS GOOD MEASUREMENTS AND SOUND SCIENCE

Uncertainties remain. This truth must be acknowledged if we are to improve management of unconventional oil and gas development. Most, though perhaps not all, of the principal risks posed to freshwater resources by unconventional development have been identified. Yet, these risks have defied quantitation. Moreover, the effectiveness of policies and practices that aim to prevent known causes of contamination has not been thoroughly demonstrated. These shortcomings are not just a Pennsylvania problem. They plague the dozens of other states that now host oil and gas extraction by hydraulic fracturing.[14] So-called expert opinion offers no remedy to this dilemma.

Management in the midst of this uncertainty should be done adaptively. Adaptive management is not new. Nor is it trial and error. Instead, adaptive management is a scientific, data-driven way of learning while doing. It is an iterative process that begins by identifying actions or management interventions that might solve a defined problem, followed by monitoring the outcomes of those interventions, and then making adjustments to resolve any of their inadequacies. The process, repeated as necessary, builds understanding and leads to continuous improvement. This adaptive framework could address numerous management goals, including reducing the risk of groundwater contamination by gas well drilling, minimizing stray gas migration from completed wells, and limiting sediment runoff to streams during well site construction.

The success of adaptive management depends on stakeholder participation. Industry must engage with managers and, in particular, scientists from the environmental community to execute it. The track record for this collaboration is not especially strong, but there are encouraging signs and legitimate reasons for hope.

## CAN WE WORK TOGETHER?

The adage "oil and water don't mix" captures the relationship between the fossil fuel industry and environmental scientists affiliated with universities and other research organizations. The nature of interactions between these two groups typically ranges from disregardful to hostile. Environmental scientists have, according to their job description, focused on unconventional oil and gas development's effects on water and air quality, with studies that show adverse effects gaining the greatest attention and industry scorn. Industry has responded to studies of water quality impacts by trying to discredit them, inviting criticism that they are more invested in covering up problems than addressing them. This adversarial relationship hurts industry and environmental scientists alike. By not cooperating, environmental scientists are excluded access to monitoring sites, operational information, and other industry data that would strengthen their research. Industry also misses out, scuttling the opportunity to partner with environmental scientists on problem-solving and giving up the chance for constructive dialogue over scientists' interpretations.[15] The tendency for each group to remain in its own silo has engendered mistrust, leading to gridlock and disagreement that can paralyze decision-making and progress toward better environmental management.

Cooperative arrangements with industry enabling scientific assessment of fracking impacts, though rare, have been forged. For example, a consortium of companies have engaged with universities (coordinated largely by the Environmental Defense Fund) in the assessment of atmospheric methane emissions from oil and gas operations.[16] On the freshwater side, researchers at Yale have leveraged a collaboration with industry to explore potential groundwater impacts of shale gas development in Pennsylvania.[17] A formal agreement with Southwestern Energy gave Yale researchers the schedules and locations of gas well projects for the company's Marcellus acreage. With this information, the Yale researchers installed groundwater monitoring wells immediately adjacent to gas wells and measured changes in water quality over two years as several gas wells were drilled, fracked, and brought into production.

### GOING FORWARD, TOGETHER

The Yale/Southwestern Energy study is a proof of concept, demonstrating that collaborative, scientific analysis of freshwater impacts of fracking-related activities is feasible. But this study is insufficient by itself. It serves as a template that must be replicated with different production companies that operate in different regions and that collectively employ a variety of practices and methodologies.

Coordination of this science is critical so that outcomes from different studies can be compared, adaptive management can proceed, and knowledge can be exchanged with policy makers. An advisory board—chaired by a delegate from the host state's department of environmental protection (or equivalent) and composed of industry members, as well as qualified scientists from universities and environmental organizations—could manage the process.

Someone has to pay for this science, of course. The Yale/Southwestern Energy study cost just over $500,000, which may seem expensive but is less than one-quarter of the cost incurred to put one Marcellus well into production. Mid-major and major production companies may elect to pay for these studies, recognizing that the investment helps build trust within local communities and contributes to science-based regulation that may be less burdensome to them. Alternatively, or additionally, state taxes on oil and gas extraction could pay for the science. Consider that just 1 percent of Pennsylvania's 2018 natural gas impact fee would pay for the first year of eight studies similar to the one conducted by Yale and Southwestern Energy.

More science is essential, but alone is not enough to either guarantee clean drinking water in areas with fracking or determine how and where unconventional oil and gas development should proceed. Policy-making institutions must listen and be responsive to new science. Policy makers must also make resources available to ensure that policies are, as they evolve, adequately enforced. And we must make a faithful accounting of fracking costs and benefits that reflects our best knowledge. Although science is only part of the solution, its proper role in the management of unconventional oil and gas development is to lead the way by providing decision makers with credible information on environmental impacts and innovative approaches for addressing them. When environmental policy builds on careful science, rigorously analyzed data, and solid facts—pursued without fear of upsetting interested parties or overturning prevailing wisdom—innovative solutions often emerge.

## NOTES

1. "U.S. Natural Gas Marketed Production," U.S. Energy Information Administration, accessed May 1, 2019, https://www.eia.gov/dnav/ng/hist/n9050us2m.htm.
2. Erica Barth-Naftilan, Noel Aloysius, and James E. Saiers, "Spatial and Temporal Trends in Freshwater Appropriation for Natural Gas Development in Pennsylvania's Marcellus Shale Play," *Geophysical Research Letters* 42, no. 15 (2015): 6348–56.
3. Jhih-Shyang Shih et al., "Characterization and Analysis of Liquid Waste from Marcellus Shale Gas Development," *Environmental Science & Technology* 49, no. 16 (2015): 9557–65.
4. Jessica M. Wilson and Jeanne M. Van Briesen, "Source Water Changes and Energy Extraction Activities in the Monongahela River, 2009–2012," *Environmental Science & Technology* 47, no. 21 (2013): 12575–82.
5. Stanley States et al., "Marcellus Shale Drilling and Brominated THMs in Pittsburgh, Pa., Drinking Water," *Journal—American Water Works Association* 105, no. 8 (2013): E432–48.

6. Lauren A. Patterson et al., "Unconventional Oil and Gas Spills: Risks, Mitigation Priorities, and State Reporting Requirements," *Environmental Science & Technology* 51, no. 5 (2017): 2563–73.

7. Brian D. Drollette et al., "Elevated Levels of Diesel Range Organic Compounds in Groundwater Near Marcellus Gas Operations Are Derived from Surface Activities," *Proceedings of the National Academy of Sciences* 112, no. 43 (2015): 13184–89.

8. Susan L. Brantley et al., "Water Resource Impacts during Unconventional Shale Gas Development: The Pennsylvania Experience," *International Journal of Coal Geology* 126 (2014): 140–56.

9. Stephen G. Osborn et al., "Methane Contamination of Drinking Water Accompanying Gas-Well Drilling and Hydraulic Fracturing," *Proceedings of the National Academy of Sciences* 108, no. 20 (2011): 8172–76.

10. Osborn et al., "Methane Contamination."

11. Susan L. Brantley et al., "Engaging over Data on Fracking and Water Quality," *Science* 359, no. 6374 (2018): 395–97.

12. "Water Supply Determination Letters," Pennsylvania Department of Environmental Protection, last modified February 2019, http://files.dep.state.pa.us/OilGas /BOGM/BOGMPortalFiles/OilGasReports/Determination_Letters/Regional _Determination_Letters.pdf.

13. Brantley et al., "Engaging over Data," 395–97.

14. U.S. Environmental Protection Agency, *Hydraulic Fracturing for Oil and Gas: Impacts from the Hydraulic Fracturing Water Cycle on Drinking Water Resources in the United States (Final Report)* (Washington, DC: U.S. Environmental Protection Agency, 2016), EPA/600/R-16/236F.

15. Katherine E. Konschnik and Mark K. Boling, "Shale Gas Development: A Smart Regulation Framework," *Environmental Science and Technology* 48, no. 15 (2014): 8404–16.

16. Ramón A. Alvarez et al., "Assessment of Methane Emissions from the US Oil and Gas Supply Chain," *Science* 361, no. 6398 (2018): 186–88, doi:10.1126/science.aar7204.

17. Erica Barth-Naftilan, Jaeeun Sohng, and James E. Saiers. "Methane in Groundwater before, during, and after Hydraulic Fracturing of the Marcellus Shale," *Proceedings of the National Academy of Sciences* 115, no. 27 (2018): 6970–75.

**PART FOUR**  RESOURCES, ECONOMICS, AND
SUSTAINABLE BUSINESS

# Next-Generation Corporate Sustainability Leadership

## NEW LINES OF ACCOUNTABILITY

Carter S. Roberts

THE ENVIRONMENTAL MOVEMENT in the United States reached its zenith in the 1960s with the passage of comprehensive regulations, and ensuing market responses, to protect our land, air, and water. Increasing challenges to federal regulations and enforcement, combined with worsening reports on climate change and natural resource losses, now raise the question: how can we ensure further progress by other means? This essay reflects on the history of non-regulatory pathways to progress; the extraordinary promise, today, of stronger accountability between investors and corporations; and the need, going forward, to transform whole sectors and begin to secure the next generation of regulatory and governance frameworks that we need.

The main conclusions are that modern-day shareholders and investors should (1) increasingly expect disclosure of long-term risks due to climate change and environmental degradation; and (2) more regularly engage, through a new generation of analysts, on the issues of emerging environmental risks and related areas of *material* financial significance in the sustainability realm. In turn, we should expect corporate leaders to (1) increasingly disclose the long-term risks of climate change and natural resource loss to their business; (2) report on progress made against relevant areas of financial "materiality"; (3) provide credible oversight through board sustainability committees and improved performance targets for line managers; and (4) work proactively to secure governance systems to reduce their business risks and the risks to the society that they serve.

In environmental protection, we have seen enduring progress when corporations follow three rules of engagement: goals (or standards), metrics, and accountability. For many years, the Clean Air Act, the Clean Water Act, the Endangered Species Act, and many other U.S. environmental regulations met those terms and helped conserve important landscapes and deliver cleaner air and water. Now, in the face of worsening reports from the 2018 Intergovernmental Panel on Climate Change (IPCC), WWF's *Living Planet Report,* and weakening federal commitment to environmental regulations, we pay increased attention to the promise of corporate initiatives and accountability as part of a new emphasis on "sub-national" initiatives at the city, state, and corporate levels. Building on the best emerging examples of corporate leadership, we have the opportunity to guide a new form of accountability that delivers even greater results on these fronts.

## THE PROGRESS AND LIMITS OF VOLUNTARY INITIATIVES AND THE EMERGENCE OF BROADER PLATFORMS

With growing attention to non-federal pathways to progress, both toward the Paris Agreement on climate change and the United Nations Sustainable Development Goals for economic and environmental progress, we increasingly look to leadership from investors and corporations. There is much on which to build. One can point to an impressive track record of accomplishments by leading corporations, often working with key nongovernmental organizations (NGOs) and government counterparts.

Beginning in the 1990s, we began to see public-private coalitions create voluntary certification programs to drive sustainable production, and avoided deforestation for scores of commodities.[1] These efforts typically blended science regarding best practices, relied on five or six key metrics, and incorporated accountability through conditional purchase agreements.[2] Leading companies, particularly those with significant brands and consumer relationships, made the most notable commitments, which grew to between 5 and 20 percent of the total market volume for commodities such as palm oil, timber, and soy. These signals played profoundly important roles in shifting broader expectations for production and approaches to sustainability. Still, a clear gap exists between 20 percent and achieving 100 percent certification of a market. Closing that gap will require more than individual commitments.

Even companies with certification standards have learned they cannot completely reach their goals (or improve the reputation of their sector) with insufficient governance, particularly where their products are grown. This specifically holds true in places of production such as the Amazon, the Brazilian Cerrado savanna, Sumatra, and Borneo, where sustainability efforts are often stymied by weak enforcement and regulation, human rights abuses, land rights violations, and corruption. Immense demand for production from those places also means that less scrupulous producers with lower environmental standards will quickly move to fill any void, with accompanying accelerating of deforestation in the region.

Solutions to this "whack-a-mole" dilemma vary. Some industries have been able to make industry-wide commitments to certification (this is easier in concentrated industries like palm oil or farmed salmon).[3] Other industries have taken a more comprehensive approach to a specific geography or ecosystem, with integrated working groups from civil society, industry, and government creating plans to reward sustainable production while keeping the functional ecological resource intact. Some of the best examples can be found in ongoing efforts to improve soy production through the Brazilian Cerrado Working Group and Unilever's actions to support local governance in Sabah, Malaysia, to accompany their commitment to sourcing palm oil that is certified by the Roundtable on Sustainable Palm Oil.[4]

These kinds of multi-stakeholder platforms reach their most impressive forms when some of the world's largest companies create more broad-based agendas that engage all their key suppliers in science-based targets and goals.[5] In 2007, The Coca-Cola Company committed to replenishing an amount of water equivalent to its sales volume, and went on to engage with almost a thousand franchised bottlers and hundreds of communities in more than fifty countries to deliver on its goal.[6] Walmart—the world's largest company by revenue[7]—recently worked with a coalition of organizations to launch Project Gigaton.[8] Project Gigaton analyzed the company's Scope 1 to 3 carbon emissions—from those directly controlled by the company to those indirectly associated with it through its supply chain—and set ambitious peer-reviewed, science-based targets. Walmart now works with NGOs to engage five hundred of its biggest suppliers in delivering a collective goal of avoiding one gigaton of emissions. McDonald's—one of the world's largest restaurant chains—set science-based targets to tackle challenging aspects outside of the company's full control, such as emissions from franchised restaurants, cattle, and feed.[9] McDonald's now pursues these targets with full board review and performance metrics for staff across the organization.

These examples demonstrate what is possible in creating multi-stakeholder platforms that employ real goals, metrics, and supplier engagement in pursuit of their commitments. The greatest challenge by far lies in indirect Scope 3 emissions, which usually exceed the scale of a company's direct emissions but rely on changing the behavior of actors across a vast array of geographies and circumstances. Inevitably these challenges motivate companies to engage in governance. Indeed, Scope 3 emission challenges have led some companies to work on a "jurisdictional approach," which seeks to identify regions with credible governance and enforcement and, in turn, takes steps to favor sourcing from those jurisdictions over time.[10]

Leverage through scale lies at the heart of other *collaborative* platforms such as the Renewable Energy Buyers Alliance, where four NGOs[11] collaborated with the largest purchasers of renewable energy in the United States.[12] This effort aims to recruit other companies to follow their lead, and to leverage the potential purchasing power of hundreds of companies to drive better enabling policies to decarbonize America's electricity system.

While multi-stakeholder efforts offer a glimpse of what we might expect of corporations of the future, they still represent the exception. Hundreds of companies have adopted science-based targets, and many more have set voluntary commitments; their initiatives matter as do their purchasing power, their political influence, and their stakeholder platforms, which take us in the right direction. But reaching the vast majority of companies—those that offer only negligible commitments beyond regulatory requirements—will require even more. The questions are: How do we close that gap where the actions of leading companies are insufficient to solve the larger problem? How do we create a more compelling set of signals and incentives to move at the speed and scale that we need?

## NEW REWARDS AND ACCOUNTABILITY FOR PROGRESS MADE

Much of the progress we have seen has relied on effective regulations, combined with private sector leadership, to solve the most pressing environmental issues we face. Our strong sense is that uptake of corporate initiatives could reach greater scale through improved external market signals and expectations. In surveying practitioners and researching, we have identified three promising areas where investors, regulators, or society can set stronger incentives for better reporting, metrics, and accountability: risk disclosure, regular reporting on areas of materiality, and board governance and performance management.

*Risk Disclosure Leading to Action.*   We have seen growing demand to require companies to disclose information relevant to environmental, social, and governance (ESG) impact. Public letters from Yale's chief investment officer David Swensen in 2014 and BlackRock's CEO Larry Fink in 2018 heightened expectations regarding ESG performance in their portfolios.[13]

In 2018, Bank of England's governor Mark Carney signaled to banks in Britain to make long-term plans for the catastrophic risks of climate change.[14] In the same year, support for the Task Force on Climate-related Financial Disclosures grew to 287 financial firms responsible for assets of nearly $100 trillion, also signaling a sectoral momentum demanding increased disclosure only fifteen months after the task force was launched.[15]

We see increasing shareholder votes by large asset managers, such as BlackRock, State Street, Fidelity, and Vanguard, to demand more climate-related disclosure from companies in which they are invested. Recent examples include ExxonMobil responding to 62 percent of shareholders' requests to increase transparency in the company's report around climate-change-related risks.[16] Shell responded to pressure from Climate Action 100+, a coalition of 310 global investors that control more than $32 trillion in U.S. assets, to set energy-sector-leading targets for climate goals linked to executive pay.[17]

Such disclosures reflect the imperative of the World Economic Forum's 2019 *Global Risk Report*. Indeed, the *Global Risk Report* lists the top five risks to the global economy—four of which relate to the environment: "failure of climate change mitigation and adaptation" (#2), "extreme weather events" (#3), "water shortages" (#4), and "severe weather conditions" (#5).[18]

But disclosure of long-term risk does not equal action when companies focus on the short-term pressures of maximizing quarterly shareholder returns. The question is: how do we create stronger signals to encourage companies to act now to address long-term risks, particularly in the face of worsening climate change and resource loss around the world? Some point to the promise of regular reporting on areas of materiality related to sustainability.

*New Skills and Improved Reporting on Progress in Areas of Materiality.*   Responding to increasing disclosure pressures, we have seen a proliferation of ESG reporting frameworks driven by individual investors and institutional asset managers seeking more sustainable investment options. Rating tools such as the Morgan Stanley Capital International and Dow Jones Sustainability Index, and reporting guidelines such as the Global Reporting Initiative or Sustainability Accounting Standards Board, allow for more transparency in reporting progress on areas of materiality. While more effort is needed to consolidate various reporting frameworks, evidence suggests that "firms with good ratings on material sustainability issues significantly outperform firms with poor ratings on these same issues."[19]

Such evidence underscores the relationship among material measures, a company's long-term profitability, and the consumers and communities it serves. These connections build the case for sector-by-sector reporting on materiality as it relates to sustainability. They also require new skills on the part of investors and their analysts to analyze these metrics as part of their quarterly reviews and to use them in developing their recommendations.

We need a new generation of analysts, fluent not just in finance but also in sustainability, to assess quarterly on areas of materiality, including sustainability, and to engage and track corporate progress on ESG metrics. Taking this one step further we are also seeing new activist investors, such as the firm ValueAct, acquire a significant stake in a company underperforming on sustainability or climate change, and as shareholders or board members, engage the CEO and board to reach more ambitious financial and ESG goals.

If investors urge companies to properly disclose risk, and trained analysts regularly insist on sustainability data, we should expect greater momentum for company boards and leadership to respond. And in turn it would reinforce the actions that the best corporate leaders take in driving stronger operational execution—and accountability—on issues fundamental to their business and reflective of their broader roles in the world.

*Moving Faster: From Reporting to Governance and Execution.*   We see increasing results from companies that create strong executive and board-level governance and management systems to act on the long-term risks to their business and to society. In companies such as McDonald's and Nike, standing board sustainability committees or key board specialists regularly review progress and hold management accountable for progress on commitments and areas of risk.[20] But only 62 percent of analyzed companies have some form of oversight for sustainability at the board level, and only 13 percent show truly active oversight practices with board mandates and regular reports on sustainability from management.[21]

Likewise, in companies such as Alcoa, Danone, and Walmart, accomplishment of sustainability goals constitutes one key measure for assessing leadership and executive compensation.[22] But only 2 percent of S&P 500 companies tie environmental metrics to executive compensation, according to a 2017 study by executive compensation and consulting firm Semler Brossy.[23]

Investors, shareholders, and the millions of individuals that invest in pension funds and sovereign wealth funds clearly play a role in signaling expectations to both executives and boards. How do we increase the percentage of boards that have stronger ESG structures? How do we motivate investors to look for board competence on sustainability—to ensure the internal metrics and incentives deliver on commitments that address risks and respond to the communities and society that they serve? In both cases, we believe investors and shareholders can productively pose basic questions when they meet with the leadership of companies, when they inquire about the credibility of systems put in place to deliver against targets, and when they ensure their analysts assess and act on relevant ESG information.

## FUTURE MARKET LEADERSHIP: SIGNALS AND ACCOUNTABILITY TO SOLVE THE LARGER PROBLEM

In conclusion, there is much to build upon in the ongoing progress by industry leaders and their evolving efforts to address environmental risks. Science-based targets, certification programs, and thoughtful multi-stakeholder platforms have shifted the direction of production and technology, given evidence of what is possible at a larger scale, and spawned innovations and learning that should guide any future systems of reporting or governance. There is now an opportunity for the most influential investors and private sector leaders to further the track record they have built and to take it to the next level. It will mean adopting goals, reporting, and metrics to solve larger environmental problems, not just a company's particular piece of the puzzle.

None of this will happen without clearer expectations from investors, consumers, and society. But the imperative is clear. The latest IPCC report documents that the threat of climate change continues to exceed expectations, as do the trajectories of deforestation and ocean destruction in the world. And the report in turn calls for an unprecedented collaboration between private and public entities, the likes of which we have not seen since the Marshall Plan for economic aid to Europe after World War II.

Regulations still matter and play the most powerful role in driving progress on environmental issues, including climate change, natural resource destruction, species extinction, and water pollution. But we also need to make better use of market mechanisms and signals to accelerate progress. More regular disclosure and reporting on risks and materiality, raised

expectations of action from investors and consumers, improved board governance and management incentives, and leadership in engaging both government and communities all promise greater speed and accountability in
solving the problems we face.

The investor of the future should signal these expectations and follow up
on them through regular meetings with corporate leadership and through
investment in a new generation of ESG-trained analysts. In turn we ought to
expect CEOs to be brilliant at demonstrably seeing and then acting on long-
term risks to their business, including those related to climate change and the
environment. One can imagine a cascading set of responses in which CFOs
are constant in reporting, quarterly, on relevant areas of materiality; boards
exercise due diligence through trained committees; and line managers are
measured by sustainability metrics and goals. In turn, these signals should
ultimately motivate external affairs teams to work with peers and associations
to build on their knowledge of risks and solutions, and to engage in creating
the regulatory and governance structures needed to solve the long-term risks
to their business, and to us all.

**NOTES**

I want to acknowledge the partnership of Katy Lai in conducting research, editing
drafts, and joining me, along with Sheila Bonini, in interviewing thought leaders
around the country and testing various ideas in different settings. This is very much a
work in progress; we look forward to updating our sense of opportunities and acting on
them accordingly.

1. Nongovernmental organizations include World Wildlife Fund (WWF), Rainforest
   Alliance, and International Social and Environmental Accreditation and Labeling
   Alliance. Industry leaders include Unilever, Mars, The Coca-Cola Company,
   Kimberly-Clark, Procter & Gamble, Walmart, McDonald's, Ikea, Nike, Pepsi, Nes-
   tle, and so on. The most well-known examples of certification programs are the
   Forest Stewardship Council, the Marine Stewardship Council, and the Roundtable
   on Sustainable Palm Oil.
2. National Research Council, *Certifiably Sustainable? The Role of Third-Party Certification Systems: Report of a Workshop* (Washington, DC: National Academies Press,
   2010), https://doi.org/10.17226/12805.
3. Roundtable on Sustainable Palm Oil has more than 4,000 members worldwide who
   represent all parts of the supply chain. "About Us," Roundtable on Sustainable Palm
   Oil, accessed January 15, 2019, https://rspo.org/about. Global Salmon Initiative
   represents approximately 50 percent of the global farmed salmon sector. "What
   Is the GSI?," Global Salmon Initiative, accessed January 15, 2019, https://global
   salmoninitiative.org/en/what-is-the-gsi/.
4. Unilever, "Walmart and Unilever Announce Forest Sustainability Initiatives at the
   Global Climate Action Summit," September 14, 2018, https://www.unilever.com

/news/press-releases/2018/walmart-and-unilever-announce-forest-sustainability
-initiatives-at-the-global-climate-action-summit.html. The Working Group includes
all the major players in the soy industry, leading NGOs, and the Brazilian government coming together to create the combination of land use plans, financial compensation to producers that forgo converting natural habitat to soy fields, and
science and market support to maintain the viability of one of the rarest and most
threatened savanna ecosystems on Earth—also one of the most profitable areas for
soy production.

5.  Definition of science-based targets: "Targets adopted by companies to reduce
    greenhouse gas (GHG) emissions are considered 'science-based' if they are in line
    with the level of decarbonization required to keep global temperature increase
    below 2 degrees Celsius compared to pre-industrial temperatures, as described
    in the Fifth Assessment Report of the Intergovernmental Panel on Climate
    Change (IPCC AR5)." "What Is a Science Based Target?," Science Based Targets,
    accessed January 15, 2019, https://sciencebasedtargets.org/what-is-a-science-based
    -target/.

6.  John Schwartz, "Coca-Cola Says It's Close to Water Replenishment Goal," *New York
    Times,* August 25, 2015, https://www.nytimes.com/2015/08/26/business/coca-cola
    -expects-to-reach-its-water-replenishment-goal-5-years-early.html.

7.  Oliver Stanley, "There's a New List of the World's 10 Largest Companies—and Tech
    Isn't on It," *Quartz,* July 19, 2018, https://qz.com/1331995/walmart-is-the-worlds
    -biggest-company-apple-isnt-in-the-top-10/.

8.  These organizations include WWF, the Environmental Defense Fund, The Sustain-
    ability Consortium, Carbon Disclosure Project, and The Nature Conservancy.

9.  Maggie McGrath, "The Largest Restaurant Companies in the World 2018: McDon-
    ald's and Starbucks at Top of Food Chain," *Forbes,* June 6, 2018, https://www.forbes
    .com/sites/maggiemcgrath/2018/06/06/the-largest-restaurant-companies-in-the
    -world-2018-mcdonalds-and-starbucks-at-top-of-food-chain/#1deead3e6fd1.

10. WWF, "Tackling Deforestation through a Jurisdictional Approach," March 7, 2018,
    https://www.worldwildlife.org/publications/tackling-deforestation-through-a
    -jurisdictional-approach.

11. WWF, World Resources Institute, Rocky Mountain Institute, and Business for So-
    cial Responsibility.

12. Lily Donge and Letha Tawney, "State of the Market" (PowerPoint presentation,
    Renewable Energy Buyers Alliance Summit, Santa Clara, CA, September 18, 2017).
    The top five renewable purchasers are Google, Amazon, Apple, Microsoft, and
    Walmart.

13. David Swensen, "2014 Letter on Climate Change," Yale Investments Office, Yale Uni-
    versity, August 27, 2014, http://investments.yale.edu/2014-letter-on-climate-change/;
    Larry Fink, "Larry Fink's 2018 Letter to CEOs: A Sense of Purpose," BlackRock Inc.,
    2018, https://www.blackrock.com/corporate/investor-relations/2018-larry-fink-ceo
    -letter.

14. John-Paul Ford Rojas, "Mark Carney Warns Banks on Climate Change Risks," Sky
    News, September 26, 2018, https://news.sky.com/story/mark-carney-warns-banks
    -on-climate-change-risks-11509476.

15. The Task Force on Climate-related Financial Disclosures, *2018 Status Report,* September 2018, https://www.fsb-tcfd.org/publications/tcfd-2018-status-report/.

16. Gary McWilliams, "Exxon Shareholders Approve Climate Impact Report in Win for Activists," *Reuters,* May 31, 2017, https://www.reuters.com/article/us-exxonmobil -climate/exxon-shareholders-approve-climate-impact-report-in-win-for-activists -idUSKBN18R0DC.

17. Ron Bousso, "Shell to Set Sector-Leading Emissions Targets after Investor Pressure," *Reuters,* December 3, 2018, https://www.reuters.com/article/us-shell-carbon/shell-to -set-sector-leading-emissions-targets-after-investor-pressure-idUSKBN1O20NK.

18. World Economic Forum, *The Global Risks Report 2019* (Geneva: World Economic Forum, January 15, 2019), https://www.weforum.org/reports/the-global-risks-report -2019.

19. Mozaffar Khan, George Serafeim, and Aaron Yoon, "Corporate Sustainability: First Evidence on Materiality," *Accounting Review* 91, no. 6 (March 2015): 1697, https:// papers.ssrn.com/sol3/papers.cfm?abstract_id=2575912.

20. "Board Committees Membership," McDonald's Corporation Investor Relations, accessed January 15, 2019, https://corporate.mcdonalds.com/content/corpmcd /investors-relations/board-committees-and-charters/committee-membership.html; Thomas Singer, "Director Notes: Linking Executive Compensation to Sustainability Performance," The Conference Board, May 2012, http://www.comunicarseweb.com .ar/sites/default/files/biblioteca/pdf/1339073125_Linking_Executive _Compensation_to_Sustainability_Performance.pdf.

21. Ceres and KKS Advisors, "Systems Rule: How Board Governance Can Drive Sustainability Performance," 2018, https://www.ceres.org/sites/default/files/reports /2018-05/Systems%20Rule%20vfinal.1.pdf.

22. Ceres, "Report on Executive Pay Links to ESG Metrics (UPS, 2018 Resolution)," 2018, https://engagements.ceres.org/ceres_engagementdetailpage?recID =a0l1H00000C4WCsQAN.

23. Seymour Burchman and Barry Sullivan, "It's Time to Tie Executive Compensation to Sustainability," *Harvard Business Review,* August 17, 2017, https://hbr.org/2017/08 /its-time-to-tie-executive-compensation-to-sustainability.

# Making Companies Work for Society

## HARNESSING GLOBAL FINANCIAL MARKETS FOR SUSTAINABILITY

Todd Cort

IN 2017, KRAFT HEINZ attempted to buy the global consumer brands company Unilever. When Unilever management refused the overture, Kraft Heinz attempted to go straight to shareholders with a hostile takeover bid. While this was one of many takeover attempts that year, observers of corporate sustainability found it particularly gripping. Unilever, led by CEO Paul Polman, had been lauded widely as a leader in corporate sustainability, championing the company's Sustainable Living Plan, which seeks to double sales while halving the company's environmental impacts. Unilever branded itself as the model for environmentally sustainable growth through prudent acquisitions, avoiding excessive reliance on debt, and focusing on the long term. To this end, Polman famously announced on his first day at the helm of Unilever that he would stop producing quarterly financial reports.

In contrast, Kraft Heinz was itself the product of an aggressive merger fueled by private equity firm 3G Capital and the Warren Buffett–owned Berkshire Hathaway. 3G Capital has showcased an ability to create value through pursuit of efficiency and optimization in the companies it owns. Specifically, the company would leverage—that is, borrow on the collateral of its subsidiaries' assets—to buy greater market access, streamline costs (including eliminating employees), and acquire more companies. This short-term growth strategy appeals to investors eager to see immediate returns. So when Kraft Heinz approached the shareholders of Unilever with the promise of aggressive, short-term growth, the sustainability world held its breath. Would Unilever's investors and the world of finance more broadly throw out the model of the "sustainable company" in the pursuit of short-term gain?

## SHAREHOLDER PRIMACY: AN UNSUSTAINABLE STATUS QUO

When asked, many people take a dim view of the moral compass that guides global financial markets. Investors, markets, and finance justifiably typify the heartless and unaccountable face of globalization. But imagine if markets and the flows of global money incentivized companies to consider the health of the planet, in addition to short-term profit and financial return. In this world of *sustainable finance,* any company, city, or nation seeking capital would need to demonstrate social and environmental responsibility.

The sustainable finance ideal and the historical realities of finance often starkly differ. A century ago, the role of the corporation was largely one of public benefit. Companies created jobs, prosperity, and economic growth that benefited a wide swath of society. The most highly regarded firms were those that demonstrated longevity and staying power. Finance flowed to established companies that sought stability and steady growth. This model of businesses as agents of broad economic benefit resulted in greater financing directed toward firms with longer-term growth models, even though their record of environmental responsibility may not have been exemplary.

Over the last 50 years, our perception of the role of companies has shifted dramatically toward a vision of companies as agents for wealth generation. More specifically, wealth generation for their shareholders. This notion of *shareholder primacy* gained significant traction in the 1970s when Milton Friedman argued that a corporate executive is "an agent serving the interests of his principal"—meaning that the management of a company must carry out the wishes of the shareholders.[1] The growth of shareholder primacy has been widely viewed as the pendulum swinging away from an earlier era of misbehavior, when companies sometimes inappropriately shunted money away from shareholders. Shareholder primacy manifests itself as greater pressure on companies to generate consistent quarterly profit by passing social and environmental costs on to society at large.[2] Under this model, the companies that pay the lowest wages and the least in environmental compliance are the winners.[3]

## INDICATORS OF CHANGE

Shareholder primacy stands in stark contrast to the ideals of sustainable finance. Whereas the ideal company under the model of shareholder primacy would theoretically maximize financial performance at the expense of environmental and social benefits, the sustainable company would seek to maximize all three simultaneously. Sustainability practitioners have increasingly pointed to "six capitals" that should be considered, valued, and grown by sustainable companies: financial, manufactured, environmental, social, intellectual, and human. In a sustainable finance world, money would flow to companies that could demonstrate benefit broadly across these six areas. For example, a company could value the natural resources (such as water) that it utilizes and replenishes to not only show investors that it is doing "good" but also demonstrate lower exposure to scarce resources and therefore lower risk of disruption if the resource becomes harder to access. Similarly, a company might demonstrate the value of its people and talent to show resilience, lower costs of recruiting talent, and increase the potential for greater innovation and productivity. The exact balance among the six capitals will vary for each company, but the more companies can demonstrate progress on all six, the greater the comfort of investors that see these capitals as important.

The tension between shareholder primacy and sustainable finance models has grown increasingly acute over the past two decades as a result of two trends. The first is a growing awareness from companies that they need to address environmental and social challenges. The number of companies that produce a voluntary sustainability report has exploded in recent years.[4] KPMG, a global consulting firm, found that approximately 75 percent of all large publicly traded companies now produce a sustainability report.[5] The second trend arises from the growing social awareness that shareholder primacy increases the gap between the wealthy and the poor.[6] The global rich-poor gap is now at levels unprecedented in modern history. People recognize that companies, as engines of economic growth, lie at the heart of this disparity by delivering wealth to a shrinking proportion of the world's population.

Given these trends and the perception that the inexorable logic of corporate finance underpins shareholder primacy, some commentators write off sustainable finance as an unrealistic dream. And yet, we are closer to a system of sustainable finance than one might expect. A variety of developments are changing the landscape of finance and providing incentives for companies to break through the model of shareholder primacy. Many of these developments are fueled by the shareholders themselves, who anticipate greater financial benefits from encouraging companies to look beyond a myopic view of short-term financial returns.

One of the compelling realities facing today's company is that over half of its market value, on average, is intangible.[7] This means that if we add up all of its concrete assets, like buildings and patents and cash, we account for only half of what the market thinks the company is worth. The other half? That half is completely dependent on the perception of a multitude of stakeholders including investors, customers, employees, and communities. We think that these companies, much like money itself, have more value than the sum of their parts, and therefore they do. But because that value depends on perception, companies must work diligently to meet the expectations of all these customers, investors, employees, and so on, lest the value slip away. The result is that if society starts to question a company's impact on the things we hold dear, such as good jobs, fair wages, clean water, and clean air, that intangible value may start to erode. The increasingly clear importance of reputation and corporate responsibility has largely driven the rise in voluntary sustainability reports, even when the tangible value of such reports may be less clear.

Investors are also keenly aware of this intangible value and have pushed companies to consider more and more social and environmental aspects of performance. Some of this pressure stems from investors seeking to align their portfolios with their own personal values. But the rapid growth in investor interest is more likely driven by thousands of studies that show positive correlations between corporate sustainability and financial performance.

However, the exact relationship between sustainability and performance remains elusive. Currently, it is hard to tell if companies that prioritize sustainability efforts create more value by avoiding risks, innovating more effectively, retaining employees, reducing costs, identifying market opportunities, or some combination of all these factors. The result is that we know sustainability can enhance the value of a company in most circumstances, but how and why are still a bit of a mystery.

## THE RISE OF SUSTAINABLE FINANCE

Because the linkages between sustainability and profit are still unclear, it is not surprising that investors are taking a wide variety of approaches to sustainable finance. Some investors see smart sustainability as an active advantage to exploit in the market and therefore seek out performance based on sustainability leadership. Other investors see sustainability as more of a risk to avoid and want to moderate the volatility of risky investments by prioritizing companies that comprehensively assess environmental risks.

Still other investors wish to use their role as shareholders for moral purposes. This approach might take the form of shareholder activism in which investors use their positions as owners to change corporate practices and thus move society toward a more sustainable future.[8] Similarly, some investors will either favor particular companies in their portfolio or screen them out to foster environmental or social impact above and beyond any financial returns. These so-called impact investors are defined by their willingness to sacrifice some level of marketplace success in the interest of sustainability results. By some estimates, as much as 25 percent of all investments today have at least one environmental or social consideration embedded in the investment strategy.[9]

The days of shareholder primacy and its consequences are not yet over, but there are clearly cracks in its armor, and the pendulum appears to be swinging back toward a vision of companies as agents of social and environmental benefit as well as financial growth. Moreover, this swing toward sustainable finance appears to be accelerating, driven by both external and internal factors.

Externally, companies are seeing the rise of a new, radical transparency. Covering up risky or irresponsible behavior—or keeping any secrets at all—is becoming more and more difficult for all companies as digital technology, social media, and the age of Big Data mature. In the 1990s, it required the work of diligent advocacy groups to uncover and bring to light the presence of children in Nike's supply chain.[10] Today, a whistleblowing employee or other observer with a cell phone can document and broadcast the same information in seconds. To gauge interest in a new product in the early 2000s, analysts would send people to the door of an Apple store to count the number of customers entering. Today, satellite images of the parking lots of every Apple store give more complete and real-time insight into the same question. It is increasingly difficult (and costly) for companies to try to control their own data. Under these circumstances, it makes more sense to change practices than to attempt to hide information. The result is greater effort from companies to align with societal expectations on sustainability in the form of better management and performance to protect people and the environment while doing business.

An internal logic for sustainable finance can also be seen in emerging form. The "fiduciary duty" of the board of directors represents the front line between companies and their investors. While the requirements of corporate law in the United States have long sharply focused the fiduciary duty of directors on shareholder value, there have been a number of recent efforts to protect boards that look beyond their narrow responsibility to shareholder financial returns. One such effort in the United States is the "benefit corporation."[11] This legal designation (similar to a 501(c)3 nonprofit organization or limited liability company) allows managers and board directors to consider social and environmental benefits in their formulation of corporate strategies. Since 2010, over 30 states have passed legislation allowing companies to register as benefit corporations, resulting in over 5,000 registered companies as of 2018.[12] While this mechanism provides protections for companies to look beyond shareholder primacy, the figurative jury is still out, as these protections have not yet been tested in courts.

More recently, professors at Harvard have proposed a mechanism for boards of directors to protect themselves by making their intentions to consider a broader suite of interests clear to shareholders. Specifically, Robert Eccles and Tim Youman have suggested that companies issue a "Statement of Significant Audiences and Materiality" as a way for boards to explicitly consider interests like social and environmental benefits—and officially notify any shareholders of this broader focus.[13]

A powerful set of forces today drives investors and companies toward more responsible behavior. The importance of reputation, intangible value, and radical transparency is forcing companies to shift toward more responsible management practices. Meanwhile, investors see sustainability information as the key to better environmental impacts, social outcomes, and financial returns. In response, governments, investors, and companies are pushing mechanisms to allow greater consideration of sustainability issues in financial decisions. A recent example is the guidance, spearheaded by major investment companies such as BlackRock, from the Task Force on Climate-related Financial Disclosures seeking greater understanding of climate-related risks faced by companies.

## IDEAS AND UNCERTAINTIES

Despite the progress toward sustainable finance, key uncertainties remain: How will companies balance financial performance with social and environmental responsibilities? Will the transition be sufficient, and sufficiently rapid, to address the pressing social and environmental concerns facing us today, such as climate change, water scarcity, pollution, income inequality, hunger, and poverty? How much can we rely on the market, investors, and companies to protect society and the environment? Government policy will largely drive the answers to these questions.

Governments have two important roles to play. First, they must enact policy frameworks and regulatory incentives to speed up the transition to a more sustainable finance model. They can promote this acceleration through more consistent financial disclosure requirements. Financial regulators can require traded companies to disclose performance on environmental and social impacts and risks. Governments can also adopt emerging guidelines on broader accounting practices that incorporate more environmental and social impacts than traditional financial accounting. While disclosure requirements should promote greater disclosure of material environmental and social issues, it would be counter-productive to be too prescriptive on the exact set of metrics they should disclose. Stakeholders need decision-useful information that identifies areas of concern, opportunities, and the company's position to either mitigate risk or take advantage. Prescriptive regulations on disclosure may, in fact, discourage investors that see environmental and social performance as an opportunity to out-perform the market.

Government policy will also need to pick up where markets leave off. Markets will protect environmental and social well-being only to the extent that it makes sense for businesses and investors. While the view of what makes sense is broadening and encompassing greater environmental and social responsibilities, it will only go so far. This is where governments must step in to protect society and the environment. One way to incentivize this protection would be to conduct assessments of the nation's environmental and social resources. This idea—to assess social and environmental capital in a manner similar to gross domestic product (GDP) calculations—is not new, but it has struggled to catch hold. Both China and India have recently made proposals to include social and environmental capital in their GDP reporting. Maryland calculates a Genuine Progress Indicator that assesses the quality of life in the state by looking at issues like income inequality, leisure time, human health, and the effects of environmental protection or degradation. Policy initiatives such as these will need to expand and grow so that governments can better understand where the greatest needs for society lie.

There is little question that we will see a more sustainable approach to finance in the future. We see this evolution playing out today in millions of investor and company decisions weighing the value of sustainability against pure financial gain. We saw it play out in the Unilever efforts to fend off the

Kraft Heinz takeover bid. In CEO Paul Polman's words, this was "clearly a clash between a long-term, sustainable business model for multiple stakeholders and a model that is entirely focused on shareholder primacy."[14] In response to the bid, Polman mobilized the Unilever shareholders most aligned with his sustainable long-term vision of growth to make it clear to Warren Buffett that this would be a clash of cultures. Polman did offer incentives to existing investors to reject the bid in the form of increased dividends, share buybacks, and higher growth projections, but activism also surged in the form of a YouGov petition and outspoken opposition from celebrities such as Bono of the band U2.[15] The takeover bid suddenly looked less attractive and less comfortable to investors. In short, the Unilever stakeholders that saw value in a sustainable business model raised their voice to claim ownership, and the takeover bid failed. That decision has been vindicated as Kraft Heinz share prices plummeted in 2019 in the wake of reports that the Securities and Exchange Commission had issued a subpoena to the company around improper accounting practices. The recognition by owners of the value of long-term and multi-stakeholder responsibility is the heart of the sustainable finance movement.

**NOTES**

1. Milton Friedman, "The Social Responsibility of Business Is to Increase Its Profits," in *Corporate Ethics and Corporate Governance*, ed. Walther Ch. Zimmerli, Markus Holzinger, and Klaus Richter (Berlin: Springer Berlin Heidelberg, 1970), 175, https://doi.org/10.1007/978-3-540-70818-6_14.

2. D. Gordon Smith, "The Shareholder Primacy Norm," *Journal of Corporation Law* 23 (1998): 277–324.

3. Lynn A. Stout, "Bad and Not-So-Bad Arguments for Shareholder Primacy," *Southern California Law Review* 75 (2002): 1189–210.

4. Ans Kolk, "Trends in Sustainability Reporting by the Fortune Global 250," *Business Strategy and the Environment* 12, no. 5 (September 2003): 279–91, https://doi.org/10.1002/bse.370.

5. KPMG, *The Road Ahead: The KPMG Survey of Corporate Responsibility Reporting*, 2017, https://assets.kpmg/content/dam/kpmg/xx/pdf/2017/10/kpmg-survey-of-corporate-responsibility-reporting-2017.pdf.

6. Paddy Ireland, "Shareholder Primacy and the Distribution of Wealth," *Modern Law Review* 68, no. 1 (2005): 49–81.

7. "Ocean Tomo's Intangible Asset Market Value Study," Ocean Tomo, accessed December 7, 2018, http://www.oceantomo.com/2013/12/09/Intangible-Asset-Market-Value-Study-Release/.

8. Daniel C. Esty and Todd Cort, "Corporate Sustainability Metrics: What Investors Need and Don't Get," in "State of ESG Data and Metrics," ed. Daniel C. Esty and Todd Cort, special issue, *Journal of Environmental Investing* 8, no. 1 (2017): 11–53,

http://www.thejei.com/wp-content/uploads/2017/11/Journal-of-Environmental
-Investing-8-No.-1.rev_-1.pdf; Nur Uysal, "The Expanded Role of Investor Relations:
Socially Responsible Investing, Shareholder Activism, and Organizational Legitimacy," *International Journal of Strategic Communication* 8, no. 3 (July 3, 2014): 215–
30, https://doi.org/10.1080/1553118X.2014.905478.

9. Laura Colby, "Global Sustainable Investments Grow 25% to $23 Trillion," Bloom-
berg Professional Services, July 24, 2017, https://www.bloomberg.com/professional
/blog/global-sustainable-investments-grow-25-23-trillion/.

10. Simon Zadek, "The Path to Corporate Responsibility," *Harvard Business Review* 82,
no. 12 (December 2004): 125–32.

11. Janine S. Hiller, "The Benefit Corporation and Corporate Social Responsibility,"
*Journal of Business Ethics* 118, no. 2 (December 1, 2013): 287–301, https://doi.org/10
.1007/s10551-012-1580-3.

12. "Benefit Corporations and the Public Markets," Benefit Corporation, accessed December 7, 2018, http://benefitcorp.net/benefit-corporations-and-public-markets.

13. Robert G. Eccles and Timothy Youmans, "Materiality in Corporate Governance:
The Statement of Significant Audiences and Materiality," Harvard Business School
Working Paper 16-023, 2015, https://www.hbs.edu/faculty/Publication%20Files/16
-023_f29dce5d-cbac-4840-8d5f-32b21e6f644e.pdf.

14. Andrew Winston, "The Top 10 Sustainable Business Stories of 2017," *Harvard Business Review*, December 22, 2017, https://hbr.org/2017/12/the-top-10-sustainable
-business-stories-of-2017.

15. Scheherazade Daneshkhu and Lionel Barber, "Paul Polman: How I Fended Off a
Hostile Takeover Bid," *Financial Times*, December 3, 2017, https://www.ft.com
/content/76cddc3e-d42e-11e7-a303-9060cb1e5f44.

# Waste and Materials Management

## FROM HARM REDUCTION TO VALUE CREATION

Marian Chertow and Matthew Gordon

FOR DECADES AMERICANS have grown up learning fundamental waste management principles: reduce, reuse, recycle. Yet, over half of what we generate from homes and businesses—known as municipal solid waste—ends up being discarded in landfills. While recycling has increased, so has our understanding of its limits. New policies and strategies can refocus waste management so that it is less costly for residents and more beneficial for the environment. In particular, twenty-first-century waste and materials policy should seek to preserve, rather than throw away, the materials and energy that go into the products we use. This priority requires a new focus on material diversion, rather than waste treatment and disposal.

## A WASTEFUL STATUS QUO

The dominant waste management strategy in place across the United States since the late 1980s and early 1990s emphasizes a "waste management hierarchy" (fig. 27.1) that promotes reuse, recycling, and energy recovery. The hierarchy, which reflects core waste management principles, dictates that people should attempt to conserve as much of the energy and material in objects as possible. The current U.S. system, however, continues to rely on landfilling for disposal and recycling for recovery (which often includes composting), with a much smaller amount of refuse sent to energy-from-waste facilities.[1]

These old favorites, however, should be seen as fragile environmentally and costly economically, especially in the United States, where the

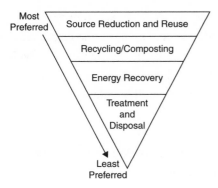

FIGURE 27.1 Waste management hierarchy. U.S. Environmental Protection Agency, "National Overview."

responsibility for waste management falls on cash-strapped local governments. It is not necessary that we achieve "zero landfill" or that we highly curtail municipal recycling. Rather, we should rely less on these strategies and more on approaches to increase the value of waste material, in a recast system that incorporates the findings of recent scientific, economic, and policy analysis and experience drawing on fields such as environmental economics, consumer behavior, operations management, and *industrial ecology*—the study of the flow of materials and energy through systems at different scales.

Looking back thirty years, we can say that at least the panic over running out of room for waste disposal has abated. In contrast to 1987, when the iconic "garbage barge" traveled eight thousand miles from New York in search of a place to dump its load, today we have a range of waste management solutions in place. Residential waste generation has leveled off over the last thirty years, at around 4.5 pounds per person per day. Landfills today are better managed environmentally, and there is significant expansion space available in many parts of the United States.[2] Interestingly, local governments have shown considerable willingness to transport waste long distances at great expense, typically to very large, privately owned landfill sites, even across multiple state borders. On the recycling front, market prices for commodities such as paper and metal are highly volatile, straining the ability of local governments to plan finances, especially when their primary duty is to deliver a healthy and sanitary collection and disposal service.

Fortunately, we also see many examples of entrepreneurial, environmentally minded firms pioneering new material management strategies and business models that create value through reuse, repair, and remanufacture with various elements of the waste stream. Without supportive policies, however, these approaches are likely to remain marginal. In an era when private firms are investing in new technology to upgrade recovery systems and create value from waste, reframing policy to focus on diversion and separation of individual materials into sub-streams can create new jobs and entrepreneurial opportunities, as well as provide life cycle environmental benefits.

## LESSONS UNLEARNED: BACK TO THE FUTURE

Upon reflection, some of the most important problems with the current waste and materials management system seem to come from forgetting three foundational lessons from the past:

1) *The "waste management hierarchy" privileges the most environmentally benign management strategies* (see fig. 27.1). The waste hierarchy holds that source reduction and reuse are preferred, in rank order, to recycling, composting, energy recovery, and treatment and disposal. Reduction comes first because it eliminates waste altogether—including the costs of collection, processing, recycling, or disposal and all of their related environmental burdens. Reuse preserves the embodied energy and materials it took to make products in the first place. Recycling, however, requires changing the physical characteristics of recovered products and materials depending on their specific composition—a process that siphons away a portion of the energy and materials it took to create the product. Waste disposal goes further yet in negating the original properties of a product or material, because in this "solution" almost all the resources it took to make and use a good are jettisoned. Worse, despite improvements in landfilling, the likelihood remains that some of the effluent from the goods can actually harm groundwater and air, create methane leakage, and provoke other problems. A reasonable critique of the hierarchy is that it has not been fully implemented.[3] As society has grown more and more consumptive, insufficient attention has gone into systematic source reduction and reuse strategies to match, and so the lion's share of U.S. municipal solid waste is recycled or landfilled.

2) *Physical separation and sorting increase recovery and reduce entropy.* Once discards are mixed together, recovering them for reuse becomes increasingly difficult from a thermodynamic perspective, because the purity of the materials diminishes as they proceed through the steps of materials processing.[4] The current Chinese waste import ban reminds us of the importance of high-quality sorting of recycling streams to maintain material value. As far back as 2013, under the "Green Fence" legislation in China, waste-exporting coun-

tries were being told to reduce the contamination in recycling loads, a common problem stemming from mixing material streams rather than keeping them isolated.

Indeed, the recent policy change in U.S. municipal recycling—from several separations for recycled materials to one mass "single-stream" recycling container—has led to *increased* waste at the back end of recycling facilities. Outgoing waste has been reported to be as high as 40 percent of incoming materials, whereas facilities accepting better-sorted materials lose as little as 5 percent. An important observation is that through policies like single-stream collection, municipalities are turning potentially valuable materials into waste, as separation after-the-fact has often proven to be economically infeasible. Business start-ups in the waste and materials space—from reusable packaging and carpet fibers to collection of used books and clothing—are more successful when they can collect their raw materials separately from other forms of waste. This reality illustrates the important contribution of infrastructure and policy in creating the conditions for market success.

3) *A life cycle view highlights that environmental impacts are higher "upstream" than "downstream."* Life cycle assessments that track the environmental impact of wastes were first released in the early 1990s.[5] They demonstrated that the largest environmental impacts from waste, by more than an order of magnitude, occur at the earlier or "upstream" stages of production, including raw material processing, manufacturing, and distribution. In contrast, the "downstream" stages following the use and discard of materials, including collection, waste recovery, and disposal, contribute a relatively small fraction of the total environmental impact. This clarifies another priority for waste and materials management: to focus on the life cycle stages with the largest environmental impacts, and to substitute recovered resources with fewer impacts for resource-intensive ones. The current ease-of-disposal paradigm encourages inexpensive, short-lived products and thus encourages more of these upstream impacts.

These facts also highlight the importance of sharpening incentives for environmental care—particularly by requiring people to pay for the harm they cause. This principle of "internalizing externalities" means that anyone producing material or using packaging that cannot be recycled should pay for its environmental costs.

In aggregate, environmental externalities, consumer behavior, and a lack of material recovery infrastructure combine to encourage the overproduction of disposable consumer products such that (1) new products are cheaper than they would be if producers had to internalize the full costs of production, and (2) disposal is cheaper than it would be if the full costs of landfilling and recycling were internalized. Such outcomes have consequences. While many environmentally minded firms are pioneering new business models that promote reuse, repair, and remanufacture, the market for such products is likely to remain limited, unless the environmental services these firms provide is reflected in the price of their goods.

## AN ECONOMIC AND ENVIRONMENTAL VALUE APPROACH TO WASTE AND MATERIALS MANAGEMENT

These three lessons point to a new imperative for twenty-first-century waste management policy: while it is important to know how much waste we produce, the more salient question may be how much is diverted before it reaches the municipal system, and how much more is diverted through a range of strategies across the product life cycle. The suggestions we provide here seek to refocus the current waste and material management system around the top rungs of the waste hierarchy, and to set priorities using systems analysis and life cycle thinking. Returning to the three lessons discussed earlier, we suggest policies to address each.

1) *Reinforcing the waste management hierarchy at the higher rungs.* In most U.S. municipalities, people do not pay for waste collection in proportion to the amount of waste they generate. This creates disincentives for reducing waste or reusing materials. A policy known as "unit-based pricing" or "pay as you throw" has been very effective at addressing these issues. While the policy is not new, the most recent data analysis from communities in Massachusetts and Connecticut finds consistent, predictable results from cities and towns. The evidence shows that these programs typically reduce solid waste disposal per capita by 40 to 48 percent.[6]

In commercial establishments, laws that require stores to charge small amounts of money for plastic bags or silverware have led to a large reduction in the use of these items. Indeed, in grocery stores across the country, just a five-cent charge for plastic bags induces a significant percentage of shoppers to bring their own reusable grocery bags. Even the simple act of requiring stores to ask a customer if he or she wants the disposable items, rather than giving them out automatically, may decrease their usage. This observation shows that it is not exclusively cost that matters but habit and salience.[7] Both of these examples clearly show how behavior changes when consumers are forced to internalize the social and environmental costs of disposal.

2) *Creating value with better sorting and separation.* Single-stream collection of recyclables essentially pits the convenience of having to handle only one recycling bag or bin against the increased value that can be achieved from the extra task of sorting recyclables. More bins can be more confusing for residents, and also work against economies of scale in collection. It is much more efficient for one truck to collect all of the waste in a neighborhood than for many trucks to collect small amounts of materials from a wider service area. Focusing on savings too narrowly, however, may preclude options that would result in higher levels of material recovery.

Cities are coming up with innovative ideas that simultaneously improve the sorting of waste and preserve its value. One example from Europe is a new system, enabled by technology, whereby residents discard waste and materials in several designated categories in distinctively colored bags. These bags, even though they carry different materials, can be collected by one truck and driven to and emptied at a recovery facility in a colorful mix. From there the material travels up conveyor belts to be optically sorted based on the color of the bags, thus enabling aggregation by type of material. Afterward, various recyclables can be recovered, food scraps and other organic materials can be digested, and refuse can be used for energy. In this system, separation occurs at the home. While there will still be some mixing that contaminates the bags, the easier the segregation, the better the recovery results and the more likely people are to participate. These systems are highly efficient, which has kept their costs down for many European cities and towns.

Another way to improve sorting and separation is to divert specific material streams before they are ever even considered waste. One interesting example of the entrepreneurial activity in this space is the effort to create a "reverse supply chain" in the apparel sector to get used clothing back to market. Today's forward-thinking apparel companies carefully preserve used garments, extending their life through repairing and resewing them until all that is left, for very worn-out garments, is thread that, in the not too distant future, using new technology, can be reclaimed for use in creating new products. Old clothing, even in the waste stream, can be very heavy. Consequently many communities are experimenting with curbside apparel pickup, so that the old clothes can re-enter "circular" supply chains, reducing waste tonnage for the cities and towns and thereby creating savings on disposal fees.

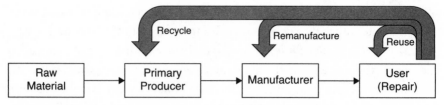

FIGURE 27.2 Material flows through the reclamation cycle. Adapted with permission from Lund and Hauser, "Remanufacturing—An American Perspective."

3) *Decreasing upstream impacts.* In some product categories, there is significant upstream benefit from replacing the need for primary production with recovered materials. The shorter loops (fig. 27.2) maintain more of the embodied energy, materials, and functionality of the product, while the longer loops require more structural rearrangement and thus degradation.[8] Mixed recycled paper and plastics, for instance, can substitute for virgin materials only in certain lower-quality applications and thus cannot fully displace the need for primary production. Reused products, on the other hand, better maintain their original functionality and thus may be better able to substitute for new goods. The infrastructure of our current waste management system corresponds primarily to the largest loop in the figure. To fully harness the environmental benefits of reuse, repair, and remanufacture, we must build or incentivize the creation of these reverse logistic chains.

**FINAL THOUGHTS**

For many countries, achieving better recycling and waste disposal would translate into significant benefits for human health and the environment, by eliminating informal dumps and garbage burning. For the United States, the focus must be on reimagining the top rungs of the waste hierarchy. The ideas highlighted here include incorporating current data around unit-based pricing of waste disposal to achieve significant reduction, reuse, and even recycling; welcoming and providing incentives to a more sustainability-oriented entrepreneurial community; using information technology and digital systems to achieve better material collection and separation; and building a sturdy reverse supply chain to fully execute on advanced cycles of reuse, repair, and remanufacture.

Over the past thirty years, the argument has changed from a tilt toward "landfilling is dangerous and recycling is a remedy" to one where, especially from a local government perspective, even if disposal is less dangerous, it is still expensive in terms of total cost. The first system alteration we need, then, is updating reduction and reuse strategies to generate greater environmental benefits. The second is reconfiguring the collection and sortation system to recognize a broader array of environmental and social welfare benefits, including incentives for job and market creation to boost the emergent entrepreneurial waste and material reuse economy.

**NOTES**

1. U.S. Environmental Protection Agency, "National Overview: Facts and Figures on Materials, Wastes and Recycling," Overviews and Factsheets, October 2, 2017, https://www.epa.gov/facts-and-figures-about-materials-waste-and-recycling/national-overview-facts-and-figures-materials.

2. Jon T. Powell, Timothy G. Townsend, and Julie B. Zimmerman, "Estimates of Solid Waste Disposal Rates and Reduction Targets for Landfill Gas Emissions," *Nature Climate Change* 6, no. 2 (February 2016): 162–65, https://doi.org/10.1038/nclimate2804.

3. Jane L. Price and Jeremy B. Joseph, "Demand Management—a Basis for Waste Policy: A Critical Review of the Applicability of the Waste Hierarchy in Terms of Achieving Sustainable Waste Management," *Sustainable Development* 8, no. 2 (2000): 96–105, https://doi.org/10.1002/(SICI)1099-1719(200005)8:2<96::AID-SD133>3.0.CO;2-J.

4. Julian M. Allwood et al., "Material Efficiency: A White Paper," *Resources, Conservation and Recycling* 55, no. 3 (January 1, 2011): 362–81, https://doi.org/10.1016/j.resconrec.2010.11.002; Timothy G. Gutowski, "Materials Separation and Recycling," in *Thermodynamics and the Destruction of Resources*, ed. Bhavik R. Bakshi, Dušan P. Sekulić, and Timothy G. Gutowski (Cambridge: Cambridge University Press, 2011), 113–32, https://doi.org/10.1017/CBO9780511976049.008; Thomas Graedel et al., "What Do We Know about Metal Recycling Rates?," *Journal of Industrial Ecology* 15, no. 3 (June 1, 2011): 355–66, https://doi.org/10.1111/j.1530-9290.2011.00342.x.

5. John Schall and Yale University Program on Solid Waste Policy, *Does the Solid Waste Management Hierarchy Make Sense? A Technical, Economic and Environmental Justification for the Priority of Source Reduction and Recycling* (New Haven, CT: Yale University School of Forestry & Environmental Studies, 1992), https://books.google.com/books?id=t-34GAAACAAJ.

6. Kristen Brown, "Comparison of Unit Based Pricing in Municipalities and Across Programs" (PowerPoint presentation, Waste Zero, Inc., December 17, 2018); Kristen Brown (VP Waste Reduction Strategy, Waste Zero, Inc.), interview by Marian Chertow, December 14, 2018.

7. Travis P. Wagner and Patti Toews, "Assessing the Use of Default Choice Modification to Reduce Consumption of Plastic Straws," *Detritus* (November 21, 2018), https://doi.org/10.31025/2611-4135/2018.13734.

8. Robert T. Lund and William M. Hauser, "Remanufacturing—An American Perspective" (paper presented at 5th International Conference on Responsive Manufacturing—Green Manufacturing, Ningbo, China, January 2010).

# Can We Define Planetary Boundaries on the Human Use of Materials?

Thomas E. Graedel

SOCIETY IS BUILT on materials. Our housing, transport, food, and communication networks depend on them to such a degree that it seems impossible to imagine life without the benefits that diverse and abundant materials provide. The result of this dependence has been an extraordinary increase in rates of material use in the past several decades.[1] However, unexpected incidents of possible materials scarcity have emerged. These trends suggest that materials sustainability should receive more attention than it has to date. In particular, in a world of rapidly growing population and personal income, it appears prudent to consider two principal goals related to materials and their use: (1) procuring the materials necessary for human society to achieve the United Nations Sustainable Development Goals, which lay out targets for sustainable and high-quality life on Earth, and (2) retaining sufficient stocks of materials to enable the continued progress of human society for many decades, to the year 2100 and beyond.

But for any given material, how do we know how much use is too much? How can we put material needs and material limits in perspective? To create a framework for understanding these limits, the concept of "planetary boundaries" for materials may offer some guidance.

Johan Rockström of the Stockholm Resilience Center and his colleagues proposed the idea of "planetary boundaries" in 2009.[2] That group of scholars attempted to define the "safe operating space for humanity with respect to the

Earth system." Their focus was on "the planet's biophysical subsystems or processes," and they defined "safe operating spaces" for several global metrics such as greenhouse gas concentrations, water use, and biodiversity loss. In other words, they argued that humans must stay below each threshold to avoid risk of dangerous environmental consequences. Although many of the detailed analytical aspects of the Rockström initiative have proven to be debatable,[3] the concept captured the imagination of the science community and has stimulated considerable debate in policy and governance circles.

Humans have been aware of the possibility of limits to the supplies of societally important materials for nearly half a century.[4] Such limits could come from the exhaustion of traditional deposits, like the depletion of oil or precious metal supplies. Alternatively, they could result from constraints related to environmental, geopolitical, or social impacts of materials use; because of cement's carbon emissions, for example, we may not be able to use all that could be available.[5]

Sustaining planetary systems is clearly a laudable goal for the future, but it is not the only goal we should consider. Society also needs to ensure the sustainable use of the planet's physical resources. As a variety of studies have clearly shown, the human appropriation of material resources is very large and is rising rapidly as populations and incomes increase throughout the world. Can rates of material supply over time balance this increasing demand? This question takes on special importance given the Sustainable Development Goals. A number of them (for example, #7: Affordable and Clean Energy and #11: Sustainable Cities and Communities) will clearly require large amounts of materials if humans around the world are going to realize them. We should thus ask whether material-based constraints might slow or reverse human progress in the future, whether defining planetary boundaries and safe operating spaces for materials might achieve some useful insight, and whether doing so would usefully contribute to discussions on sustainability.

## BOUNDARIES FOR THE PLANET AND ITS MATERIALS

The basic framework of the original planetary boundary concept involved several steps: (1) identifying a small number of critical processes that regulate the Earth system and that keep the planet in a stable condition that allows life to thrive, (2) identifying human disturbances to these processes, and (3) specifying levels of perturbation below which destabilization risk is low. This list raises some immediate issues. First, how large is a "small number of critical processes," and how should they be chosen? Second, what exactly is meant by "perturbation"? Third, can the perturbation be measured, and are we already doing so? For the original planetary boundaries project, a useful response to these questions appeared to require a combination of scientific evidence and professional judgment. Will Steffen, Rockström, and colleagues in 2015 pictured global-level perturbations as changes to a damage indicator (for example, climate change) related to a specific cause (for example, atmospheric carbon dioxide concentrations).[6] They then delineated a structured progression of steps to evaluate human environmental impacts: a "safe operating space," a "zone of uncertainty," and a "zone of danger."

Rockström and colleagues found that some indicators appeared to be within the safe operating space limits, some were in the zone of uncertainty, and some were in the high-risk territory. To the degree that the authors' choices of the variables and their evaluations accurately reflect current stresses, the planetary boundary exercise appears to have considerable potential as a tool to help guide environmental policy and governance.

With this framework as a starting point, how might the planetary boundary concept be applied to the human use of materials? Doing so would require choosing the materials or material groups important for human functioning, identifying potential rates of demand over time for those materials, and specifying safe operating demand, zones of uncertainty, and thresholds of high-risk demand for each. The intent of this exercise would be to define levels of resource use that are sustainable over the long term (say to 2100 or beyond) while simultaneously permitting progress toward realization of the Sustainable Development Goals for humanity.

### POTENTIAL MATERIALS OF CONCERN

Although the number of different materials used by humans is vast, a suitable list of "potentially critical" materials should be modest in order to be tractable. Such a list would presumably include those materials humans use most widely, those with lower use rates but that appear crucial in enabling sustainable technologies, and those for which processing and product fabrication result in large environmental impacts. A first attempt at such a list, containing six material groupings, is given in Table 28.1.

*Major Metals.* "Major metals" are the most widely used metals for constructing and maintaining the foundational entities of human society: buildings,

**Table 28.1**

Initial list of potential materials groupings to be considered in creating the planetary boundaries for materials

| MATERIAL | POSSIBLE BASIS FOR ASSESSMENT |
|---|---|
| Major metals | Anticipated demand as fraction of known resources |
| Alloy metals | Anticipated demand as fraction of known resources |
| Polymers | Potential for recovery and reuse |
| Construction minerals | Local and regional resources as fractions of anticipated demand |
| Composite materials | Potential for recovery and reuse |
| Mass timber | Anticipated demand as a fraction of annual forest growth |

infrastructure, transportation, and so on. A list of metals important to human society would surely include iron, aluminum, and copper and perhaps others such as manganese, nickel, and zinc. It is very difficult to identify appropriate substitutes for these metals in most of their applications should their supplies become scarce, both because of their unique material properties and because they are so heavily used that it is unclear whether sufficient quantities of possible substitutes could ever be made available.

Geological processes, over millennia, determine the ultimate availability of the major metals. One could imagine, however, constraints other than geological ones. For example, the processing of aluminum is very energy intensive, and a legislated limit to greenhouse gas emissions, were lawmakers to enact it, could severely constrain the supplies of aluminum. Similar concerns involve other metals that possess high embodied energy, such as the platinum and palladium used as catalysts in chemical manufacturing.

*Alloy Metals.*    Alloy metals are metals that we add to other metals (often major metals) in order to enhance the physical properties of a material. In many cases alloys enable such artifacts of modern life as aircraft engines, batteries for portable electronics, and magnets for renewable energy applications. Because metal usage is generally in alloy form, and because the level of use of alloy metals in critical applications is often modest, we should consider evaluating the alloy metals that are widely employed in modern society. The list could include tungsten (cutting tools), vanadium (lightweight, high-strength alloys), and neodymium (magnets for renewable energy), among many other possible choices.

A unique aspect of many alloy metals is that we often mine them as by-products of major metals rather than extracting them for themselves. For example, there are no indium mines; indium is produced as a by-product of zinc. A consequence of this geological occurrence is that alloy metal availability is not closely linked to price, because the income from alloy metals is too small to influence a decision on whether to open or close a mine whose financial plan is based on the parent metal. Should demand for the parent metal decrease significantly, therefore, alloy metal supply could also decrease regardless of demand.

*Polymers.* In the second half of the twentieth century, polymers (for example, polyethylene and polyvinyl chloride) became very widely used in consumer products, packaging, high-performance industrial products, and elsewhere. Their low cost, diverse physical and chemical properties, and relative ease of processing have rendered them the obvious choice for many applications. The wide variety of polymers that are a common feature of modern life are produced from just 2 to 3 percent of petroleum and natural gas production. Accordingly, potential supply issues do not play a dramatic role in the availability of polymers. However, polymers disperse widely into their surroundings, are difficult to distinguish from one another without extensive analysis, and are prone to loss into the environment.[7] It is increasingly clear that they do long-term damage to marine ecosystems when they are discarded. For this reason, it seems likely that we should explore limits on—or transformations of—polymer use because of environmental impacts rather than limitations based on physical or chemical properties.

*Construction Minerals.* Construction minerals consist of cement, sand, and crushed stone—the default materials used worldwide to create roads, buildings, and infrastructure. These minerals have generally been widely available and society has used them extensively, but in recent years their per capita rates of use have increased dramatically as construction has intensified around the world.[8] Because of the weight of sand and crushed stone, construction materials are seldom exported or imported over long distances.

A planetary boundaries approach to materials should consider three major concerns regarding the use of construction minerals: (1) the production of cement is highly energy intensive—it generated some 1.5 petagrams of planet-warming carbon dioxide emissions in 2014, a bit more than 4 percent of the global total; (2) sand has become so scarce in some parts of the world that illegal sand mining has emerged; and (3) the limited availability of crushed stone in some regions results in costly mining and shipping from elsewhere. As a consequence of these concerns, materials experts are increasingly discussing alternative approaches to the use of construction materials. There is thus a challenge in defining the safe operating space, a metric that would almost certainly vary with location around the world.

*Composite Materials.* A composite material, or "composite," is formed from two or more materials that have significantly different physical or chemical properties. The goal is that, when combined, the composite will have salutary characteristics that derive from the combination of the two substances. Such materials have become widely used in applications that include construction (glass fiber insulation), automobiles (body panels, components), and aircraft (fuselages, wing skins). In fact, the annual global use of composite materials is roughly equivalent in mass to that of certain major metals, such as lead.

Unlike metals, alloys, and plastics, composites are very challenging to recycle after use, largely because their material properties depend on close bonding of dissimilar materials.[9] However, recent progress in developing recycling approaches for carbon fiber composites suggests that this challenge can be overcome in at least some cases.[10] Overall, therefore, the inclusion of composite materials in a planetary boundary assessment would be difficult to conceptualize but would be a potentially important insight into sustainable worldwide materials use in the future.

*Mass Timber.* Innovative forest products—such as cross-laminated ("mass") timber made from multiple layers of wood—are increasingly used in buildings and related structures. Mass timber typically originates from trees, but engineered bamboo can be used in similar ways. Because bamboo grows largely in temperate climates, where population growth is likely to be the highest in the next several decades, it will be important as a building resource in those regions. With anticipated rapid development around the world to house growing urban populations,[11] mass timber appears likely to see robust and increasing demand in the coming years.[12] For this reason, it may be an important resource to consider when assessing material planetary boundaries.

## DEVELOPING A PROVISIONAL PLANETARY BOUNDARY FRAMEWORK FOR MATERIALS

The work of Rockström and his colleagues on planetary boundaries addresses whether humans are crossing sustainability thresholds in a number of important areas. Such an approach usefully evaluates the present but says nothing about how human activity might evolve in the future. In the case of materials, most of which are ultimately limited in quantity, it seems more important to compare current and future demand with anticipated supply over time. Supply would, of course, be limited not only by the absolute availability of the resources themselves but also by the rates of technology development that enable or inhibit acquisition, processing, and use of the materials. Accordingly, the development of material-centered planetary boundaries would likely build on frameworks such as the recently developed Shared Socioeconomic Pathways,[13] an effort by scholars to imagine future global economic and demographic change. Evaluating future scenarios for materials is a longer-term and more involved process than assessing the present state of material use. The project may need an organizational structure that encompasses a small full-time research staff together with frequent workshops that involve external experts, so as to generate ongoing evaluations of the state of materials use relative to planetary boundaries.

If, as I suggest here, a list of planetary boundaries for the human use of materials would have value in assessing global sustainability for the next several decades and beyond, we should ask how such a quantified list could be created. As with the original planetary boundaries concept, a materials version of this activity should be viewed as a community effort rather than one performed by a single scholar or research group. One could imagine the starting point being to convene, for perhaps a week, twenty or thirty worldwide scholars with deep knowledge about natural resources, the implications of material resource use from a sustainability perspective, and potential material resource constraints under various possible global futures. The goal would be to assess the framework outlined in this essay, revise and improve it, explore what materials to track and how to measure their boundaries, and then generate a proposal for review and assessment by the global scientific community. Given anticipated trends in economic development and development's increasingly clear materials dependence, establishing planetary boundaries for materials would seem to be imperative.

**NOTES**

1. Heinz Schandl et al., *Global Material Flows and Resource Productivity* (Paris: United Nations Environment Programme, 2016).
2. Johan Rockström et al., "A Safe Operating Space for Humanity," *Nature* 461 (2009): 472–75.
3. "Earth's Boundaries?," *Nature* 461 (2009): 447–48; Jose Montoya, Ian Donohue, and Stuart Pimm, "Planetary Boundaries for Biodiversity: Implausible Science, Pernicious Policies," *Trends in Ecology & Evolution* 33 (2018): 71–73.
4. Brian J. Skinner, "Earth Resources," *Proceedings of the National Academy of Sciences of the United States* 76 (1979): 4212–17.
5. Saleem H. Ali et al., "Mineral Supply for Sustainable Development Requires Resource Governance," *Nature* 541 (2017): 367–72.
6. Will Steffen et al., "Planetary Boundaries: Guiding Human Development on a Changing Planet," *Science* 347 (2015), https://doi.org/10.1126/science.1259855.
7. Roland Geyer, Jenna R. Jambeck, and Kara Lavender Law, "Production, Use, and Fate of All Plastics Ever Made," *Science Advances* 3, no. 7 (2017), https://doi.org/10.1126/sciadv.1700782.
8. Alessio Miatto et al., "Global Patterns and Trends for Non-metallic Minerals Used for Construction," *Journal of Industrial Ecology* 21 (2016): 924–37.
9. Amar K. Mohanty et al., "Composites from Renewable and Sustainable Resources: Challenges and Innovations," *Science* 362 (2018): 536–42.
10. Fanran Meng et al., "Environmental Aspects of Use of Recycled Carbon Fiber Composites in Automotive Applications," *Environmental Science & Technology* 51 (2017): 12727–36.
11. Mark Swilling et al., *The Weight of Cities: Resource Requirements of Future Urbanization* (Nairobi, Kenya: United Nations Environment Programme International Resource Panel, 2018).
12. Michael H. Ramage, "The Wood from the Trees: The Use of Timber in Construction," *Renewable and Sustainable Energy Reviews* 68 (2017): 333–59.
13. Brian C. O'Neill et al., "The Roads Ahead: Narratives for Shared Socioeconomic Pathways Describing World Futures in the 21st Century," *Global Environmental Change* 42 (2017): 169–80.

# Natural Capital, Equity, and the Sustainable Development Challenge

Eli P. Fenichel

FOR MOST OF OUR species' existence, prior generations left sufficient resources for the generations that followed to flourish. Societies typically passed forests, soils, and waters from generation to generation in a similar condition and added complementary technologies. The degradation of natural resources since the Industrial Revolution has led policymakers to focus on the questions of *sustainable development* and *conservation*. Sustainable development and conservation consist of two core challenges: (1) how to meet the needs of the current generation and (2) how to do so without compromising the ability of future generations to meet their own needs (the primary focus of conservation).[1]

Policymakers have long attempted to address these challenges separately, but they are fundamentally linked. Any present-day use and distribution of a forest, an ocean, or an oil reserve shapes the availability of those resources for future generations. Any present-day restriction on resource use shapes how people meet their present needs. To ensure equitable use of the resources that sustain society, *natural capital*, society needs to pay greater attention to the difficult trade-offs between use of resources now and how resources are saved for the future.

## SOCIETY'S PRINCIPAL AND INTEREST

Resource use by preceding generations seldom compromised the ability of later generations to meet their needs—at least at a general scale.[2] In part, natural resources available were vast, and the human demands put on them—given a limited population—were relatively low. Various cultures also imposed rules and norms that led to conservation.

It is harder to argue that past societies met their own needs—especially by modern standards. At no time in history has a smaller fraction of the global population lived in abject poverty than in the present. In 1820, over 95 percent of people lived in extreme poverty, but less than 10 percent do today.[3] At no time in history have children had a greater probability of surviving to adulthood; today 95 percent of children survive until at least age five.[4] Meeting the needs of the present, addressing *intragenerational equity,* was the historical challenge. In some places, this remains the challenge. However, the cost of meeting the needs of the next member of the current generation, whose needs are not yet met, is likely rising. It appears harder and harder to reach those still in extreme poverty.

Despite continued intragenerational challenges, the assumption that the next generation will be able to meet its needs cannot be taken for granted. Natural resource consumption by current generations—including using the environment to store waste products such as climate-warming carbon dioxide—may be compromising the ability of future generations to meet their needs.

Past generations passed wealth and opportunities to current generations through a portfolio of *capital assets* shared and divided up among members of society. These capital assets are often classified into produced capital, such as infrastructure and buildings; human capital, such as health and knowledge; and natural capital, such as water, forests, minerals, and a stable climate. The total value to society of these capital assets is called *inclusive wealth.*[5] Sustainable development requires the current generation to leave future generations with capital endowments, measured as inclusive wealth, at least as large as they received. Said in the terms we would use to describe a financial endowment, equity between generations requires not letting society's "principal balance" decline.

Natural capital holds a special place in the set of "capitals" that contribute to inclusive wealth. Humanity's initial endowment was largely in the form of natural capital, and natural capital is largely shared by humanity. People consumed natural capital and converted it into the other forms of capital. For example, people converted forests into buildings and wild animals into livestock, which enhanced human nutrition. Or people converted oil into light that enabled learning and generated knowledge. People continue to benefit from natural capital without extraction—for example, through recreation, flood protection, and aesthetics. The process of converting natural capital has heightened concerns about conservation of natural resources. President The- odore Roosevelt articulated this concern as early as 1910, stating: "The nation behaves well if it treats the natural resources as assets which it must turn over to the next generation increased, and not impaired, in value; . . . That is all I mean by the phrase, Conservation of natural resources. Use them; but use them so that as far as possible our children will be richer, and not poorer, because we have lived."[6]

It is not a forgone conclusion that all societies everywhere are better off converting more natural capital into produced capital or human capital. Con- suming or converting natural capital has global impacts. Cutting down trees and using them for fuel results in greenhouse gas emissions and global warming. In many places, people still feel a need to convert natural capital to consumption to meet their needs. Thus, they cut trees to have wood fuel with which to cook. But such actions affect the ability of future populations glob- ally to meet their needs. Reconciling local and global difference remains a major challenge.

## MEASURING NATURAL CAPITAL

The discussion about intra- versus intertemporal allocation requires a com- mon set of facts—they require measurement of the change in value of natural capital stocks. Nobel laureate Robert Solow argued that "talk [of sustainability] without measurement is cheap . . . a few numbers, even approximate num- bers, would be much more effective in turning the discussion toward con- crete proposals and away from pronunciamentos."[7]

Focusing on "a few numbers" may lead to measurement of the things that are easy to measure. Since World War II, economists have been focused on measuring "economic growth." Oddly, despite natural capital's historical role in human development, natural capital has been largely ignored since formal measurement of "economic growth" and social progress began. Nobel laureates William Nordhaus and James Tobin pointed out as early as the 1970s that this effort, aimed exclusively at measuring produced capital and perhaps human capital, fails to measure human well-being and instead fo- cuses on production while leaving out environmental degradation.[8] For ex- ample, society focuses on keeping track of the money made catching fish to a much greater extent than it keeps track of how many fish are left in the ocean and the future fishing opportunities those fish enable. Recently, Nobel laureates Joseph Stiglitz and Amartya Sen, along with Jean-Paul Fitoussi, renewed concerns about the ability to measure and track through time whether needs of current generations are being met, with a focus on natural capital, human capital, and inequality.[9]

The World Bank, United Nations Environment Programme, and others are paving the way toward measuring changes in natural capital and inclusive wealth.[10] Current versions of the inclusive wealth metric—the measure of all resources society is leaving future generations—do not inform whether the current needs are met. Rather, the inclusive wealth approach assumes that the only concern is maintaining an equally valuable set of opportunities for the next generation. Still, it is informative, but perhaps unsurprising given environmental pressures and increasing social concern about poverty, that the World Bank reports that over the past twenty years global inclusive wealth has grown; though in many low-income countries, per capita wealth has declined. That is, these poor countries are wealthier, but there are more people among which to divide those riches, resulting in less per person. The World Bank's analysis includes only the easiest-to-measure stocks of natural capital, but still finds that "getting rich is not about liquidating natural capital."[11] The World Bank does find declines in natural capital wealth, but these are compensated for with increases in human and produced capital.

Change in inclusive wealth depends on changes in quantities of capital assets (for example, acres of forest, gallons of oil in reserves, or tons of fish in the sea), multiplied by an asset price, or "marginal value."[12] For example, a country's forest natural capital goes up either because there is more forest (assuming the price stays constant) or because the asset price of the forest increases, perhaps because of more foresighted management. It is not enough to simply measure how much land forests cover, because as technologies and economies change, the price or marginal value of natural capital resources can change over time. Whale oil was once highly valued for lighting lamps in homes, but the discovery of kerosene and other fuels reduced the value of whales for future lighting while the value of living whales increased for other reasons (for example, tourism).

A challenge associated with achieving a full accounting for natural capital is that many important stocks are not traded in markets. So how can those stocks be priced? Economists must *impute* prices based on how people conserve and use natural capital stocks[13]—do people treat forested land like a valuable resource, or do they act as if it is expendable? Regardless of how people feel about stocks, the asset price for accounting depends on actual actions.

The process of inferring these prices reveals that whether or not inclusive wealth is declining depends on how and to whom resources are allocated.[14] Who has access to natural capital stocks impacts asset prices. How the owners of forests manage their land greatly impacts how much of that form of natural capital gets passed on to future generations. It means that, in practice, the questions of intra- and intergenerational equity concerns raised in the sustainability discussion cannot be addressed separately.

## CONNECTING PRESENT AND FUTURE

There are two reasons why natural capital connects present and future questions of equity. First, who manages a stock of natural capital and how it is managed shape how much of it ends up being conserved for future generations. Forgone conservation impacts the well-being of people in the present. Consider if to provide a clean atmosphere for future generations, society agreed to suddenly stop all oil extraction, effective immediately. Future generations would reap the benefits of a stable climate. Current generations would face economic chaos as people tried to figure out how to power their cars or heat their homes—and this burden would fall disproportionately on rural and poor populations. This is an extreme example, but it highlights how natural capital management connects present and future.

Within the first challenge is the challenge that investment in the future requires a right that enables exclusion of others. Inevitably, either future or present generations have the right to use any particular stock of natural capital. Without the right of exclusion, one individual's restraint becomes another individual's opportunity to use now—"use it or lose it." This may sound perverse, but water allocations in the dry western United States work this way. The shared nature of many forms of natural capital, which provide broad and diffuse benefits, makes addressing the right of exclusion especially challenging. But, "use it or lose it" or "first come, first served" approaches exclude the future in favor of the present, while strong preservation excludes the present in favor of the future. There is no fully inclusive solution.

Second, public policy decisions involve aggregating effects across people. Even if stocks of resources stay constant, the human population can change, so aggregate inclusive wealth misses something important. The most common approach is to think of per person or per capita wealth measures. Imagine a society of only two people. Consider a reallocation of resources: if one individual were made sufficiently better off and could compensate the other, who might be made worse off without the compensation, but is at least indifferent with the compensation, both parties should *voluntarily agree* to the change. This "potential compensation criterion" maintains freedom and lacks coercion.

Sustainability, however, is not just about having the ability to potentially meet the needs of the current generation. Nobel laureate Sen argues that the potential compensation criteria cannot credibly be evoked as the ethic associated with voluntary exchange when there is no intention or attempt to compensate those made worse off. Furthermore, it is possible to allocate resources so as to distribute gains to the wealthy at the expense of the poor while still increasing the average. The philosopher John Rawls advocated focusing on the least well-off person in society, but such a criterion does not address intergenerational concerns, because the current generation may well be the least well-off, and then there is little that future generations can do.[15] A democratic approach, based on majority rule, might lead to a focus on changes in the inclusive wealth of the median individual. But focusing on the median clearly would not ensure that the needs of all members of the current generation are met.

As Roosevelt advised, societies need policies that protect the value of natural capital. First, societies, from the level of communities to nations, need to develop a set of accounts to begin to track changes in the value of inclusive wealth, especially inclusive wealth that is collectively "owned," like most forms of natural capital. This is imperative to developing a commonly agreed-upon set of facts.

Second, a sort of "pay as you go" rule needs to be developed, so that declines in value of some stocks are offset with investment in other stocks.[16] If society chooses to increase current fish harvests, then society needs to compensate future generations for the value of lost fishing opportunities. An important and outstanding question is, what offsetting investments should "count"?

Third, failing to achieve intragenerational fairness often translates into pressure on and degradation of natural resources and lost opportunities for future generations. Society needs to find ways to help current generations meet their needs while, at the same time, storing opportunities for the future. The need to compensate current generations for their forbearance requires new ways to move future collectively held wealth to the neediest members of the current generations. A conservation bond program could be one path

forward. Bonds would transfer financial conservation costs to future generations, who likely will have greater financial resources. While it seems unfair
to saddle future generations with excess financial debt, it also seems unfair to
saddle them with a woefully unbalanced portfolio of assets and eroded endowment. Conservation bonds would in effect allow future generations to pay
present generations to protect natural capital on their behalf. A conservation
bond program would increase financial debt but reduce the declines in the
principal balance of collectively held assets, such as natural capital. Understanding this balance underscores why accounting systems for natural capital
and inclusive wealth are needed.

When the stakes are real, sharing is hard. But the golden rule we all
learned as small children still applies, with a bit of extra nuance—treat future
generations as you would like your generation treated, and treat others in your
generation as you would like to be treated in the future (or perhaps have your
children treated). Thus, those who are frustrated by the lack of environmental
action—for example, on climate change—might wish to ensure that the policies they advance to address greenhouse gas emissions include a deeper commitment to intragenerational equity. Specifically, they might want to promote
much greater support for those in the present whose well-being could suffer
as the transition to clean energy unfolds—coal miners in Appalachia, for example. Remember, the golden rule works within and through time. Therefore, selective application to the future at the expense of the present, and vice
versa, is not application of the golden rule at all.

## NOTES

1. World Commission on Environment and Development, *Our Common Future* (New York: Oxford University Press, 1987).
2. Past generations achieved this feat because subsequent generations "repaired" damage and migrated. However, those past generations often endowed descen-dants with the technology and knowledge to make those repairs or migrate.
3. Max Roser and Esteban Ortiz-Ospina, "Global Extreme Poverty," Our World in Data, last modified March 27, 2017, https://ourworldindata.org/extreme-poverty.
4. Max Roser, "Child Mortality," Our World in Data, accessed January 14, 2019, https://ourworldindata.org/child-mortality.
5. Glenn-Marie Lange, Quentin Wodon, and Kevin Carey, *The Changing Wealth of Na-tions 2018: Building a Sustainable Future* (Washington, DC: World Bank, 2018); Shunsuke Managi and Pushpam Kumar, eds., *Inclusive Wealth Report 2018: Measur-ing Progress towards Sustainability* (New York: Routledge, 2018). Terminology here is a bit muddled. The terms "comprehensive wealth" and "genuine wealth" are also used. "Wealth" is sometimes replaced with the word "savings."

6. Theodore Roosevelt, "Speech at Denver before the Colorado Live Stock Association," in *A Compilation of the Messages and Speeches of Theodore Roosevelt*, ed. Alfred Henry Lewis (New York: Bureau of National Literature and Art, 1906), 52.

7. Robert Solow, "An Almost Practical Step towards Sustainability," *Resources Policy* 19, no. 3 (1993): 171.

8. William Nordhaus and James Tobin, "Is Growth Obsolete?," *Economic Research: Retrospect and Prospect* (National Bureau of Economic Research) 5 (1972): 1–80.

9. Joseph E. Stiglitz et al., *Mis-measuring Our Lives: Why GDP Doesn't Add Up* (New York: New Press, 2010).

10. The absolute value of inclusive wealth is meaningless, which means that it is of little use for assessing how current generations are doing. Changes in inclusive wealth through time are helpful for assessing concerns about intergenerational equity and whether opportunities for future generations are being protected.

11. Lange, Wodon, and Carey, *Changing Wealth of Nations*, 9.

12. Arrow et al. and Dasgupta show this formal relationship. Fenichel et al. provide a graphical explanation as to why the prices must be weighted. Kenneth Arrow et al., "Are We Consuming Too Much?," *Journal of Economic Perspectives* 18, no. 3 (Summer 2004): 147–72; Partha Dasgupta, *Human Well-Being and the Natural Environment* (New York: Oxford University Press, 2007); Eli Fenichel et al., "Wealth Reallocation and Sustainability under Climate Change," *Nature Climate Change* 6 (February 2016): 237–44.

13. Eli Fenichel, Joshua K. Abbott, and Seong Do Yun, "The Nature of Natural Capital and Ecosystem Income," in *Handbook of Environmental Economics, Volume 4*, ed. Partha Dasgupta et al. (North Holland: Elsevier, 2018), 85–142.

14. Eli Fenichel and Yukiko Hashida, "Choices and the Value of Natural Capital," *Oxford Review of Economic Policy* 35, no. 1 (January 2019): 120–37.

15. John Rawls, *A Theory of Justice* (Cambridge, MA: Harvard University Press, 1971); Robert Solow, "Intergenerational Equity and Exhaustible Resources," *Review of Economic Studies* 41, no. 5 (1974): 29–45.

16. Economists typically refer to this as the Hartwick rule, based on the writings of John Hartwick. "Intergenerational Equity and the Investing of Rents from Exhaustible Resources," *American Economic Review* 67 (1977): 972–74.

# International Carbon Pricing

## THE ROLE OF CARBON CLUBS

William Nordhaus

EACH DISCIPLINE VIEWS the threat of climate change from a different vantage point. Economics sees it as a massive global externality, one whose sources are global and whose reach spans the Earth but also stretches into the distant future.

Unlike many other global externalities, climate change has a simple solution: make people pay for the harm they cause. For any policy to be effective, it must raise the market price of carbon dioxide and other greenhouse gas emissions. Putting a price on emissions corrects for the underpricing of the externality in the marketplace.

Prices can be raised by putting a regulatory tradable limit on the amount of allowable emissions ("cap and trade") or by levying a tax on carbon emissions (a "carbon tax"). Both of these price signals would create incentives for changed behavior. A central lesson of economic history is the power of incentives. To slow climate change, everyone must have an incentive to replace their current fossil-fuel-driven consumption with low-carbon activities— millions of firms and billions of people spending trillions of dollars. The most effective incentive for change is a high price for carbon.

Raising the price of carbon will achieve four goals.[1] First, it will provide signals to consumers about which goods are carbon-intensive and should, therefore, be used more sparingly. Second, it will provide signals to producers about which inputs are carbon-intensive (such as coal and oil) and which use less or no carbon (such as natural gas or wind power), thereby inducing firms to move to low-carbon technologies. Third, it will give market incentives for inventors and innovators and investment bankers to invent, fund, develop, and introduce new low-carbon products and processes. Finally, a carbon price will economize on the information that is required to undertake all these tasks.

However, we have learned that raising the price of carbon in one country or one region will not be sufficient to slow global warming, and surely one country implementing a Green New Deal or other ambitious proposals will not attain the goals of limiting temperature change to 1.5 or 2 degrees Celsius if some free ride on the actions of others. Rather, it will be necessary for virtually all major countries to act collectively to overcome the free-riding that has plagued all international climate change agreements.

As a means of projecting carbon pricing into the international space, I have proposed a "climate club."[2] The notion is that nations can overcome the syndrome of free-riding if they adopt the club model rather than voluntary arrangements such as the Kyoto Protocol and the Paris Agreement on climate change. A climate club is an agreement by participating countries to undertake harmonized emissions-reduction policies, but the central new feature is that nations would be penalized if they did not meet their obligations. The club proposed here centers on an "international target carbon price" that is the focal provision of the agreement. Under this plan, countries would agree to implement policies that produce a minimum domestic carbon price of, say, $50 per ton of carbon dioxide.[3]

One important feature of the carbon club is that it organizes policies around a target carbon price rather than emissions reductions (emissions limits being the approach of the Paris Agreement and the Kyoto Protocol). One reason for focusing on prices rather than quantities is the structure of the costs and benefits. However, the more important reason, emphasized by Martin Weitzman,[4] involves the low dimensionality of the decision process for prices.

The international community is a long way from adopting a climate club or an analogous arrangement that will slow the ominous march of climate change. Indeed, most discussions are still focused on the doomed voluntary model. Other obstacles include ignorance, the distortions of democracy by anti-environmental interests and political contributions, free-riding among those looking to the narrow interests of their country, and short-sightedness among those who discount the interests of the future. A way forward includes the dual approaches of carbon pricing and carbon clubs.

**NOTES**

1. This description of carbon pricing draws on and builds on William D. Nordhaus, *The Climate Casino: Risk, Uncertainty, and Economics for a Warming World* (New Haven, CT: Yale University Press, 2013).

2. William D. Nordhaus, "Climate Clubs: Overcoming Free-Riding in International Climate Policy," *American Economic Review* 105, no. 4 (2015): 1339–70.

3. Daniel C. Esty and Michael E. Porter, "Pain at the Pump? We Need More," *New York Times*, April 27, 2011, https://www.nytimes.com/2011/04/28/opinion/28esty.html.

4. Martin Weitzman, "Voting on Prices vs. Voting on Quantities in a World Climate Assembly," *Research in Economics* 71, no. 2 (June 2017): 199–211.

# Hip-Hop Sustainability

## TOWARD DIVERSITY IN ENVIRONMENTAL COMMUNICATION

Thomas RaShad Easley

IMPORTANT CONVERSATIONS about environmental issues sometimes take place without all of the affected parties at the table. As Michelle Bell's essay in this volume discusses, people of color in the United States face elevated risk from environmental harms such as flooding, air pollution, and hazardous waste. But people of color are often underrepresented in conversations about how to solve these problems. A 2014 report by the University of Michigan professor Dorceta Taylor surveyed environmental nonprofit entities, foundations, and government agencies and found that even though people of color make up 36 percent of the U.S. population, they constitute no more than 16 percent of the workforce of any environmental organization.[1] The result, the report argues, is a disproportionately white "green insiders' club." To bring more people into the conversation about how we achieve a sustainable future, we need to rethink how we communicate about the environment. We should use more diverse communications modes, styles, and interests to get a more complete set of individuals and groups engaged in conversations about climate change, pollution, food, water, toxic exposures, and other important issues.

Though many factors shape who participates in environmental conversations, how we communicate emerges as a fundamental driver of whether people feel included or excluded from the give-and-take. Discussions about the environment often occur in spaces not all people go to—such as universities or academic conferences—and not all people communicate in the manner common in these settings. These conversations can also happen through articles or texts like this book, where authors have a certain approach to writing and idea formation that is largely derived from academic traditions. Just as there are other voices that can contribute to this discussion from other perspectives and nontraditional settings, the authors of this book have chosen *intentionally* to try to be more inclusive—and, in this essay, I address the dynamics of this challenge.

At a 2019 discussion on environmental issues with residents of New Haven, Connecticut—a city with a high proportion of low-income residents and residents of color—a group of Yale students and faculty asked residents if they see ways their lives are impacted by climate change, air quality, and other environmental issues. One person offered a common response to such a question: "We don't think about that here, we're just thinking about our survival. That doesn't matter to us." And then the individual listed other pressing issues such as jobs and safety. I decided to reframe the discussion and asked the group, Do more people of color die from gun violence or from diabetes? I further asked the question, Are there more people of color in college or in prison? The reply was not shocking to me, because I hear the same responses to these questions pretty commonly. In response to the first question, most people say guns cause more deaths than diabetes, and both answers to the second question come up frequently. This led us on a different discussion, where we considered race and class, economics, and politics as they relate to the environment. Then we talked about their access to healthy foods and clean water, but we spoke more about the conditions of our unhealthy and impoverished aspects of our community that contribute to our perception and our focus on survival. As an African American, I feel that we have to focus on survival because of the circumstances that are against us, and we show this mentality through how we treat one another, which results in us continuing the cycle of focus on survival instead of topics like the environment.

The group paused. They were undoubtedly familiar with diabetes, a disease prevalent in communities of color across the country. People likely had relatives dealing with the disease, and maybe even some people in the room were dealing with it. I think my answers to the two questions—that more of us die from diabetes than from guns, and that there are more of us in college than in prison—contributed to their pause, because they were hearing a different narrative. This framing got the audience's attention and reveals the importance of how environmental topics are communicated. Audiences like this one in New Haven may not relate much to a term like "air quality," which might seem secondary compared with the many other immediate challenges in peoples' lives. But the same audience likely knows that their families and their communities struggle with asthma, a problem directly tied to air quality. A conversation about soil health and soil pollution may seem foreign, but people are much more likely to identify with a conversation about the nutritional quality of food available in a community. Once these connections were made, our group in New Haven not only was able to discuss topics about the environment but also started talking about how people learn about these conditions and their environment. This outcome led to another scheduled meeting between our students and the community leaders who were speaking with us to continue this discussion and create ways to rectify these problems together as one community and not as Yale and New Haven.

A clear, overarching lesson comes through: we need to communicate about environmental issues in ways that connect with a specific audience—and tie those issues to concepts that are important in people's daily lives. We need to find more such ways to speak people's *language* and to their values. There are a variety of ways we can make this happen.

## COMMUNICATING THROUGH HIP-HOP FORESTRY

When environmental conversations happen in a vacuum, it is not because environmental professionals do not want to speak to people of color or speak to new audiences. What is notable is that people of color are very interested in these topics when they are part of the conversation. But we are accustomed to talking to a smaller group of people, one that knows how to speak a specialized language, and they usually look the same (white). How can we make this communication easier and more effective? One example I am working on illustrates some principles for doing so—what I call "hip-hop forestry," which uses the art of hip-hop to communicate about the discipline of forestry. Hip-hop forestry introduces forestry to hip-hop listeners and can also help forestry practitioners make sense of hip-hop. When I taught an introductory class at North Carolina State University, my students knew that I rapped, because they had researched my music and me before they entered my class. Being a musician made me cool to the students, and it also opened a door to connect with the students.

On the other hand, when my colleagues (mostly white) found out that I rapped, they would ask me, "Do you have any songs that address forestry and nature?" Then I started putting thoughts together; when I worked in the community with youth, it was the hip-hop that hooked them. When I went to recruit or speak and opened up with hip-hop, the audience held on to my every word. That was when I decided to try to put something together, because these two communities do not often connect. But I know that they both care about the planet. And they intersect in me! So, I work to embrace the connections, and I hope that hip-hop forestry—or more broadly *hip-hop sustainability*—can do the same. Here are some lyrics from my song "Hip-Hop Forestry":

> *This hip-hop forestry and poetry It's getting late let's floetry*
> *This academic superstar gone Plant a seed and grow a tree*
> *In my front yard Locally or on my block hopefully*
> *Make others do it globally, now fresh air its more for me*
> *I'm thankful for oxygen a TREE HUGGER!!! NOT AGAIN*
> *But trees my family, you see I lost a lot of friends*[2]

I address culture and academics and give instruction on impacting our planet just in these lines. It is the last line that is the most important to me: "but trees my family, you see I lost a lot of friends." In some indigenous cultures, trees are not commodities but family, because they add to our lives and we can learn just from observing them.[3] It is not enough to just mention culture, but when people feel that you are aware of diversity, that may open the door for more conversation. The goal is to bring these two communities together in pursuit of greater understanding about their environmental impacts—and common interests. In one song, I talk about air quality from the standpoint of the absence of trees and the abundance of concrete in a public housing project. I tie the concrete—as well as the violence some people see on that concrete—to emerging research about how the lack of green space shapes human psychological well-being.[4] Many people in such situations may not even realize that they are dealing with some of the environmental issues that mostly get discussed in science classrooms. By talking about this subject from the familiar starting point of concrete urban landscapes and saying it in a way that sounds hip, I can draw people in to listen.

Hip-hop forestry builds on the success that hip-hop has already had in starting conversations about important issues. In the 1990s, popular hip-hop artists brought attention to the challenges facing impoverished communities in American cities. Other artists have begun to weave environmental themes into their work. Mos Def has a song on his *Black on Both Sides* album entitled "New World Water," in which he breaks down the challenges some communities face in getting clean water, especially in urban environments, since he is from Brooklyn, New York. I am now seeing more people interested in learning about hip-hop forestry across the academy, which is exciting; but to understand hip-hop forestry, one needs to appreciate diversity and inclusion, and recognize that we all want to be heard and valued.

### PRINCIPLES FOR INCLUSION

Hip-hop forestry offers just one example of a creative new way to communicate environmental messages. But it highlights some of the key principles for making sure conversations about the environment resonate with all audiences.

First, better environmental communication should be *tailored* to the specific audience we are looking to reach. For example, hip-hop is a form of expression created by the marginalized communities of color I am trying to connect with about forestry. We have to think about how to speak the right language. This does not mean that an audience cannot understand other forms of communication or that people will only listen to an idea if it is in a hip-hop song. Rather, the point is that using a medium an audience already cares about and understands will likely lead to more interest.

Second, people in the environmental movement should look for more *engaging* ways to communicate. In their book *Walk Out Walk On*, the authors Margaret J. Wheatley and Deborah Frieze discuss examples of communities around the world that have come up with innovative solutions to environmental and social challenges.[5] In many of the cases, this work began through communities having fun together, which stimulated the creativity that led to solutions. For instance, Wheatley and Frieze in their book describe how they went to Brazil to learn of a community that transformed its trash into a children's garden. Wheatley and Frieze called this initiative Warriors Without Weapons, because play evoked the passion for the people to overcome their challenges. The people called their work upcycling because they reimagined how to use their waste to benefit them.

Creativity helps spread ideas as well. Hip-hop as an art form has enormous power, and the backing of a multibillion-dollar industry. If a song strikes the right note and the right nerve at the right time, even an amateur artist can get his or her work streamed millions of times online. We do not have to talk about the environment only in classrooms, journals, and books. Many of the most successful examples of raising environmental awareness have come from documentaries, but the environmental field has not penetrated pop culture as much as areas like medicine and criminal justice. There are, however, artists who focus on the Earth. Will.i.am of the Black Eyed Peas wrote the song "S.O.S.," where we call on the Almighty to heal the world's ailing environment. How can we better use arenas such as film to raise awareness about sustainability?

Successful communication also needs grounding in the issues important to peoples' lives. In the New Haven example I described, diabetes served as an effective starting point for discussing the health impacts of environmental conditions because it was indeed a pressing problem for the people in the room. It is not that people do not care about sustainability. Instead, they often dismiss environmental concerns because they have other pressing issues in their lives and perceive that the environment is disconnected from those issues. The right communication needs to demonstrate how the environment is in fact connected to those other problems. Existing frameworks for community engagement often recognize these principles. A toolkit from the Metropolitan Washington Council of Governments on environmental justice, for example, highlights the importance of two-way dialogue, flexibility, and accessibility.[6] This grounding also requires elevating the importance of listening. We find out what matters to people not by studying them but rather by talking to them. We need to let them lead the conversation and tell us.

## NEW SOLUTIONS

As Samara Brock, Austin Bryniarski, and Deepti Chatti note in their essay in this book, a lack of understanding of local contexts—essentially due to *poor communication*—can lead policy makers to create policies that fail to address underlying problems and perhaps even cause harm to communities. Better communication can broaden conversations and highlight important problems that may not otherwise be visible. But even more importantly, it can shed light on previously unrecognized solutions.

A TED Talk by the guerrilla gardener Ron Finley illustrates this dynamic. Finley lives in South Central Los Angeles, which has been described as a *food desert*—an area without adequate access to affordable and healthy food. "People are dying from curable diseases in South Central Los Angeles," Finley said. "For instance, the obesity rate in my neighborhood is five times higher than, say, Beverly Hills, which is probably eight, ten miles away."[7]

The area also faced problems due to vacant land—the city of Los Angeles owns over twenty-six square miles of it, Finley said. So, he decided to address the health issues in the community by planting fruits and vegetables on the city-owned vacant land near his house. Finley created a garden with volunteers and the organization LA Green Grounds. "I have witnessed my garden become a tool for the education, a tool for the transformation of my neighborhood," he said in the TED Talk. "You'd be surprised how kids are affected by this. Gardening is the most therapeutic and defiant act you can do, especially in the inner city."

But because this work took place on land owned by the city, Finley received a ticket, which threatened to turn into a warrant for his arrest. Finley was trying to improve his community and ran into a legal barrier. On the other hand, the laws in place allowed for the persistence of vacant land and posed an impediment to communities that wanted to improve their health and the environment around them. After starting a petition and getting media attention, Finley fought off the ticket. The fact remained, though, that vacant land policies in Los Angeles reflect poor communication about local needs. The absence of inclusive conversations in developing these laws leads to policies that are less likely to serve people well.

Finley's work is based on community needs. Environmental policy should be too. The principles for inclusive communication described here—tailored, entertaining messages built on understanding of peoples' lives—can help us have conversations that engage all people about the environment. The good news is that many of us are already doing some of this: people have to talk about their profession all the time to people who may work in a different field. Those experiences can be the foundation for beginning to have broader conversations. If discussions only include insiders, and environmental policy ideas only get feedback from insiders, we are more likely to end up with the unintended consequences that we see in arenas like vacant land policy in Los Angeles. Through better and more diverse modes of communication—including *hip-hop sustainability*—we can create solutions that improve the environment as well as improve people's quality of life.

## NOTES

1. "The State of Diversity in Environmental Organizations," Green 2.0, July 2014, https://www.diversegreen.org/the-challenge/.
2. RaShad Eas, artist/author, produced by Joe Tea the Producer, recorded at Pershing Hill Sound Studio, Raleigh, NC. Permissions granted by Easley Branch, LLC.
3. "Trees and Religion: Worldwide Indigenous Religions," Arboriculture, last modified December 17, 2016, https://arboriculture.wordpress.com/2016/12/17/trees-and-religion -worldwide-indigenous-religions/.

4. Matthias Braubach et al., "Effects of Urban Green Space on Environmental Health, Equity and Resilience," in *Nature Based Solutions to Climate Adaptation in Urban Areas* (New York: Springer, September 2017): 187–205, https://link.springer.com/chapter/10.1007/978-3-319-56091-5_11.

5. "From Power to Play," Walk Out Walk On, accessed April 18, 2019, http://walkoutwalkon.net/brazil/.

6. Metropolitan Washington Council of Governments—Air and Climate Public Advisory Committee, *Environmental Justice Toolkit* (Washington, DC: Metropolitan Washington Council of Governments, 2017), https://www.mwcog.org/file.aspx?D=zM1V6GN72J2Hlmkbp7IzaQXZVwxUkV9ME1zuHj8CYWI%3d&A=dgZH9iahDgEHw34oTjVu9dCxjxbXTr3wL8%2f8AJRIFsM%3d.

7. Ron Finley, "A Guerrilla Gardner in South Central LA," filmed February 2013 at TED2013, video, https://www.ted.com/talks/ron_finley_a_guerilla_gardener_in_south_central_la/transcript?language=en#t-13435.

# Driving Systems Change through Networks

Bradford S. Gentry

INCREASINGLY SEVERE STORMS hitting cities across the globe. Loss of biodiversity and natural areas around the world. Growing plastic garbage patches in the Pacific and on beaches everywhere.

What do these and the many other "systemic," global environmental risks have in common? Simply put, no individual nor any single organization is going to be able to address them successfully on their own. Rather, we will need networked response strategies that bring individuals and groups together to pool their capacities and resources in new and unusual ways across locations, scales, areas of knowledge, institutional structures, communities, jurisdictional boundaries, and many other dimensions.

Networks for environmental change are not a new concept—for example, while landscape-scale land conservation networks are in a growth phase, their origins in the United States can be traced back to the turn of the twentieth century.[1] What is new is their increasing ability to drive change. First, technological advances are allowing us to connect global and local in amazing new ways—from the collection of biophysical data around the world and its mapping at extremely fine, local resolutions (see Karen Seto's essay in this volume) to the use of social networks and global online communications platforms as a way for individuals to exchange ideas and build enduring relationships across locations. Second, management research on what makes networks effective continues to grow, offering new insights on how this information and these relationships can be used to make change.

In exploring why and how networks can be used to address many of society's most pressing global sustainability challenges, a quick review of the need for a *systems* perspective is provided below—looking, for example, at the energy-water-food nexus. Recognition of the interconnected elements of such global systems is critical to making them "actionable" at a human scale, say through efforts to build more resilient cities, more sustainable supply chains, and more inclusive business models. Since no one government or company or nonprofit or academic discipline or individual can achieve these goals by working alone, networks are increasingly being used to help deliver an integrated response. As more attention focuses on such networks, more lessons are being learned about how best to build and use them.

One of the greatest challenges facing networks as a source of sustainability solutions is the need for participants to make the time to understand, respect, and build from their differences—rather than engaging only with people who are like them. Progress on society's most pressing and complicated sustainability challenges requires people to engage with others whose experiences, perspectives, strengths, and weaknesses are different but who share common goals that can be achieved only if they work together.

## THE NEED FOR GLOBAL SYSTEMS CHANGE

As resource flows become more global and our technological capacity to track them continues to expand, more scientists and policy makers are seeing that systems-level analyses best capture the most important sustainability dynamics. Many of the approaches to this type of analysis span biophysical, social, and political dimensions, including:

- Industrial ecology, which tracks flows of physical resources through industrial and urban systems around the world (see Marian Chertow and Matthew Gordon's essay in this volume, on waste and materials).
- The energy-water-food nexus, which demonstrates how interconnected these resources are—for example, how much energy, water, and land are used in our food system and vice versa.[2]
- The planetary boundaries concept, which identifies key resources and systems on which life depends and then estimates where we are already exceeding safe levels of resource use (see Thomas Graedel's essay in this volume).
- The coupled natural and human systems framework,[3] which brings in the human institutions that enable and support flows of natural

resources, such as legal, tax, financial, market, income support, and other social structures.

- The World Economic Forum's annual *Global Risks Report,* which combines biophysical, social, and economic dimensions and, in 2018, named three environmental risks with huge social and economic impacts—extreme weather events, natural disasters, and failure to address climate change—as the greatest risks facing the world.[4]
- The United Nations' Sustainable Development Goals, which reflect a global, political agreement on how humankind should address these systemic economic, social, and environmental issues.[5]

These systemic analyses suggest that (1) humans are putting unsustainable pressures on the natural resources and planetary systems on which we all rely; and (2) the global economic and social systems we use to allocate these resources bring wealth to some but yield inequitable results for many. We must ask, therefore, how these global-level analyses can be brought to a human scale and used to inform actions that will put the world on a more sustainable trajectory.

## MAKING THE ENERGY-WATER-FOOD NEXUS "ACTIONABLE" AT A HUMAN SCALE

Energy-water-food nexus thinking highlights how interconnected the global resource systems on which we all rely are. Not only are these linkages critical at the local level, but they are essential to understand at a planetary scale given the global reach of our current economic structures. Because no single organization really "governs" the global economy, what are the levers one might pull to change the patterns of global resource flows—say to improve resource use efficiency, increase reuse, find renewable substitutes, and reduce greenhouse gas emissions? Or, to put it differently, what activities are individual humans pursuing around the world that, if one could put them on more sustainable paths, might help relieve these pressures on global resource flows?

Urbanization emerges as a key starting point. As Karen Seto notes in her essay in this volume, the pace of urbanization has grown dramatically in recent years. As more and more people move to cities, they consume more resources and generate more waste in urban areas. Urbanization demonstrates the interconnectedness of energy-water-food challenges and how single-sector approaches are insufficient for addressing such a networked problem.

As more people and wealth concentrate in cities, urban areas face both chronic stresses (such as rising housing costs, unemployment, and crime) and acute shocks (such as hurricanes, flooding, droughts, and heat waves). These challenges are leading to rapid growth in efforts to build more resilient and sustainable cities—including planning for floodable areas, ensuring the durability of telecommunications and emergency services, and connecting people to jobs near where they live (see Amanda Brown-Stevens's essay in this volume).

At the same time, cities do not exist in isolation—they are dependent on many other parts of the world for the resources they need to function, including food, water, electricity, building materials, and many others. In a global economy, many of those locations are distant, while others surround particular cities. Keeping critical resource supply chains open is key for urban resilience. Resilience thinking also suggests that local and regional supply chains will play even greater roles in the future to help address the shocks facing cities.

This is where efforts to build more sustainable and resilient supply chains come into play. Some of this work can be done between private parties—buyers and producers—such as through certification programs and requirements in purchasing contracts. Others are likely to require coordinated action by both public and private actors, such as supporting the development of "circular" economies or the revitalization of regional supply chains. To interlink these efforts, effective collaboration is essential.

Making cities more resilient and supply chains more sustainable also requires creating more inclusive wealth models. If the majority of citizens do not feel that they are receiving their fair share of resources, cities will not be socially or politically resilient and supply chains will not be sustained as social unrest and crime increase. Efforts to generate wealth in more inclusive manners require new ownership and organizational structures, community investing platforms, and related innovations.

## EXAMPLES OF EMERGING ACTION NETWORKS

In response, networks are already emerging to move such efforts forward by combining resources, as well as by sharing lessons being learned across contexts, locations, perspectives, and other differences. For example, various networks are dedicated to making cities more resilient. The 100 Resilient Cities program helps cities across the world communicate and share resources about social and environmental challenges.[6] The C40 Cities network convenes mayors committed to meeting the targets of the 2015 Paris Agreement on climate change.[7] And the ICLEI—Local Governments for Sustainability Network brings together over 1,500 cities to tackle sustainability questions.[8] Many other national and regional networks of cities are doing related work around the world.

Networks are also working to make supply chains more sustainable, including the Forest Stewardship Council and the many other organizations offering certification programs for more sustainably produced goods and services.[9] The World Business Council for Sustainable Development and others are also mapping and working to increase the resilience of global supply chains.[10] So are many others across sectors and locations.

On the economic front, the New Economy Coalition brings people together to build "a future where people, communities, and ecosystems thrive."[11] Other networks seek to spread wealth more inclusively as well. The Rural Development Innovation Group—convened by the Aspen Institute, the Northern Forest Center, and the U.S. Endowment for Forestry and Communities—brings together experts and communities to work on generating jobs and prosperity in rural areas.[12] Many other networks are also working to reform or replace existing economic structures with more equitable ones.

All of these networks use differences in perspectives among their participating groups and individuals to clarify issues and sharpen the focus on critical choices that must be made. Each participant's perspectives, scale of analysis, or priorities add to those of the others. One member's assets fill another member's needs and vice versa. One member has credibility and influence with certain communities, another member with a different set of communities. Such networks are also usually built around the voluntary participation of individuals and organizations. This means that something needs to bind the networks together—and that is usually a shared goal that individual members recognize they cannot achieve by acting alone.

These differences raise a question. How different can members' goals or values be while still bringing the network together and making it effective in its work? Networks of like-minded people certainly have a place, but we also need to build more networks that cut across differences in values and life experiences. Admittedly, this is even harder to do in these politically divisive times. But, for example, might more environmentalists find shared goals and ways to work with Christian evangelicals to address pollution and expand the use of clean energy—such as with the Evangelical Environmental Network?[13] Independence-minded Tea Party activists to promote solar and wind energy?[14]

Fossil fuel investors to reduce methane leaks—such as the Environmental Defense Fund's work with pension funds and other investors?[15] Or many other organizations and individuals with whom they might disagree on most everything—other than addressing critically important shared needs or risks?

Building wider, more inclusive networks is critical both for creating new sustainability solutions and for expanding the influence of new coalitions implementing those solutions in effective ways that fit local contexts around the world.

## LESSONS BEING LEARNED ABOUT BUILDING EFFECTIVE ACTION NETWORKS

Some foundational logic underlies the need for more networks that seek out and build from the differences of their members. We need the creativity of diverse teams to come up with new approaches for the "wicked problems" we face—those involving contested science as well as contested values.[16] We need to find ways to harness the power of "weak ties" between acquaintances to engage with many people in many different ways.[17] People listen to messengers whom they see as credible—given the size of the coalitions needed to make systemic change, we need the engagement of many different messengers.[18] And, people listen to messages that are consistent with their values—so we need to understand, respect, and find areas where our values overlap around particular solutions.[19]

There are also a number of basic structural requirements for effective networks.

*Networks Start with Individuals, Not Organizations.* Given their voluntary nature, durable networks center on personal relationships that the participants value for achieving goals they otherwise cannot. Clearly, a spectrum of motivations drives network involvement, from being paid to engage to doing so as a way to achieve organizational objectives that participants also personally value. Once an individual engages in a network, they are the ones that pull others in their organization along with them.

*Network Members Need Complementary Strengths and Weaknesses.* If individuals can do what they need to do alone, they will—working with others is always more complicated. To justify those additional costs, network members need to help each other fill gaps in their resources and abilities, by providing complementary assets and capacities in ways that help achieve their overlapping goals.

*Networks Need to Use Processes That Build Engagement and Ownership.* As networks are primarily voluntary structures, members need to feel that they are part-owners of their group's work and can influence its trajectory. Digital platforms are certainly helping to keep members of far-flung networks in contact with each other. At the same time, we should never forget how important it is for members to deepen their relationships by periodically breaking bread together in person. Networks also need to recognize that they will evolve over time, as progress is made and people change.

As more action networks emerge, more research has generated models for how best to put these foundational principles into action. For example, in *Connecting to Change the World,* Peter Plastrik, Madeleine Beaubien Taylor, and John Cleveland analyzed over 20 networks working for social change.[20] They derived several "orienting thoughts" about how best to build them, including recognizing that networks are different from other organizational forms, designing them intentionally by weaving connections, improving the network's function through regular assessments, and preparing to have the network evolve over time.

In an influential series of articles describing "The Collective Action Framework," John Kania and Mark Kramer identified five areas to focus on when thinking about coordinated action in pursuit of social change: (1) having a common agenda, (2) sharing measurements of progress on that agenda, (3) engaging in mutually reinforcing (rather than duplicative) activities, (4) staying in continuous communication, and (5) having a "backbone" support organization with the incentive to focus on helping the network achieve the shared agenda.[21] While backbone organizations are critically important, they can offer an interesting tension over time between keeping network members focused on achieving shared goals and preserving the jobs in the backbone organization as the network evolves.

Ultimately, however, network effectiveness comes down to the level of participant engagement. To keep members of networks engaged over time, the network researchers Jane Wei-Skillern and Nora Silver advise putting the network's shared mission ahead of growing one's own member organization; building on trust, not control; promoting the work of others rather than one's self; and building constellations, not just stars.[22]

## APPLYING NETWORK LESSONS FOR CHANGE

Clearly, such networked approaches will never provide a one-size-fits-all, silver bullet solution to the critical sustainability problems facing the planet. But "silver buckshots" across differences—that is, bringing together many different responses across locations, institutions, and communities—have an essential role to play, both in making progress today and in finding new ways forward for the future.

Differences within networks offer an important way to address several key challenges. To build urgency for sustainability action, networks can focus on addressing threats and opportunities that are visible to a wide variety of constituencies. To overcome resistance to change, they can focus on finding opportunities for small victories to build capacity and confidence, as well as widening the scope of the coalitions pushing for change. Moreover, to accelerate learning and creativity, they can support both local action and actions across wider geographic scales. They can also use examples of successes to build support for interested policy makers, both as they become and when they are ready to act. For example, the Land Trust Alliance (already a network of over 1,200 members) is consciously embarking on a "listening campaign" to hear how a wider range of communities value access to natural areas and to explore new ways they might work together to conserve them.[23]

To increase the number and capacity of such action networks we will need to:

- Support individuals' willingness and ability to reach out to others who face a shared threat and engage with them—even in these deeply conflicted times
- Create more opportunities for individuals to address pressing needs with partners who are different from them—possibly through new networks of convening organizations (for example, educational institutions, think tanks, government agencies, business associations, or neighborhood groups)
- Develop new metrics for measuring the success of such networking activities, as part of the effort to attract more funding to support creating, building, and maintaining them—not just the resulting projects and solutions[24]
- Encourage people to start small and build big—across values, perspectives, locations, and scales

A networked strategy for environmental change involves a huge amount of decentralized, hard-to-coordinate experimentation and action. Given the need for creative new solutions, as well as for broader political coalitions, however, it also offers an essential pathway to a sustainable future.

## NOTES

1. Network for Landscape Conservation, *Assessing the State of Landscape Conservation Initiatives in North America,* March 2018, http://landscapeconservation.org/wp-content/uploads/2018/04/NLC-2017-Survey-Report_Final-Report.pdf.

2. For example, see the Water, Energy, and Food Security Resource Platform, https://www.water-energy-food.org/nexus-platform-the-water-energy-food-nexus/.

3. For example, a description of the U.S. National Science Foundation's funding program for work on coupled natural and human systems can be found at https://www.nsf.gov/pubs/2018/nsf18503/nsf18503.htm#summary.

4. World Economic Forum, *The Global Risks Report 2018, 13th Edition* (Geneva: World Economic Forum, 2018), http://www3.weforum.org/docs/WEF_GRR18_Report.pdf.

5. "Sustainable Development Goals," United Nations Knowledge Platform, accessed March 3, 2019, https://sustainabledevelopment.un.org/?menu=1300.

6. "About Us," 100 Resilient Cities, accessed March 3, 2019, http://www.100resilientcities.org/about-us/.

7. "About C40," C40 Cities, accessed March 3, 2019, https://www.c40.org/about.

8. "About Us," ICLEI—Local Governments for Sustainability, accessed March 3, 2019, https://iclei.org/en/About_ICLEI_2.html.

9. "What We Do," Forest Stewardship Council, accessed March 3, 2019, https://us.fsc.org/en-us/what-we-do.

10. World Business Council for Sustainable Development, *Building Resilience in Global Supply Chains,* December 2015, https://www.wbcsd.org/Programs/Climate-and-Energy/Climate/Resources/Building-Resilience-in-Global-Supply-Chains.

11. "Mission and Vision," New Economy Coalition, accessed March 4, 2019, https://neweconomy.net/about.

12. "Rural Development Innovation Group," The Aspen Institute, accessed March 4, 2019, https://www.aspeninstitute.org/team/rural-development-innovation-group/.

13. "Our Witness," Evangelical Environmental Network, accessed March 4, 2019, https://www.creationcare.org/.

14. Carolyn Kormann, "Greening the Tea Party," *New Yorker,* February 17, 2015, https://www.newyorker.com/tech/annals-of-technology/green-tea-party-solar.

15. Environmental Defense Fund + Business, *Risking Risk: Improving Methane Disclosure in the Oil and Gas Industry,* January 2016, http://business.edf.org/files/2016/01/rising_risk_full_report.pdf.

16. For example, see David Rock and Heidi Grant, "Why Diverse Teams Are Smarter," *Harvard Business Review,* November 4, 2016, https://hbr.org/2016/11/why-diverse-teams-are-smarter; Horst W. J. Rittel and Melvin M. Webber, "Dilemmas in a General Theory of Planning," *Policy Sciences* 4, no. 2 (June 1973): 155–69.

17. For example, see Mark Granovetter, "The Strength of Weak Ties: A Network Theory Revisited," *Sociological Theory* 1 (1983): 201–33.

18. Aristotle is credited with first using the terms "ethos," "pathos," and "logos" to describe major modes of persuasion—with ethos going to a speaker's credibility. More information can be found in many sources, such as "Ethos, Pathos, and Logos," Nature of Writing, https://natureofwriting.com/ethos-pathos-logos/.

19. For example, see Matthew Feinberg and Robb Willer, "From Gulf to Bridge: When Do Moral Arguments Facilitate Political Influence?," *Personality and Social Psychology Bulletin* 41, no. 12 (October 2015): 1–17.

20. Peter Plastrik, Madeleine Taylor, and John Cleveland, *Connecting to Change the World: Harnessing the Power of Networks for Social Impact* (Washington, DC: Island Press, 2014).

21. John Kania and Mark Kramer, "Collective Impact," *Stanford Social Innovation Review* (Winter 2011): 36–41, https://ssir.org/articles/entry/collective_impact.

22. Jane Wei-Skillern and Nora Silver, "Four Network Principles for Collaboration Success," *Foundation Review* 5, no. 1 (2013): 121–29.

23. The website for Land Trust Alliance can be found at https://www.landtrustalliance.org/.

24. Leigh Goldberg Consulting, *Capacity Building for Collaboration: A Case Study on Building and Sustaining Landscape-Scale Stewardship Networks in the 21st Century,* 2018, landscapeconservation.org/wp-content/uploads/2017/12/CLSN_Case-Study_11_30_18_Print_Ready.pdf.

# Moral and Spiritual Contributions to a Flourishing Earth Community

Mary Evelyn Tucker and John Grim

HOW MIGHT WE ENCOURAGE broader understanding of our current environmental challenges, especially existential threats such as climate change? Can and should these challenges be seen as moral issues? And will people be moved from self-interest to embrace a wider perspective on the well-being of the Earth and future generations? In answering these questions, we need to engage the religions of the world. These traditions are embraced by 85 percent of the world's peoples, shaping their spiritual attitudes and moral values toward nature. How can some two billion Christians, over a billion Muslims, and more than a billion Hindus, for example, be drawn into environmental policy and action?

Moral influence, spiritual perspectives, educational capacities, and institutional resources of the religions of the world are poised to make a difference in delivering effective responses to sustainability challenges. In a variety of ways, the emerging alliance of religion and ecology has the potential to shift environmental discourse toward action. When moral and spiritual perspectives are brought to bear on social or environmental problems, innovative solutions often arise.

These solutions are emerging because the environmental crisis is being seen as a spiritual issue, not just as contained in science or policy. Religious leaders such as Pope Francis and the Dalai Lama are speaking out about our shared planetary future, while local religious communities are reducing their carbon footprint, cleaning up waterways, and planting trees. Now every religious tradition has affirmed the value of nature as well as engaged in environmental projects on the ground. These principles and practices are beginning to change the conversation regarding an integrated ecology embracing both people and the planet, from the global to the local levels. So how can this potential of the religions of the world be further realized?

## PROBLEMS AND PROMISE OF RELIGIONS

Religions offer a number of resources, both moral and practical, to bring to bear on environmental issues.[1] Religions can help protect our Earth by wielding moral force—seeing the loss of biodiversity and the effects of climate change as ethical issues that impact the well-being of both people and the planet.[2] From a moral outlook, climate change is altering Earth's ecosystems and adversely affecting the poor.[3] In response, traditions like Catholicism are increasingly seeing "the cry of the Earth and the cry of the poor" as one struggle.[4] The World Council of Churches has been working for decades to join humans and nature in its program focused on Justice, Peace, and the Integrity of Creation.

The religions can also activate spiritual perspectives on the value of the Earth as sacred, from indigenous peoples to Christian and Buddhist groups. From this perspective the religions may foster protection, wise use, or restoration of land, forests, and water by encouraging a spirituality of mutually enhancing human-Earth relations. The Ecumenical Patriarch Bartholomew, for example, has held international symposia on religion, science, and the environment since 1995 elevating the sacred dimension of water.

As the United Nations Environment Programme (UNEP) has recognized for decades, religions constitute the largest nonprofit organizations on the planet.[5] In 2000, UNEP published *Earth and Faith: A Book of Reflections for Action.*[6] This volume was followed by conferences and seminars in various parts of the world. In 2017 the organization launched a major Interfaith Rainforest Initiative engaging indigenous peoples and other religious groups in the Amazon, the Congo, and Indonesia for rainforest protection.

Because of their expansive scope, the educational capacities of the religions of the world are immense. From schools and universities to seminaries and adult learning centers, the religious potential for transforming environmental consciousness and conscience is unsurpassed. Awareness and action can be elevated through these institutions to mitigate degradation of the planet and subsequent suffering of people. A Green Seminary Initiative is working to make this potential a reality through greening of seminary curricula and institutions. Catholic universities around the world are now incorpo-rating the Pope's encyclical *Laudato Si* in their curriculum.

The institutional resources of the religions, along with their land hold-ings and investment portfolios, are also significant game changers. Indeed, many religious communities are involved in socially and ecologically respon-sible investment led by the Interfaith Center on Corporate Responsibility. Through such initiatives, millions of dollars have already been committed to divestment from fossil fuels and investment in renewable energies.

Scientists such as Tom Lovejoy, E. O. Wilson, Jane Lubchenco, Peter Ra-ven, and Ursula Goodenough have recognized the importance of religious and cultural values when discussing solutions to environmental challenges. This includes evangelical scientists such as Katharine Hayhoe. Eleanor Ster-ling at the American Museum of Natural History has developed a biocultural approach to conservation. Other scientists such as Paul Ehrlich and Donald Kennedy at Stanford have called for studies of human behavior and values in relation to environmental issues.[7] This proposal then morphed into the Mil-lennium Alliance for Humanity and the Biosphere. Since 2009, the Ecologi-cal Society of America has established an Earth Stewardship Initiative with yearly panels and publications. Numerous environmental studies programs, including Yale School of Forestry & Environmental Studies, are now seeking to incorporate these broader ethical and behavioral approaches into the cur-riculum.

Religions are dynamic, diverse living traditions. They are far from mono-lithic or impervious to change, and instead are often syncretic and hybrid. We should note several qualifications regarding the various roles of religion in human life. First, no one religious tradition has a privileged ecological per-spective. Rather, multiple interreligious perspectives may be most helpful in identifying contributions to the flourishing of life.

We also acknowledge that there is frequently a disjunction between principles and practices: ecologically sensitive ideas in religions are not always evident in actual practices. Many cultures have overused their environments, with or without religious sanction. Finally, religions have all too frequently contributed to tensions and conflict between groups of people, both histori-cally and at present. Dogmatic rigidity, inflexible claims of truth, and misuse of institutional and communal power by religions have led to tragic conse-quences in many parts of the globe.

Nonetheless, while religions have preserved traditional cultures, they have also provoked social change. They can be limiting but also liberating in their outlooks. In the twentieth century, for example, religious leaders helped to birth progressive movements such as civil rights for minorities and social justice for the poor. The challenge now is a broadening of their ethical perspectives from human concerns to Earth concerns. Traditionally, the religions developed ethics for homicide, suicide, and genocide. Currently they need to respond to biocide, ecocide, and geocide. How can they expand their ethical embrace to respond to humans, other species, and ecosystems? Can a planetary ethics—such as the Earth Charter, a global declaration for ecology, justice, and peace—become functional with the help of the religions of the world?

### RETRIEVAL, REEVALUATION, AND RECONSTRUCTION

While religions have always been involved in meeting contemporary challenges over the centuries, it now seems clear that the global environmental crisis is larger and more complex than anything in recorded human history. Thus, a simple application of traditional ideas to contemporary problems is unlikely to be either possible or adequate. To address ecological problems properly, religious and spiritual leaders, laypersons, and academics have to be in dialogue with scientists, environmentalists, economists, businesspeople, policy makers, and educators.[8]

With these qualifications in mind we can identify three approaches in the emerging alliance of religion and ecology—retrieval, reevaluation, and reconstruction. Retrieval involves the scholarly investigation of scripture, commentaries, and rituals to clarify religious perspectives regarding human-Earth relations. This work requires that historical and textual studies uncover resources latent within a given tradition. For example, new interpretation of the description of human dominion over nature in the biblical book of Genesis has led to fresh ideas regarding care for creation.[9] In addition, retrieval can identify forgotten ethical codes and ritual customs of a tradition in order to discover how these teachings can be put into practice to address environmental questions. Traditional environmental knowledge is an important part of this for all the world religions, especially indigenous traditions.

Through the reevaluation approach, traditional teachings are reexamined for their relevance to contemporary circumstances. Are the spiritual or ethical teachings in these traditions relevant for shaping more ecologically sensitive attitudes and sustainable practices? Reevaluation also questions ideas that may lead to inappropriate environmental practices. For example, are certain religious tendencies reflective of otherworldly or world-denying orientations that may cause some followers of that tradition to discount pressing ecological issues in this world? The approach asks as well whether the material world of nature has been devalued by a particular religion. In other words, is the world seen as fallen and thus redeemable only by otherworldly salvation?

Finally, reconstruction suggests ways that religious traditions might adapt their existing spiritual and moral teachings to current circumstances in new and creative ways. These teachings may result in new syntheses or in creative modifications of traditional practices to suit modern modes of expression. Reconstruction has led to Hindu environmental ethics for tree planting (like the Chipko movement by people in India to physically embrace trees to prevent them from being felled, or the distribution of tree saplings at temples to be planted as *prasad,* or religious offerings), as well as Buddhist ordination of trees in Southeast Asia to protect forests. Similarly, the Greenbelt Movement in Africa founded by the Nobel laureate Wangari Maathai draws on both traditional African religions and Christian stewardship to encourage tree planting. Many more examples of engaged projects can be seen around the world.[10]

## RELIGIOUS ECOLOGIES AND RELIGIOUS COSMOLOGIES

As part of the environmental retrieval, reevaluation, and reconstruction of religions, we identify "religious ecologies" and "religious cosmologies" as ways that religions have functioned in the past and can still function at present. Religious ecologies are means of orienting and grounding whereby humans, acknowledging the limitations and suffering inherent in life, undertake specific practices of nurturing and transforming self and community. Humans pursue religious ecologies in a particular cosmological context of stories in which they experience the larger mystery through which life arises, unfolds, and flourishes. These are what we call religious cosmologies. These two, namely religious ecologies and religious cosmologies, can be distinguished but not separated. Together they provide a context for navigating life's challenges and affirming the rich spiritual value of human-Earth relations.

Human communities until the modern period sensed themselves as grounded in and dependent on the natural world. This sense gave rise to religious ecologies. Even when the forces of nature were overwhelming, the regenerative capacity of the natural world opened a way forward. Humans experienced the processes of the natural world as interrelated, both practically and symbolically. These understandings were expressed in traditional environmental knowledge—namely, in hunting and agricultural practices such as the appropriate use of plants, animals, and land. Such knowledge was integrated in symbolic language and practical norms, such as prohibitions, taboos, and limitations on ecosystems' usage. All this was based in an understanding of nature as the source of nurturance and kinship. The Lakota people and other native peoples speak of "all my relations," *mitakuyasin,* as an expression of this kinship.

Such perspectives will need to be revitalized and incorporated into strategies to solve environmental problems. Humans are part of nature, and their cultural and religious values are critical dimensions of the solutions. This is becoming clear in the rapidly emerging area of environmental humanities, which complements science and policy approaches.[11]

## THE EMERGENCE OF ENVIRONMENTAL HUMANITIES

Environmental humanities is a growing and diverse area of study within humanistic disciplines. In the past several decades, new academic courses and programs, research journals, and monographs have blossomed. At Yale alone, there are over 100 courses in this area. This broad-based movement of environmental humanities has sparked creative investigation into multiple ways, historically and at present, of understanding and interacting with nature and the cosmos.

One project that has emerged within this framework is *Journey of the Universe,* an Emmy Award–winning film that we produced in 2011, as well as a book, a series of conversations, and online classes involving over 24,000 people.[12] This project involves both science and the humanities in the telling of the epic of evolution. The aim is to awaken awe and wonder in a way that helps humans see their role in this "great story" and their responsibility for the "great work" needed for its continuation. The Sisters of Earth, a group of religious women, for example, sponsors ecoliteracy centers and community-supported agriculture drawing on the integrated ecological vision of Thomas Berry, Brian Swimme, and *Journey of the Universe.*[13]

The field of religion and ecology is part of this broader emergence of environmental humanities. While the environmental study of history, literature, and philosophy is some four decades old, the field of religion and ecology is newer, beginning two decades ago. We organized a three-year international conference series to identify and to map religiously diverse attitudes and practices toward nature. Ten conferences with over 800 participants were held at the Harvard Center for the Study of World Religions from 1996 to 1998 that resulted in a ten-volume book series (1997–2004). In 1998, at a culminating conference at the United Nations, the Forum on Religion and Ecology was founded and is now located at Yale. The forum has sponsored two dozen more conferences, developed a website, and created a newsletter that is sent to over 12,000 people around the world.

## THE FORCE OF RELIGIOUS ENVIRONMENTALISM

For the past several decades all of the religious traditions have been groping—through the practice of retrieval, reevaluation, and reconstruction—to find the languages, symbols, rituals, and ethics for sustaining both ecosystems and humans. Thus, as the field has developed within academia, so has the force of religious environmentalism emerged around the planet. One of the first expressions of this was in 1986 at Assisi, Italy, when the World Wildlife Fund, under the leadership of Prince Philip, convened religious leaders to pray for the environment. In 1990 John Paul II released his message "Peace with God the Creator, Peace with All of Creation."[14] In 1991 the U.S. Catholic Bishops issued a statement on global warming called "Renewing the Earth."[15] The Alliance for Religion and Conservation, the Forum on Religion and Ecology, and GreenFaith have been working on these issues since 1995. The Parliament of World Religions has included panels on the environment since 1998 in Chicago, and most expansively focused on climate change in 2018 in Toronto. It is clear, then, that an alliance of religion and ecology is emerging around the planet. In many settings around the world, practitioners are drawing together religious ways of respecting place, land, and life with an understanding of environmental science and the needs of local communities.[16]

Even amid the industrial growth that grips China, there are calls from many in politics, academia, and nonprofits to draw on Confucian, Daoist, and Buddhist perspectives for environmental change. The Harvard volumes on these traditions have been translated into Chinese. In 2008 we met with Pan Yue, China's deputy minister of the environment, who has studied these traditions and sees them as critical to Chinese environmental ethics. In India, another fast-growing economy, Hinduism is faced with the challenge of cleanup of sacred rivers, such as the Ganges and the Yamuna. To this end, in 2010 we organized a conference of scientists and religious leaders in the cities of Delhi and Vrindavan to address the pollution of the Yamuna River.

Many religious groups are focused on climate change and energy issues. For example, the U.S.-based Interfaith Power and Light and GreenFaith are calling on religious communities to reduce their carbon footprint. The Evangelical Environmental Network and groups in other denominations are emphasizing climate change as a moral issue that is disproportionately affecting the poor. Earth Ministry in Seattle is joining with indigenous peoples in protests against oil pipelines and shipping terminals. In Canada and the United States, the Indigenous Environmental Network is speaking out against damage caused by resource extraction, pipelines, and dumping on First Peoples' Reserves and beyond. All of the major world religions have made statements that climate change is a moral issue.[17] They were strongly represented in the landmark People's Climate March in New York in September 2014 (some 10,000 people amid the 400,000) and in negotiations of the Paris Agreement on climate change in December 2015.

Striking examples of religious ecological perspective have arisen from the Islamic world as well. One of the earliest spokespersons for the joining of religion and ecology is the Iranian scholar Seyyed Hossein Nasr. Fazlun Khalid in England founded the Islamic Foundation for Ecology and Environmental Science. In Indonesia in 2014 there was an Islamic legal fatwa ruling against killing endangered species. And in 2001 and 2005 we attended conferences sponsored by the Islamic Republic of Iran (then led by President Seyyed Mohammad Khatami) and the UNEP in Tehran. They were focused on Islamic principles and practices for environmental protection. A third conference was convened by President Hassan Rouhani in 2016. The Iranian Constitution mobilizes Islamic values for ecological protection and threatens legal sanctions against those who violate them. In 2019 in Rhodes the first interreligious workshop of its kind was jointly organized by Daniel Weiner, vice president for global affairs at the University of Connecticut, and the Yale Forum on Religion and Ecology, titled "Abrahamic Traditions and Environmental Change."

Traditional values within the religions now cause them to awaken to the environmental crises in ways that are strikingly different from science or policy. But they may find interdisciplinary ground for dialogue in concerns for eco-justice, sustainability, and cultural motivations for transformation. One of the greatest difficulties, of course, is that some religious communities are often preoccupied with narrow sectarian interests. However, many people, including the Pope, are calling on the religions to go beyond these interests in their efforts to become moral leaven for environmental and social change.

## ECOLOGICAL RENEWAL THROUGH *LAUDATO SI*, "ON CARE FOR OUR COMMON HOME"

Pope Francis has highlighted an integral ecology that brings together concern for humans and the Earth—offering a paradigmatic example of how religious leaders and laity can drive the environmental movement forward.[18] He makes it clear that the environment can no longer be seen as an issue for scientific experts or government agencies alone. Rather, he invites all people, programs, and institutions to realize that complicated environmental and social problems require integrated solutions beyond a "technocratic paradigm" that values an easy fix. Within this framework, he urges bold new solutions.

In this context, Francis suggests that ecology, economics, and equity are intertwined. Healthy ecosystems depend on a just economy that results in well-being for people. An exploitative economic system is endangering ecosystems and causing immense human suffering and inequity. In particular, the world's poorest and most vulnerable are especially threatened by climate change, even though they are not the major cause of the climate change problem. Francis calls for believers and non-believers alike to both help renew the vitality of Earth's ecosystems and expand systemic efforts for equity.[19]

In short, he calls for an "ecological conversion" from all the world's religions. He is making visible the emerging worldwide force of religious environmentalism on the ground, as well as the field of religion and ecology in academia developing new eco-theologies and eco-justice ethics. This diverse movement is evoking a change of mind and heart, consciousness, and conscience. Its expression will be seen more fully in the years to come, especially as Jesuit schools and universities around the world make *Laudato Si* central to their curriculum.

Religions cannot ignore how challenging this contemporary call for ecological renewal will be. Nor can they answer it simply with traditional doctrine, dogma, scripture, devotion, ritual, belief, or prayer. It cannot be addressed by any of these well-trod paths of religious expression alone. Moreover, like so much of our human cultures and institutions, the religions may be necessary for our way forward but not sufficient in themselves for the environmental changes we need. Yet one of the richest sources of environmental ethics and moral transformation is arising within the religious traditions. Individual religions are working to grow and to contribute to this creative period of environmental engagement that is upon us.[20] In this process they may again empower humans to embrace values that sustain life and contribute to a vibrant Earth community.

**NOTES**

This essay draws on and builds on the authors' extensive prior scholarship on religion and ecology, including "The Movement of Religion and Ecology: Emerging Field and Dynamic Force," in Willis Jenkins, Mary Evelyn Tucker, and John Grim, eds., *Routledge Handbook of Religion and Ecology* (New York: Routledge, 2016), 3–12; and John Grim and Mary Evelyn Tucker, *Ecology and Religion* (Washington, DC: Island Press, 2014).

1. Grim and Tucker, *Ecology and Religion*.
2. Mary Evelyn Tucker, "Can Science and Religion Respond to Climate Change?," *Zygon* 50, no. 4 (2015): 949–61, https://doi.org/10.1111/zygo.12221.
3. Jim Antal, *Climate Change, Climate World: How People of Faith Must Work for Change* (Lanham, MD: Rowman and Littlefield, 2018).
4. Leonardo Boff, *Cry of the Earth, Cry of the Poor* (Maryknoll, NY: Orbis Books, 1997). This book was a major influence on the 2015 encyclical from Pope Francis titled *Laudato Si*. It is part of the Ecology and Justice Series at Orbis Books that we help edit.
5. "Faith for Earth Initiative," United Nations Environment Programme, accessed January 15, 2019, https://www.unenvironment.org/about-un-environment/faith-earth-initiative.
6. Libby Bassett, *Earth and Faith: A Book of Reflection for Action* (Nairobi, Kenya: UNEP/Earthprint, 2000).
7. Paul R. Ehrlich and Donald Kennedy, "Millennium Assessment of Human Behavior," *Science* 309, no. 5734 (2005): 562–63, https://doi.org/10.1126/science.1113028.
8. For more on engaging with the business community, see the Interfaith Center on Corporate Responsibility, accessed March 8, 2019, https://www.iccr.org.
9. This critique was first made by Lynn White in his widely read article "The Historical Roots of Our Ecologic Crisis," *Science* 155, no. 3767 (1967): 1203–7. Ted Heibert challenged the dominion interpretation in Genesis in his book *The Yahwist's Landscape: Nature and Religion in Early Israel* (New York: Oxford, 1996).
10. "Forum on Religion and Ecology at Yale," Yale University, accessed March 8, 2019, http://fore.yale.edu.
11. Willis Jenkins, Mary Evelyn Tucker, and John Grim, eds., *Routledge Handbook of Religion and Ecology* (New York: Routledge, 2016).
12. Brian Thomas Swimme and Mary Evelyn Tucker, *Journey of the Universe* (New Haven, CT: Yale University Press, 2011). For film and conversations, see journeyoftheuniverse.org and Yale/Coursera online classes (https://www.coursera.org/specializations/journey-of-the-universe).
13. Thomas Berry, *The Sacred Universe*, ed. Mary Evelyn Tucker (New York: Columbia University Press, 2009); Thomas Berry, *The Great Work* (New York: Bell Tower, 1999).
14. See Global Catholic Climate Movement work and statements: "Statements on Climate Change from the Popes," June 10, 2015, https://catholicclimatemovement.global/statements-on-climate-change-from-the-popes/.
15. See U.S.-based Catholic Climate Covenant work on this issue: "U.S. Bishops," accessed March 8, 2019, https://catholicclimatecovenant.org/teachings/us-bishops.
16. "Engaged Projects of Religious Grassroots Environmentalism," Yale University, accessed March 8, 2019, http://fore.yale.edu/engaged-projects; "Center for Earth Ethics at Union Theological Seminary," Union Theological Seminary, accessed March 8, 2019, https://centerforearthethics.org.

17. "Climate Change Statements from the World Religions," Yale University, accessed March 8, 2019, http://fore.yale.edu/climate-change/statements-from-world-religions/.

18. Pope Francis, *Encyclical Letter Laudato Si' of the Holy Father Francis, on Care for Our Common Home* (Vatican: Libreria Editrice Vaticana, 2015), http://w2.vatican.va /content/francesco/en/encyclicals/documents/papa-francesco_20150524_enciclica -laudato-si.html.

19. Mary Evelyn Tucker and John Grim, "Integrating Ecology and Justice: The Papal Encyclical," *Quarterly Review of Biology* 91, no. 3 (September 2016): 261–70; Mary Evelyn Tucker and John Grim, "How to Read Pope Francis on the Environment," interview by Robert McMahon, *Council on Foreign Relations*, June 18, 2015, http://www.cfr .org/holy-seevatican/read-pope-francis-environment/p36665.

20. Mary Evelyn Tucker, *Worldly Wonder: Religions Enter Their Ecological Phase* (Chicago: Open Court, 2003).

# The Public Health Science of Environmental Justice

Michelle L. Bell

IN 1978, the Ward Transformer Company disposed of about 30,000 gallons of oil containing polychlorinated biphenyls (PCBs) along the sides of roads in North Carolina. This disposal was illegal. Often used in electrical equipment, PCBs are associated with damage to neurological, reproductive, and immune systems. The U.S. Environmental Protection Agency considers PCBs carcinogenic to humans. The state government selected Warren County, two counties north of the Ward Transformer Company headquarters, as the location for a disposal site for the contaminated soil.

Local residents questioned why their community was chosen. Around this time, the county was 60 percent African American, compared with 22 percent for the state, and a quarter of the families were in poverty. After many hearings, North Carolina moved forward with the landfill, and truckloads of contaminated soil began to arrive. Religious and civil rights activists joined local citizens in peaceful protests. Chanting "Dump Hunt in the Dump," referring to North Carolina governor Jim Hunt, hundreds of protestors marched from Coley Springs Baptist Church to the remediation site, and hundreds were arrested, including religious and political leaders.

In the end, the dump was built, and unfortunately the residents' concerns were founded, as later tests showed that the landfill had begun to leak. Yet their efforts were not in vain. The landfill's safety standards and groundwater surveillance were likely more stringent than they would have been otherwise. The demonstrations brought together those interested in environmental, political, community, and civil rights in a way that had not been seen before, and their activities gained national attention. The events of Warren County were covered nationally, with reports in the *New York Times, Washington Post,* and other major news outlets. The Warren County activists laid a foundation for community-scale environmental action that would be built on throughout the country and spark the "environmental justice" movement across the United States as other predominantly minority communities fought against being forced to suffer disproportionate health outcomes from harmful environmental exposures.

## THE EVOLUTION OF ENVIRONMENTAL JUSTICE

An intersection of the civil rights and environmental movements, these early environmental justice efforts involved individuals, religious organizations, community groups, and others. They engaged in grassroots and then larger efforts to protest and lobby governments and industry to address environmental contamination in communities of color. As in Warren County, they were primarily concerned about the human health consequences of environmental pollution. This aspect of the environmental justice movement differs substantially from historical, conservation-oriented environmental movements as it focuses primarily on human health, as opposed to other important environmental concerns such as endangered species protection or ecological preservation. Other differences are that the environmental justice movement has largely minority leadership compared with the traditionally white leadership of the original mainstream environmental movements.

Grassroots community groups continue to be central to the pursuit of environmental justice, although they have undergone major transformations since Warren County. Many groups have formalized their organizations as legal entities, developed partnerships with other associations, leveraged networks to enhance influence, and expanded their mission to include broader environmental and health issues such as green space.[1] Through education, lawsuits, protests, and lobbying, community environmental justice groups have impacted regulations and policies for local and federal governments.[2] The communities and subpopulations involved have broadened to include occupational workers, especially in agriculture, which can differentially impact workers of Hispanic origin. Environmental justice is also critically important for Native Americans and indigenous people who have suffered displacement and discriminatory practices relating to the development of their land and their environment.

The U.S. federal government has acknowledged environmental justice in several ways, notably through Executive Order 12898, signed by President Bill Clinton in 1994. The order notes that "each Federal agency shall make achieving environmental justice part of its mission by identifying and addressing, as appropriate, disproportionately high and adverse human health or environmental effects of its programs, policies, and activities on minority populations and low-income populations."[3] An associated memorandum highlighted the need for public participation through the National Environmental Policy Act, which has governed federal environmental work since 1970, and for U.S. federal agencies to consider the implications of their actions with respect to environmental justice for low-income and minority communities.[4]

The executive order also created the Interagency Working Group on Environmental Justice, which still functions today and includes 17 federal agencies. The group aims to support a coordinated national response to environmental injustice, implement associated policies, and provide technical assistance to federal agencies. In 2011, the Interagency Working Group issued a Memorandum of Understanding on environmental justice and the executive order, which formalizes the collaboration among federal agencies to address environmental justice. The memorandum outlines features such as the need for federal agencies to make an environmental justice strategy publicly available and ensure meaningful public involvement.

Today the concept of environmental justice extends beyond the distribution of environmental harms for communities based on race, ethnicity, and socioeconomic status. Other terms have been introduced: environmental injustice, environmental racism, environmental prejudice, environmental equity, and environmental inequity. Herein, the term "environmental justice" is used to encompass these concepts generally, although the terms can have subtle differences and distinct connotations. The various terminology is not applied with perfect consistency and seems to be evolving and expanding as additional aspects of environmental justice are uncovered. The U.S. Environmental Protection Agency defines environmental justice as "the fair treatment and meaningful involvement of all people regardless of race, color, national origin, or income, with respect to the development, implementation, and enforcement of environmental laws, regulations, and policies,"[5] and has extended the concept of fair treatment to consider the distribution of benefits as well as burdens from pollution. While no standard definition exists, common themes are that environmental justice incorporates fairness, inclusion of communities in a meaningful way, access to the decision-making processes, equal application of laws and regulations such as fines for violations, and access to the benefits of a quality environment (for example, green space such as parks).

## DATA ON INJUSTICE

While the environmental justice movement began because some communities perceived that they were exposed to more harmful pollutants than other, whiter, and in some cases richer communities, a wealth of scientific research has since confirmed their fears. The earliest research studies on environmental justice examined residential *proximity*—the concept that some persons live closer to hazardous sites and facilities and thereby face higher exposures and associated adverse health outcomes. One of the first large-scale studies was commissioned by the United Church of Christ, which formed a Commission for Racial Justice. The church's report, *Toxic Wastes and Race in the United States: A National Report on the Racial and Socio-Economic Characteristics of Communities with Hazardous Waste Sites,* presented findings on commercial hazardous waste facilities and uncontrolled toxic waste sites in relation to race in the United States. Of the variables it considered, race was the most significantly associated with the sites of commercial hazardous waste facilities.[6] Communities with more than one such facility averaged 24 percent minority population versus 12 percent for other communities. The authors concluded that while race and socioeconomic status (as measured by indicators such as household income or home value) were important for proximity to hazardous sites, race was a larger factor.

Early explorations of environmental justice were criticized for simplistic approaches and methodological choices, such as their spatial unit of analysis (for example, ZIP code) and statistical choices in the interpretation of results. Additional research in the past three decades, however, largely confirms the themes of the initial studies. Scientists have made substantial advances in the methods used to investigate environmental justice,[7] establishing that it is a real concern. In fact, an updated version of the United Church of Christ study, conducted 20 years later, found that neighborhoods with commercial hazardous waste facilities are 56 percent people of color compared with 30 percent for other neighborhoods.[8] Poverty rates in such neighborhoods were 1.5 times higher than elsewhere. Race remained a significant and robust predictor of the location of commercial hazardous waste facilities, even when socioeconomic factors were considered.

Proximity remains a key feature of environmental justice questions, as those of lower income and racial/ethnic minorities are more likely than others to work and live near hazardous conditions. In these studies, proximity to environmental hazards is used as a proxy for exposure to the relevant contaminants, with the reasonable assumption that higher exposure is associated with greater health effects. Whereas the initial analyses evaluated proximity to hazardous waste facilities, more recent work also considers disproportionate burdens from noise, traffic pollution, power plants, ambient air pollution, flooding, confined animal feeding operations (CAFOs), and other potential sources of environmental exposures. For instance, non-Hispanic blacks were over-represented in U.S. urban counties with poor air quality. In inland areas, economically disadvantaged populations were more likely to live in flood zones, whereas in coastal zones wealthy and older persons were more likely to live in flood zones (perhaps indicating that beachfront property is valuable despite flood risk).[9] A study focused on Florida found that chemical spills were more likely to occur near areas with high African American and low-income populations than near white and richer communities.[10]

Living and working in the vicinity of an environmental hazard is not the only type of environmental justice concern, although it remains the most studied.[11] Violations of environmental laws can result in lower penalties in low-income and minority communities, although results are less consistent across studies for this type of disparity than for other categories of environmental justice questions. One study found that environmental fines were about $50,000 higher for violations in white and affluent areas compared with non-white and poorer communities.[12] An investigation of the U.S. Pacific Northwest found that the severity of fines for noncompliance with environmental regulations was lower for facilities in low-income communities.[13]

This type of study addresses environmental crimes, finding that the protections from environmental laws and regulations are not applied uniformly across communities, thus depriving some persons from equal protection under the law. Some subpopulations face greater health effects from conditions related to specific environmental exposures, and documented higher exposures for known harmful environmental contaminants.[14] For example, African American children have substantially higher blood lead levels than other children,[15] resulting from exposure to lead paint in older housing.[16]

## CAUSE AND EFFECT

Those unfamiliar with the literature on environmental justice may ponder whether the links between race/ethnicity and environmental conditions are a function of the correlation between race/ethnicity and socioeconomic status. Indeed, strong patterns of overlap exist for race and income in the United States, with a 65 percent higher median household income for non-Hispanic whites than blacks, and blacks more than 2.5 times more likely to live in poverty.[17] Blacks further have lower rates of upward economic mobility than whites, leading to a perpetuation of these inequities.[18] In other words, black children tend to earn less in adulthood than white children with the same family economic history. The relationship between race and socioeconomics was recognized by the earliest environmental justice community leaders and researchers, who noted that higher levels of environmental exposures were experienced by both minority and poorer communities. Still, the scientific literature consistently shows that while both factors are relevant, race/ethnicity is more strongly tied to environmental conditions than is socioeconomic status.

Another question may be, which came first, the environmental deterioration or the community's demographics? Most studies have been cross-sectional, examining the relationship between demographics and environmental conditions at a given point in time, without incorporating temporal trends. The environmental disparities identified by such work could result from (1) worsening environmental quality in communities that are already predominantly communities of color, indigenous persons, and/or those of lower income, or (2) the link between property values and related economic shifts that can occur after undesirable conditions (for example, poor air quality or the presence of a hazardous waste treatment facility) are placed on a community and the demographic changes that follow. These processes have been labeled (1) "disparate siting" and (2) the "move-in hypothesis"[19] or "post-siting demographic change,"[20] although environmental justice concerns can result from many processes other than siting of potentially harmful facilities.

Although many studies support the hypothesis that "disparate siting" occurs, the overall scientific evidence is inconsistent with limited longitudinal investigations. Disparate siting relates to outright discrimination and to social or political theories that sites are placed in communities with low political power. Likely both processes play some role. One of the first national studies on the timing of the siting of commercial hazardous waste facilities found evidence for both disparate siting and post-siting demographic change.[21] Using national data for the United States over almost three decades, the authors found the strongest evidence for disparate siting, and post-siting demographic changes were largely part of long-term trends for communities that were already undergoing demographic transitions prior to a polluting facility's arrival. The authors concluded that disparate siting explained present-day conditions for environmental injustice. Importantly, the relevant populations (that is, communities of color, indigenous populations, low-income persons) suffer the health burden of environmental contamination regardless of which process, or both, is taking place.

The dimensions of environmental justice are multifaceted, involving many significant issues too numerous to discuss here—the long history of injustices to Native Americans and current environmental disparities;[22] the intergenerational and temporal dimensions of climate change, as the consequences of today's carbon emissions will be felt in the future, and further as some populations will be more affected by climate change's health impacts than others;[23] and the global realm such as the export of wastes from industrialized nations to less developed regions such as in Africa or Asia.[24]

Environmental justice has reshaped environmentalism, redirecting the priorities toward human health and bridging the civil rights, public health, and environmental communities. Yet much work needs to be done. The underlying causes of environmental injustice are rooted in social, cultural, and economic paradigms of racism. While scientific research has shown that environmental justice concerns are real, more understanding is needed on how to address these issues, which strategies are successful, and the progress environmental movements have made.[25]

Further attention to environmental justice is greatly needed in the policy arena—as we now understand that disproportionate exposure of disadvantaged communities to pollution has emerged as a major public health matter. While there are many areas of environmental law and policy that aim to protect human health from contaminants, many of these rules and practices do not directly address issues of environmental justice. Some laws, such as the U.S. Clean Air Act, require health-based regulations to be set at a level adequate to protect sensitive populations, which can be interpreted to indirectly protect communities and individuals impacted by environmental justice problems. In this case, however, Congress may have been referring to biologically sensitive populations such as asthmatics as opposed to those who are potentially vulnerable in relation to socioeconomic status or race/ethnicity.

Even where the law calls for special focus on vulnerable communities, such a provision may not address the full spectrum of environmental justice issues, such as inconsistencies in regulatory enforcement.

Specific laws and policies to address environmental justice are therefore needed—along with resources and organizations to ensure attention to the scientific underpinnings and public health and environmental tracking systems needed to support them.

## NOTES

1. Alejandro Colsa Perez et al., "Evolution of the Environmental Justice Movement: Activism Formalization and Differentiation," *Environmental Research Letters* 10, no. 10 (October 2015), https://iopscience.iop.org/article/10.1088/1748-9326/10/10/105002/pdf.

2. Robert D. Bullard and Glenn S. Johnson, "Environmental Justice: Grassroots Activism and Its Impacts on Public Policy Decision Making," *Journal of Social Issues* 56, no. 3 (Fall 2000): 555–78.

3. Executive Order No. 12898, "Federal Actions to Address Environmental Justice in Minority Populations and Low-Income Populations," 59 Federal Register 7629 (February 16, 1994).

4. Council on Environmental Quality, *Environmental Justice: Guidance under the National Environmental Policy Act* (Washington, DC: Council on Environmental Quality, Executive Office of the President, 1997).

5. "Toolkit for Assessing Potential Allegations of Environmental Injustice," United States Environmental Protection Agency, accessed March 8, 2019, https://www.epa.gov/sites/production/files/2015-04/documents/toolkitej.pdf.

6. United Church of Christ Commission for Racial Justice, *Toxic Wastes and Race in the United States: A National Report on the Racial and Socio-Economic Characteristics of Communities with Hazardous Waste Sites* (New York: United Church of Christ, 1987).

7. Michael Buzzelli and Michael Jerrett, "Comparing Proximity Measures of Exposure to Geostatistical Estimates in Environmental Justice Research," *Global Environmental Change Part B: Environmental Hazards* 5, no. 1 (2003): 13–32; Jayajit Chakraborty, Juliana A. Maantay, and Jean D. Brender, "Disproportionate Proximity to Environmental Health Hazards: Methods, Models, and Measurement," *American Journal of Public Health* 101, no. S1 (2011): S27–S36; Bryan Comer and Sharon Moran, "The Evolution of Empirical Environmental Justice Research Methods: A Call for Greater Use of Geographically Weighted Regression," *Environmental Justice* 10, no. 1 (2017): 11–17; G. Scott Mills and K. Sieglinde Neuhauser, "Quantitative Methods for Environmental Justice Assessment of Transportation," *Risk Analysis* 20, no. 3 (2000): 377–84; Katherine S. Nelson, Mark D. Abkowitz, and Janey V. Camp, "A Method for Creating High Resolution Maps of Social Vulnerability in the Context of Environmental Hazards," *Applied Geography* 65 (2015): 89–100; Marie S. O'Neill et al., "Health, Wealth, and Air Pollution: Advancing Theory and Methods," *Environmental Health Perspectives* 111, no. 16 (2003): 1861–70.

8. Robert D. Bullard et al., *Toxic Waste and Race at Twenty, 1987–2007: A Report Prepared for the United Church of Christ Justice and Witness Ministries* (Cleveland, OH: Justice and Witness Ministries, United Church of Christ, 2007).

9. Paul Stretesky and Michael J. Lynch, "Environmental Justice and the Predictions of Distance to Accidental Chemical Releases in Hillsborough County, Florida," *Social Science Quarterly* 80, no. 4 (1999): 830–46.

10. Stretesky and Lynch, "Environmental Justice."

11. Phil Brown, "Race, Class and Environmental Health: A Review and Systematization of the Literature," *Environmental Research* 16 (1995): 15–30; Robert D. Bullard, "Environmental Justice in the United States," *International Encyclopedia of the Social & Behavioral Sciences* 7 (2015): 756–62.

12. Marianne Lavelle and Marcia Coyle, "Unequal Protection: The Racial Divide on Environmental Law," *National Law Journal* 15, no. 3 (1992): S1–S12.

13. Joseph Kremer, "Environmental Sentencing in the United States Pacific Northwest 2007-2011: A Story of Disparity," *Sociological Perspective* 59, no. 3 (2016): 528–42.

14. David R. Williams and Chiquita Collins, "U.S. Socioeconomic and Racial Differences in Health," in *Race, Ethnicity, and Health: A Public Health Reader,* ed. Thomas A. LaVeist (San Francisco: Jossey-Bass, 2002), 391–431.

15. Andrea E. Cassidy-Bushrow et al., "Burden of Higher Lead Exposure in African-Americans Starts in Utero and Persists into Childhood," *Environment International* 108 (2017): 221–27; Rachel B. Kaufmann et al., "Elevated Blood Lead Levels and Blood Lead Screening among US Children Aged One to Five Years: 1988–1994," *Pediatrics* 106, no. 6 (2000): E79; James L. Pirkle et al., "Exposure of the U.S. Population to Lead, 1991–1994," *Environmental Health Perspectives* 106, no. 11 (1998): 745–50.

16. Bruce P. Lanphear and Klaus J. Roghmann, "Pathways of Lead Exposure in Urban Children," *Environmental Research* 74, no. 1 (1997): 67–73.

17. Jessica L. Semega, Kayla R. Fontenot, and Melissa A. Kollar, *Income and Poverty in the United States: 2016* (Washington, DC: United States Census Bureau, 2017).

18. Raj Chetty et al., "Race and Economic Opportunity in the United States: An Intergenerational Perspective," NBRE Working Paper No. 24441, 2018.

19. Manual Pastor, Jr., Jim Sadd, and John Hipp, "Which Came First? Toxic Facilities, Minority Move-in, and Environmental Justice," *Journal of Urban Affairs* 23, no. 1 (2001): 1–21.

20. Paul Mohai and Robin Saha, "Which Came First, People or Pollution? A Review of Theory and Evidence from Longitudinal Environmental Justice Studies," *Environmental Research Letters* 10 (2015): 1–8.

21. Mohai and Saha, "People or Pollution?"

22. John T. Doyle et al., "Challenges and Opportunities for Tribal Waters: Addressing Disparities in Safe Public Drinking Water on the Crow Reservation in Montana, USA," *International Journal of Environmental Research and Public Health* 15, no. 4 (2018): E567; Ronald Pope, Jianguo Wu, and Christopher Boone, "Spatial Patterns of Air Pollutants and Social Groups: A Distributive Environmental Justice Study in the Phoenix Metropolitan Region of USA," *Environmental Management* 58, no. 5 (2016): 753–66; Jamie Vickery and Lori M. Hunter, "Native Americans: Where

in Environmental Justice Research?," *Social and Natural Resources* 29, no. 1 (2015): 36–52.

23. Abhishek Kumar Awasthi et al., "Environmental Pollution and Human Burden from Improper Recycling of E-waste in China: A Short Review," *Environmental Pollution* 242, Part B (2018): 1310–16; Rachel Bick, "The Global Environmental Injustice of Fast Fashion," *Environmental Health* 17 (2018): 92; Mehreen Iqbal et al., "E-Waste Driven Pollution in Pakistan: The First Evidence of Environmental and Human Exposure to Flame Retardants (FRs) in Karachi City," *Environmental Science and Technology* 51, no. 23 (2017): 13895–905.

24. Jia Coco Liu et al., "Who among the Elderly Is Most Vulnerable to Exposure to and Health Risks of Fine Particulate Matter from Wildfire Smoke?," *American Journal of Epidemiology* 186, no. 6 (2017): 730–35; Yoland J. McDonald et al., "A Scalable Climate Health Justice Assessment Model," *Social Science Medicine* 133 (2015): 242–52; Jouni Paavola, "Health Impacts of Climate Change and Health and Social Inequalities in the UK," *Environmental Health* 16, Suppl. 1 (2017): 113.

25. David Naguib Pellow and Robert J. Bruelle, "Power, Justice and the Environment: Toward Critical Environmental Justice Studies," in *Power, Justice, and the Environment,* ed. David Naguib Pellow and Robert J. Bruelle (Cambridge, MA: MIT Press, 2005), 1–19.

# Science by and for Citizens

## A HISTORICAL PERSPECTIVE

Deborah R. Coen

SUSTAINABILITY IN THE twenty-first century will depend on a re-orientation of scientific research toward support for policy decision-making, particularly when it comes to climate change. The Intergovernmental Panel on Climate Change, for instance, was created to translate science into policy, but it has focused on long-term predictions of global temperature rather than on shorter-term, regional-scale predictions that could help guide local policies.[1] The climate change crisis calls on us to do science differently. How can scientists ensure that their work serves the needs of their communities? Generating actionable climate science will require incorporating the knowledge, experience, and values of those impacted by climate change into the process of producing and evaluating new research.

Several recent initiatives stake a strong claim to producing "usable" climate science. Among these are "climate services," or the provision of custom-made, local, seasonal forecasts, which can help agricultural communities and public health agencies plan for climate variability. Another example is "attribution studies," which evaluate the role of global warming in extreme weather events, useful to the insurance industry and potentially for decisions about legal liability. Some new endeavors go even further toward tailoring research to the needs of a given community. For instance, the American Geophysical Union's Thriving Earth Exchange pairs scientists with local communities and supports their collaborative efforts to achieve local goals. The organization has connected water managers with regional climate scientists, giving them access to locally detailed rainfall measurements that make it possible to plan for droughts. In another case, a community in the vicinity of a coal-burning power plant is seeking a scientist to help it quantify the impact of coal ash pollution by monitoring soil, water, and fish-tissue contamination.

As examples like these indicate, "usable" knowledge to support both climate-change adaptation and mitigation is increasingly emerging from research that is "collaborative" or "participatory," produced jointly by scientists and citizens. Thus the international research consortium Future Earth, which supports studies of global environmental change in relation to urgent social issues, now requires research to be "co-designed" by scholars and "stakeholders." When the consortium announced this policy in 2012, its leaders proclaimed it a "stepchange in making the research more useful and accessible for decision-makers."[2]

Indeed, strong claims are being made for the novelty of these modes of generating climate knowledge. If "normal science," following the historian of science Thomas Kuhn, refers to a highly technical, esoteric form of knowledge, one that is inherently resistant to public communication, then these new forms of research arguably constitute "post-normal science."[3] Jerome Ravetz, the sociologist who coined this term, has insisted that doing science in the age of anthropogenic warming "demands something rather different from scientists" than the responsibilities they bore in earlier periods. "Not only must scientific knowledge about climate change be publicly owned . . . but . . . the very practices of scientific enquiry must also be publicly owned."[4] Indeed, confronting climate change demands a more collaborative way of doing science.

However, these initiatives face pressing questions. Which areas of research will benefit from this grassroots approach, and which areas might instead need more centralized, top-down direction? What are the criteria for success when the goal is not truth but usefulness? What mechanisms of assessment are appropriate when evaluating knowledge made for and in part by non-expert users? What is to be done when users' goals or values conflict with those of the scientists they're partnering with?

These questions suggest that we should proceed with caution and in full cognizance of the lessons of history. In fact, the precedents for involving non-experts in scientific research date back to the very birth of professional science in the eighteenth century. If we want to reimagine science as a collaborative and publicly owned endeavor, we need to attend to the long and largely neglected history of non-expert participation in the Earth and environmental sciences—and to the sheer variety of ways in which collaboratively produced knowledge has, in fact, proved "usable."

## THE ORIGINS OF USABLE EARTH SCIENCE

The turn to usable climate science has its immediate roots in the United States in the 1980s. In that era, calls for citizen participation in science tended to come not from scientists or the state but from grassroots movements concerned with issues such as women's health, carcinogenic waste, and the AIDS epidemic. Their legacies live on today, including achievements like the self-published women's health manual *Our Bodies, Ourselves,* the exposure of cancer clusters, and the reform of clinical trials. These were radical movements that pushed researchers to turn their attention to the concerns of neglected populations and that challenged scientists' claims to exclusive expertise.[5]

Yet those movements were a world apart from the Cold War–era Earth sciences, which were effectively shielded from public scrutiny due to their military value. The impetus for usable climate science came instead from U.S. development policy. By the mid-1980s, critics of development economics were increasingly drawing attention to social concerns like nutrition and health.[6] In that year, Mark Cane and Steve Zebiak announced that they had built a coupled atmosphere-ocean model that could produce reasonably reliable forecasts of El Niño events over a year in advance. It was not long before regional climate services were channeling this information to scientists, policy makers, and farmers in regions where agriculture, fisheries, water resources, and public health were highly sensitive to intraseasonal climate variability. The term "usable science" was first applied to this work in 1993.[7] The goal was to "link climate science with challenges associated with sustainable development and risk management in developing countries."[8] Subsequent experience convinced scientists that their work was not complete once they had produced accurate predictions; it was also necessary to study the social and cultural contexts in which local decision makers operated and to work closely with them to translate forecasts into policy. In the intervening decades, climate services providers have developed nuanced, interdisciplinary methods that are emphatically "iterative," incorporating feedback from users to producers of knowledge.[9]

In this context, "usable science" has come to be defined as knowledge that facilitates the management of risk, whether by planning for disaster or

insuring against it. So firmly embedded were climate services in the paradigm of finance-based risk management that their providers tended to think of
cultural difference primarily as a matter of variations in levels of risk aversion.

But the geosciences have not always worked with such a narrow definition of usable knowledge. Before their entanglement with military strategy in
World War II, the Earth sciences were emphatically public-facing. The U.S.
Weather Bureau relied on a network of volunteer observers that included not
only physicians, teachers, and clergymen but also a significant proportion of
storekeepers and farmers, as well as women, who typically took over when a
husband or father was absent. Both the American Meteorological Society
(AMS) and the Seismological Society of America (SSA) were founded in the
Progressive Era around the turn of the twentieth century with the explicit
goal of enlisting lay observers in the production and dissemination of socially
useful knowledge. As the AMS's first bulletin explained in 1920, the "extension of meteorological knowledge and its applications require *cooperation* between amateur and professional meteorologists on the one hand, and teachers,
business and professional meteorologists on the other hand."[10] The SSA,
founded in 1906, turned to the public in order to supplement seismographic
measurements with naked-eye observations. The society hoped that the
charge of reporting on tremors would build public support for seismic safety
measures in the wake of the recent catastrophe in San Francisco. The group's
president wrote to citizens across California, explaining with disarming hu-
mility that "none of us knows much about earthquakes, but if we all try to
find out we hope to know something after a while."[11]

In the end, neither organization sustained this populist project for long.
The AMS lost most of its amateur members after raising its annual dues from
one to two dollars in 1922. And the SSA, following a series of false predictions
of a major earthquake in the 1920s, turned from public outreach to backdoor
lobbying in its campaign to influence local building codes.[12]

Still, this earlier era of participatory science has left an instructive legacy.
By the late nineteenth century, rural Americans increasingly demanded forecasts of future weather and agricultural yields.[13] And yet predictive knowledge was not the only form that usable science took at the time. Alongside
short-term forecasts, meteorological networks in Europe also generated information about regional climates over the long term and their characteristic
variability. These forms of usable climate science were not tools for calculating risk; rather, they were guides to what contemporaries understood as the
mutual influence between people and land. A climatic map, for instance,

could be compared with a map of forest cover, highlighting regions where industrialization had depleted forest cover and raising questions about deforestation's climatic repercussions. Climatographies, or regional climatic descriptions, allowed readers to identify which crops a region could best support, as well as its suitability for health cures or seasonal recreation. Usable knowledge in these forms encouraged sustainable adaptations to long-term climatic constraints, as opposed to financial management of near-term risks.[14]

By the same token, seismologists of the late nineteenth and early twentieth centuries produced usable knowledge while hardly ever issuing predictions. Instead, in the wake of an earthquake, they examined the field site and interviewed eyewitnesses in order to produce thick descriptions of the impact of the event and its destruction. Their final output consisted of maps of historical seismicity, which the public could use to make decisions about future construction. With improvements in seismographs, seismic maps also came to serve as the basis for assigning moral responsibility for damages. Comparison between the distribution of "intensity" (a tremor's effects according to structural damage and subjective impressions) and the distribution of "magnitude" (the tremor's physical force) could reveal an unsuspected geography of vulnerability and exposure. In this sense, nineteenth-century usable science taught the lesson that "natural disasters" are always partly social in origin. In the 1930s, seismologists dropped their outreach campaign and began relying exclusively on instrumental measures of magnitude. The result was a knowledge vacuum when it came to the human-made determinants of seismic vulnerability.[15]

## WHAT KIND OF CLIMATE SCIENCE DO CITIZENS WANT?

This history matters to the future of the science of climate change. In the course of the twentieth century, atmospheric science came to rely on automated instruments for its data, and its models and theories grew increasingly remote from ordinary experiences of weather and climate. Today, the Earth sciences are still feeling the effects of the abandonment of citizen-observers and the hardening of the risk-management paradigm circa World War II. This has recently become evident in studies of "detection and attribution." For the past decade, most such studies have posed the question: how does anthropogenic climate change influence the risks associated with extreme weather events? However, as the philosophers of science Elisabeth Lloyd and Naomi Oreskes have recently observed, there is no reason to assume that this is the question most citizens are asking.

After all, usable knowledge takes many forms besides calculations of risk. Lloyd and Oreskes draw our attention to an alternative approach to detection and attribution, known as "storylines," which seeks instead to make intuitive the causal (not merely statistical) relationship between a known effect of anthropogenic warming and the occurrence of a particular extreme event. For a given storm, for instance, this approach makes it possible to evaluate the relative significance of the factors that determined the event's human impact, including the added moisture in the atmosphere due to anthropogenic warming and the local geography of settlement that left some residents more vulnerable than others. The "usability" of this approach can be enhanced by allowing users' questions about the plausible impacts of climate change to guide the modeling of new scenarios.

And yet, as Lloyd and Oreskes suggest, environmental science today remains so firmly in the grip of the risk management paradigm that it has yet to recognize the value of the storylines approach. Instead, its proponents have been attacked for failing to do what they did not set out to do, namely to calculate risks.[16]

In fact, the virtues of storylines become all the more apparent when juxtaposed with the Earth sciences of the Progressive Era. Like the thick descriptions and maps generated by nineteenth-century climatology and seismology, the storylines approach foregrounds the mutual relationship between environment and society. Its scenarios illustrate not only how human-made warming can affect the toll of extreme weather but also how possible courses of action might allow a community to protect against future damage. By focusing on causal rather than statistical relationships, the storylines approach addresses a key concern of the Progressive Era: how to hold public and private authorities accountable for the harm that has resulted from their mismanagement or neglect. While the global scale of the Intergovernmental Panel on Climate Change's analysis diffuses moral responsibility, the storylines approach is an important step toward pinpointing it.[17]

## BEYOND USABILITY

This history holds important implications for present-day efforts to draw users into the process of making policy-relevant science. Researchers tend to assume they know what kind of information users want. Thus, nearly all recent proposals to make climate science "usable" focus on the provision of seasonal forecasts. But history reminds us that there are many different ways for science to be useful. Useful knowledge should open up a new range of possibilities for action rather than merely propping up the status quo.

Above all, we need to reconsider what we mean by usability. Before the technocratic turn of the mid-twentieth century, collaborative research in the Earth sciences supported not only instrumental goals but also broad civic ideals—not only the management of risk but also principled resistance to un-fettered industrialization. The storylines approach holds an analogous poten-tial, precisely because it moves beyond the risk-management paradigm to support long-term, communal, and ethical decision-making. Today, most pro-posals for the assessment of participatory science ask about the uptake of knowledge by users and its application in foreseeable ways. Yet even very re-cent history reveals cases where the cause of sustainability was served instead by citizens who rejected scientists' conclusions and refused to act on them. Consider the Japanese citizen-scientists who measured their own radiation exposures after the Fukushima nuclear disaster in the absence of govern-ment data, or the citizens of Flint, Michigan, who trusted their own senses over official measurements of drinking water safety. In place of a model that prioritizes the smooth and efficient provision of information, these episodes suggest that friction is sometimes essential to producing actionable knowl-edge for sustainability. In cases like these, the most useful forms of knowl-edge might be those that serve ethical reasoning rather than calculations of self-interest. In short, we need a broader vision of what "usable" science will mean for the twenty-first century.

## NOTES

1. Clark A. Miller, "Climate Science and the Making of a Global Political Order," in *States of Knowledge: The Co-Production of Science and the Social Order* (New York: Routledge, 2004), 46–66, https://doi.org/10.4324/9780203413845; Mike Hulme, "1.5°C and Climate Research after the Paris Agreement," *Nature Climate Change* 6 (February 2016): 222–24, https://doi.org/10.1038/nclimate2939; Jasmine E. Liv-ingston, Eva Lövbrand, and Johanna Alkan Olsson, "From Climates Multiple to Cli-mate Singular: Maintaining Policy-Relevance in the IPCC Synthesis Report," *Environmental Science and Policy* 90 (December 2018): 83–90, https://doi.org/10.1016/j.envsci.2018.10.003.

2. "Future Earth Initial Design Report Executive Summary," Future Earth, accessed November 15, 2018, http://futureearth.org/media/future-earth-initial-design-report-executive-summary.

3. Silvio O. Funtowicz and Jerome R. Ravetz, "Science for the Post-Normal Age," *Futures* 25 (1993): 739–55, https://doi.org/10.1016/0016-3287(93)90022-L; Tuomo M. Saloranta, "Post-Normal Science and the Global Change Issue," *Climatic Change* 50 (2001): 395–404, https://doi.org/10.1023/A:1010636822581.

4. Mike Hulme and Jerome Ravetz, "'Show Your Working': What 'ClimateGate' Means," *BBC News,* December 1, 2009, http://news.bbc.co.uk/2/hi/8388485.stm.

5. Bruno J. Strasser et al., "'Citizen Science'? Rethinking Science and Public Participation," *Science & Technology Studies* (forthcoming).

6. Joseph Hodge, "Writing the History of Development. Part 1: The First Wave," *Humanity* 6 (2015): 433.

7. "Workshop on Usable Science: Food Security, Early Warning, and El Niño," accessed January 25, 2019, http://www.ilankelman.org/glantz.html#usable.

8. Lisa Farrow Vaughan et al., "US Investments in International Climate Research and Applications: Reflections on Contributions to Interdisciplinary Climate Science and Services, Development, and Adaptation," *Earth Perspectives* 1 (2014): 5, https://doi.org/10.1186/2194-6434-1-23.

9. Lisa Dilling and Maria Carmen Lemos, "Creating Usable Science: Opportunities and Constraints for Climate Knowledge Use and Their Implications for Science Policy," *Global Environmental Change* 21 (2011): 680–89, https://doi.org/10.1016/j.gloenvcha.2010.11.006; Catherine Vaughan and Suraje Dessai, "Climate Services for Society: Origins, Institutional Arrangements, and Design Elements for an Evaluation Framework," *WIREs Climate Change* 5 (2014): 587–603, https://doi.org/10.1002/wcc.290.

10. Deborah R. Coen, *The Earthquake Observers: Disaster Science from Lisbon to Richter* (Chicago: University of Chicago Press, 2013), 239.

11. Coen, *Earthquake Observers,* 232.

12. Carl-Henry Geschwind, *California Earthquakes: Science, Risk, and the Politics of Hazard Mitigation* (Baltimore: Johns Hopkins University Press, 2001), 118.

13. Jamie L. Pietruska, *Looking Forward: Prediction and Uncertainty in Modern America* (Chicago: University of Chicago Press, 2017), 85.

14. Deborah R. Coen, *Climate in Motion: Science, Empire, and the Problem of Scale* (Chicago: University of Chicago Press, 2018), 144–70.

15. Coen, *Earthquake Observers,* 215–66.

16. Elisabeth A. Lloyd and Naomi Oreskes, "Climate Change Attribution: When Is It Appropriate to Accept New Methods?," *Earth's Future* 6 (2018): 311–25, https://doi.org/10.1002/2017EF000665; Theodore G. Shepherd et al., "Storylines: An Alternative Approach to Representing Uncertainty in Physical Aspects of Climate Change," *Climatic Change* 151 (2018): 555–71.

17. Theodore G. Shepherd and Adam H. Sobel, "Prediction and Uncertainty," *Public Culture* (forthcoming).

# In the Calm before the Storm

## PRIORITIZING PREPAREDNESS FOR NATURAL DISASTERS

Courtney Durham

CLIMATE CHANGE POSES an existential threat to communities across the country and around the world. Greenhouse gas emissions are climbing, temperatures are rising, and these changes threaten to cause disruptions at a scale we have never experienced before.[1] The Intergovernmental Panel on Climate Change suggests that as temperatures rise, stronger and more unpredictable weather patterns will bring forth more dangerous natural disasters like hurricanes, fires, and floods.[2] Sea levels will continue to rise, precipitation patterns will change, and longer and more severe droughts will likely occur. Aside from physical and ecological damage, the conventional economic and geopolitical system could be challenged as resource scarcity becomes a possible facet of everyday life. Economic inequality, political strife, mass migration, and new threats to human health may arise.[3]

Traditional approaches to disaster response were not built for the challenges of this new world. We need a new prioritization of *resilience*—built on novel approaches to finance, coordinate, monitor, and evaluate disaster preparedness measures. Across the globe, disaster management needs a course correction away from its current reactive framework and toward a more proactive approach that anticipates disasters before they strike.

## BACKGROUND CONSIDERATIONS

Disasters, both natural and human-made, can be defined as the occurrence of a *hazard* striking a system (for example, when a hurricane strikes a coastal community). Either suddenly or slowly over time, the system releases pressure compounded by root causes, stressors, and vulnerabilities (for example, lack of building codes, sea walls, or early warning systems) that often exist long before the hazard arrives. Mounting weaknesses from social, political, and economic segments of a system run alongside physical exposure to natural hazards. In other words, risk can be a function of human-made pressures generating vulnerability that continually builds over time in the system. This definition of disaster refutes the idea that disasters are simply a result of where a population lives, underscoring that their intersection with underlying human-made vulnerabilities is just as foundational.

Adapting and managing for known deficiencies on the front end offers more time and money to save lives once a disaster hits.[4] Thus, preparedness can contribute to effective response measures by understanding conditions specific to a location and bolstering capacities that improve outcomes post-hazard.

## PROBLEM STATEMENT

Currently, the world does not adequately finance disaster risk reduction measures that protect communities and build resilience to climate change. Between 1991 and 2010, total global aid for economic development amounted to about $3 trillion, of which about $107 billion went to disaster-related aid. Of that total, only $13.5 billion went to disaster risk reduction.[5] The rest went to disaster-related relief after harms had struck. Moreover, the available assistance is unequally distributed. In fact, the ten countries that received the most disaster risk reduction funding got nearly $8 billion in the 1991–2010 period, and the remaining 144 countries got only $5.6 billion combined.[6] Remarkably, middle-income countries receive the bulk of the money, leaving the world's least developed countries—those often dealing with the most severe climate-change-fueled natural disasters—underfunded when it comes to disaster risk reduction measures. Granted, these countries have many pressing needs, such as health and education, that compete for funding from governments and international donors.

Even where efforts prioritize disaster preparedness over post-disaster response, they are often too centralized to respond effectively to extreme events. Local communities experience disaster impacts first and are inherently attuned to their strengths and vulnerabilities. For example, amid a disaster, community members could quickly point out houses that include small children or the elderly in their neighborhoods, advise about road or airstrip conditions, or gain access to areas that may not be accessible to responders.

Development agencies, nonprofits, and other outside entities may overlook or misinterpret critical data without local partners gathering, analyzing, interpreting, and disseminating information. By training and using local implementers in disaster risk reduction, policy makers can appropriately ground-truth outside perspectives. Communities can also offer innovative solutions that fit local context and culture.[7]

Next, a lack of sufficient long-term planning, across all sectors but especially national governments, prevents the creation of adequate investment plans that carve out funding for disaster risk reduction. Long-term planning, especially investment planning, does not always consider a changing climate.[8] Further, most disaster response is reactive. Two reasons may drive this focus. On the donor side, it is politically more appealing to show the tangible results of disaster relief funding, and response efforts are highly visible events. In addition, taxpayers may be less willing to finance disaster risk reduction because they struggle to visualize the importance of contingency planning and may perceive it as potentially unnecessary since there remains a possibility that a disaster does not materialize.

What is more, lack of coordination across disaster risk reduction efforts— between sectors and levels of government as well as the international community—is hindering progress. From the global to local levels, plans and measures (especially from international development aid) to address disaster risk reduction frequently exist in silos.[9] Too often, fragmented coordination translates into policy incoherence. Sometimes uncoordinated efforts may duplicate or even undermine other initiatives, largely due to the absence of planning and engagement with all relevant stakeholders.[10] Even within national governments, agencies may not coordinate effectively or frequently enough to secure a whole-of-government approach to sustainable development, let alone disaster risk reduction. For example, a government planning or finance agency determining the details of a costly new highway project should crossfertilize the plan with the environment department to consider things like projections for sea level rise. National governments may not have sufficient funding for disaster risk reduction either, irrespective of inter-agency coordination and political will. National priorities and development strategies may not align with those of international donor partners or local communities, and vice versa.

Finally, and crucially, traditional disaster risk reduction and response does not adequately gather, interpret, and base decisions on the best available data. Several potential gaps lead to this flaw, but to begin with, there is no central place to access data on disaster-risk-reduction-related information that incorporates climate change. Planners and implementers are unable to sort through data that may help them develop early warning systems and monitor trends for future impacts. Many countries may also need to overcome capacity constraints to encourage the proper analysis and development of disaster prediction models.

Promising examples of effective disaster risk reduction through preparedness do exist. The island nation of Fiji, for instance, serves as a case study for building resilience and improving disaster coordination supported by local community members.

## FIJI CYCLONES: CONTEXT-SPECIFIC, COMMUNITY-BASED RESPONSE

Empowering communities to make change in the wake of climate-change-induced natural disasters can lead to improved disaster response. Communities are easier to mobilize in the short windows of time before sudden-onset natural disasters hit, and they provide valuable information in the golden hours of response thereafter. The Fijian government, following horrific damages from Tropical Cyclone Winston in 2016, has been revising its National Disaster Management Act to identify priorities for risk reduction across ministries and local communities. Particularly, the government seeks to address needs of vulnerable groups and put preparedness structures in place ahead of disasters.[11] Considering the needs of local communities means examining their specific local contexts while leveraging strengths and targeting deficiencies.

Linking communities through technology can greatly assist disaster response measures. Technologies like social media, Geographic Information System (GIS) mapping, virtual reality, and improved internet connectivity across the globe can speed up communication to diffuse populations in times of crisis. Many of these technologies, however, can become disconnected or obsolete if a disaster damages cell towers or other infrastructure. Sufficient capital for technology investment may also mean that local community members do not always have these tools at their disposal. In these instances, more accessible technologies like radios, pre-positioned around a vulnerable area, may provide similar benefits.

Organizations in the Pacific island nation of Fiji have taken steps to increase preparedness by harnessing affordable and reliable technology and partnering with local communities. The Fiji Women's Weather Watch,[12] launched in 2009 in response to severe flooding, is a community radio station aimed at empowering women to be agents of change in disaster risk management. The island nation, particularly vulnerable to cyclones, consists of approximately three hundred islands with many remote populations. To relay necessary early warning information, Fiji Women's Weather Watch has given a series of radios to communities so that they can exchange information about incoming weather systems and impacts. The program provides capacity building to local women to understand the technology and has successfully engaged many communities. This level of proactivity offers just one way to improve information flows to save lives.

## IMPROVING DISASTER READINESS WORLDWIDE

Considering the current impediments to disaster risk reduction and growing risk from climate change, a number of policies can help nations shift the balance from reactivity to proactivity. First, disaster managers should build contingency plans for a variety of disaster scenarios, drawing on the Sendai Framework for Disaster Risk Reduction, a United Nations document that provides guidelines for disaster readiness.[13] These plans should come from the national level but should incorporate sub-national and local levels in their implementation. At a minimum these preparations should include four elements: funding for disaster risk reduction, localized disaster readiness projects, improved coordination across areas of government, and continuous learning and improvement.

*Increase the Amount of Disaster Risk Reduction Funding from a Variety of Sources.*    Disaster risk reduction needs new and additional funds from a variety of sources. To begin with, the global community needs to diversify sources of funding for disaster readiness projects, representing the multitude of donors that would consider prioritizing disaster risk reduction given its cost-effectiveness. These funders could include United Nations agencies such as the United Nations Office for Disaster Risk Reduction or the United

Nations Development Programme, multilateral development banks such as Inter-American Development Bank, national donor governments, private companies, and credit agencies. A comprehensive package of disaster readiness funding could include grants and loans, insurance mechanisms like the international Caribbean Catastrophe Risk Insurance Facility, and in-kind contributions like staff secondments.[14]

Funds for these efforts must be made accessible for developing countries especially. Donors to disaster readiness efforts need to avoid red tape in the form of complex applications and lengthy response times. At the country level, national governments need to carve out public finances for disaster risk reduction in annual budgets. Dedicated budget line items can encourage the private sector to join with public-private partnerships. Proactive funding also provides nations with the agency to determine exactly how, where, and to whom money will flow and ease the burden of international fund-raising, bidding, and reporting.

*Incorporate Communities in the Design and Implementation of Disaster Readiness Efforts.*    Disaster planners also need to develop the volunteer response capacity of local community stakeholders. "Boots on the ground" in an affected area allows leaders to deploy initial response measures immediately after a natural disaster hits. Routinely, decision makers wrongfully presume that local communities lack adequate knowledge and expertise, and overlook the vast potential that community members have in disaster responses. Disaster risk reduction plans need to prioritize local pre-positioning of supplies; training local staff to mobilize before, during, and after disasters; modeling risk using local knowledge; and pooling risk among community members. Disaster risk reduction can also become a major component of local school curriculums. Stakeholder mapping can enlist residents to ground-truth and verify information. These data should incorporate the latest technologies like GIS and other satellite imagery to understand who is at risk and who is able to provide assistance.

Participatory disaster readiness planning represents not only a *logistical* necessity but also an *ethical* necessity. Giving agency to those who bear the brunt of climate change impacts and face increasingly intense natural disasters is the right thing to do. Incorporating their voices into planning and implementing disaster management offers important context, history, and creative solutions for effective disaster risk reduction. Strong relations with community members can enable adequate access, outreach, and response measures. A human-rights approach to disaster risk reduction may improve agency and empower local communities.[15]

*Mainstream Long-Term Planning for Disaster Risk Reduction and Improve Coordination.*   Governments also need to build institutional and personnel capacity to manage funds from all sources. It is not enough to just receive money for disaster readiness; funds must be effectively channeled to project sites. Long-term planning, in the form of improved regulatory and legal frameworks, can build resilience and save lives and livelihoods as it places disaster risk reduction squarely into national development planning. Thus, governments should avoid the trappings of near-term planning, often marred by changing political tides, and work toward long-term planning based on common consensus that sustainable development benefits everyone. Disaster managers also need to emphasize capacity building at all levels, especially regionally and locally.

Disaster risk management plans should prioritize effective stakeholder engagement that improves coordination, lines of communication, and collective decision-making. A stakeholder in disaster readiness is anyone who considers themselves a stakeholder, not a predefined, select group of actors. To better engage on the front end, for example, U.N. groups that normally respond after disasters strike could meet on a routine basis to exchange information and best practices. Coordination will also grease the proverbial wheels when it is response time and introduce a chain of command to enforce when a disaster strikes. This organizational structure can include community members, nonprofits, U.N. agencies, and other vested stakeholders that can respond with clear value-add.

*Monitor and Evaluate.*   Sufficient disaster risk reduction plans will require monitoring and evaluation that effectively communicate successes and challenges. Building such frameworks requires not pre-judging which measures matter most from the top down. Rather, feedback mechanisms that capture the issues and stories that are most important to stakeholders should be built in. In developing monitoring and evaluation frameworks, knowledge management, and learning strategies, disaster planners should consider a combination of qualitative and quantitative approaches. Planners should also develop ongoing, informal opportunities for partners to communicate with each other laterally (not only through formal reporting mechanisms shared "up" that often do not get distributed widely). Peer-to-peer exchange platforms, virtual gathering opportunities (such as webinars, conference calls, and newsletters), and network-based capacity building tools can all connect to overall disaster readiness monitoring strategies. Such an approach can help build capacity, develop ownership, and cement accountability.

## EQUITABLE AND SUSTAINABLE DISASTER READINESS

The era of certain uncertainty ushered in by climate change requires disaster preparedness unlike that seen before. We can equitably and sustainably build resilience to climate change impacts only when we include local communities and address root causes of vulnerability. Resources channeled toward preparation will save money in the long run, upward of four-fold.[16] A new era of disaster risk reduction depends on planning with real-time data, along with continually improved monitoring and evaluation of disaster readiness efforts. Beyond the clear financial savings and technical advancements that make this new approach smarter, we have a moral imperative to help those experiencing very real climate change impacts today.

## NOTES

1. Intergovernmental Panel on Climate Change (IPCC), *Global Warming of 1.5 Degrees C: A Summary for Policymakers*, 2018, http://report.ipcc.ch/sr15/pdf/sr15_spm_final.pdf.
2. IPCC, *Global Warming*.
3. Tamma A. Carleton and Solomon M. Hsiang, "Social and Economic Impacts of Climate," *Science* 353, no. 6304 (2016): http://science.sciencemag.org/content/353/6304/aad9837.
4. Cheney M. Shreve and Ilan Kelman, "Does Mitigation Save? Reviewing Cost-Benefit Analyses of Disaster Risk Reduction," *International Journal of Disaster Risk Reduction* 10A (December 2014): 213–35, https://www.sciencedirect.com/science/article/pii/S2212420914000661?via%3Dihub.
5. Jan Kellett, *The Future Framework for Disaster Risk Reduction: A Guide for Decision-Makers*, Overseas Development Institute, November 2014, https://www.odi.org/sites/odi.org.uk/files/odi-assets/publications-opinion-files/9230.pdf.
6. Jan Kellett and Alice Caravani, *Financing Disaster Risk Reduction: A 20-Year Story*, Overseas Development Institute, September 2013, https://www.odi.org/sites/odi.org.uk/files/odi-assets/publications-opinion-files/8574.pdf.
7. Syed Sobri Zubir and Hafiz Amirrol, "Disaster Risk Reduction through Community Participation," in *Ravage the Planet III: Management of Natural Resources, Sustainable Development, and Ecological Hazards* (Ashurst, UK: WIT Press, 2011), https://www.witpress.com/Secure/elibrary/papers/RAV11/RAV11019FU1.pdf.
8. Lindsey Jones et al., *Promoting the Use of Climate Information to Achieve Long-Term Development Objectives in Sub-Saharan Africa: Results from the Future Climate for Africa Scoping Phase*, Climate and Development Knowledge Network,

February 2015, https://reliefweb.int/sites/reliefweb.int/files/resources/CDKN_FCFA _synthesis.pdf.

9. François Bourguignon and Jean-Philippe Platteau, "The Hard Challenge of Aid Coordination," *World Development* 69 (2015): 86–97, https://ideas.repec.org/a/eee /wdevel/v69y2015icp86-97.html.

10. Homi Kharas, "Trends and Issues in Development Aid" (working paper, Brookings Institution, 2007), https://www.brookings.edu/wp-content/uploads/2016/06 /11_development_aid_kharas.pdf.

11. Pacific Community, "Fiji Government Reviews National Disaster Management Act and Plan," May 18, 2018, https://www.spc.int/updates/news/2018/05/fiji-government -reviews-national-disaster-management-act-plan.

12. "Women's Weather Watch," FemLINKPacific, accessed March 15, 2019, https://www .femlinkpacific.org.fj/index.php/en/what-we-do/2015-01-20-00-16-09.

13. United Nations Office for Disaster Risk Reduction, *Sendai Framework for Disaster Risk Reduction,* March 2015, https://www.unisdr.org/we/coordinate/sendai-frame work.

14. "About Us," Caribbean Catastrophe Risk Insurance Facility, accessed March 15, 2019, https://www.ccrif.org/.

15. Karen da Costa and Paulina Pospieszna, "The Relationship between Human Rights and Disaster Risk Reduction Revisited: Bringing the Legal Perspective into the Discussion," *Journal of International Humanitarian Legal Studies* 6, no. 1 (2015): 64–86, https://doi.org/10.1163/18781527-00601005.

16. Reinhard Mechler, "Reviewing Estimates of the Economic Efficiency of Disaster Risk Management: Opportunities and Limitations of Using Risk-Based Cost–Benefit Analysis," *Natural Hazards* 81, no. 3 (2016): 2121–47, https://www.doi.org/10 .1007/s11069-016-2170-y.

# Planetary Sustainability in the Urban Century

Karen C. Seto

THE FUTURE OF the planet depends on how we operate and maintain existing cities as well as how and where we build cities over the next twenty to thirty years. There are five urbanization trends that present significant challenges for sustainability: (1) urban greenhouse gas emissions and climate change; (2) demands for materials and energy required to build and operate cities; (3) loss of biodiversity when urban growth occurs; (4) loss of prime agricultural land and changes in urbanizing diet that have implications for food systems; and (5) growing climate change threats to cities.

## IMPACTS OF URBANIZATION

Cities are engines of economic growth and hubs of innovation, but they are also hotspots of energy use and greenhouse gas emissions. According to the Intergovernmental Panel on Climate Change (IPCC), urban areas account for between 71 percent and 76 percent of carbon dioxide emissions from global final energy use.[1] Urban greenhouse gas emissions are driven by a variety of physical, economic, and social factors, development levels, and urbanization histories specific to each city. Key influences on urban greenhouse gas emissions include income, population dynamics (including household size), urban form, location (which affects the demand for heating and cooling), and economic structure. Cities in the U.N. Framework Convention on Climate Change's "Annex I" countries (industrialized countries and economies in transition) generally have lower per capita energy use and greenhouse gas

335

emissions than national averages, whereas per capita energy use and emissions of cities in non–Annex I countries (low-income and developing countries) tend to be higher than national averages. Several factors explain this disparity. First, in Annex I countries, cities are primarily service-sector industries, which do not use energy intensively. Additionally, most Annex I countries have access to modern energy such as electricity. In contrast, cities in the Global South are manufacturing hubs, which are energy and emissions intensive. Moreover, the rest of these countries likely use lower-quality energy such as from fuelwood or animal by-products. Thus, compared with the national average, Global South cities use a lot of energy.

Yet, the IPCC made its estimates for cities that already exist. They do not include the new cities that have yet to be built or the new urban population of tomorrow. Consider this: today, about 52 percent of the world's population—roughly 4.2 billion people—lives in urban areas. By the middle of this century, the urban population will increase by another 2.5 billion people, bringing the global proportion to 68 percent.[2] This growth translates to building a new urban area of 1.3 million every week. The increase in urban population will be paralleled with the expansion of urban land areas. Our research has estimated that new urban areas built during the first three decades of the twenty-first century will be equivalent to twenty thousand American football fields converted to urban land *every day*.[3] This increase will mean an urban land area equal in size to the combined areas of Germany, France, Spain, and Italy constructed between 2000 and 2030.

These new cities will require tremendous amounts of raw materials and energy to construct and operate. Efficiency gains through construction materials such as better insulation or improved heating and cooling systems are often seen as a panacea for high energy use associated with urbanization. However, whereas efficiency gains do reduce energy and material use locally, the sheer magnitude of future urbanization can overwhelm efficiency gains. For example, in China, the energy required to manufacture concrete has decreased by 25 percent over a twenty-year period. But during this same period, concrete use has increased by 300 percent. Similarly, the average air conditioner might use 35 percent less energy than earlier models, but in the last twenty years, annual carbon dioxide emissions from heating and cooling alone increased 2,800 percent.[4] Thus, increasing urban density and resource-use efficiency can reduce energy demands or carbon dioxide emissions on a per capita basis. These savings, however, are likely outweighed by the overall increase in urban areas and urban population. China is not exceptional in this regard. All around the world, increases in construction and urban expansion far outweigh gains in energy efficiency. Moreover, the build-up of future urban infrastructure is expected to produce cumulative emissions of between 3,000 and 7,400 gigatons of carbon dioxide during the remainder of the twenty-first century.[5] Thus, constructing and operating the built environment requires enormous energy and carbon emissions.

Historically, the expansion of urban areas has been a major cause of habitat loss and declines in biodiversity. Between 1992 and 2000, urban expansion was responsible for the loss of 190,000 square kilometers of natural habitat. If current rates of urban expansion continue, it is estimated that about 290,000 square kilometers of natural habitat will be destroyed between 2000 and 2030.[6] Nearly one-third of this habitat loss will occur in tropical moist forests while another one-third of habitat will be lost in temperate forests. Urban expansion not only leads to habitat loss but also results in habitat fragmentation, which in turn can lead to a decline in species richness and abundance. Biodiversity loss due to urbanization is forecasted to be geographically concentrated, with 78 percent of endemic species threatened by urban growth occurring in just thirty priority ecoregions. Many of these ecoregions are on islands, such as Sri Lanka, Puerto Rico, Hispaniola, and Jamaica. The spatial concentration of biodiversity impacts could have positive effects: it suggests that the right policies in just a few places could have overwhelmingly disproportionate positive effects on biodiversity.

In addition to the loss of habitat, urban expansion often results in the loss of cropland. Future urban land expansion is expected to take place on prime cropland that is nearly two times the global average in productivity; in mega-urban regions in Asia and Africa the productivity of land lost is often more than twice as high as national averages.[7] About 75 percent of global cropland loss from urban expansion will take place in Asia and Africa; Asia will experience the highest absolute loss in productive cropland, with prime agricultural land loss especially around mega-urban regions.

Urbanization's impact on food systems goes well beyond just loss of farmland.[8] On the demand side, it is well documented that urban and higher-income societies consume land-, water-, and energy-dense diets. With few exceptions, highly urbanized countries eat higher-footprint diets with more animal protein than the world average in the form of pork, poultry, beef, and dairy products. Globally, the average person consumes about 37 kilograms per year (kg/year) of meat per capita, but levels vary significantly between countries, with higher-income countries consuming about 82 kg/year per capita compared with 18 kg/year in lower-income countries. In the United States, where 81 percent of the population lives in cities, the average person consumes 90 kg/year of meat. In China, per capita meat consumption quadrupled between 1970 and 2015, a period when the urban population increased from 17 percent to 56 percent. Other countries experiencing high rates of urbanization are undergoing similar dietary transitions. It is important to point out that changes in diet include not only increased meat consumption but also shifts in quality, composition, and sources of caloric intake. In general, changes in diet can be characterized as a shift from complex carbohydrates, grains, vegetables, and fruits to a higher proportion of animal proteins, refined fats, refined sugars, alcohol, and oils. Thus, urbanization is transforming all aspects of food systems, from production on the farm, to food processing and packaging, to distribution and retail, to consumption at the table.

## BUILDING FOR THE FUTURE

Given these trends, we clearly cannot build cities of tomorrow using nineteenth- or twentieth-century technologies and methods. The magnitude and pace of urbanization are central to the future of the world's ecosystems, farmlands, climate, and biodiversity. In order for cities to transition toward sustainability, we need to develop scalable solutions based on sound evidence, good design, the best science, and innovative critical thinking about equity, culture, and society—not just for a few cities but for all cities, towns, and regions worldwide. What are the opportunities for urbanization to be part of the sustainability solution, especially given that about 75 percent of the urban infrastructure expected to be in place by 2050 has not yet been built? How do we do this?

First, urban and land use planning and multi-pronged land-based strategies must form part of the solution. Infrastructure and urban form are strongly linked and affect urban transport and building greenhouse gas emissions. Thus, to reduce urban greenhouse gas emissions, urban areas should invest in a combination of public transit, a higher mix of land uses, mobility demand management strategies, and co-locating people near jobs.[9] A key principle is to increase accessibility, a concept that combines proximity and travel time. Accessibility means providing people with access to places, or destinations and origins, whether these are jobs, housing, services, shopping, or recreation. Increasing accessibility can substantively reduce greenhouse gas emissions. Additionally, designing more compact and walkable cities—concepts related to accessibility—can also reduce urban sprawl and save land for nature, be it farmland or habitat. Walkable and accessible cities are a vital component of sustainable urbanization.

Second, we must build differently. Buildings account for 32 percent of global final energy use and 19 percent of energy-related greenhouse gas emissions.[10] Future buildings must be low-carbon, low in embodied energy, and low in operational energy. Yet numerous barriers hinder the large-scale uptake of new building technologies, including inadequate financing and fragmentation of the building industry. Ample evidence indicates that market forces alone will be insufficient to transition to low-carbon, low-energy buildings without adequate policy interventions. Resources to construct the built environment must be selected with information about their origin, manufacturing, and disposal, also known as cradle-to-grave accounting. These criteria aim not only to source materials that are low in embodied carbon and energy but also to reduce pressure on the ecosystems from which these resources are extracted, mined, and harvested.

Not only must we use low-carbon materials; we must also reassess the size and location of what we build. In the United States, the size of new homes has steadily increased despite declining household size. According to the U.S. Census, in 1973, the average new home in the United States was around 150 square meters. Today, it is over 241 square meters. During this same period, household size in the United States fell from about 3.1 to 2.5 people. Building, heating, and cooling large homes is extremely energy, material, land, and resource intensive.

Additionally, climate change and associated impacts require that we rethink *where* we build the new cities of tomorrow. Coastal zones are especially vulnerable to sea level rise and storm surges. However, even urban areas located far from the coast are threatened by the increasing number and intensity of heat waves, wildfires, and power outages. How can we make our existing cities more resilient and build our future cities to be away from harm?

Third, we need to strengthen institutions and governance that can implement sound sustainable urban development. While there is tremendous opportunity to shape the cities of tomorrow, the bulk of future infrastructure and urban growth will likely occur in small- to medium-size cities in developing countries, where technical, institutional, governance, and finance capacities are often limited or weak.[11] Leapfrog innovations in governance and rapid global spread of new ideas could result in large-scale positive outcomes. To craft and implement sound urban design for sustainability, we need to align institutional arrangements and governance mechanisms. In many cities, institutional fragmentation limits the ability to coordinate or implement sustainable urbanization strategies. We must invest in building capacity in urban management, budgeting and accounting, urban planning, finance, and project supervision across administrative scales but especially at the urban level.

Urbanization presents unique opportunities to transition to sustainability. Mass-transit alternatives to the automobile demand high population densities and compact urban design.[12] Co-located high residential and employment densities can reduce energy consumption and greenhouse gas emissions. Concentrated populations can also save land for agriculture, wildlife, and habitat by using less land for urban development. The trade-offs between environmental challenges and opportunities will depend in large part on how and where urban areas expand, urban lifestyles and consumption patterns, and the ability of institutions and governance structures to adequately address these challenges. Given the rate and magnitude of urbanization, there is a small window of opportunity to shape urbanization trajectories.

**NOTES**

This essay builds on the author's extensive research on urban sustainability over two decades, including Karen C. Seto et al., "IPCC Fifth Assessment Report: Mitigation of Climate Change, Chapter 12: Human Settlements, Infrastructure, and Spatial Planning," in *Mitigation of Climate Change, Fifth Assessment Report* (Berlin: Intergovernmental Panel on Climate Change, 2014); Burak Güneralp and Karen C. Seto, "Environmental Impacts of Urban Growth from an Integrated Dynamic Perspective: A Case Study of Shenzhen, South China," *Global Environmental Change* 18, no. 4 (2008): 720–35, https://doi.org/10.1016/j.gloenvcha.2008.07.004; Burak Güneralp and Karen C. Seto, "Can Gains in Efficiency Offset the Resource Demands and $CO_2$ Emissions from Constructing and Operating the Built Environment?," *Applied Geography* 32, no. 1 (2012): 40–50; Christopher Bren d'Amour et al., "Future Urban Land Expansion and Implications for Global Croplands," *Proceedings of the National Academy of Sciences of the United States of America* 114, no. 34 (2017): 8939–44, https://doi.org/10.1073/pnas.1606036114; Karen C. Seto and Navin Ramankutty, "Hidden Linkages between Urbanization and Food Systems," *Science* 352, no. 6288 (2016): 943–45; Karen C. Seto, Roberto Sánchez-Rodríguez, and Michail Fragkias, "The New Geography of Contemporary Urbanization and the Environment," *Annual Review of Environment and Resources* 35 (2010): 167–94.

  1. Seto et al., "IPCC Fifth Assessment Report."
  2. U.N. Department of Economic and Social Affairs, *World Urbanization Prospects: The 2011 Revision* (New York: United Nations, Department of Economic and Social Affairs, Population Division, 2012).

3. Karen C. Seto et al., "A Meta-Analysis of Global Urban Land Expansion," *PLoS One* 6, no. 8 (2011): e23777, https://doi.org/10.1371/journal.pone.0023777.

4. Güneralp and Seto, "Gains in Efficiency."

5. Daniel B. Müller et al., "Carbon Emissions of Infrastructure Development," *Environmental Science & Technology* 47, no. 20 (2013): 11739–46, https://doi.org/10.1021/es402618m.

6. The Nature Conservancy, "Nature in the Urban Century" (2018), https://www.nature.org/en-us/what-we-do/our-insights/perspectives/nature-in-the-urban-century/.

7. Bren d'Amour et al., "Future Urban Land Expansion."

8. Seto and Ramankutty, "Hidden Linkages."

9. Seto et al., "IPCC Fifth Assessment Report."

10. Oswaldo Lucon et al., "IPCC Fifth Assessment Report: Mitigation of Climate Change, Chapter 9: Buildings," in *Mitigation of Climate Change, Fifth Assessment Report.*

11. Seto et al., "IPCC Fifth Assessment Report."

12. Seto, Sánchez-Rodríguez, and Fragkias, "New Geography."

# Reimagining the City and Park for a Sustainable Urban Future

Alexander J. Felson

URBAN ENVIRONMENTS, projected to be home to two-thirds of the global population by 2050,[1] will continue to place additional demands on the aging and often-failing city infrastructure systems, as well as on the green spaces that support cities and people. Twenty-first-century city parks must be designed to absorb these added pressures while also addressing current health challenges and issues stemming from factors including urban heat islands, stormwater management, and habitat loss. To address this demand, we need to view urban green space as a high-priority area of investment, a primary driver of urban redevelopment, and a critical asset for facilitating climate change adaptation. With a growing awareness of the value of having humans live in more nature-like environments,[2] we need to reconceptualize twenty-first-century park systems as extensive and fundamental components of the city fabric to be integrated at multiple scales into every aspect of urban land use.

## A REFUGE FROM THE CITY

Parks have long played a key role in providing a refuge from the city and fulfilling urban infrastructural needs. Frederick Law Olmsted (1822–1903), a founding father of modern landscape architecture, designed parklands that also served critical water management and infrastructural functions in a number of cities. Two examples are Boston's Back Bay Fens (completed in 1879), a drainage and management landscape system that helps control flooding along the Charles River floodplain, and Louisville, Kentucky's extensive park system consisting of eighteen parks and six parkways over twenty-six miles (initiated in the 1880s).[3] Amid the unsanitary urban conditions created by the Industrial Revolution, Olmsted understood the value of exposing urban dwellers, particularly working-class populations, to parks with rural and natural landscapes.[4] Building on medical and healing trends of the time, he saw the value of natural scenery to the physical and spiritual health of urban residents.

Similar efforts were applied extensively to the development of large public park projects in the nineteenth century, including Central Park (1857) and Prospect Park (1867) in New York City and Golden Gate Park (1871) in San Francisco. In this "large park movement," workers brought in soil, plants, and trees to reconstruct naturalized environments as spaces for urban dwellers to frequent and inhabit. These parks became inextricably linked to and highly influential on the character and identity of the cities they occupy. The spaces functioned for recreation, cultural events, and civic life.[5] Other early advocates of parks sought to counter the harsh environmental changes created by industrialization and urbanization through the application of engineering, regional planning, and design strategies to urban landscapes—and sculpting the land through earthwork and planting.[6]

Parkland and green space, though often treated as secondary to the more traditional "built environment," in fact make up the ecological lifeblood of cities. They provide city dwellers numerous, diverse benefits—some intentional and others accidental. Some ecological benefits may be visible to the public, such as the seasonal migration of birds with stopovers in New York City's Central Park.[7] Other benefits can be less visually apparent—but no less important—such as the way park vegetation improves air quality and parks host microbial soil communities that support insect populations and associated food webs.[8] Moreover, by providing opportunities for active and passive recreation in natural settings, urban parks have a positive impact on human health and well-being. And by supporting water quality treatment and urban ecosystems, they strengthen urban infrastructure as well.

In many cities, however, only a fraction of the municipal budget supports parks and greening strategies. Parkland currently composes less than 10 percent of the total land area of an average U.S. city.[9] Research scientists, including public health experts and urban ecologists, are sounding alarms at this under-investment, as they recognize the risks of exposure to harsh urban and industrial environments faced by the public.[10] Cities should increase the budget and land area for green space in order to expand the functional contributions to urban residents and public health.

## THE UTILITY OF ECOLOGY FOR THE CITY

To continue to serve communities in these critical ways, cities of the future must become more *biophilic,* or nature-like.[11] Doing so requires a reinterpretation of urban surfaces, with an emphasis on incorporating greening strategies at multiple scales into all forms of urban land use, including city infrastructure, transportation systems, and commercial spaces. This includes developing more permeable surfaces for infiltration and making existing building and roadway surfaces more environmentally friendly. In addition to expanding recreational and civic activities, public open spaces must also be developed as networks across cities. Restructuring buildings, blocks, and neighborhoods to incorporate green space can expand pedestrian access to healthy spaces. Expanded green spaces can also help to integrate energy and water infrastructure into distribution systems and stormwater treatment systems that allow local residents to support cutting-edge water recapture, advanced treatment, and reuse strategies. Additionally, green space should be designed to help protect urban water supplies by providing stormwater retention and groundwater infiltration.[12] Establishing indoor–outdoor exchanges for buildings and public spaces will also be critical in order to work toward on-site sustainable solutions.

Similarly, reimagined streets could incorporate robust planting of trees and other vegetation, reflective and permeable pavements, and other design elements that make cities more environmentally friendly. To achieve these physical changes and support changed urban lifestyles, we need to modernize zoning regulations to promote mixed-use areas that blend green space with commercial and residential activities. We will also need new financing options to ensure that twenty-first-century cities have adequate green spaces and appropriate investment in environmentally advanced infrastructure and maintenance.

While many historic urban parks are the outcome of conservation planning, such as Forest Park in Portland, Oregon (1890s), new parkland development in dense urban areas tends to occur in the *interstitial* spaces between other land uses, especially with the constraints of private property and developmental pressures. These remnant landscapes may occur along waterways, in brownfields, or on steep slopes. Remnant landscapes can provide opportunities for green infrastructure strategies, where buffers can provide ecological benefits such as water quality treatment or erosion control, or facilitate the natural succession from one ecological community to another. Examples include portions of the approximately 8,700 acres that constitute the Forever Wild Nature Preserves (2001) of forest, grasslands, and shrublands in New York City. This parkland system was established by the New York City Department of Parks and Recreation and the Natural Resources Group to preserve lands of the highest ecological value across the city's five boroughs.

To achieve the goals outlined above, we will need to prioritize the creation of parks and other green spaces—and work to intentionally reincorporate nature into our cities. We need to proactively green cities through the conversion of hard surfaces and add park use functionality to infrastructure and transportation areas. In doing so, we can diversify and enliven extensive areas of urban space for both ecological gains and social benefits.[13] What if we followed the recent trend of establishing large parks designed to transform cities focusing on post-industrial sites such as Brooklyn Bridge Park (2005) or Louisville Waterfront Park (1999), when these parcels become available? And what if, at the same time, we expanded parkland running along waterways, steep slopes, conservation lands, and interstitial spaces to create park networks building on projects such as the Atlanta Beltline (2006) and Boston's Emerald Necklace park system?

This type of landscape architecture could transform our relationship to nature by creating more robust ecological systems and incorporating elements from nature into new inventions in the act of building. Opportunities exist to continue to explore and build reciprocal and complex feedback loops between people and natural systems. Novel ecosystems—those engineered by humans—are a new approach to consider as part of our urbanized landscapes.[14] Recent studies into the side effects of urbanization, and especially their implications for humans, have led to a fresh wave of proactive research that will better guide how we urbanize. It is essential that we deepen our understanding of urban ecological dynamics to improve critical services that support human welfare and maintain ecological systems. We need to reconsider our approach to building and managing cities, not as separate human or natural systems but as overlapping and integrated *socioecological systems*.[15]

Achieving this vision requires a reconceptualization of our approach to building and managing cities. We first must recognize that our ancestral relationships with nature have been remade by intense urbanization. We have modified our environments to cater to our needs and have harvested natural resources to address basic sustenance and generate economic growth. We have drastically changed our environments to manage issues such as waste disposal, disease, and health concerns to the point that there is no return to an original nature. However, we still rely on exchanges with our biological world. Reconstructing the biologically rich environment that humans as species have evolved to inhabit requires a strategic combination of increased investments, smart construction practices, adaptability, novel ecosystems, technology, regulations, education, and awareness. We need to explore the trade-offs associated with fostering greater connection to nature in urban life. But given the utopian nature of this vision, we must ask ourselves, is it practical? Retrofitting cities as integrated human and natural systems requires reexamining the major infrastructural and ecological systems within urban environments from the standpoint of water supply, public health concerns, microclimates, biodiversity, and maintenance and operations practices. Within each area, we must shift our conceptualization of the city from a stand-alone entity to a contextualized environment embedded in a larger landscape.

*Water Quality.*   In the past, inventive thinking around water management and sewage treatment made the management of urban drinking water possible. Tactics included broad watershed management and control of sewage treatment to reduce water pollution. In the early 1900s, New York City coupled upland watershed protection with gravity-fed tunnels and a water grid that now supports over 9.5 million people.[16] The infrastructural marvel made New York City one of five cities nationally (along with Boston, San Francisco, Seattle, and Portland) able to obtain federal and state waivers that allowed them to supply unfiltered water and avoid costly filtration requirements. Without these waivers, New York City might have had to spend over $10 billion to construct a filtration plant with an annual upkeep cost of at least $100 million for operations and maintenance.[17] This innovative nature-based solution illustrates the benefits of investing in natural systems in combination with hard infrastructure. In principle, this approach should inform all infrastructure projects, and can contribute additional parks and conservation land to cities and urban regions.

However, present water quality issues call for further innovation in urban water systems. Engineered water management systems alter the flow of traditional watersheds. They channel water through above- and below-ground infrastructure. Urbanization further alters the water cycle by paving and developing the land. As a result, urban watersheds are dominated by impervious surfaces, which prevent the infiltration of rainfall into the ground and generate more runoff. Urban water systems typically collect surface water runoff in underground sewer systems, which—depending on the age of the city—may either be separate from or combined with wastewater systems. Along the way, urban surface water runoff picks up and concentrates pollutants: sediment, nutrients, pathogens, and toxic substances such as pesticides and heavy metals. To address such *non-point source pollution*, cities are actively developing green infrastructure systems for water catchment and treatment. Such water catchment systems can catch and partially clean water before it enters into waterways. In leveraging nature-based systems, they not only provide infrastructure services for cities but also expose inhabitants to more biophilic conditions.[18]

Through design, cities can create urban treatment chains to keep clean water (roof water, for example) separate from water contaminated through contact with roads; cities can strategically reuse the cleaner water or discharge it into adjacent, separate waterways. Like the Sustainable Urban Drainage Systems in the United Kingdom, which mimic natural water flows, stormwater treatment chains provide for both the management of weather events and a water treatment system.[19] Building on these precedents, we have an opportunity to transform hidden underground infrastructure into a visible, dynamic feature of cities. Cities can incorporate the dynamic and aesthetic qualities of natural infrastructure to diversify and enliven urban spaces for ecological and social health.

*Public Health.* Public health issues in urbanized areas are a serious concern and are becoming more severe in the face of climate change and natural disasters. Vulnerable populations face chronic health concerns. Critical facilities, such as hospice care facilities and hospitals, face physical risks during extreme weather events that curtail their ability to provide health care services. Natural disasters exacerbate already-overlooked mental health issues. They also contribute to the public health challenges that urban dwellers face, including chronic and infectious diseases, mental health conditions, and injuries, as well as issues such as power outages, heat risk, and food insecurity.[20]

To improve urban health, we need to facilitate collaborative efforts that build on technological advances and educate people about critical public health concerns. We must also promote social equity and community cohesion while fostering ecosystem function and resiliency. We have gained insights about urban public health through novel studies capturing public health data as well as through new technologies—along with standardized data collection strategies, more systematic analysis, and synthesis of big datasets. Better reporting and augmented approaches to working with communities are increasing the quality and availability of primary data. All of these changes improve our understanding of the impact of urbanized areas on our behavior and ultimately our health and well-being. Urban transformation efforts should prioritize equitable, strategic, timely, and cost-conscious adaptations to address public health concerns, particularly in the face of climate change.

*Urban Microclimates.*   Cities are often described as "urban heat islands" because they are substantially warmer than surrounding suburban or rural areas. The dense concentration of impervious pavements, buildings, and other hard surfaces in cities absorbs and retains heat, raising temperatures by anywhere from 1.8 to 5.4 degrees Fahrenheit.[21] These elevated temperatures result in both higher levels of air pollution and increased energy costs. In times of intense summer heat and drought, this extra heat can significantly impact public health and cause heat-related illnesses and mortality to spike. Climate change is predicted to cause frequent, more intense, and longer heat waves, and will exacerbate these conditions. Disadvantaged citizens, including those lacking air conditioning or who work outdoors, will be especially affected.

In an effort to mitigate urban heat islands, many cities are implementing natural cooling solutions, including additional tree planting, which produces shade to counteract the temperature-amplifying effects of concrete. For example, the MillionTreesNYC campaign that began in 2007 established an extensive planting program across New York City focusing on planting street trees and increasing tree canopy in parkland. Similar programs have been initiated across the country. Cities are also beginning to establish "cool corridors" with dense plantings in key areas of the city, and to repurpose certain streets as green streets exclusively for pedestrians. A growing emphasis on recreation and commuting by bike helps drive these trends.

*Biodiversity and Habitat Connectivity.*   Urban biodiversity matters as much for people as it does for wildlife. Cities and suburbs can coexist with ecologically active environments. While urbanization has displaced ecological communities, cities also have conserved, disturbed, and recovered landscapes as well as novel ecosystems. Across the country, many cities are developing a new generation of green infrastructure, parkland, and public spaces that incorporate biodiversity into landscapes. In establishing landscape biodiversity through restoration practices, it is critical to determine whether these actively built novel ecosystems carry out their intended functions. To function effectively and support biodiversity, city ecosystems have to contend with invasive species and habitat fragmentation.

Restoration practices must also be monitored and adaptively managed. Cities have more recently begun pursuing extensive afforestation programs, such as the MillionTreesNYC effort mentioned above. These landscape-scale projects have the potential to transform the urban landscape, but they require ongoing monitoring and management. They can fail to supply the *ecosystem services* to humans they were designed to provide and may have unintended negative consequences.[22] For example, the MillionTreesNYC project planted native tree species to promote regional biodiversity and support wildlife, but the survival of these trees will depend upon their ability to withstand planting in highly altered soils and remain resistant to invasive species, which draw away water and nutrients.

*Maintenance and Operations.*   Urban green spaces require extensive maintenance and operational support. While all vegetation requires upkeep, urban settings place additional stress on plants, as the built environment increases temperatures and changes hydrological conditions. Cities are highly modified and controlled environments with constrained biological functions. Where biological systems have complex food webs consisting of soil microbial activity, food chains, and feedbacks between species, urban areas reduce this complexity with impervious surfaces, managed water flows, and limited vegetation and wildlife. This reduction in ecological diversity—coupled with ongoing management through the collection of trash, wastewater, and other materials—produces an environment with limited biological depth. This is not a necessary state for cities, but reintroducing more biological function will require careful consideration, given the trade-off between maintenance to organize city life and the potential messiness of adding biological richness.

## FUTURE GREEN CITY

To reshape American parks, we need fundamental changes to the way we regulate, conceptualize, build, manage, and remake our cities. Still, even small investment approaches can produce meaningful results. Consider New York City's Privately Owned Public Spaces program, initiated in 1961, which provides zoning incentives that allow private developers to construct larger or taller buildings in exchange for the construction of indoor and outdoor public spaces.[23] Although the program has garnered criticisms for the amount of benefit it has provided to real estate developers,[24] it has also facilitated the construction of over 3.8 million square feet of additional public space across 550 projects. Such incremental strategies, where carefully orchestrated, could foster park development as well.

Policy changes should focus on implementing multifunctional greening strategies that strengthen the ecosystem services nature provides, in addition to expanding green areas. We should encourage smart real estate and construction practices that create more sustainable and walkable neighborhoods. Positive trends are already occurring, such as Philadelphia's efforts to expand green space, the Trust for Public Land's national efforts to promote parks, programs such as the Sustainable Sites Initiative design system to improve land development practices, and the Leadership in Energy and Environmental Design Neighborhood Development program to certify urban sustainability efforts, but further incentives are needed.[25]

To build on this work, we must promote infrastructure investments, zoning law amendments to change how construction occurs, and municipal financing strategies that more adequately address risks at the neighborhood scale and encourage effective adaptation to climate change. These strategies will help to expand green space within cities and develop green spaces that provide utility and infrastructure functions as well as recreational and aesthetic benefits. Our approach should introduce resiliency and redundancy in infrastructure systems and couple green systems with infrastructure in the face of an uncertain and dynamic future. We must also define metrics for monitoring urban ecosystems over time using adaptive experimental strategies to guide design, maintenance, and operations.[26] Through such changes, parks can address a wider spectrum of physical and mental human needs. A reimagined next generation of urban parks will facilitate sustainable future cities that will be very different from the urban centers we inhabit today.

## NOTES

1. "68% of the World Population Projected to Live in Urban Areas by 2050, Says UN," United Nations, Department of Economic and Social Affairs, May 16, 2018, https://www.un.org/development/desa/en/news/population/2018-revision-of-world-urbanization-prospects.html.
2. See, for example, Kurt Beil and Douglas Hanes, "The Influence of Urban Natural and Built Environments on Physiological and Psychological Measures of Stress—a

Pilot Study," *International Journal of Environmental Research and Public Health* 10, no. 4 (2013): 1250–67; Marc G. Berman, John Jonides, and Stephen Kaplan, "The Cognitive Benefits of Interacting with Nature," *Psychological Science* 19, no. 12 (2008): 1207–12.

3. Olmsted worked on the Boston park systems with others including Charles Eliot (1859–1897), who developed a comprehensive regional park system for Boston. This citywide park system introduced the idea of a citywide scale multi-park network that integrated ecology, infrastructure, and civic values. See Cynthia Zaitzevsky, *Frederick Law Olmsted and the Boston Park System* (Cambridge, MA: Belknap Press of Harvard University Press, 1982). For Louisville, see Olmsted Parks Conservancy, accessed June 17, 2019, https://www.olmstedparks.org.

4. Frederick Law Olmsted, "Parks, Parkways and Pleasure Grounds," *Engineering Magazine* 9, no. 2 (May 1895): 253–54.

5. Charles E. Beveridge, Paul Rocheleau, and David Larkin, *Frederick Law Olmsted: Designing the American Landscape* (New York: Universe Publisher, 1998).

6. Good examples of this are the English landscapes designed by landscape architects including Capability Brown and Humphry Repton.

7. Jennifer Nalewicki, "The Best Places in the U.S. to See Spring's Migrating Birds," *Smithsonian Magazine*, March 2017, https://www.smithsonianmag.com/travel/best -places-america-see-spring-migration-180958494/.

8. Rachel Nuwer, "The Ants of Manhattan," *New York Times*, December 1, 2014, https://www.nytimes.com/2014/12/02/science/the-ants-of-manhattan.html.

9. Margaret Walls, "Parks and Recreation in the United States: Local Park Systems," Resources for the Future Issue Brief (Washington, DC: 2009), 1–22, https://www .rff.org/publications/issue-briefs/parks-and-recreation-in-the-united-states-local -park-systems/.

10. Nick Watts et al., "The Lancet Countdown on Health and Climate Change: From 25 Years of Inaction to a Global Transformation for Public Health," *The Lancet* 391 (2018): 581–630, https://doi.org/10.1016/S0140-6736(17)32464-9.

11. Stephen R. Kellert, Judith Heerwagen, and Martin Mador, *Biophilic Design: The Theory, Science, and Practice of Bringing Buildings to Life* (Hoboken, NJ: John Wiley, 2008).

12. Greg Kats and Keith Glassbrook, *Achieving Urban Resilience: Washington DC* (Capital E, 2017), https://www.coolrooftoolkit.org/wp-content/uploads/2016/12 /Kats-SmartsurfacesDC-FullReport.pdf.

13. Myla F. J. Aronson et al., "Biodiversity in the City: Key Challenges for Urban Green Space Management," *Frontiers in Ecology and the Environment* 15, no. 4 (2017): 189–96.

14. Richard Hobbs et al., "Managing the Whole Landscape: Historical, Hybrid, and Novel Ecosystems," *Frontiers in Ecology and the Environment* 12, no. 10 (2014): 557–64, https://doi.org/10.1890/130300; Ingo Kowarik, "Novel Urban Ecosystems, Biodiversity, and Conservation," *Environmental Pollution* 159, nos. 8–9 (2011): 1974–83.

15. J. Morgan Grove, "Cities: Managing Densely Settled Social-Ecological Systems," in *Principles of Ecosystem Stewardship*, ed. F Stuart Chapin III (New York: Springer, 2009), 281–94.

16. See Winnie Hu, "A Billion-Dollar Investment in New York's Water," *New York Times*, January 19, 2018, https://www.nytimes.com/2018/01/18/nyregion/new-york-city-water-filtration.html; Emily S. Rueb, "How New York Gets Its Water," *New York Times*, March 24, 2016, https://www.nytimes.com/interactive/2016/03/24/nyregion/how-nyc-gets-its-water-new-york-101.html.

17. Hu, "Billion-Dollar Investment."

18. Todd S. Bridges et al., "Use of Natural and Nature-Based Features (NNBF) for Coastal Resilience" (Field Report ERDC SR-15-X, U.S. Army Engineer Research and Development Center, Vicksburg, MS, 2014).

19. Nigel Dunnett and Andy Clayden, *Rain Gardens: Managing Water Sustainably in the Garden and Designed Landscape* (Portland, OR: Timber Press, 2007).

20. June J. Cheng and Peter Berry, "Health Co-Benefits and Risks of Public Health Adaptation Strategies to Climate Change: A Review of Current Literature," *International Journal of Public Health* 58, no. 2 (2013): 305–11.

21. "Heat Island Effect," U.S. Environmental Protection Agency, accessed February 25, 2019, https://www.epa.gov/heat-islands.

22. Alex Felson et al., "Constructing Native Urban Forests as Experiments to Evaluate Resilience," *Scenario Journal* 4 (Spring 2014), https://scenariojournal.com/article/constructing-native-urban-forests/.

23. "New York City's Privately Owned Public Spaces," New York City Department of City Planning, accessed February 25, 2019, https://www1.nyc.gov/site/planning/plans/pops/pops.page.

24. Sarah Schindler, "The 'Publicization' of Private Space," *Iowa Law Review* 103 (2018): 1093–153, https://ssrn.com/abstract=2960320.

25. "The Sustainable Sites Initiative," The Sustainable Sites Initiative, accessed February 25, 2019, http://www.sustainablesites.org/; "Getting to Know LEED: Neighborhood Development," U.S. Green Building Council, January 1, 2014, https://www.usgbc.org/articles/getting-know-leed-neighborhood-development.

26. Alexander J. Felson, Mark A. Bradford, and Tim Terway, "Promoting Earth Stewardship through Designed Experiments," *Earth Stewardship Special Issue—Frontiers in Ecology* 11, no. 7 (2013): 362–67.

# Built to Learn

FROM STATIC TO ADAPTIVE ENVIRONMENTAL POLICY

Lori S. Bennear and Jonathan B. Wiener

MANY POLICIES HAVE been deployed over the last half century to improve our air quality, water quality, and ecosystem health. We have learned from experience that some have been more successful than others. This book is replete with big ideas to address problems that were left unsolved or that are newly emerging. Together this represents a remarkable effort to apply accumulated learning to devise new and better policies.

Although learning has undoubtedly occurred over the past fifty years of environmental protection, each policy can often effectively be a one-time decision, difficult to revise except over long time periods. It may take centuries to amend the Constitution, decades to amend a statute, years to change a final agency rule. Political gridlock adds delay. Human psychology often supposes that a single action will be an enduring solution.[1] Agencies may try to work around these constraints, but these tactics may be limited and criticized for skirting required procedures for public input.[2]

There are significant limitations to this static approach to environmental policy because—inevitably—the world changes. With new scientific understanding, new technology, new environmental outcomes, and new social patterns and values, past policies can become mismatches with changing conditions. These mismatches can grow over time and prove harmful, undermining environmental protection, risking disasters, inhibiting innovation, and fostering frustration and political opposition.

For example, in 1976 Congress passed the Toxic Substances Control Act, authorizing the Environmental Protection Agency (EPA) to develop regulations on chemicals. But since 1976, the number of chemicals in use has grown dramatically, with over eighty thousand chemicals currently on the market. Furthermore, our understanding of the relationship between chemical exposure and human health has advanced substantially. The 1976 law may have been a good fit when it was enacted, but over time it became ill suited to deal with evolving realities in the risk assessment and management of both new and old chemicals. To overcome this growing mismatch, changes to the regulations governing chemicals required congressional action. The Lautenberg Chemical Safety Act finally passed both houses of Congress in 2016, forty years after the initial law and even after Senator Lautenberg's death. Change did happen, but even with bipartisan support, this change happened very slowly.

We propose to better incorporate learning directly into the policy process itself, not just to take stock of and amend laws every few decades but to design environmental policies to be built to learn and update over time.[3] Adaptive learning can foster better environmental protection at lower cost. And by offering the prospect of repeated reviews, this approach could also help overcome interest group impasses that can block initial adoption of sound policies. Adaptive updating would help environmental policy better deal with what we know has occurred in the past, and what we know to expect in the future: change.

An adaptive approach to environmental policy is especially compelling when we expect to learn a lot after the initial adoption of a policy. Advancing technologies can offer both benefits and risks. For example, automated vehicles, hyperloops, gene editing, better batteries, advanced nuclear energy, solar geoengineering, space exploration, and other emerging technologies may improve human health and environmental quality, but may also pose risks of adverse effects. A traditional static approach to regulation of these emerging technologies would invest a great deal of effort in a single decision—yes-no, go–no go. Yet emerging technologies pose significant uncertainties, and we know we will learn more over time. These and other technologies may warrant an adaptive policy approach that is built from the outset to learn and update over time.

Still, adaptive regulation may pose its own drawbacks. First, there is the cost of data collection, which may incur both public expenditures and private burdens and pose privacy and data access concerns. Second, the analysis and review of a policy may be costly, in agency staff time and in the opportunity costs of other policies not addressed. Third, despite the need for regulation to adapt to changes in the world, there is also value in the predictability of legal rules. Roscoe Pound recognized both sides of this trade-off when he counseled that "law must be stable, and yet it cannot stand still."[4] Policy instability can impose costs, especially if unanticipated. Moreover, if adaptive regulation looks too facile, it may erode the credibility of the government's commitment to stick to the initial rules, thereby undermining compliance.[5]

Thus, we suggest that adaptive approaches to environmental policy will be warranted in many though not all cases. And, adaptive policy is not just one thing; there are several ways to incorporate learning over time. The challenge is to identify which type of adaptive approach makes the most sense in each case. The options vary in at least two key ways: whether the adaptive updating is unplanned or planned, and whether it is discretionary or automatic.

### UNPLANNED VERSUS PLANNED ADAPTIVE POLICY

Truly static regulation would remain rigid despite the world changing. In reality we do see some legal change over time, as illustrated in the eventual revisions to the Toxic Substances Control Act discussed above. But many policy changes are "unplanned adaptive," in the sense that the learning process was not initially envisioned, and no plan was adopted to collect monitoring data and undertake periodic reviews. Some "unplanned adaptive" regulatory changes occur only after surprises—crisis events that upend past static regulation.[6] For example, the landmark Superfund legislation that requires cleanup of toxic waste sites was passed by Congress in 1980 after the Love Canal incident—in which toxic waste was discovered under a residential neighborhood in upstate New York. There are many other examples of crisis-driven policy change, in areas as diverse as oil and chemical spills, nuclear power accidents, transportation accidents, workplace safety accidents, foodborne disease outbreaks, air pollution incidents, drinking water contamination, hazardous waste discoveries, and more. Such "policy shocks" can dramatize the need for regulatory change, reveal the arguable shortcomings of past regulation, spark contested framings of blame, and open windows of political opportunity for policy entrepreneurs to advance new approaches.[7]

Regulatory change after a surprise or crisis can be needed, indeed overdue, to address neglected or festering problems. But where it lacks careful preparation and analysis, such unplanned adaptive regulatory change can be wrenching, can make errors of diagnosis and remedy, and can yield new rules that are poorly designed, inadequately effective, and excessively costly, as well as generate adverse ancillary impacts (countervailing risks). For example, the Superfund legislation has been responsible for the clean-up of just over four hundred contaminated sites across the United States during its forty-year existence, but over one thousand sites remain to be remediated. The Superfund program has been criticized as overly costly where it requires clean-up to essentially pristine conditions regardless of the eventual future land use. Often the highest costs are associated with the very last units of clean-up. Those extra costs may make sense if the land will be used for a children's playground, but may not make sense if the land will be used as an industrial site.[8]

A potential improvement over unplanned reaction—recognizing that we cannot predict all disasters and that there will be some surprises—is to "prepare to learn" from a crisis by creating a standing "safety board" or investigative body in advance.[9] Such a standing safety board is ready to diagnose causes and recommend policy changes whenever a surprise occurs, accumulating institutional expertise over time. It can be a significant improvement over either an agency reaction (potentially hasty under intense pressure, and also potentially inhibited by fidelity to the agency's own past policies) or an ad hoc commission of inquiry (created anew from scratch and lacking institutional memory).[10] Examples of such standing bodies include the U.S. National Transportation Safety Board, which investigates transit-related accidents, and the Dutch Safety Board, which has a broader mandate to investigate not just transportation-related accidents but also food contamination, health care accidents, and other incidents. A step forward in U.S. environmental policy could be the creation of an independent-standing Environmental Safety Board or Environmental Crisis Investigation Body, equipped with expert staff and ready to make findings and recommendations—prepared to learn.

Going further, we could build learning even more deliberately into the policy process—planning to adapt. This would mean that the initial regulation incorporates processes for data collection, analysis, review, and potential policy changes. In short: planned adaptive regulation.[11]

One option for planned adaptive regulation is "retrospective review" (also called follow-up evaluation or ex post impact assessment), which can helpfully identify useful policy changes. But in practice this has typically meant a single look-back at one point in time, often with no initial plan to monitor and analyze data, and often focused on reducing costs rather than on increasing benefits or learning to improve the accuracy of ex ante impact assessments.[12]

Even more adaptive would be planned periodic review: a series of ongoing monitoring, data collection, and analysis, with periodic evaluation of the consequences through recurring impact assessments and iterative updating/revision. For example, the U.S. Clean Air Act requires EPA—advised by a special panel, the Clean Air Science Advisory Committee—to undertake periodic reviews of the national ambient air quality standards for regional air pollutants (such as ozone and particulate matter) every five years, and to determine whether revisions to the rule are warranted. As scientific understanding of these air pollutants and human health has advanced, EPA has tightened many of these air quality standards over time based on these periodic reviews. Some other environmental policies have adopted this periodic review approach to planned adaptive regulation. The Lautenberg Chemical Safety Act, discussed above, requires EPA to review its policies every five years. The Corporate Average Fuel Economy Standards for automobiles and the energy efficiency standards for appliances are subject to periodic reviews. The Paris Agreement on climate change also calls for periodic "stocktakes."

## DISCRETIONARY VERSUS AUTOMATED ADAPTIVE POLICY

Another choice in designing adaptive environmental policy is whether the learning and updating involve discretionary action by the regulator, or whether these adjustments are automatic. In discretionary adaptive regulation, like the examples mentioned above, the policy mandates the collection of data and evidence and the subsequent review of that evidence by the regulator; with that review, the regulator can decide whether to revise the policy.

Alternatively, adaptive regulation could be automated. An initial regulation, anticipating change in key variables, could establish trigger values that, if reached, would automatically adjust the policy. For example, cap-and-trade systems allocate a finite number of permits for pollutant emissions and then allow emitters to trade those permits. In any such cap-and-trade system, a key parameter that is unknown to the regulator—and often to the regulated entities themselves—is the actual cost of reducing the pollution. To optimize societal net benefits, the goal is to reduce emissions until the marginal benefit (the benefit of another unit of reduction) equals the marginal cost of that reduction. But there is significant uncertainty over both marginal benefits and marginal costs. If marginal costs turn out to be much lower than originally anticipated (due, perhaps, to rapid technological change), or marginal benefits much greater (due, perhaps, to more severe environmental damages), then to maximize net benefits the policy should be made more stringent—requiring greater emissions reductions. Alternatively, if marginal costs turn out to be much higher than anticipated or marginal benefits much lower, then maximizing net benefits would imply that the policy should be more lenient, requiring less emissions reductions.

Following this approach, the Regional Greenhouse Gas Initiative of several U.S. states has pre-set price floors and price ceilings that, if reached in the market for emissions permits, automatically adjust the allowable amount of emissions. If the price of a permit rises to the price ceiling (reflecting higher than expected costs), the agency issues additional permits at that price. This increases the number of permits available and effectively makes the policy less stringent. Or, if the price of a permit falls to the price floor (indicating lower than expected costs), the agency buys up permits at that price. This reduces the number of permits available and effectively makes the policy more stringent. The key here is that the adaptive mechanism, including the price floor and ceiling, is established earlier and takes effect automatically. No discretionary policy decisions need to be made to adjust the policy when the costs change.

Automated adaptive regulation could go further, through the use of algorithms, machine learning, and artificial intelligence to revise policy in response to new information and a changing world.[13] Such automated adaptive regulation could be more rapid in responding to multiple kinds of change, but may also raise questions of transparency, explainability, accountability, embedded bias, and other concerns. These drawbacks must be compared with the shortcomings of discretionary human decisions—neither is perfect.[14]

The choice between automated and discretionary adaptive policy implicates both the speed and breadth of the adaptation. Under discretionary adaptive regulation, the agency or legislature can review its policy and make changes based on a broad set of information about impacts and options, but this process requires more time. In contrast, automated adaptive regulation is quicker but usually more narrowly focused on only one or two key variables identified at the outset. There can also be hybrid combinations of automated and discretionary policy. Indeed, the Regional Greenhouse Gas Initiative requires periodic review of the price ceilings and floors, thereby combining the benefits of quick automatic adjustments with the benefits of broader discretionary adjustments.

## MOVING FORWARD

There have already been some moves from a static approach toward a more adaptive approach to environmental policy. The potential gains from wider adoption of adaptive approaches appear to be large, and much work needs to be done to assess where adaptive approaches, and which types, would be most desirable. Among the key parameters in the move from static toward adaptive are the frequency of review, the scope of information to be assessed, and who is the decision maker among agencies or other bodies.

As to frequency, it is worth questioning why many policies call for review every five years; that might be ideal, but it might also be that learning will advance on different timelines for different issues, warranting different periods of review. Policy makers should be thoughtful in their choice of review period, to ensure that the timing is frequent enough to avoid stagnant policy mismatches and reap the gains of learning, but not so frequent that it poses undue burdens of data collection and instability.

As to scope of information, the monitoring and review should try to assess not only the policy's intended benefits and possible costs but also the unintended consequences (such as co-benefits or countervailing harms) that are important enough to warrant policy change.

As to who decides, one choice is whether the relevant regulatory agency (such as EPA), an executive oversight body (such as the Council on Environmental Quality or the Office of Management and Budget), or another institution (such as a National Academies of Sciences panel, the Government Accountability Office, or a new commission) should undertake the adaptive review. This choice is not one-size-fits-all. There may be a trade-off between topical expertise, which is typically concentrated in regulatory agencies, and independent evaluation expertise, which is typically concentrated in the other bodies mentioned above. More work is needed to develop criteria and evidence that would help determine when an outside review leads to better outcomes than a review within an agency itself.

To learn more, we should test and compare several options for monitoring, analysis, review, and updating of policies, especially where change is rapid and learning is significant. The environment is dynamic and adaptive, as are human societies, technologies, and science; likewise, environmental policies can be made more adaptive over time. Environmental laws and institutions can be built to learn.

## NOTES

1. Jordi Quoidbach, Daniel T. Gilbert, and Timothy D. Wilson, "The End of History Illusion," *Science* 339 (2013): 96–98.
2. Robin Craig and J. B. Ruhl, "Designing Administrative Law for Adaptive Management," *Vanderbilt Law Review* 67 (2014): 1–87; Wendy Wagner, William West, Thomas McGarity, and Lisa Peters, "Dynamic Rulemaking," *New York University Law Review* 92 (2017): 182–266.
3. Daniel A. Farber, "Environmental Protection as a Learning Experience," *Loyola Los Angeles Law Review* 27 (1994): 791–807; Justin R. Pidot, "Governance and Uncertainty," *Cardozo Law Review* 37 (2015): 112–84.
4. Roscoe Pound, *Interpretations of Legal History* (Cambridge: Cambridge University Press, 1923), 1.
5. John Coffee, "The Political Economy of Dodd-Frank: Why Financial Reform Tends to Be Frustrated and Systemic Risk Perpetuated," *Cornell Law Review* 97 (2012): 1019–82; Richard J. Lazarus, "Super Wicked Problems and Climate Change: Restraining the Present to Liberate the Future," *Cornell Law Review* 94 (2009): 1153–233; Aaron L. Nielsen, "Sticky Regulations," *University of Chicago Law Review* 85 (2018): 85–143.
6. Thomas A. Birkland, *Lessons of Disaster: Policy Change after Catastrophic Events* (Washington, DC: Georgetown University Press, 2006).
7. Edward J. Balleisen, Lori S. Bennear, Kimberly D. Krawiec, and Jonathan B. Wiener, eds., *Policy Shock: Recalibrating Risk and Regulation after Oil Spills, Nuclear Accidents, and Financial Crises* (Cambridge: Cambridge University Press, 2017).
8. James T. Hamilton and W. Kip Viscusi, *Calculating Risks? The Spatial and Political Dimensions of Hazardous Waste Policy* (Cambridge, MA: MIT Press, 1999).
9. Balleisen et al., *Policy Shock*.
10. Edward J. Balleisen, Lori S. Bennear, David Cheang, Jonathon Free, Megan Hayes, Emily Pechar, and A. Catherine Preston, "Institutional Mechanisms for Investigating the Regulatory Implications of a Major Crisis: The Commission of Inquiry and the Safety Board," in *Policy Shock*, ed. Edward J. Balleisen et al. (Cambridge: Cambridge University Press, 2017): 485–539.
11. Lawrence E. McCray, Kenneth A. Oye, and Arthur C. Petersen, "Planned Adaptation in Risk Regulation," *Technological Forecasting & Social Change* 77 (2010): 951–59.
12. Cary Coglianese, "Moving Forward with Regulatory Lookback," *Yale Journal on Regulation Online* 30 (2013): 57–66; Maureen Cropper, Art Fraas, and Richard Morgenstern, "Looking Backward to Move Regulations Forward: Rigorous Ex Post Analyses Can Improve Regulatory Policies," *Science* 355 (2017): 1375–76; Cass R. Sunstein, "The Regulatory Lookback," *Boston University Law Review* 94 (2014): 579–602; Jonathan B. Wiener and Daniel L. Ribeiro, "Environmental Regulation Going Retro: Learning Foresight from Hindsight," *Journal of Land Use & Environmental Law* 32 (2016): 1–72.
13. Cary Coglianese and David Lehr, "Regulating by Robot: Administrative Decision Making in the Machine-Learning Era," *Georgetown Law Journal* 105 (2017): 1147–223.
14. Joshua A. Kroll, Joanna Huey, Solon Barocas, Edward W. Felten, Joel R. Reidenberg, David G. Robinson, and Harlan Yu, "Accountable Algorithms," *University of Pennsylvania Law Review* 165 (2017): 633–705.

# Why Big Ideas So Often Fail

Samara Brock, Austin Bryniarski, and Deepti Chatti

BIG IDEAS OFTEN FAIL—especially in the environmental arena. The initial promise of a bright green future often degrades quickly under the weight of unforeseen negative consequences. Our research identifies a number of reasons why this outcome is so common. Fundamentally, big idea thinking often runs afoul of place-based realities. By paying attention to local cultures, histories, economies, and ecologies, big ideas can be made less prone to failure. We note, in particular, that getting clarity on the full context of an issue can help mitigate the risk of misalignment between the solutions offered and on-the-ground circumstances. It may seem ironic to have this analysis embedded in a book about big ideas, but we do not think so. To the contrary, policy progress depends on learning from past mistakes—and on a commitment to continuous improvement.

## LESSONS FROM POLITICAL ECOLOGY

Political ecology examines the link among ecological, social, economic, and political issues—and can provide a foundation for considering the nuanced implications of big ideas. To enrich the conversation on big ideas, it is vital to examine this extensive body of social science research, to gain insights from a discipline that has for many decades demonstrated how environmental change initiatives fail to meet their grand aims. Political ecology first focused on examining environmentally motivated development initiatives taking place in the Global South, and has since come to interrogate all manner of attempts to solve environmental problems. Here, we outline some themes the discipline has uncovered.

*Not Analyzing Underlying Power Dynamics Can Lead to a Misdiagnosis of a Problem.*   In his seminal political ecology analysis of the failure of international development efforts to curb soil erosion in Nepal, the geographer Piers Blaikie argues that the failure of these initiatives often stems from the initial framing of the problem. Governments and aid agencies often think ecological degradation emerges from careless use of resources by local communities. But this assumption misses the broader trends that push impoverished people to live on marginal lands in the first place.[1] Any projects that do not address the underlying power dynamics that lead to such marginalization are, according to Blaikie and subsequent authors, doomed to failure. Emphasis on the broader context of issues remains important today: understanding how a problem emerges in the first place can more fully account for inequities that often lead to environmental degradation. Thus, the question of who benefits and who loses from the events that lead to environmental problems needs to be carefully examined. And who might benefit and who might lose from the proposed solution must also be explored to avoid solutions that further disempower marginalized groups.

*Global, Bird's-Eye-View Framing Can Exclude Local Knowledge and Make a Problem Worse.*   How we view "nature" itself, and how that view shapes environmental problem-solving, must also be understood. We caution against relying solely on a "global" view of nature where humans transcend it and the world becomes merely property or resources to be managed for the public good.[2] Writers such as James C. Scott and Bruno Latour contend that this global "view from above" all too often leads to abstraction and simplification by experts at centers of power.[3] In oversimplifying the complex dynamics of local ecologies and politics into abstractions that can be managed from afar, managers may lose local perspectives. Further, local places themselves become obscured when they are understood through statistics: they become managed to meet abstract metrics, rather than with place-based knowledge in mind. Scott highlights examples—from planned forests in Germany to mono-crop farming in European colonies—where distant metrics-driven managers unknowingly destroyed local biological and cultural diversity in the name of productive and efficient land use.[4] The political scientist Timothy Luke argues that seeing nature as such a globalized system under threat invites expert managerial oversight.[5] He suggests that a top-down understanding of the global environment—through expert mapping, monitoring, measuring, and managing nature for the public good—may pave over more successful democratic environmental problem-solving. While some problems, such as global climate change, require a global understanding, that understanding must also consider the potential failures this framing may invite.

*External Intervention Begets More External Intervention.*   When failure does occur in environmental projects, policy makers[6] often think the solution is to double down on outside intervention. A number of authors have argued that, post-failure, policy makers often offer a "technical fix" as the solution rather than a more integrated place-based intervention.[7] For example, the solution for low yields in agriculture becomes greater dependence on external inputs of fertilizer, machinery, pesticides, and new seed varieties for commodity crops. Such framing may preclude consideration of what crops and cropping systems may be best adapted to local microclimatic conditions, management histories, and cultural needs. Attention to metrics like crop yield may sideline a range of other diverse and sustainable forms of agriculture.[8] The more external solutions are to communities, the less control, involvement, and, often, buy-in communities have in them. This can ultimately lead to failure.

## BIG IDEAS, BIG PROBLEMS? COOKSTOVES AND FOOD WASTE

To succeed, environmental policies and projects must pay attention to how policy makers frame a problem, what kind of management these framings invite, and who gains and who loses through the intervention proposed. Not paying attention to these key issues can ultimately undermine seemingly well-meaning environmental initiatives and lead to failure of big ideas. Two case studies from our research explore these lessons.

*Cookstove Programs in India.*   The case of household energy transitions in rural India helps us analyze these issues. Governments, nonprofits, and international aid organizations have sought to intervene in the cooking technologies and practices of low-income families for decades. So-called "traditional" cookstoves, used by three billion people around the world, are usually made locally and use solid biomass fuels such as wood, crop residue, and animal dung. Burning solid biomass in enclosed cooking spaces leads to household air pollution, which has local public health and global climate change consequences. Development organizations such as the United States Agency for

International Development, Germany's GIZ development agency, and the Global Alliance for Clean Cookstoves and the national governments of countries such as India and China have attempted to transition low-income families to "clean" cooking technologies. In this case, we examine the rhetoric surrounding two national energy programs in India that attempted to facilitate a clean cooking energy transition. While the development world commonly considers one of them a failure and the other a success, there are multiple programmatic similarities between the two that illustrate important lessons about big ideas.

The National Program on Improved Cookstoves, a national energy program launched in India in 1984, is generally characterized as a failure. India launched the program to distribute improved biomass cookstoves to low-income families across the country. The new "improved" cookstove technologies were supposed to replace traditional cookstoves, which governments and development agencies considered inefficient, as well as drivers of global deforestation. This claim is now known not to be true, as numerous studies have shown that poor households are not the perpetrators but rather the victims of deforestation. However, this erroneous claim helped frame early "big" solutions to the problem.[9]

The "improved" technologies were primarily designed to reduce fuelwood demand and were thought to have the additional benefits of reducing drudgery for rural women and generating livelihoods in rural areas. Between 1984 and 2001, the government disseminated thirty-four million stoves to rural Indian households, making the National Program on Improved Cookstoves the second-largest stove program in the world, after China's.[10] The new technologies used the same fuels that households were already using for cooking. But by the late 1990s, policy researchers and academics were discussing the program as a failure, although conclusive reasons were not evident. Some researchers concluded that the "improved" biomass cookstoves were deeply unpopular with intended beneficiaries of the program. And yet others concluded that the technologies were popular and would have been continually used if policies had been in place for repair and maintenance. Regardless, by 2002 the Indian national government discontinued its active support of the program.

While the National Program on Improved Cookstoves is remembered as a failure, the latest household energy program in India is seen as a success. The Pradhan Mantri Ujjwala Yojana is an ambitious energy program that expands fossil fuel cooking energy in the form of liquefied petroleum gas (LPG) access to families below the poverty line. This program launched in May 2016, and in the two and a half years since, India has given out 57.6 million new LPG connections to low-income families. Similar to the previous household energy effort, this program also aims to intervene in the cooking technologies of India's poor, and specifically aims to provide clean cooking fuels to ameliorate the health impacts of woodfuel smoke. Private franchisees of the state-owned oil companies distribute the fuels, under direction from the Indian national government to expand their services to low-income families.

Both of the Indian national programs are big ideas. Neither of them has yet achieved the health benefits of access to energy that does not cause indoor air pollution. So why has one emerged as a success and the other a failure? One of the key differences in the perception of the contemporary program as a success derives from the belief that the new program is scalable. It is, in other words, seen as a *bigger idea* than the earlier program. Development groups believe that the structure of the new program—relying on private franchisees to distribute petroleum—is amenable to rapid expansion. The new program also uses one standard technology—the LPG stove—as opposed to a variety of locally appropriate "improved biomass cookstoves."[11] The health, environmental, and social benefits of clean cooking fuels, however, are achieved only when the stove is used, and success can become evident in subsequent years only if families keep purchasing the fuel. The success of this program in meeting its desired objectives is therefore contingent on many of the same variables as the previous one. The project, though hailed as a success, may fall prey to a similar lack of long-term support for an initial big idea, as the National Program on Improved Cookstoves did. Long-term support for families who want to use LPG could include a plethora of policies to ensure reliable availability, accessibility, and affordability of the fuel.

In short, charismatic big ideas—like providing low-income families with clean cooking fuels—will succeed only when supported by a confluence of seemingly small and mundane ideas to ensure that families can continue to access the fuel. A key danger of relying on the excitement of a big idea approach is that it may obscure the very groundwork that needs to be done to make it succeed. Our point here is that the early excitement that the LPG big idea is receiving could obscure the fact that—as past efforts have shown—it may need many small, ongoing interventions to maintain it over the long term.

*Food Waste Reduction Efforts.*    The case of food waste allows us to ask similar questions about another big idea unfolding in real time: a constellation of contemporary efforts to reduce food waste. We note that big ideas are not always discrete projects like India's cookstove program—big ideas can also be conceptual. For example, in this volume, "conservation" and "natural capital" offer good examples of conceptual big ideas. Food waste is one such concept worth analyzing due to its growing popularity as an environmental issue. The way we measure food waste renders it a "big" problem: an oft-cited paper reports that the United States wastes up to 40 percent of its post-harvest food supply, much of it at the consumer level.[12] Another study notes that, in a country where 14 percent of people struggle to access food at some point in the year, the United States throws away around 1,250 calories worth of food per person each day.[13]

This presentation of food-waste-as-crisis has mobilized philanthropic organizations, nonprofits, and venture capitalists alike. Donors and investors have put hundreds of millions of dollars toward food waste programming. Environmental nongovernmental organizations have taken up food waste as a major issue. Supermarket chains have sought to link donations of would-be-wasted food to soup kitchens through initiatives with names such as Zero Hunger, Zero Waste. Even the federal government has caught food waste fever: the Trump administration announced a food waste reduction initiative in October 2018. "Sadly, each day too many American families struggle to meet their nutritional needs," Food and Drug Administration (FDA) commissioner Scott Gottlieb said in a press release announcing the program. "We at the FDA recognize the important role that reducing food waste can play in filling this critical gap," he said.[14]

Food waste's alluring bigness might be understood as a framing of the issue that comes with its own set of unintended consequences. Food waste's large-scale thinking runs the risk of overshadowing approaches to environmental and social problem-solving that are more sensitive to context and place. It obscures approaches that might be more politically complex but ultimately more durable. Attempts to pair reducing food waste with reducing hunger illustrate this well. In her book *Sweet Charity*, the sociologist Janet Poppendieck argues that charitable efforts to redistribute food to the impoverished, well-meaning as they may be, have perpetuated the rolling back of state-based food security protections like food stamps.[15] Some food bank operators have applied this analysis to the redistribution of wasted food. They have named food waste as a distraction and called instead for greater emphasis on public policy and localized approaches that address the root causes of poverty.[16]

Thinking big about food waste's environmental impacts might ultimately have little effect on reducing those impacts too. Even if the 40 percent of food wasted in this country were eaten, greenhouse gas emissions from across the food supply chain would remain relatively similar without any intervention to reduce emissions where they occur. Food production is inherently place-based, as are its impacts, yet food waste as a focus tells us very little about these contexts. Instead of focusing on wasting less of food that is grown in unsustainable ways, what if we incentivized growing food more sustainably to begin with? Rather than addressing the power dynamics that structure food systems in ways that make them unsustainable, food waste reduction efforts focus on individualized, consumer-driven solutions that do not call these dynamics into question, and therefore may not adequately mitigate the environmental consequences of food production, processing, and distribution.[17]

Focusing on reducing the quantity of wasted food also eclipses more qualitative questions we might ask that depend on harder-to-quantify variables, like, how can we make access to food more just?[18] The big idea of reducing food waste channels attention—not to mention philanthropic dollars, political will, and human capital—away from social and environmental problems that look different at local scales and therefore might demand different approaches.

### HOW TO MAKE BIG WORK?

Big ideas, by their nature, rally attention to urgent problems of seemingly universal significance. Their scale and audacity make them compelling—but may also be part of what makes them particularly vulnerable to failure. The best way to avoid some of the most common pitfalls is to be aware of them and plan for them in problem diagnosis, project design, and implementation. Bent Flyvbjerg, a professor of planning at Oxford's Saïd Business School, who studies why big-idea-style projects often go awry, outlines a framework called "phronetic" research, ideal for studying complex social dynamics. Using Aristotle's outline of three basic knowledges—scientific (*episteme*), technical (*techne*), and *phronesis* (often translated as "practical wisdom")—he asserts that truly predictive theories cannot be found in the study of human affairs. Trying to understand social dynamics through *episteme* or *techne* can lead alternately to gross simplification or gross generalization. We can generate more meaningful knowledge from context-dependent analysis that can then be used to reveal critical insights in other contexts. Flyvbjerg says we should do so "in full knowledge that we cannot find ultimate answers to these questions or even a single version of what the questions are."[19]

Rather than solely generating critique and stopping there, the aim of phronetic research is to ask incisive questions that can engender localized and sensitive solutions. We therefore offer the following analytical frames derived from the case studies discussed above: those looking to implement big ideas should reflect on whether their schemes may (1) fail to understand local context, (2) misidentify the problem, (3) privilege short-term technological approaches over longer-term democratic ones, (4) over-emphasize metrics to the detriment of on-the-ground diversity and complexity, and (5) fail to build trust between those most affected by an intervention and that intervention's proponents.

One small exercise those who seek to employ the lessons of this volume would do well to use is to constantly ask "for whom?" If policy makers describe food waste reduction as socially beneficial, we might ask "beneficial for whom?" Certainly not those who would prefer the dignity of self-provisioning food than accept the charity of a supermarket chain. If the LPG cookstove program is deemed a "success," we might ask "successful for whom?" Without a suite of complementary policies to sustain it, the program will not be a long-term success for the low-income families it aims to benefit. Habitually asking "for whom?" can be an important step in proactively addressing the five cautionary points raised here. This approach can help down-scale from sweeping, universalized prescriptions toward more contextualized sets of small responses. It is also important that practitioners who bring big ideas into being not fear failure so much as use it to learn about how sensitivities to context, place, people, and perspectives may get glossed over. By treating such failures as opportunities to become more reflective and adaptive to these sensitivities, the ultimate result will be more durable over the long run. The purchase of the "big idea"—and this volume—is its ability to present a clear and agreed-upon goal in light of environmental change. The big idea here is that reaching this goal might require many more small ideas along the way.

## NOTES

1. Piers Blaikie, *The Political Economy of Soil Erosion in Developing Countries* (London: Routledge, 1985).
2. Tim Ingold, *The Perception of the Environment: Essays on Livelihood, Dwelling and Skill* (London: Routledge, 2000).
3. James C. Scott, *Seeing Like a State: How Certain Schemes to Improve the Human Condition Have Failed* (New Haven, CT: Yale University Press, 1998); Bruno Latour,

*Science in Action: How to Follow Scientists and Engineers through Society* (Cambridge, MA: Harvard University Press, 1987).

4. These aspects are echoed in Anastas and Zimmerman's essay in this volume, in which they argue that systems thinking may allow environmental practitioners to move past reductionist approaches to environmental problem-solving—the example of growing crops for fuel parallels Scott's examples.

5. Timothy W. Luke, "Developing Planetarian Accountancy: Fabricating Nature as Stock, Service, and System for Green Governmentality," in Harry F. Dahms, ed., *Nature, Knowledge and Negation (Current Perspectives in Social Theory, Volume 26)* (Bingley, England: Emerald Group Publishing, November 2009), 125–59.

6. We use the term "policy maker" here to refer broadly to those working not only in government but also in nongovernmental organizations and the private sector as well.

7. Timothy Mitchell, *Rule of Experts: Egypt, Techno-Politics, Modernity* (Berkeley: University of California Press, 2002).

8. Michael Dove, "Theories of Swidden Agriculture and the Political Economy of Ignorance," *Agroforestry Systems* 1, no. 2 (1983): 85–99.

9. Called the "other energy crisis" by Erik Eckholm, it was believed at the time that low-income families around the world were causing deforestation by burning up too many trees to cook their food. Erik Eckholm, "The Other Energy Crisis: Firewood" (Worldwatch paper 1, Worldwatch Institute, Washington, DC, 1975); Bina Agarwal, *Cold Hearths and Barren Slopes: The Woodfuel Crisis in the Third World* (Riverdale, MD: Riverdale, 1986); James Fairhead and Melissa Leach, *Misreading the African Landscape: Society and Ecology in a Forest-Savanna Mosaic* (Cambridge: Cambridge University Press, 1996).

10. Douglas F. Barnes, Priti Kumar, and Keith Openshaw, *Cleaner Hearths, Better Homes: New Stoves for India and the Developing World* (New Delhi: Oxford University Press and World Bank, 2012).

11. It was the responsibility of Technical Back-up Units for each state to designate a menu of improved biomass cookstoves that were appropriate for the state, based on an analysis of the types of solid fuels usually used by local families, the state cuisine, and local cooking practices.

12. Kevin D. Hall et al., "The Progressive Increase of Food Waste in America and Its Environmental Impact," *PLoS One* 4, no. 11 (2009): e7940.

13. Marie L. Spiker et al., "Wasted Food, Wasted Nutrients: Nutrient Loss from Wasted Food in the United States and Comparison to Gaps in Dietary Intake," *Journal of the Academy of Nutrition and Dietetics* 117, no. 7 (2017): 1031–1040.e22.

14. "Trump Administration Launches 'Winning on Reducing Food Waste' Initiative," United States Department of Agriculture, October 18, 2018, accessed December 10, 2018, https://www.usda.gov/media/press-releases/2018/10/18/trump-administration-launches-winning-reducing-food-waste.

15. Janet Poppendieck, *Sweet Charity: Emergency Food and the End of Entitlement* (New York: Viking, 1998).

16. Echoing Leiserowitz's contribution to this volume on the importance of building political will, critics of food waste donations illustrate how building political will around environmental and social issues can expand the field of possibility around

what is considered politically feasible. On the other hand, big ideas are often championed because they are already politically feasible, and therefore may not challenge those boundaries of possibility.

17. Julie Guthman, *Weighing In: Obesity, Food Justice, and the Limits of Capitalism* (Berkeley: University of California Press, 2011).

18. To borrow terms from Anastas and Zimmerman in this volume, approaches to reduce food waste tend more to "symptoms" of the way food systems are structured rather than to the underlying challenges those structures pose.

19. Bent Flyvbjerg, *Making Social Science Matter: Why Social Inquiry Fails and How It Can Succeed Again* (Cambridge: Cambridge University Press, 2001), 140.

# Epilogue

HOW TO MAKE BIG IDEAS WORK

Ingrid C. Burke and James Cameron

THIS VOLUME CONTAINS a range of ideas and perspectives on how to move society toward a more sustainable future—as has the collaborative Yale Environmental Dialogue process that helped shape this book. We hope the essays in *A Better Planet* will inspire ongoing conversation in government departments, communities, corporate boardrooms, media centers, laboratories, nongovernmental organizations, classrooms, and beyond. Diversity of thought, and even disagreement, builds a foundation for strong policy.

We are aware of the dangers *big ideas* pose. They have led to breakthroughs in the past, but also disasters. The development of synthetic nitrogen fertilizer in the early 1900s, for instance, has helped feed a growing planet but has also damaged aquatic ecosystems, polluted drinking water, and led to hypoxia in estuaries all over the world. Nonetheless, big ideas provide essential structure for society and necessary frameworks for battling big problems in the environment. We all must therefore learn—and learn well—how to bring big ideas forward while being aware of the risks they pose, how to make them last and evolve, and how to bring people along to implement them because they find them useful, or because they connect to them emotionally.

A few important principles stand out for translating big ideas into practice and ensuring that they endure over time. First, sustainable solutions for the future are likely to require disruptive innovation. We are in the midst of nonlinear changes in the environment with human impacts on critical ecosystems increasing, sometimes at exponential rates. Our responses require proportional action and impact. Such disruption must take a number of forms—new technologies, new leaders, systems approaches, organizational structures, and activism.

Second, while technological innovation can—and must—contribute to creating the solutions equivalent to the challenges we face, we need a broader view of *innovation*. Educating tomorrow's leaders can generate new breakthroughs, rapidly multiply impact, and contest existing orthodoxies. Such a spirit of fresh thinking has driven the effort to put together this book. Institutions such as the Yale School of Forestry & Environmental Studies help create the kinds of leaders who can go into both the corporations and the nonprofit organizations of America to provide challenging voices, diversity of perspectives, systems thinking, and creative solutions.

Third, serious barriers to turning big ideas into reality exist—and must be addressed. "Culture eats strategy for lunch," as the saying goes. Big ideas that shine on paper can quickly be derailed when they run into the inertia associated with complex local conditions. Building a middle ground to overcome these barriers requires networking and better-organized work, motivated by a vision for the future, and strong appreciation for local culture. This action must take place at multiple scales, from global to local—and cities, states, and other sub-national entities have a central role to play in crafting sustainability solutions. Discussions at a Yale Environmental Dialogue event provided numerous examples of the need for context-specific applications of big ideas—for small farms, water treatment, waste management solutions, indoor air quality associated with cookstoves, and more. To turn ideas into enduring practices that deliver transformative change, we must not assume that the critical breakthroughs will take the same form across different contexts.

Fourth, to implement and sustain big ideas, we should also consider how we communicate with each other. As some of the essays in this volume articulate, the right language is crucial for translating scientific or technical knowledge into that which can be received and acted on more broadly. For example, politicians in many parts of the world, especially in representative democracies, have said that the majority of voters do not actively prioritize climate change. They say people do not often write letters to their member of Congress or Parliament asking them to address climate change. Instead, they write about health, jobs, transport, immigration, parks, or any number of other points. These legislators are failing to understand that climate change underlies many of the issues citizens *do raise*. Truly advancing big ideas requires that we explain the connection between these vital "everyday" concerns and climate change—and to communicate clearly and without alienating jargon why and how the solutions to climate change can also address concerns about housing, health, transport, and jobs. In the next breath, those that sense creativity and constraint are always connected can innovate, display real examples, and reveal a better and more attractive pathway to a sustainable future for that constituency.

Fifth, and on a similar note, change driven by big ideas requires collaborative processes, stakeholder engagement, and thoughtful conversations. Such ideas succeed only through networks of people that can identify the challenges to be overcome, explain the opportunities, and help tackle the thorny issues that inevitably arise as the process of change unfolds. We recognize that it will not be easy to get people to work together in a context where vested interests, deeply held (but sometimes opposing) beliefs, and different lived experiences make alignment difficult. But a commitment to cooperation, which clearly emerges as a core theme of this book, can aid in balancing social, economic, and environmental priorities—and getting all hands on deck to deliver a sustainable future. Jane Wei-Skillern and Nora Silver's principles for collaboration success—highlighted in Bradford S. Gentry's essay in this volume—resonate here: establishing shared goals, building trust but not control, promoting others before yourself, and creating constellations and not stars.

Finally, big ideas require attention to the rule of law—itself a very big idea—as well as to principles of justice and questions of power. Those most in direct need of environmental protection, those exposed to pollution or climate change impacts today, tend to be in much less powerful positions. Much climate change action, for example, comes from grassroots organizations, and these disparities mean they often struggle to make a major impact at the national or international level. The push for fairness through collaboration and engagement of those who are not traditionally brought to the table should also consider fairness between generations, and justice for the other biological organisms on the planet. Intergenerational concerns especially matter in making sure big ideas stand the test of time. Our ideas will not last—nor should they—if they do not consider the well-being of young people and their descendants. Along with social justice, though, advancing big ideas for sustainability requires that powerful interests see incentives for themselves to change too. This broader perspective is the only way to make the transformations demanded by the environmental threats we face.

Big ideas help construct a story of our future that is both challenging and promising—allowing us to feel that we *can* overcome the difficulties that we face. In this story, we can see both the necessity and the possibility of confronting and averting environmental crises including climate change, mass human migration, water scarcity, cities at risk, biodiversity loss, toxic exposures, and others. An expansive view of the future allows us, moreover, to better appreciate the natural wealth that we have inherited and the resources we have been provided with which to improve the state of the world. Our mission is not just to forestall environmental damage and suffer a little bit less, but rather to rise to today's challenges and build a better future.

## ACKNOWLEDGMENTS

This book would not have been possible without the help of an enormous number of people. Not only are we grateful for the inspiring essays of our fifty-three authors, but we also deeply appreciate the guidance and feedback from hundreds of others who participated in the Yale Environmental Dialogue events that led up to the publication of this volume. We are especially appreciative of the more than one hundred thought leaders who came from across the country and around the world to New Haven, Connecticut, in February 2019 to participate in a workshop at which the draft essays were reviewed and critiqued—in a spirit of open debate and commitment to finding the best possible path toward a sustainable future. We would also like to thank the Aspen Institute for its crucial partnership in organizing and hosting Dialogue events.

No project of this kind could proceed without resources. We are especially grateful in this regard to Marne Obernauer, Jr., and to William Kunkler and Susan Crown, for their leadership support of the Dialogue and this volume, and various other friends of the Yale School of Forestry & Environmental Studies who are leading efforts to share the ideas produced by the Dialogue around the country.

*A Better Planet* reflects Yale's commitment to playing a central role in providing a base of knowledge on which a sustainability action agenda might be built as well as a venue for dialogue over how best to move the world forward on the spectrum of environmental, energy, land use, conservation, and natural resource management issues that must be addressed. Within the Yale School of Forestry & Environmental Studies, Dean Indy Burke has provided extraordinary leadership in getting this project launched and helping to sharpen the focus of the Yale community on the need to play a major role in advancing society toward a sustainable future. At Yale University Press, Jean Thomson Black offered essential guidance and played a critical part in shaping the manuscript above and beyond the usual role of the editor. Michael Deneen provided key assistance at every step of the publication process. Mary Pasti at Yale and Brian Ostrander at Westchester Publishing Services ensured the manuscript's smooth progress through editing and production.

This book is the product of a dedicated team working long hours over many months, including Timothy J. Mason, associate director of the Yale Center for Environmental Law and Policy; Chris Lewis, editorial director of the Yale Environmental Dialogue project; Melanie Quigley, director of strategic initiatives for the School of Forestry & Environmental Studies; Kristin Floyd, assistant dean for development and alumni services at the Yale School of Forestry & Environmental Studies; Jamerlyn Brown, senior administrative assistant at the Yale Center for Environmental Law and Policy; and an incredible team of Yale students including Hannah Abelow, Maria A. Martinez, Robert Little, Margaret Ferrato, Jonathan Silverthorne, Alix Kashdan, Laura Brush, Liz Bourguet, Hayley Lemoine, Sam Faries, Lucas Isakowitz, Pallavi Sherikar, Kate Donatelli, Rebecca L. McLean, Mai Ichihara, and Christina Ospina.

The Yale Environmental Dialogue grew out of the Yale School of Forestry & Environmental Studies strategic planning initiative carried out in 2017 and 2018. A dedicated committee of faculty, staff, and students worked over many months to shape the Dialogue's direction—and in this regard we are grateful for the work of Minna Brown, Gary Dunning, Kristin Floyd, Nicholas Olson, Melanie Quigley, John Wargo, Kevin Dennehy, Marian Chertow, Viveca Morris, Claire Lafave, and Maria A. Martinez.

Daniel C. Esty
New Haven, Connecticut

The jacket for this book includes a background motif consisting of keywords that highlight many of the critical concepts, new frameworks, and biggest ideas for a sustainable future discussed in the forty essays. We were inspired to develop this list as one outcome of our first readings of the contributors' essays, and it grew as we received feedback from the Yale Environmental Dialogue workshop held in February 2019 in New Haven, Connecticut.

We now share this list with you, our readers, and hope these words and the ideas embedded within them spur discussion, lay the foundation for reimagined and reinvigorated environmental policies, and lead to action. But the conversation does not end here. Please share your thoughts and big ideas with us at http://environment.yale.edu/dialogue.

Adaptive Learning
Agriculture
Algorithmic
    Governance
Anthropocene
Big Data
Biodiversity
Bioremediation
Borders

Carbon Pricing
Circular Economy
Cities
Clean Energy
Climate Change
Climate Change Justice
Collective Action
Communication
Community

Conservation
Context
Cooperation
Coordination
Corporate
    Sustainability
Design
Disruption
Diversity

Ecology
Ecosystems
Energy
Environmental
   Education
Environmental Justice
Equity
Ethics
Externalities
Extreme Weather
Fairness
Finance
Fisheries
Forests
Found Water
Future
Genomics
Global Governance
Green Banks
Green Chemistry
Green Lights
Harm Charges
High Yield Farming
Human Rights
Implementation
Incentives
Indigenous Knowledge
Industrial Ecology

Infrastructure
Innovation
Intensification
Interdisciplinary
Intergenerational
Landscapes
Leadership
Local-Regional-Global
Machine Learning
Markets
Materiality
Materials Management
Materials Science
Morality
National Climate
   Service
Natural Capital
Networks
Next Generation
Oceans
Paris Agreement
Parks
Place
Planetary Boundaries
Policy
Population Growth
Preparedness
Price Signals

Private Lands
Public Health
Public-Private
   Partnerships
Reform
Regulation
Renewable Power
Religion
Resilience
Responsibility
Rights
Risk
Rule of Law
Science
Sea Level Rise
Spirituality
Stewardship
Sustainability
Systems Thinking
Technology
Transformation
Values
Waste
Waste Management
Wastewater
Wilderness

ALEXIA AKBAY holds a Master of Public Health from Yale School of Public Health. Her research focuses on the effect of petroleum-based materials on human reproductive health. She was one of 20 candidates nominated for the Pritzker Emerging Environmental Genius Award in 2018.

SALEEM H. ALI is the Blue and Gold Distinguished Professor in Energy and the Environment at the University of Delaware, a Senior Fellow at Columbia University's Center on Sustainable Investment, and a Professorial Research Fellow at the University of Queensland. Professor Ali is a member of the United Nations International Resource Panel and the Scientific and Technical Advisory Panel of the Global Environment Facility. His research and practice focuses on resolving ecological conflicts and exploring novel ways of peace-building between corporations, governments, and communities.

FREDERICK W. (DERRY) ALLEN served at the U.S. Environmental Protection Agency (EPA) in various roles for 37 years, focusing on a wide range of environmental and sustainability issues. He was presented with the agency's Distinguished Career Service Award upon retirement. He also served at several other federal agencies—and as elected leader of three nonprofit organizations in Washington, DC. He serves on the board of the EPA Alumni Association, co-chairing a project on the future of environmental protection and EPA.

PAUL T. ANASTAS is a synthetic chemist at Yale School of Forestry & Environmental Studies, Yale School of Public Health, Chemistry Department, School of Engineering and Applied Sciences, and School of Management. He is the founding director of the Yale Center for Green Chemistry and Green Engineering; his research focuses on the design of sustainable products. Anastas has served in the administrations of four U.S.

379

presidents, most recently as assistant administrator for R&D at the U.S. Environmental Protection Agency. He is recognized as the "Father of Green Chemistry" and has received three honorary doctorates, two honorary professorships, the Heinz Prize, the Jeyes Medal, the Rachel Carson Award, and the E. O. Wilson Prize.

MARK S. ASHTON is Morris K. Jesup Professor of Silviculture and Forest Ecology at Yale School of Forestry & Environmental Studies, where he has served as the Director of School Forests since 2001. He researches the biological and physical processes governing the regeneration of natural forests and the creation of their agroforestry analogs. He is the author of *Basis for Agroforestry Systems* and *The Practice of Silviculture: Applied Forest Ecology*.

MICHELLE L. BELL is Mary E. Pinchot Professor of Environmental Health at Yale School of Forestry & Environmental Studies, School of Public Health, and School of Engineering and Applied Science. Bell's research—based in epidemiology, biostatistics, and environmental engineering—investigates how human health is affected by atmospheric systems. She has received the Prince Albert II de Monaco / Institut Pasteur Award, Rosenblith New Investigator Award, and the NIH Outstanding New Environmental Scientist Award.

LORI S. BENNEAR is Juli Plant Grainger Associate Professor of Energy Economics and Policy at Nicholas School of the Environment, with additional appointments at the Sanford School of Public Policy, and Economics Department at Duke University. She is the Associate Director for Educational Programs at the Duke University Energy Initiative. Her research focuses on evaluating the effectiveness of flexible environmental policies.

SUSAN BINIAZ served for over thirty years in the Legal Adviser's Office at the U.S. Department of State, including as a Deputy Legal Adviser. She was the lead U.S. lawyer, and a negotiator, for the climate change negotiations from 1989 until early 2017 and for many years ran the legal office responsible for environmental, scientific, and ocean affairs. She has held fellowship, lecturer, or research positions at various think tanks and universities, including Yale. She is currently a Senior Fellow at the U.N. Foundation, a Senior Adviser at the Center for Climate and Energy Solutions, and a Distinguished Senior Fellow at Climate Advisers.

SAMARA BROCK is a Ph.D. candidate at Yale School of Forestry & Environmental Studies researching organizations attempting to transform the future of the global food system. She has worked to establish urban agriculture projects in Cuba and Argentina, as a food systems planner for the City of Vancouver, and more recently as a program officer for the Tides Canada Foundation.

CRAIG R. BRODERSEN is an associate professor of physiological plant ecology at Yale School of Forestry & Environmental Studies. His work focuses on the structure and function of plants, especially how plants efficiently utilize two of the most limiting resources on Earth: water and light. His work is aimed at developing a better understanding of the trade-offs faced by plants in assembling transport systems that are both safe and efficient.

AMANDA BROWN-STEVENS is CEO of the Greenbelt Alliance, working throughout the San Francisco Bay Area to protect the region's iconic natural areas and encourage climate-smart development. Prior to this role, she oversaw Resilient by Design—a collaboration that brings innovative design solutions to sea level rise impacts around San Francisco Bay. Brown-Stevens has helped communities throughout California raise hundreds of millions of dollars in funding for open space and essential infrastructure.

GARY W. BRUDVIG is Benjamin Silliman Professor of Chemistry and professor of molecular biophysics and biochemistry at Yale. He is founding director of Yale Energy Sciences Institute, where he oversees the development of new research programs and facilities related to renewable energy, alternative fuels, and carbon management. He researches the chemistry of solar energy conversion in photosynthesis and works to develop artificial bio-inspired systems for solar fuel production. He has published over 400 papers on these topics.

AUSTIN BRYNIARSKI received a Master of Environmental Science from Yale School of Forestry & Environmental Studies. At Yale, he worked with the Yale Sustainable Food Program and conducted policy research as a Kerry Fellow. He serves as chair of the New Haven Food Policy Council.

INGRID C. "INDY" BURKE is Carl W. Knobloch, Jr. Dean at Yale School of Forestry & Environmental Studies. She was a University Distinguished Teaching Scholar and Professor at Colorado State University, and dean of the Haub School of Environment and Natural Resources at the University of Wyoming before joining the Yale faculty in 2016. Dr. Burke is an ecosystem ecologist whose research has focused on carbon and nitrogen cycling in dryland ecosystems. Her work with graduate students, postdoctoral associates, and colleagues has addressed how drylands are influenced by land use management, climatic variability, and regional variability. Burke has served on numerous committees and boards for national and international environmental science organizations, including the National Science Foundation, the National Research Council, and the Environmental Protection Agency's Science Advisory Board, UNESCO SCOPE, the International Geosphere-Biosphere Programme, the Dahlem Conference, and others.

JAMES CAMERON is an Executive Fellow at Yale Center for Environmental Law & Policy. He is currently chairman of the Overseas Development Institute and Senior Adviser at Systemiq, and previously was the founder and chairman of Climate Change Capital. Cameron has spent much of his legal career working on climate change matters, including negotiating the UNFCCC and Kyoto Protocol as an adviser to the Alliance of Small Island States.

DEEPTI CHATTI is a Ph.D. candidate at Yale School of Forestry & Environmental Studies and certificate candidate in Women's, Gender, and Sexuality Studies. Her doctoral research ethnographically analyzes household energy transitions in rural India. She has served as coordinator for the "Energy and the Humanities" initiative and served on the steering committee for the Environmental Humanities at Yale.

MARIAN CHERTOW is a professor of industrial environmental management at Yale School of Forestry & Environmental Studies, Yale School of Management, and National

University of Singapore. Her research and teaching focus on industrial ecology, business/environment issues, circular economy, waste management, and urban sustainability. She serves on the External Advisory Board of the Center for Energy Efficiency and Sustainability at Ingersoll Rand, the Board of Directors of Terracycle US Inc., and the Board of the Alliance for Research in Corporate Sustainability (ARCS).

DEBORAH R. COEN is a professor of history and chair of the Program in History of Science and Medicine at Yale University, as well as a member of the steering committee of Yale's Environmental Humanities Program. Her research interests include the history of the physical and environmental sciences and the intellectual and cultural history of modern central Europe. Her most recent book is *Climate in Motion: Science, Empire, and the Problem of Scale*.

CARY COGLIANESE is Edward B. Shils Professor of Law and professor of political science at the University of Pennsylvania, and director of the Penn Program on Regulation. He specializes in the study of regulation and regulatory processes, with an emphasis on the empirical evaluation of alternative regulatory strategies and the role of public participation, technology, and business-government relations in policy making. His most recent books include *Achieving Regulatory Excellence, Does Regulation Kill Jobs?*, and *Regulatory Breakdown: The Crisis of Confidence in U.S. Regulation*.

TODD CORT is a lecturer at Yale School of Management and faculty co-director for Yale Center for Business and the Environment. He also serves as co-director of the Yale Initiative on Sustainable Finance. He serves on multiple advisory boards, including the Connecticut Fund for the Environment, BlueSky Asset Management, and JUST Capital. He has over 15 years of experience in global corporate settings advising on sustainability matters including metrics, risk management, and auditing practices.

COURTNEY DURHAM received a Master of Environmental Management at Yale School of Forestry & Environmental Studies. She currently works as the Senior Associate, Coastal Wetlands and Coral Reefs for The Pew Charitable Trusts. She has also worked with World Resources Institute and the German Development Cooperation (GIZ).

THOMAS RASHAD EASLEY is the Assistant Dean of Community and Inclusion at Yale School of Forestry & Environmental Studies. He assists with enhancing diversity by promoting access to education, and developing programming around workplace equity. Before Yale, he served as the diversity director of the College of Natural Resources at North Carolina State University for 13 years, where he taught courses, advised students, engaged in community activism, and consulted with faculty and staff on programming inclusive to all populations.

DANIEL C. ESTY is Hillhouse Professor at Yale University with primary appointments at Yale Law School and the School of Forestry & Environmental Studies and a secondary appointment at the School of Management. He serves as director of the Yale Center for Environmental Law and Policy (www.yale.edu/envirocenter) and is on the Advisory Board of the Yale Center for Business and Environment (cbey.yale.edu), which he founded in 2006. Professor Esty is the author or editor of eleven books and dozens of articles on environmental protection, energy, and sustainability—and their connections to policy, regulatory reform, corporate strategy, performance measurement, competitiveness, trade, and economic success. His book *Green to Gold: How Smart Companies Use Environmental Strategy to Innovate, Create Value, and Build Competitive Advantage* has been named the top-selling "green business" book of the past decade. Prior to taking up his Yale professorship in 1994, he served in a variety of senior positions at the U.S. Environmental Protection Agency (where he helped to negotiate the 1992 Framework Convention on Climate Change) and was a senior fellow at the Peterson Institute for International Economics in Washington, D.C. From 2011 to 2014, he served as commissioner of Connecticut's Department of Energy and Environmental Protection, where he helped to launch the Connecticut Green Bank and earned a reputation for policy innovation.

ALEXANDER J. FELSON is a senior certified ecologist and a registered landscape architect. He is the deputy executive director of the Connecticut Institute for Resilience and Climate Adaptation and serves as the Director of Resilience Design with the State of Connecticut. He is an associate research scientist in the University of Connecticut's Department of Marine Sciences. He founded and directs the Urban Ecology and Design Lab and Ecopolitan Design.

ELI P. FENICHEL is an associate professor of bioeconomics and ecosystem management at Yale University. Professor Fenichel conducts quantitative research that connects economics, natural science, and sustainable development. His research approaches natural resources as capital assets. He has published over 60 papers on natural resource management and economics in outlets including *Proceedings of the National Academy of Sciences, Journal of the Association of Environmental and Resource Economists,* and *Proceedings of the Royal Society B.*

ERIN FITZGERALD serves as CEO of the U.S. Farmers & Ranchers Alliance, which represents farmer- and rancher-led organizations, and food and agricultural partners, with a common vision to further global sustainable food systems. She previously served as Senior Vice President, Global Sustainability, for the Innovation Center for U.S. Dairy. Fitzgerald has been recognized in Chicago's 40 under 40 and is a White House Champion of Change for Sustainable and Climate-Smart Agriculture and an Aspen Institute First Movers Fellow.

BRADFORD S. GENTRY is Senior Associate Dean for Professional Practice at Yale School of Forestry & Environmental Studies, a Professor in the Practice at the Yale School of Management, and a director of the Yale Center for Business and the Environment. Trained as a biologist and a lawyer, his work focuses on strengthening the links between private investment and improved environmental performance. He has worked on land, water, energy, industrial, and other projects in over 40 countries for private, public, and not-for-profit organizations.

GREG GERSHUNY leads the Energy and Environment Program at The Aspen Institute. Greg previously served as the associate director for the U.S. Department of Energy's Office of Energy Policy and Systems Analysis, as well as Director of Energy and Environment at the White House Office of Presidential Personnel. He also worked as a policy aide to the Associate Director for Science at the White House Office of Science and Technology Policy.

KENNETH GILLINGHAM is an associate professor at Yale School of Forestry & Environmental Studies, Department of Economics, and School of Management. In 2015–2016 he served as the Senior Economist for Energy and the Environment at the White House Council of Economic Advisers. He is an energy and environmental economist who has published widely on consumer decisions and policy in transportation, energy efficiency, and renewable energy.

MATTHEW GORDON is a Ph.D. candidate at Yale School of Forestry & Environmental Studies, where he studies the environmental and human impacts of urban infrastructure systems and waste policy. Previously he worked for the New York City Economic Development Corporation.

THOMAS E. GRAEDEL is Clifton R. Musser Professor Emeritus of Industrial Ecology at Yale School of Forestry & Environmental Studies. His research focuses on developing and enhancing industrial ecology and the resource aspects of the Anthropocene. His textbook *Industrial Ecology and Sustainable Engineering* was the first book in its field. Graedel's books (17) and papers (about 390) have resulted in a citation record in the top 1 percent of all active scientists. He was elected to the U.S. National Academy of Engineering in 2002.

JOHN GRIM is a senior lecturer and research scholar at Yale School of Forestry & Environmental Studies, Yale Divinity School, and the Department of Religious Studies. He co-directs the Forum on Religion and Ecology at Yale. He has published *The Shaman: Patterns of Religious Healing Among the Ojibway Indians*. With Mary Evelyn Tucker, he published *Ecology and Religion* and *Thomas Berry: A Biography*. They also produced the Emmy Award–winning film *Journey of the Universe* (journeyoftheuniverse.org).

BARRY E. HILL is a visiting scholar at the Environmental Law Institute and an adjunct professor of law at Vermont Law School. Professor Hill is the author of the four editions of *Environmental Justice: Legal Theory and Practice*. He was the director (1998–2007) of the Office of Environmental Justice at the U.S. Environmental Protection Agency. He is the recipient of distinguished achievement awards and a distinguished alumni award for his teaching, research, and leadership on environmental justice and sustainable development.

MEHA JAIN is an assistant professor in School for Environment and Sustainability at the University of Michigan. Her research examines the impacts of environmental change on agricultural production, and strategies that farmers adopt to reduce negative impacts. Her work also examines how to increase food production while limiting environmental impacts. She combines remote sensing with household-level and census datasets to examine farmer decision-making and behavior across large spatial and temporal scales.

ANTHONY LEISEROWITZ is director of the Yale Program on Climate Change Communication and a senior research scientist at the Yale School of Forestry & Environmental Studies. He is an expert on public opinion and engagement with climate change and the environment. Leiserowitz is a board member of the KR Foundation and advisor to the U.N. Foundation, the Ad Council, Years of Living Dangerously, and the China Center for Climate Change Communication, and host of Climate Connections, broadcast daily on more than 500 radio stations nationwide.

THOMAS E. LOVEJOY, "the godfather of biodiversity," has conducted research in the Brazilian Amazon since 1965, where his experiment on forest fragmentation has run since 1980. He has worked at the interface of science and public policy with various positions at the World Wildlife Fund, Smithsonian Institution, and other organizations. He currently is University Professor of Environmental Science and Policy at George Mason University and leads its Institute for a Sustainable Earth. He is credited with coining the term biological diversity.

THE HONORABLE JANE LUBCHENCO, University Distinguished Professor at Oregon State University, is a marine ecologist with expertise in the ocean, climate change, and interactions between the environment and human well-being. She served (2009–2013) as Under Secretary of Commerce for Oceans and Atmosphere and as Administrator of the National Oceanic and Atmospheric Administration (NOAA), as part of President Barack Obama's Science Team, and as the first U.S. Science Envoy for the Ocean with the State Department (2014–2016). She is one of the "most highly cited" ecologists in the world, with eight publications as "Science Citation Classics." She has received numerous awards, including 23 honorary doctorates, the highest honor given by the National Academy of Sciences (the Public Welfare Medal), and the highest honor from the National Science Board (the Vannevar Bush Award). She co-founded The Leopold Leadership Program, COMPASS, and Climate Central.

MONICA MEDINA is the founder and publisher of *Our Daily Planet*, an environmental e-mail newsletter; an adjunct professor in the School of Foreign Service at Georgetown University; and an independent policy consultant. Medina served as Special Assistant to the Secretary of Defense (2012–2013). She previously served as the Principal Deputy Undersecretary of Commerce for Oceans and Atmosphere at the National Oceanic and Atmospheric Administration (2009–2012). In 2013, Ms. Medina was awarded the Department of Defense Distinguished Public Service Medal.

G. TRACY MEHAN, III is Executive Director for Government Affairs at the American Water Works Association (AWWA). Mehan served as Assistant Administrator for Water at the U.S. Environmental Protection Agency (2001–2003), director of the Michigan Office of the Great Lakes (1993–2001), and director of the Missouri Department of Natural Resources (1989–1992). Mehan served on the Committee on the Mississippi River and the Clean Water Act for the National Research Council of the National Academies. He is currently an adjunct professor at Antonin Scalia Law School at George Mason University.

WILLIAM NORDHAUS is Sterling Professor of Economics at Yale University and a member of the faculty at Yale School of Forestry & Environmental Studies. From 1977 to 1979, he was a member of President Carter's Council of Economic Advisers. Dr. Nordhaus is a member of the National Academy of Sciences, a Fellow of the American Academy of Arts and Sciences, a Fellow of the Econometric Society, and a past president of the American Economic Association. His research has encompassed environmental economics, climate change, health economics, augmented national accounting, the political business cycle, and productivity. He was awarded the 2018 Nobel Prize in Economics for his work on climate change economics.

JOHN REEDER is an Executive in Residence at American University, visiting from the Environmental Protection Agency, where he has held several senior leadership positions, including Deputy Chief of Staff and Director of Congressional Affairs. He has also served as a U.S. Senate staffer during consideration of environmental reforms. He received EPA's Gold Medal, the agency's highest honor, for his leadership in reforming federal drinking water safety laws.

DAVID REJESKI has worked at the interface of public policy and emerging technologies for a wide range of organizations, including the Environmental Law Institute, Woodrow Wilson Center, White House Council on Environmental Quality, White House Office of Science and Technology Policy, and Environmental Protection Agency. He is a fellow of the National Academy of Public Administration and has served on advisory boards at the NSF, FDA, EPA, DARPA, AAAS, and the UK Open Plant Project.

PAUL RINK is a graduate of Yale Law School and Yale School of Forestry & Environmental Studies. He focuses on using legal strategies to promote climate change justice. His essay on climate change litigation received a silver medal in the Centre for International Sustainable Development Law's 2018 climate change law and governance essay competition.

CARTER S. ROBERTS is president and CEO of World Wildlife Fund (WWF) in the United States. As CEO, Roberts has built globally recognized programs to engage multinational corporations like Walmart, Mars, and McDonald's in scaling up certification and science-based targets to reduce emissions and deforestation, along with many other initiatives spanning finance, supply chain sourcing, protected areas, and regulation. Roberts serves on the board of the Nicholas Institute for Environmental Policy Solutions at Duke University and is a member of the Council on Foreign Relations and the International Finance Corporation's Advisory Panel on Sustainability and Business.

JAMES SAIERS is Clifton R. Musser Professor of Hydrology at the Yale School of Forestry & Environmental Studies, where he studies water quality and supply. He runs experiments, collects observations, and develops models to illuminate how human activities affect the chemical composition of drinking water resources and alter freshwater flows within aquifers, wetlands, and river basins. Professor Saiers's teaching addresses various applied and theoretical aspects of surface water and groundwater hydrology.

OSWALD J. SCHMITZ is Oastler Professor of Population and Community Ecology at Yale School of Forestry & Environmental Studies. His research aims to make sense of nature's complexity that comes from interdependencies among the variety of carnivore, herbivore, decomposer, and plant species within ecosystems. He uses these insights to teach about stewardship to enhance the sustainability of ecosystem functions and services.

LARRY SELZER is president and CEO of the Conservation Fund. Prior to being named president and CEO in 2001, Selzer led the Fund's efforts to integrate economic and environmental goals, including its efforts in mitigation, working forest conservation, and small business investing. He serves as the chairman of the American Bird Conservancy and is on the board of Weyerhaeuser and Manomet. He served as chairman of the Outdoor Foundation and twice served as chair of the Sustainable Forest Initiative, Inc.

KAREN C. SETO is one of the world's leading experts on contemporary urbanization. An urban and land change scientist, her research has generated new insights on the links between urbanization and climate change, food systems, biodiversity, and energy use. She co-led the chapter on urban mitigation for the 2014 United Nations IPCC climate change report and will co-lead the same chapter for the IPCC Sixth Assessment Report. She is co-editor in chief of the journal *Global Environmental Change*. She is an elected member of the U.S. National Academy of Sciences, the Connecticut Academy of Science and Engineering, and the American Association for the Advancement of Science.

BALWINDER SINGH is a systems agronomist based in New Delhi, India, with the International Maize and Wheat Improvement Center. He has made significant contributions in developing technologies and strategies for addressing the productivity and sustainability challenges in cereal systems in India. He explores how farmers can sustainably increase agricultural productivity while addressing issues like labor shortages, water scarcity, soil fertility loss, land degradation, rising temperatures, and other impacts from climate change.

MARY EVELYN TUCKER is a senior lecturer and research scholar at Yale University, where she has appointments in the School of Forestry & Environmental Studies as well as the Divinity School and the Department of Religious Studies. She co-edited *Confucianism and Ecology, Buddhism and Ecology,* and *Hinduism and Ecology.* She has co-authored *Ecology and Religion* and *Thomas Berry: A Biography* with John Grim. With Brian Thomas Swimme, she wrote *Journey of the Universe* and was the executive producer with John Grim of the Emmy Award–winning *Journey* film. In 2015, she was awarded the Inspiring Yale teaching award.

VASILIS VASILIOU is Susan Dwight Bliss Professor of Epidemiology and the chair of the Department of Environmental Health Sciences at the Yale School of Public Health. His research interests include mechanisms of cellular responses to environmental stress, gene-environment interactions, alcohol toxicity, and the evolution of gene families. Vasiliou has published over 190 papers, is the editor of *Human Genomics,* and serves on the editorial boards of several toxicology and visual sciences journals.

JONATHAN B. WIENER is Perkins Professor of Law and professor of public policy and environmental policy at Duke University, where he co-directs the Center on Risk. He is a University Fellow of Resources for the Future. He was president of the Society for Risk Analysis in 2008 and co-chair of the World Congress on Risk held in Sydney, Australia, in 2012. Previously he served at the White House Council of Economic Advisers, the Office of Science and Technology Policy, and the Environment Division of the U.S. Department of Justice.

JULIE B. ZIMMERMAN is an internationally recognized engineer whose work is focused on advancing innovations in sustainable technologies. Dr. Zimmerman is a professor in the Yale Department of Chemical and Environmental Engineering and School of Forestry & Environmental Studies, where she also serves as the Senior Associate Dean for Academic Affairs. Her work established the fundamental framework for her field with her seminal publications on the "Twelve Principles of Green Engineering" in 2003. Professor Zimmerman is co-author of *Environmental Engineering: Fundamentals, Sustainability, Design,* associate editor of *Environmental Science and Technology,* and a member of the Connecticut Academy of Sciences.